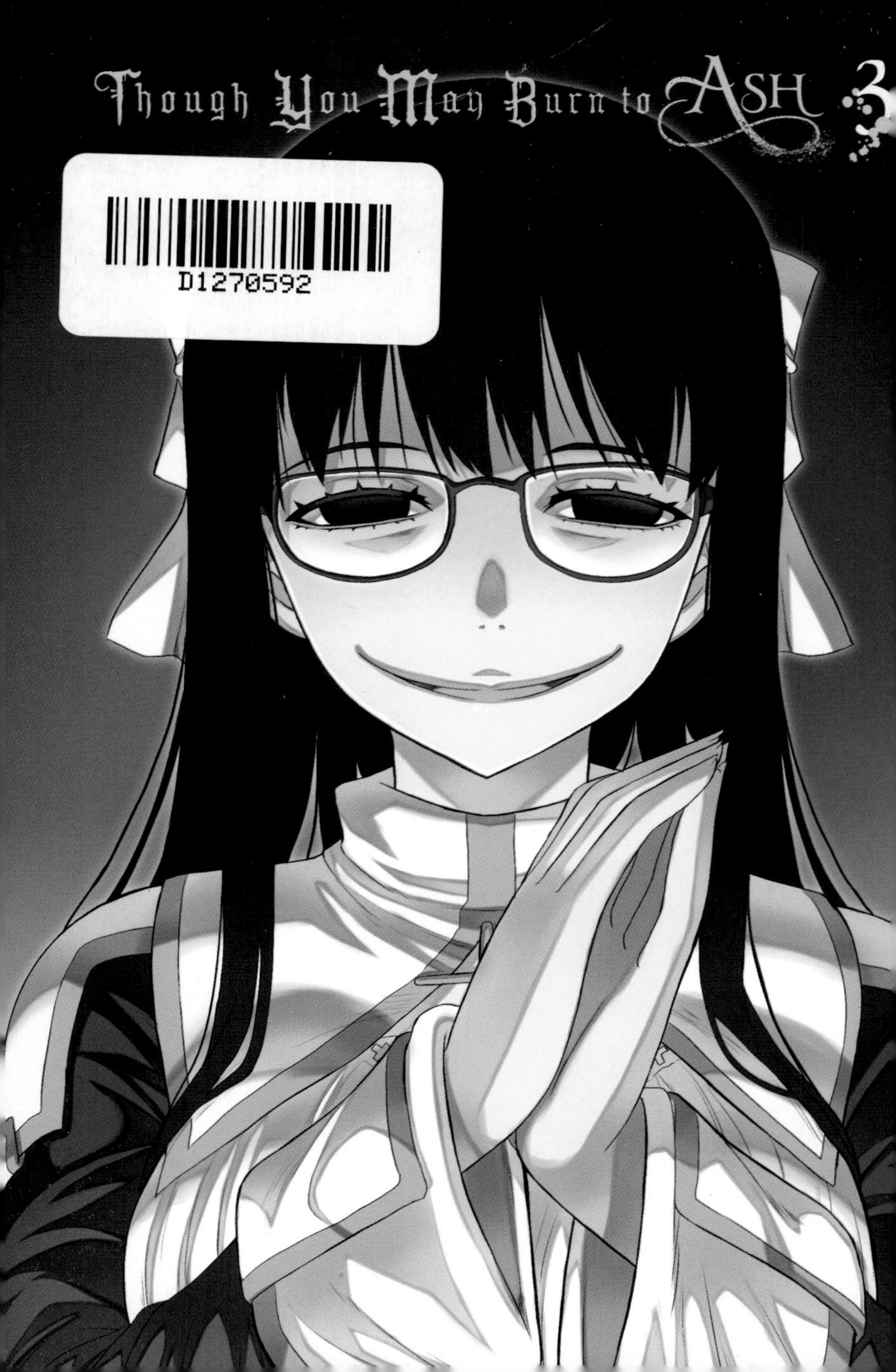
Though You May Burn to ASH 3

## Contents



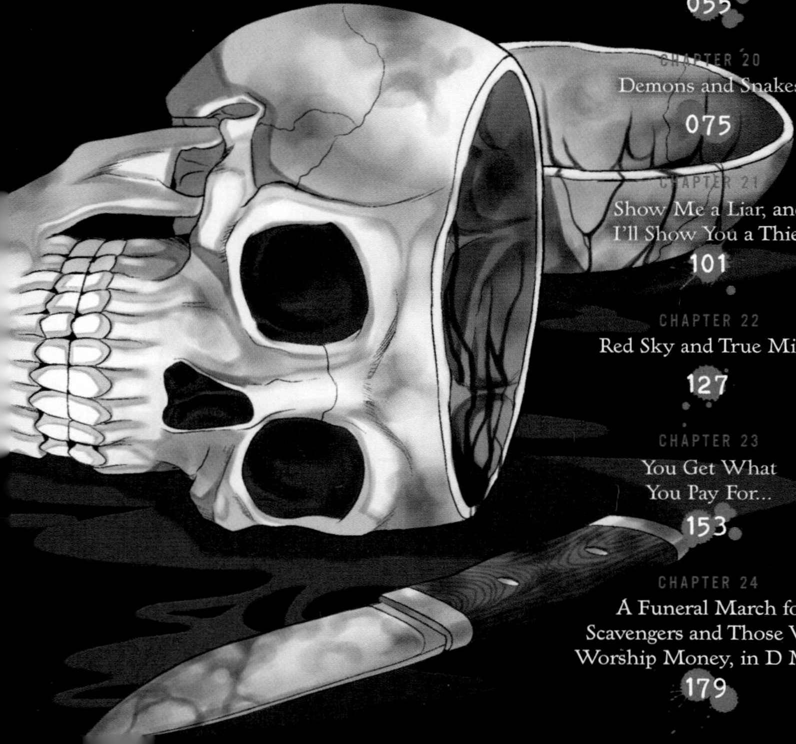

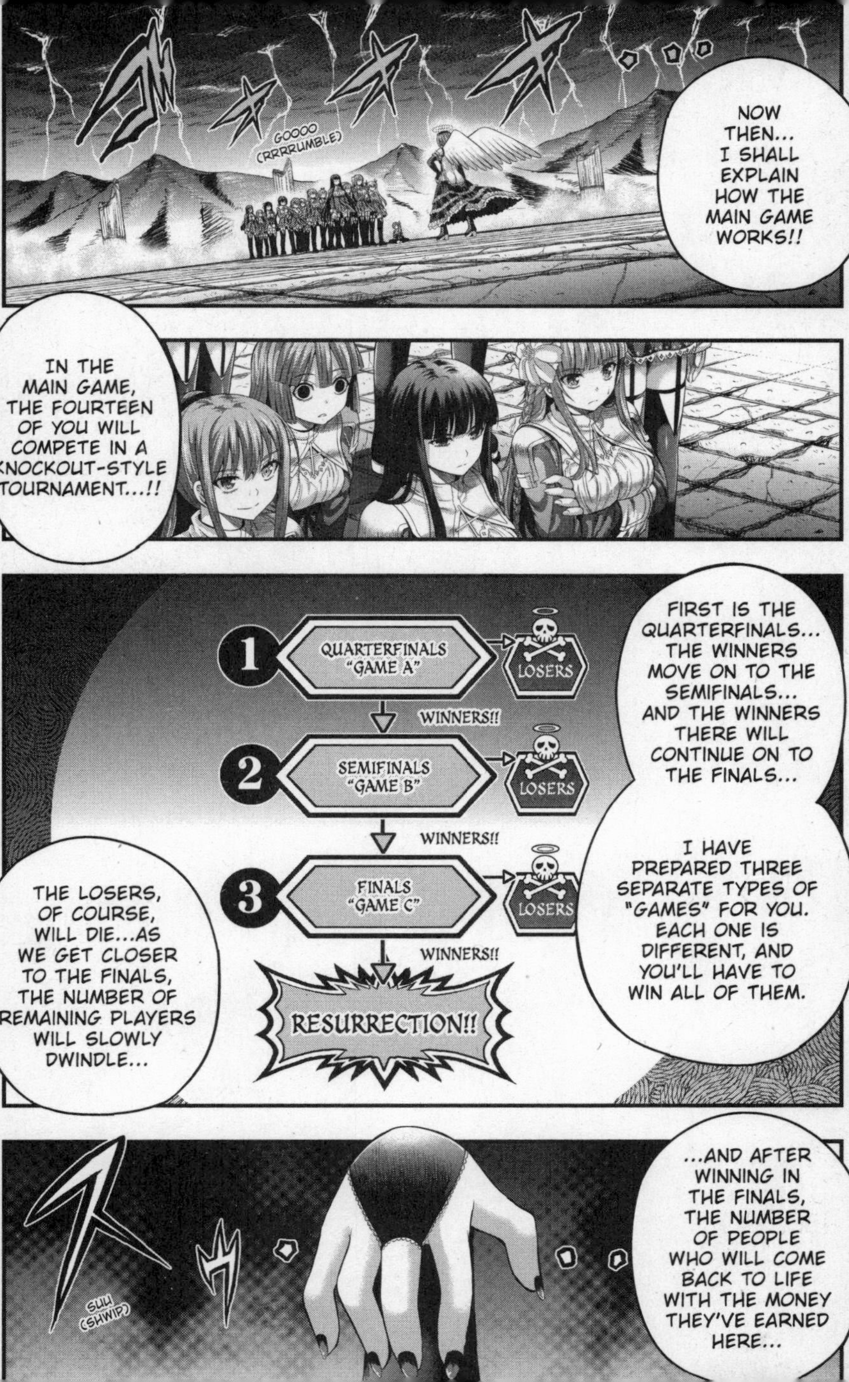
NOW THEN... I SHALL EXPLAIN HOW THE MAIN GAME WORKS!!
GOOOO (RRRRUMBLE)
IN THE MAIN GAME, THE FOURTEEN OF YOU WILL COMPETE IN A KNOCKOUT-STYLE TOURNAMENT...!!
FIRST IS THE QUARTERFINALS... THE WINNERS MOVE ON TO THE SEMIFINALS... AND THE WINNERS THERE WILL CONTINUE ON TO THE FINALS...
1
QUARTERFINALS "GAME A"
LOSERS
WINNERS!!
2
SEMIFINALS "GAME B"
LOSERS
WINNERS!!
3
FINALS "GAME C"
LOSERS
WINNERS!!
RESURRECTION!!
I HAVE PREPARED THREE SEPARATE TYPES OF "GAMES" FOR YOU. EACH ONE IS DIFFERENT, AND YOU'LL HAVE TO WIN ALL OF THEM.
THE LOSERS, OF COURSE, WILL DIE...AS WE GET CLOSER TO THE FINALS, THE NUMBER OF REMAINING PLAYERS WILL SLOWLY DWINDLE...
...AND AFTER WINNING IN THE FINALS, THE NUMBER OF PEOPLE WHO WILL COME BACK TO LIFE WITH THE MONEY THEY'VE EARNED HERE...
SUU (SHWIP)

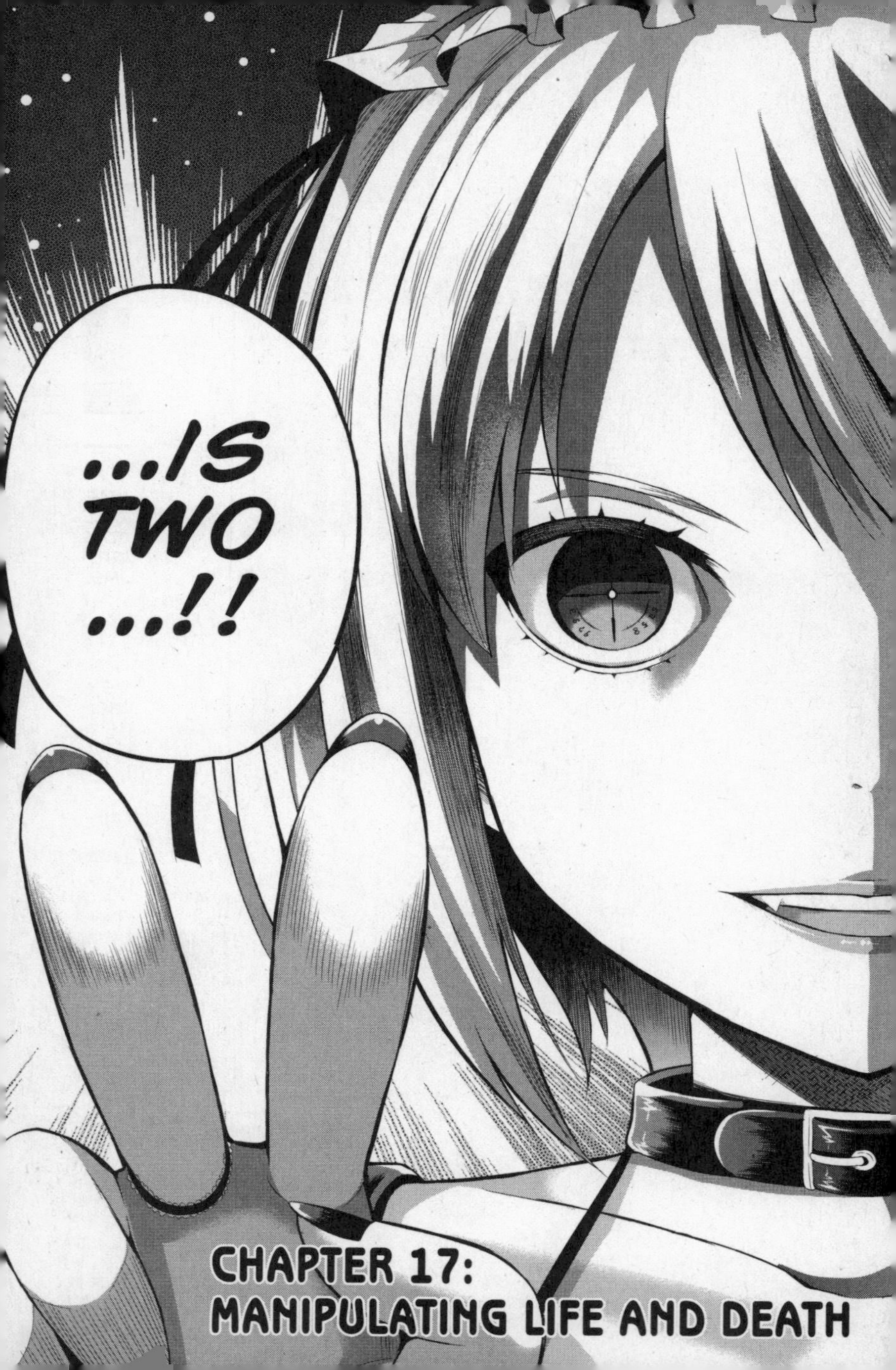
...IS TWO ...!!

# CHAPTER 17: MANIPULATING LIFE AND DEATH

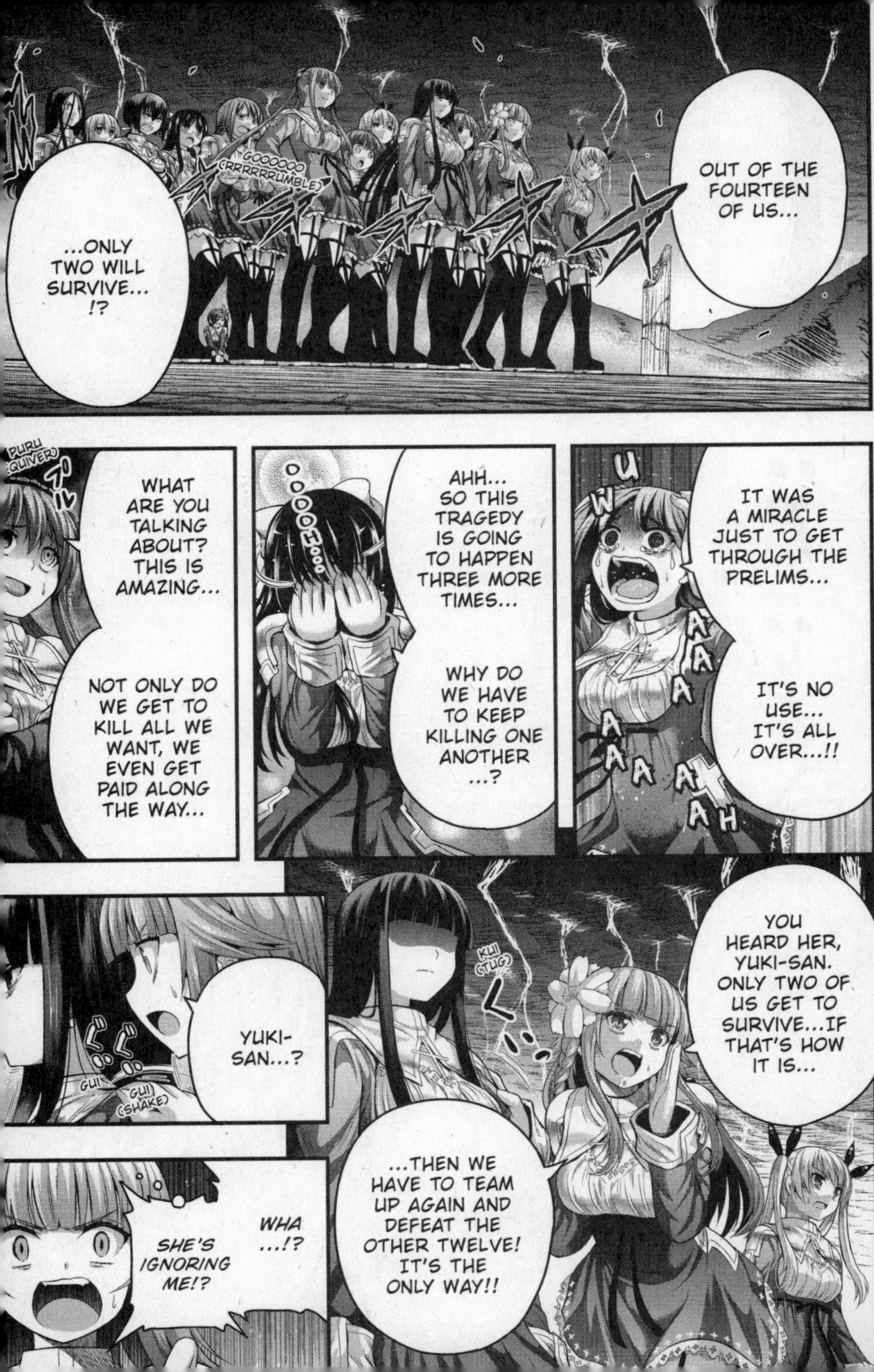

OUT OF THE FOURTEEN OF US...
GOOOOOOO (RRRRRRRUMBLE)
...ONLY TWO WILL SURVIVE... !?
IT WAS A MIRACLE JUST TO GET THROUGH THE PRELIMS...
UWAAAAAAAAAH
IT'S NO USE... IT'S ALL OVER...!!
OOOOH...
AHH... SO THIS TRAGEDY IS GOING TO HAPPEN THREE MORE TIMES...
WHY DO WE HAVE TO KEEP KILLING ONE ANOTHER ...?
PURU (QUIVER)
WHAT ARE YOU TALKING ABOUT? THIS IS AMAZING...
NOT ONLY DO WE GET TO KILL ALL WE WANT, WE EVEN GET PAID ALONG THE WAY...
YOU HEARD HER, YUKI-SAN. ONLY TWO OF US GET TO SURVIVE...IF THAT'S HOW IT IS...
KUI (TUG)
...THEN WE HAVE TO TEAM UP AGAIN AND DEFEAT THE OTHER TWELVE! IT'S THE ONLY WAY!!
YUKI-SAN...?
GUI GUI (SHAKE)
WHA ...!?
SHE'S IGNORING ME!?

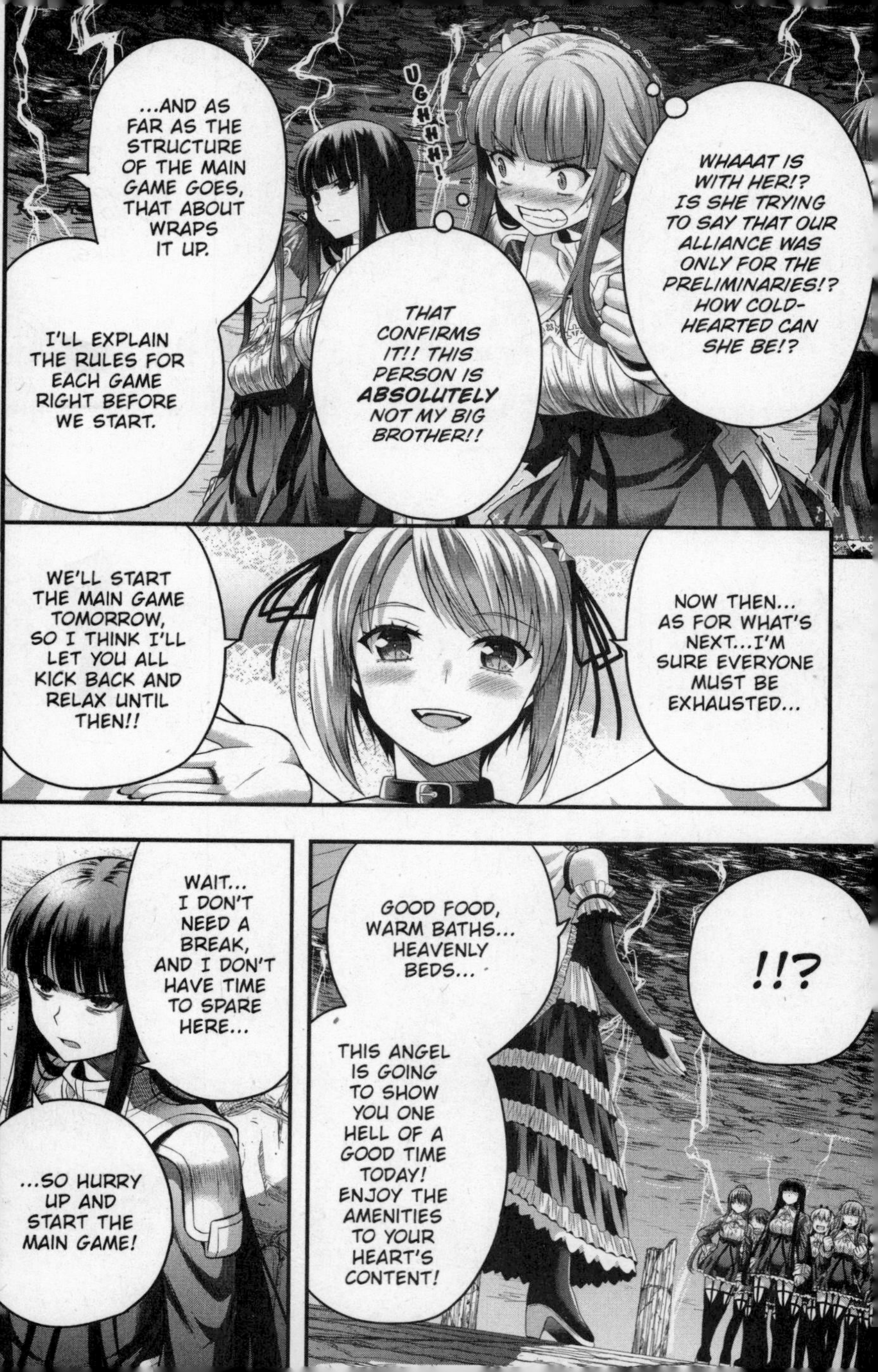
UGHHH!
WHAAAT IS WITH HER!? IS SHE TRYING TO SAY THAT OUR ALLIANCE WAS ONLY FOR THE PRELIMINARIES!? HOW COLD-HEARTED CAN SHE BE!?
...AND AS FAR AS THE STRUCTURE OF THE MAIN GAME GOES, THAT ABOUT WRAPS IT UP.
THAT CONFIRMS IT!! THIS PERSON IS **ABSOLUTELY** NOT MY BIG BROTHER!!
I'LL EXPLAIN THE RULES FOR EACH GAME RIGHT BEFORE WE START.
NOW THEN... AS FOR WHAT'S NEXT...I'M SURE EVERYONE MUST BE EXHAUSTED...
WE'LL START THE MAIN GAME TOMORROW, SO I THINK I'LL LET YOU ALL KICK BACK AND RELAX UNTIL THEN!!
GOOD FOOD, WARM BATHS... HEAVENLY BEDS...
THIS ANGEL IS GOING TO SHOW YOU ONE HELL OF A GOOD TIME TODAY! ENJOY THE AMENITIES TO YOUR HEART'S CONTENT!
!!?
WAIT... I DON'T NEED A BREAK, AND I DON'T HAVE TIME TO SPARE HERE...
...SO HURRY UP AND START THE MAIN GAME!

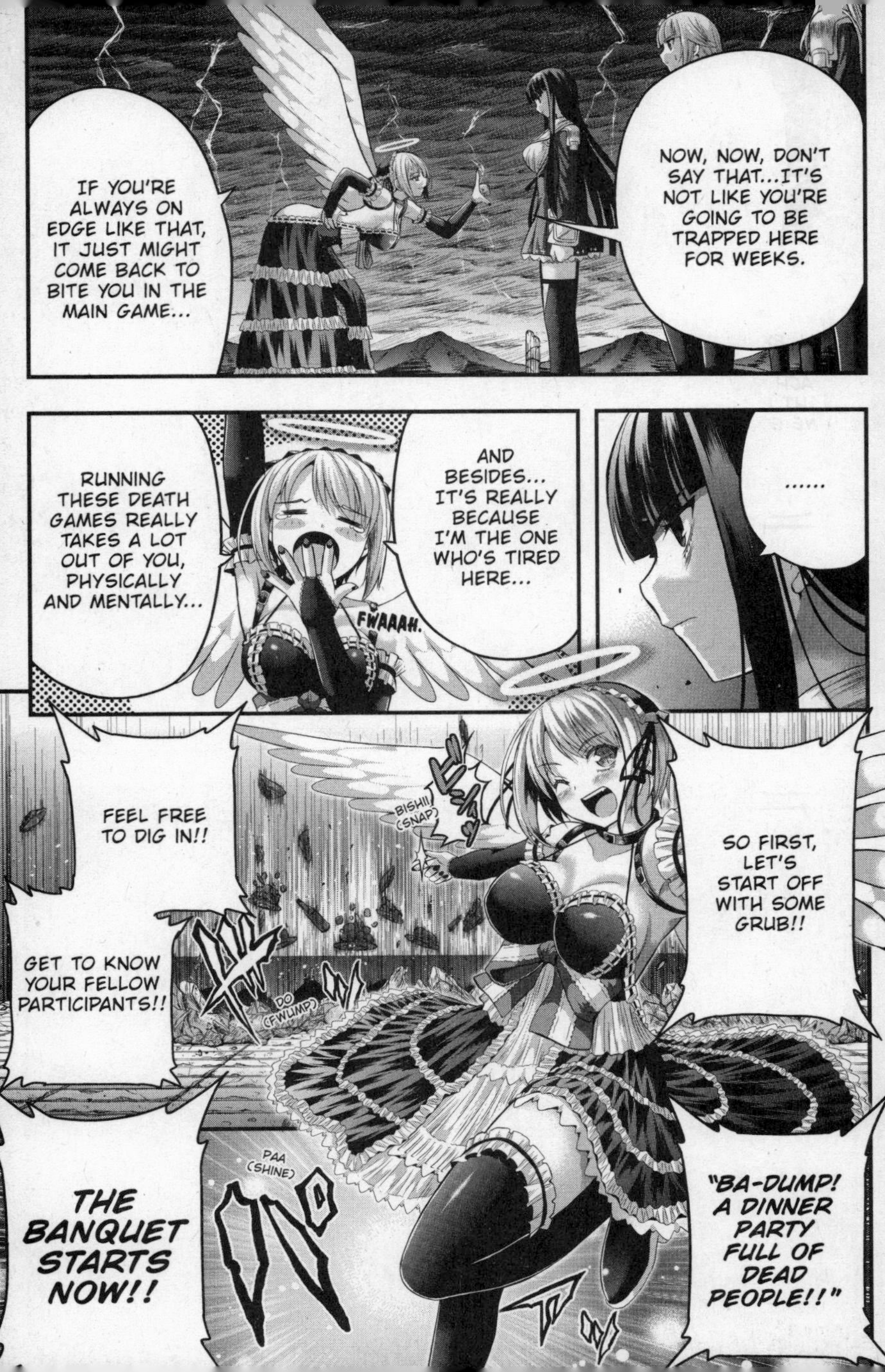
NOW, NOW, DON'T SAY THAT...IT'S NOT LIKE YOU'RE GOING TO BE TRAPPED HERE FOR WEEKS.
IF YOU'RE ALWAYS ON EDGE LIKE THAT, IT JUST MIGHT COME BACK TO BITE YOU IN THE MAIN GAME...
......
AND BESIDES... IT'S REALLY BECAUSE I'M THE ONE WHO'S TIRED HERE...
RUNNING THESE DEATH GAMES REALLY TAKES A LOT OUT OF YOU, PHYSICALLY AND MENTALLY...
FWAAAH.
SO FIRST, LET'S START OFF WITH SOME GRUB!!
BISHI (SNAP)
FEEL FREE TO DIG IN!!
GET TO KNOW YOUR FELLOW PARTICIPANTS!!
DO (FWUMP)
"BA-DUMP! A DINNER PARTY FULL OF DEAD PEOPLE!!"
PAA (SHINE)
THE BANQUET STARTS NOW!!

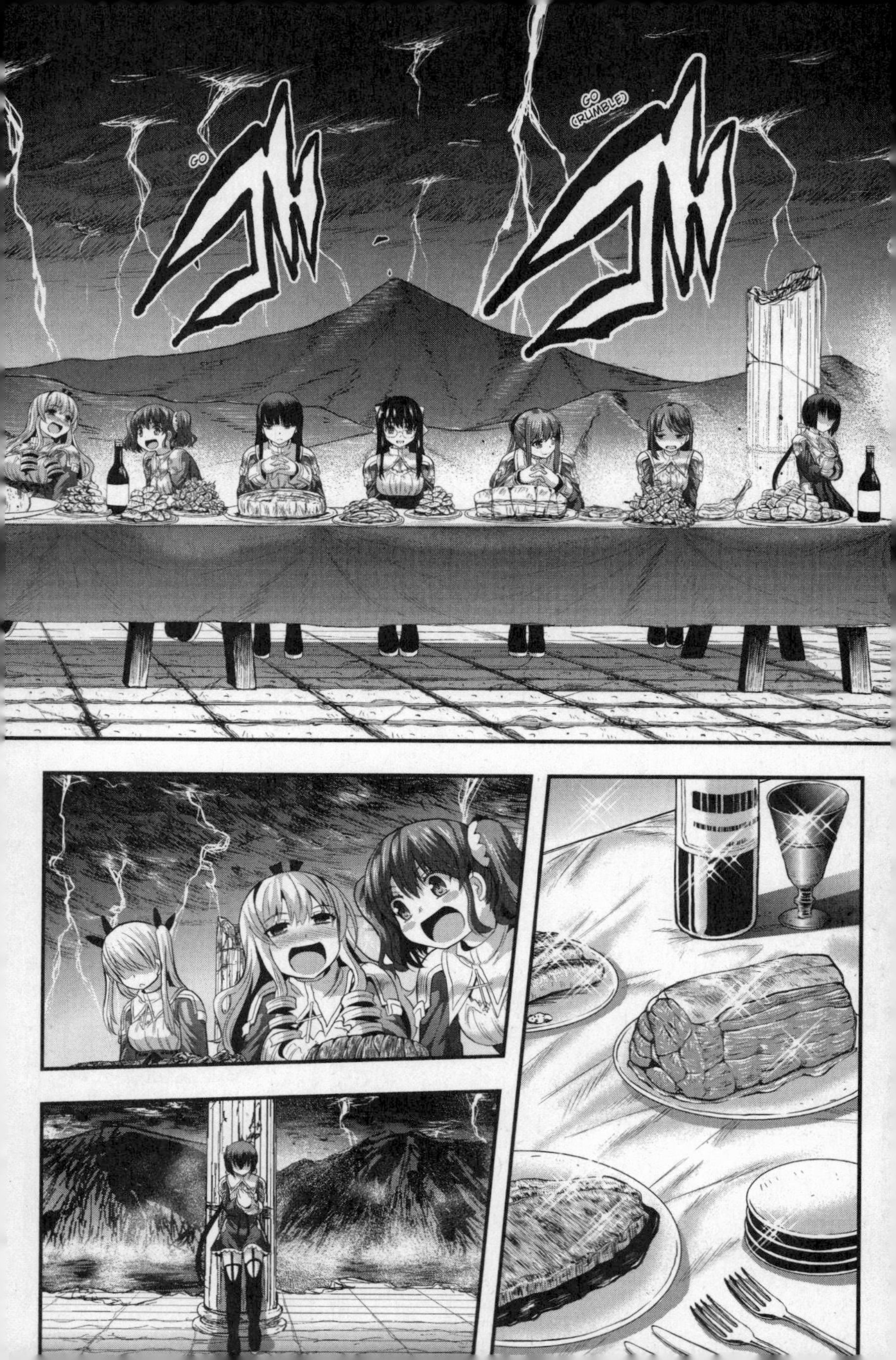
GO (RUMBLE)
GO

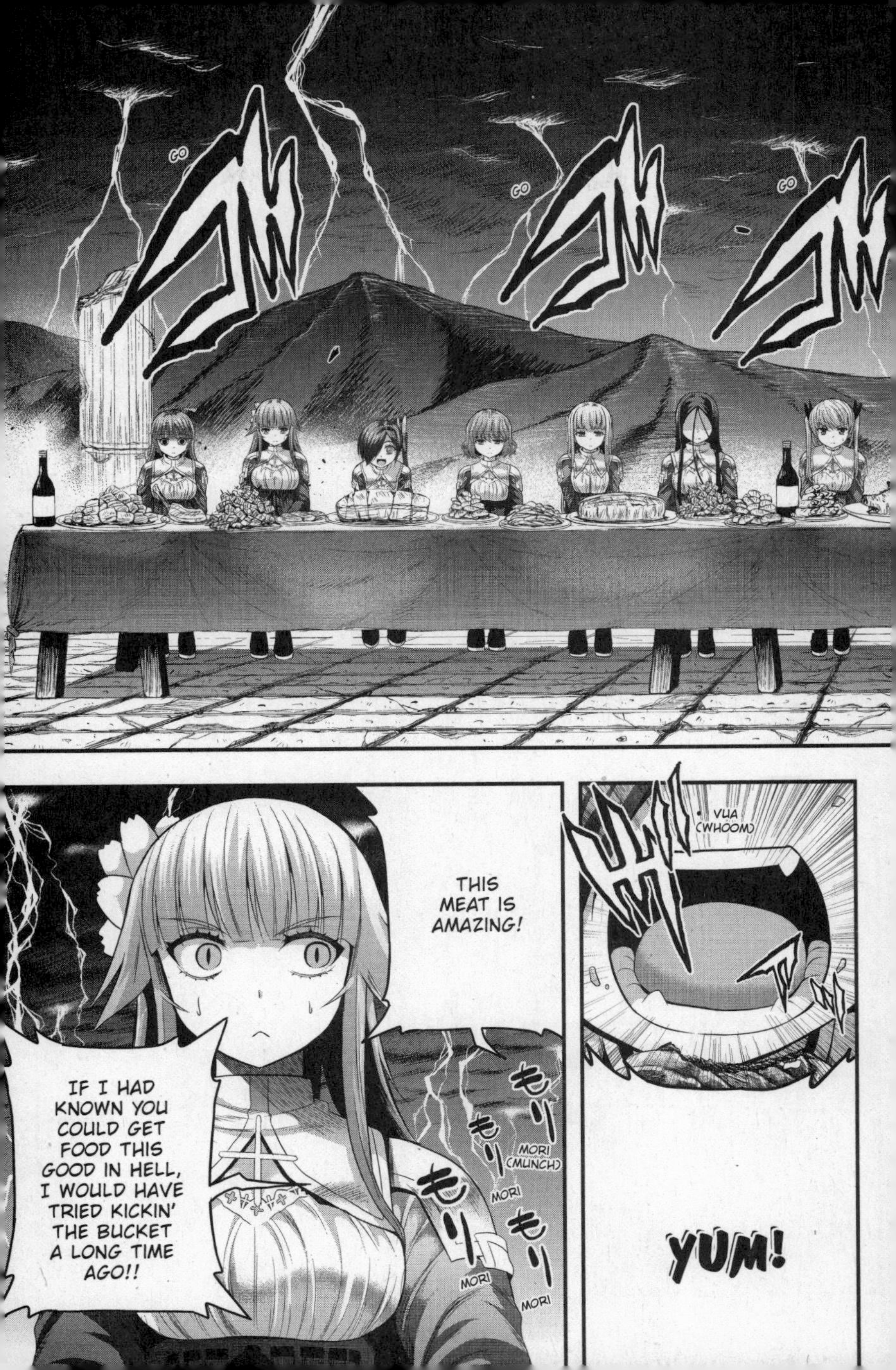
GO
GO
GO
VUA (WHOOM)
YUM!
THIS MEAT IS AMAZING!
IF I HAD KNOWN YOU COULD GET FOOD THIS GOOD IN HELL, I WOULD HAVE TRIED KICKIN' THE BUCKET A LONG TIME AGO!!
MORI (MUNCH)
MORI
MORI
MORI

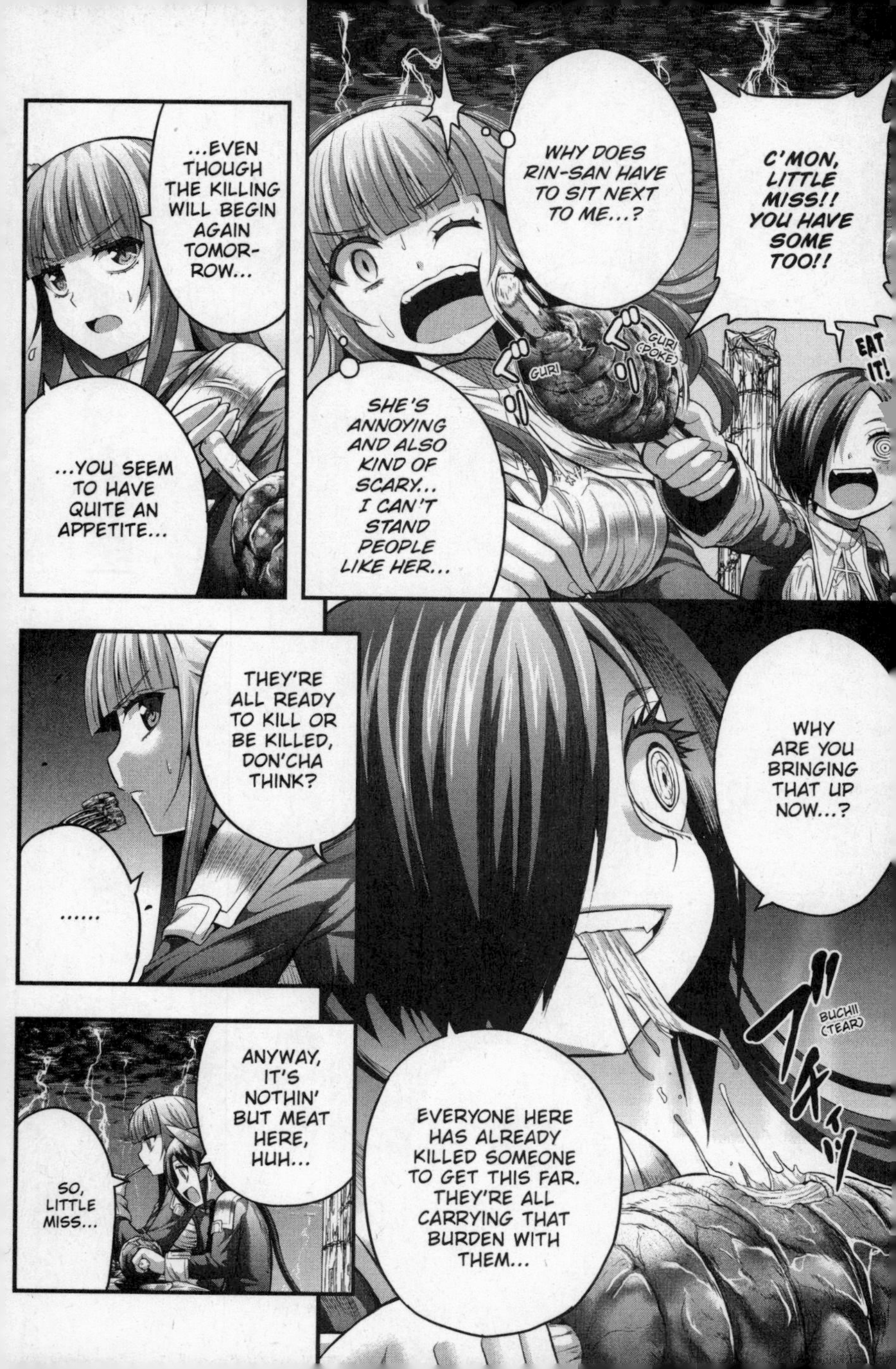

C'MON, LITTLE MISS!! YOU HAVE SOME TOO!!
EAT IT!
GURI (POKE)
GURI
WHY DOES RIN-SAN HAVE TO SIT NEXT TO ME...?
SHE'S ANNOYING AND ALSO KIND OF SCARY... I CAN'T STAND PEOPLE LIKE HER...
...EVEN THOUGH THE KILLING WILL BEGIN AGAIN TOMOR-ROW...
...YOU SEEM TO HAVE QUITE AN APPETITE...
WHY ARE YOU BRINGING THAT UP NOW...?
BUCHII (TEAR)
EVERYONE HERE HAS ALREADY KILLED SOMEONE TO GET THIS FAR. THEY'RE ALL CARRYING THAT BURDEN WITH THEM...
THEY'RE ALL READY TO KILL OR BE KILLED, DON'CHA THINK?
......
ANYWAY, IT'S NOTHIN' BUT MEAT HERE, HUH...
SO, LITTLE MISS...

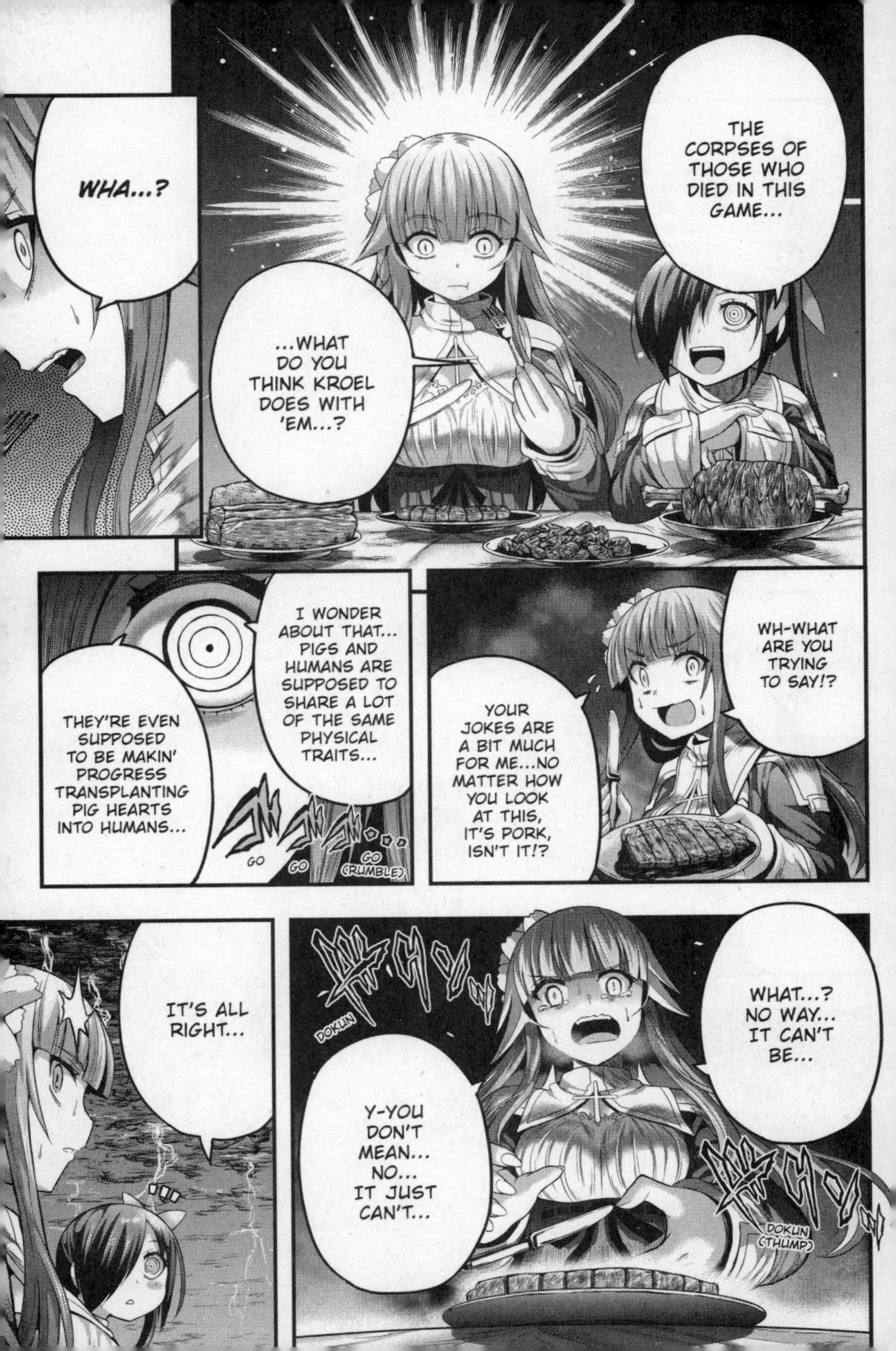
THE CORPSES OF THOSE WHO DIED IN THIS GAME...
...WHAT DO YOU THINK KROEL DOES WITH 'EM...?
WHA...?
WH-WHAT ARE YOU TRYING TO SAY!?
YOUR JOKES ARE A BIT MUCH FOR ME...NO MATTER HOW YOU LOOK AT THIS, IT'S PORK, ISN'T IT!?
I WONDER ABOUT THAT... PIGS AND HUMANS ARE SUPPOSED TO SHARE A LOT OF THE SAME PHYSICAL TRAITS...
THEY'RE EVEN SUPPOSED TO BE MAKIN' PROGRESS TRANSPLANTING PIG HEARTS INTO HUMANS...
GO GO GO (RUMBLE)
DOKUN
WHAT...? NO WAY... IT CAN'T BE...
Y-YOU DON'T MEAN... NO... IT JUST CAN'T...
DOKUN (THUMP)
IT'S ALL RIGHT...

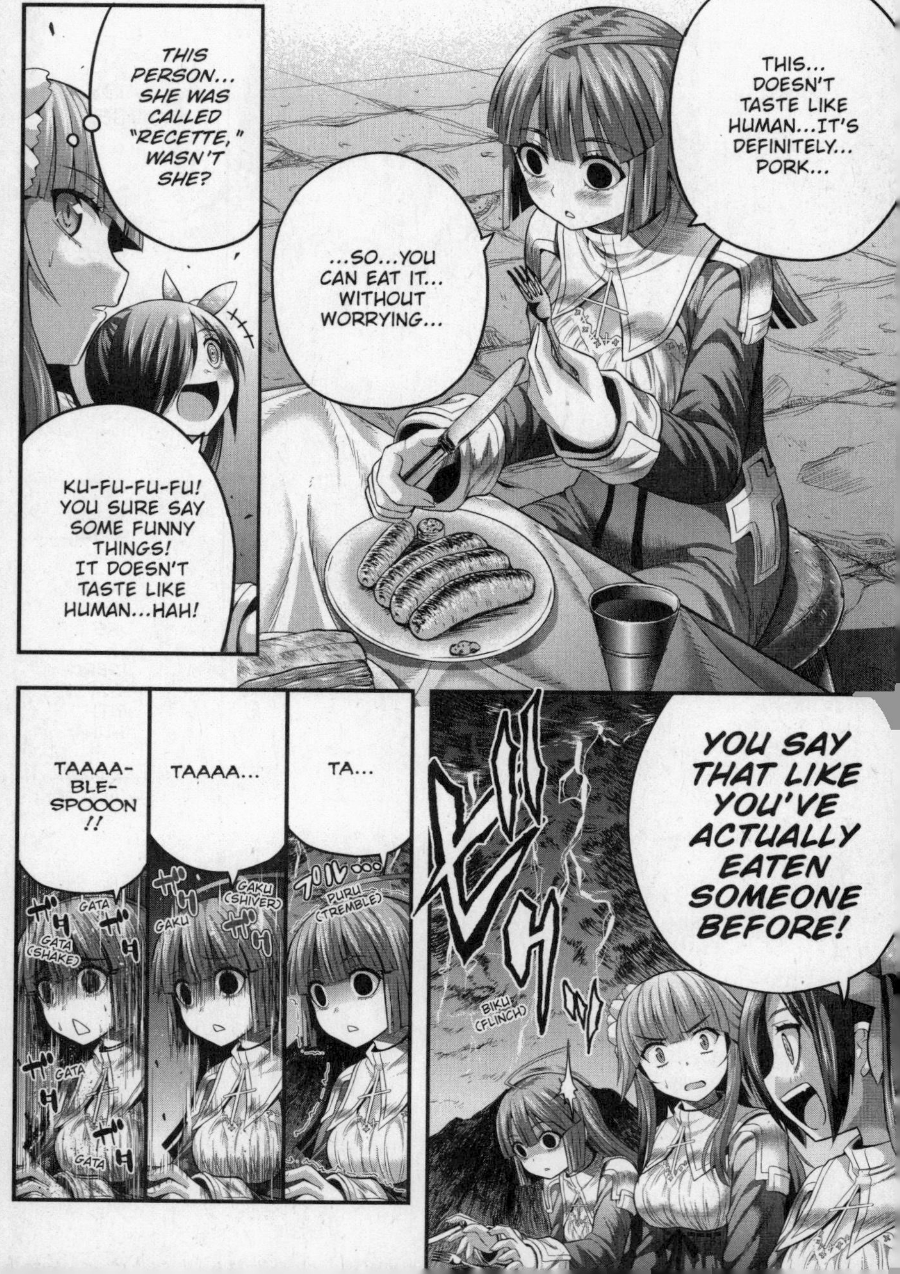
THIS... DOESN'T TASTE LIKE HUMAN...IT'S DEFINITELY... PORK...
...SO...YOU CAN EAT IT... WITHOUT WORRYING...
THIS PERSON... SHE WAS CALLED "RECETTE," WASN'T SHE?
KU-FU-FU-FU! YOU SURE SAY SOME FUNNY THINGS! IT DOESN'T TASTE LIKE HUMAN...HAH!
YOU SAY THAT LIKE YOU'VE ACTUALLY EATEN SOMEONE BEFORE!
BIKU (FLINCH)
TA...
PURU (TREMBLE)
TAAAA...
GAKU (SHIVER)
GAKU
TAAAA-BLE-SPOOON!!
GATA
GATA (SHAKE)
GATA
GATA

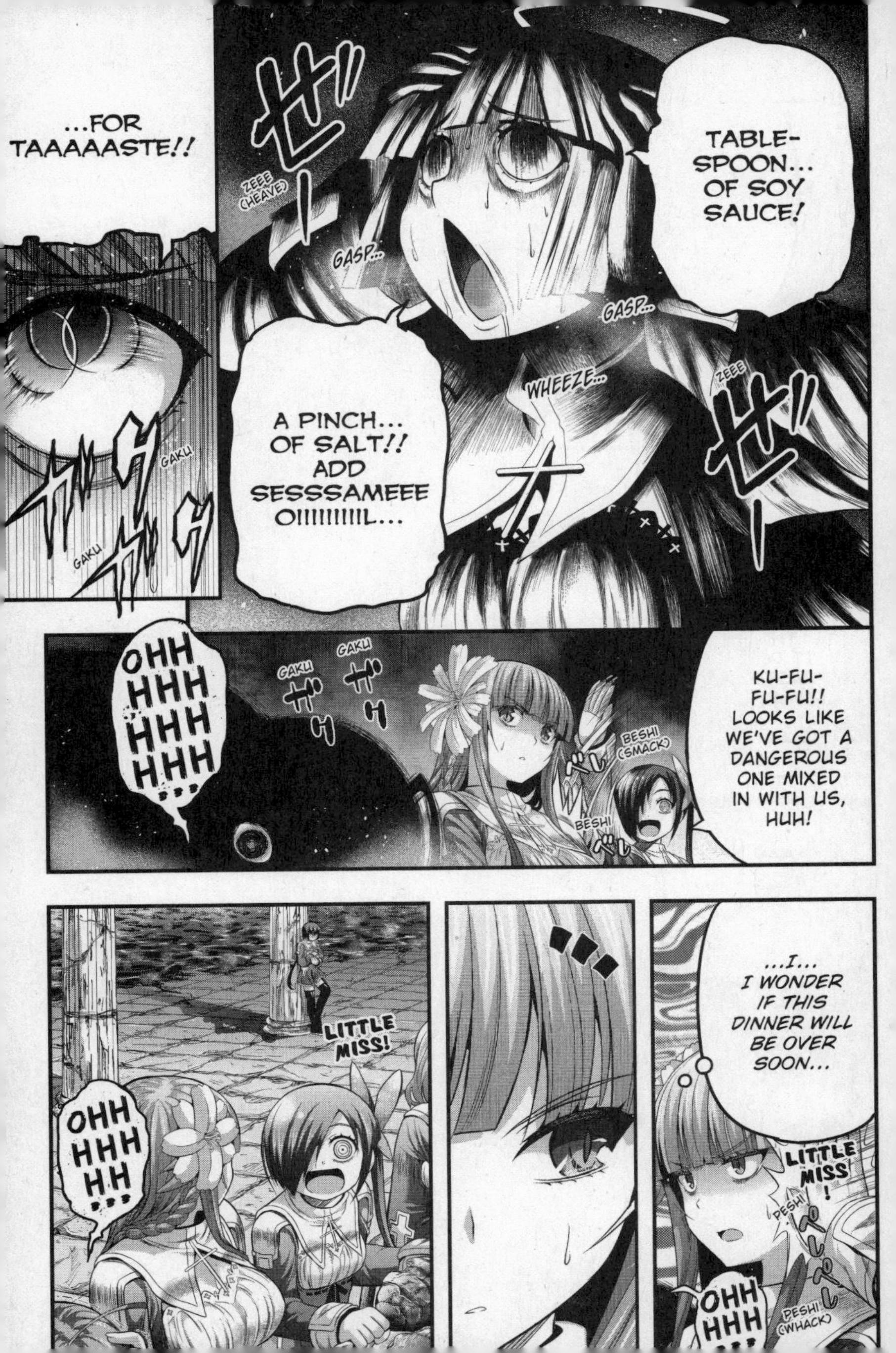

TABLE-SPOON... OF SOY SAUCE!
ZEEE (HEAVE)
GASP...
GASP...
A PINCH... OF SALT!! ADD SESSSAMEEE OIIIIIIIIIL...
WHEEZE...
ZEEE
...FOR TAAAAASTE!!
GAKU
GAKU
KU-FU-FU-FU!! LOOKS LIKE WE'VE GOT A DANGEROUS ONE MIXED IN WITH US, HUH!
BESHI (SMACK)
BESHI
GAKU
GAKU
OHHHHHHHHHHHHH...
...I... I WONDER IF THIS DINNER WILL BE OVER SOON...
LITTLE MISS!
PESHI
PESHI (WHACK)
OHHHHHHHH
...
LITTLE MISS!
OHHHHHHHH...

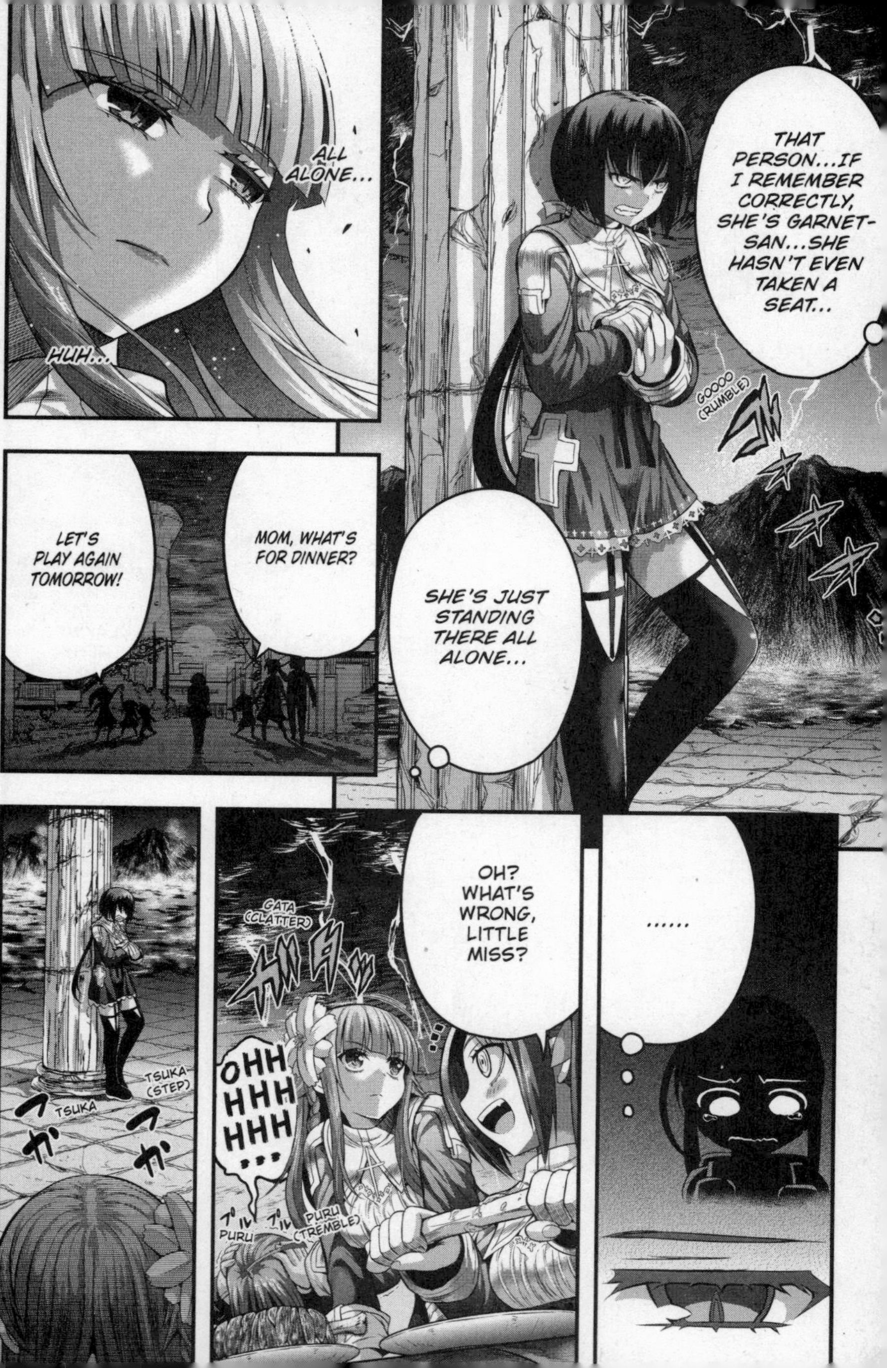
THAT PERSON...IF I REMEMBER CORRECTLY, SHE'S GARNET-SAN...SHE HASN'T EVEN TAKEN A SEAT...
GOOOO (RUMBLE)
SHE'S JUST STANDING THERE ALL ALONE...
ALL ALONE...
HUH...
MOM, WHAT'S FOR DINNER?
LET'S PLAY AGAIN TOMORROW!
......
OH? WHAT'S WRONG, LITTLE MISS?
GATA (CLATTER)
OHHHHHHHHH
PURU (TREMBLE)
PURU
TSUKA (STEP)
TSUKA

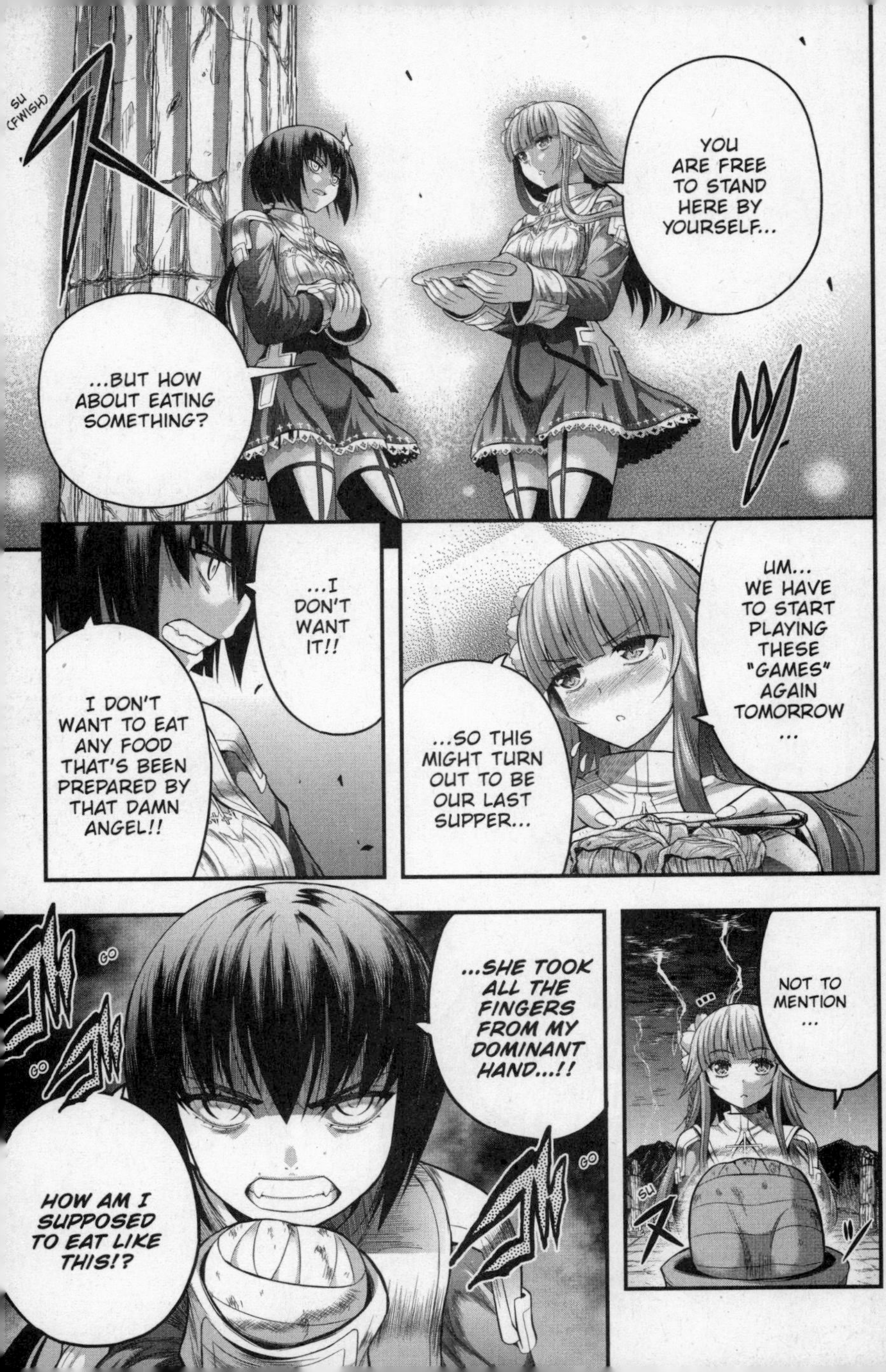
YOU ARE FREE TO STAND HERE BY YOURSELF...
SU (FWISH)
...BUT HOW ABOUT EATING SOMETHING?
UM... WE HAVE TO START PLAYING THESE "GAMES" AGAIN TOMORROW ...
...SO THIS MIGHT TURN OUT TO BE OUR LAST SUPPER...
...I DON'T WANT IT!!
I DON'T WANT TO EAT ANY FOOD THAT'S BEEN PREPARED BY THAT DAMN ANGEL!!
NOT TO MENTION ...
SU
...SHE TOOK ALL THE FINGERS FROM MY DOMINANT HAND...!!
GO
GO
HOW AM I SUPPOSED TO EAT LIKE THIS!?
GO

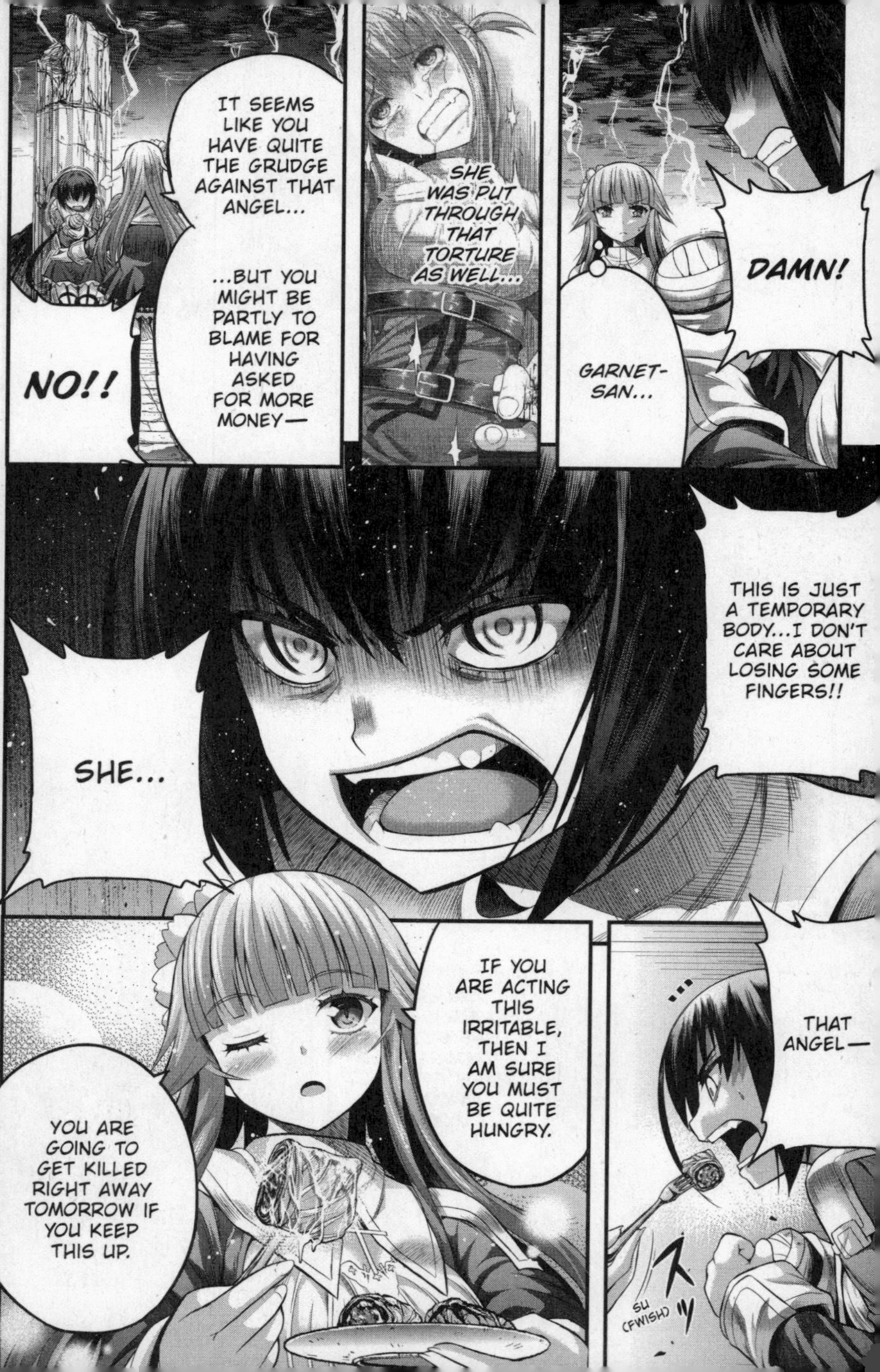
DAMN!
GARNET-SAN...
SHE WAS PUT THROUGH THAT TORTURE AS WELL...
IT SEEMS LIKE YOU HAVE QUITE THE GRUDGE AGAINST THAT ANGEL...
...BUT YOU MIGHT BE PARTLY TO BLAME FOR HAVING ASKED FOR MORE MONEY—
NO!!
THIS IS JUST A TEMPORARY BODY...I DON'T CARE ABOUT LOSING SOME FINGERS!!
SHE...
...
THAT ANGEL—
ス
SU (FWISH)
IF YOU ARE ACTING THIS IRRITABLE, THEN I AM SURE YOU MUST BE QUITE HUNGRY.
YOU ARE GOING TO GET KILLED RIGHT AWAY TOMORROW IF YOU KEEP THIS UP.

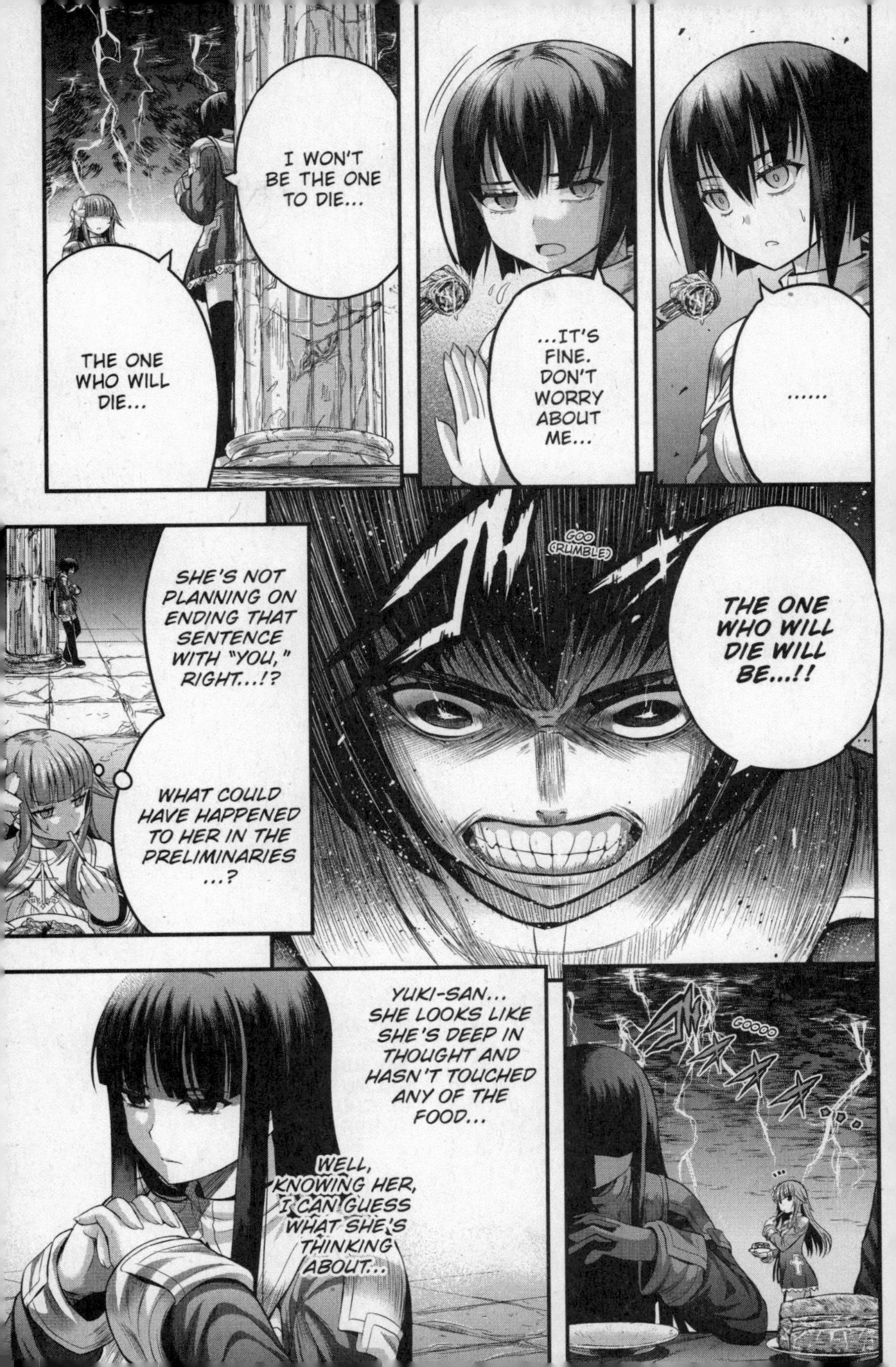
......
...IT'S FINE. DON'T WORRY ABOUT ME...
I WON'T BE THE ONE TO DIE...
THE ONE WHO WILL DIE...
GOO (RUMBLE)
THE ONE WHO WILL DIE WILL BE...!!
SHE'S NOT PLANNING ON ENDING THAT SENTENCE WITH "YOU," RIGHT...!?
WHAT COULD HAVE HAPPENED TO HER IN THE PRELIMINARIES...?
GOOOO
YUKI-SAN... SHE LOOKS LIKE SHE'S DEEP IN THOUGHT AND HASN'T TOUCHED ANY OF THE FOOD...
WELL, KNOWING HER, I CAN GUESS WHAT SHE'S THINKING ABOUT...

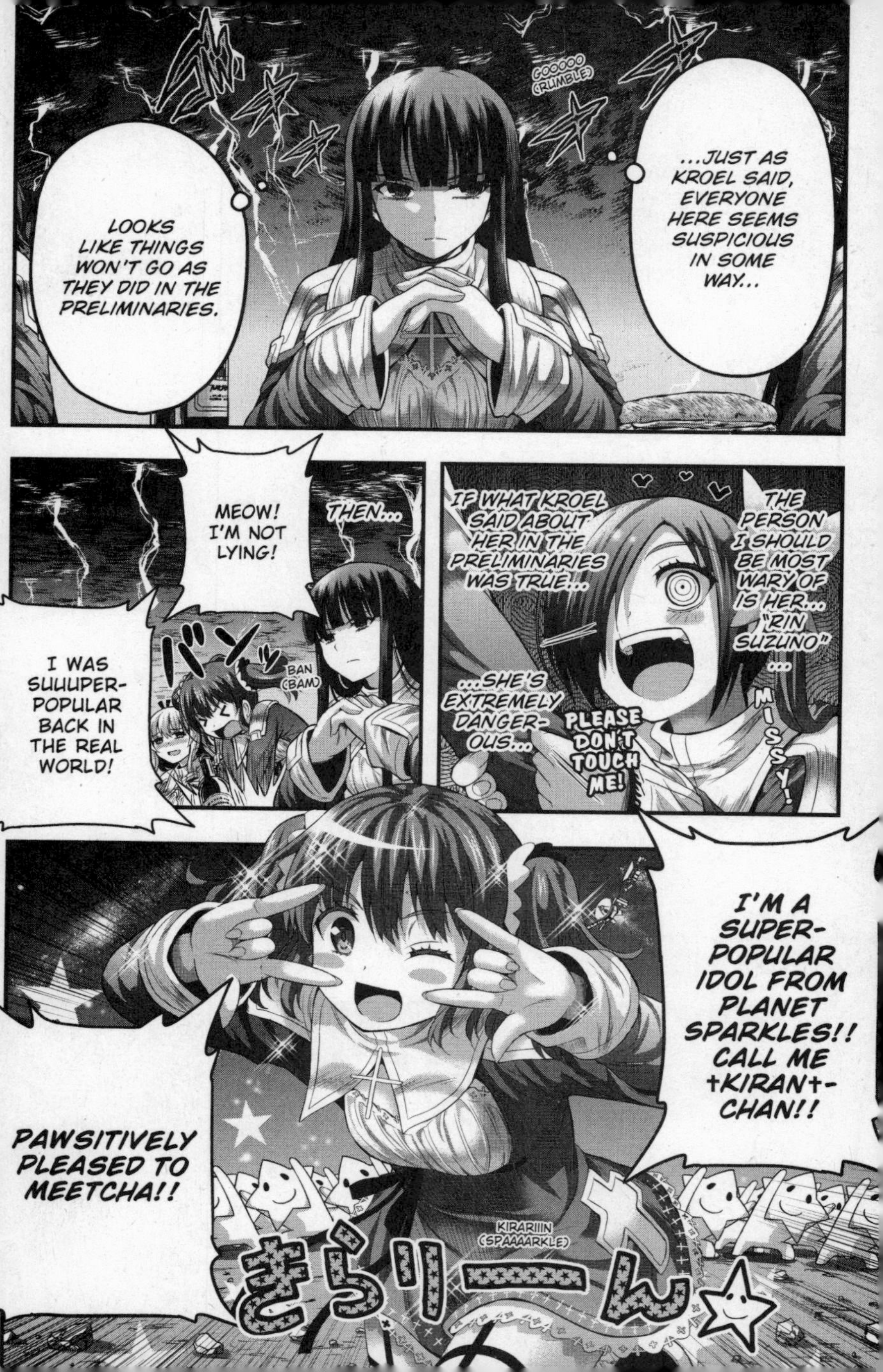
GOOOOO (RUMBLE)
...JUST AS KROEL SAID, EVERYONE HERE SEEMS SUSPICIOUS IN SOME WAY...
LOOKS LIKE THINGS WON'T GO AS THEY DID IN THE PRELIMINARIES.
THE PERSON I SHOULD BE MOST WARY OF IS HER... "RIN SUZUNO"...
IF WHAT KROEL SAID ABOUT HER IN THE PRELIMINARIES WAS TRUE...
...SHE'S EXTREMELY DANGER-OUS...
PLEASE DON'T TOUCH ME!
MISSY!
THEN...
MEOW! I'M NOT LYING!
BAN (BAM)
I WAS SUUUPER-POPULAR BACK IN THE REAL WORLD!
I'M A SUPER-POPULAR IDOL FROM PLANET SPARKLES!! CALL ME +KIRAN+-CHAN!!
PAWSITIVELY PLEASED TO MEETCHA!!
KIRARIIIN (SPAAAARKLE)
きらりーーーん☆

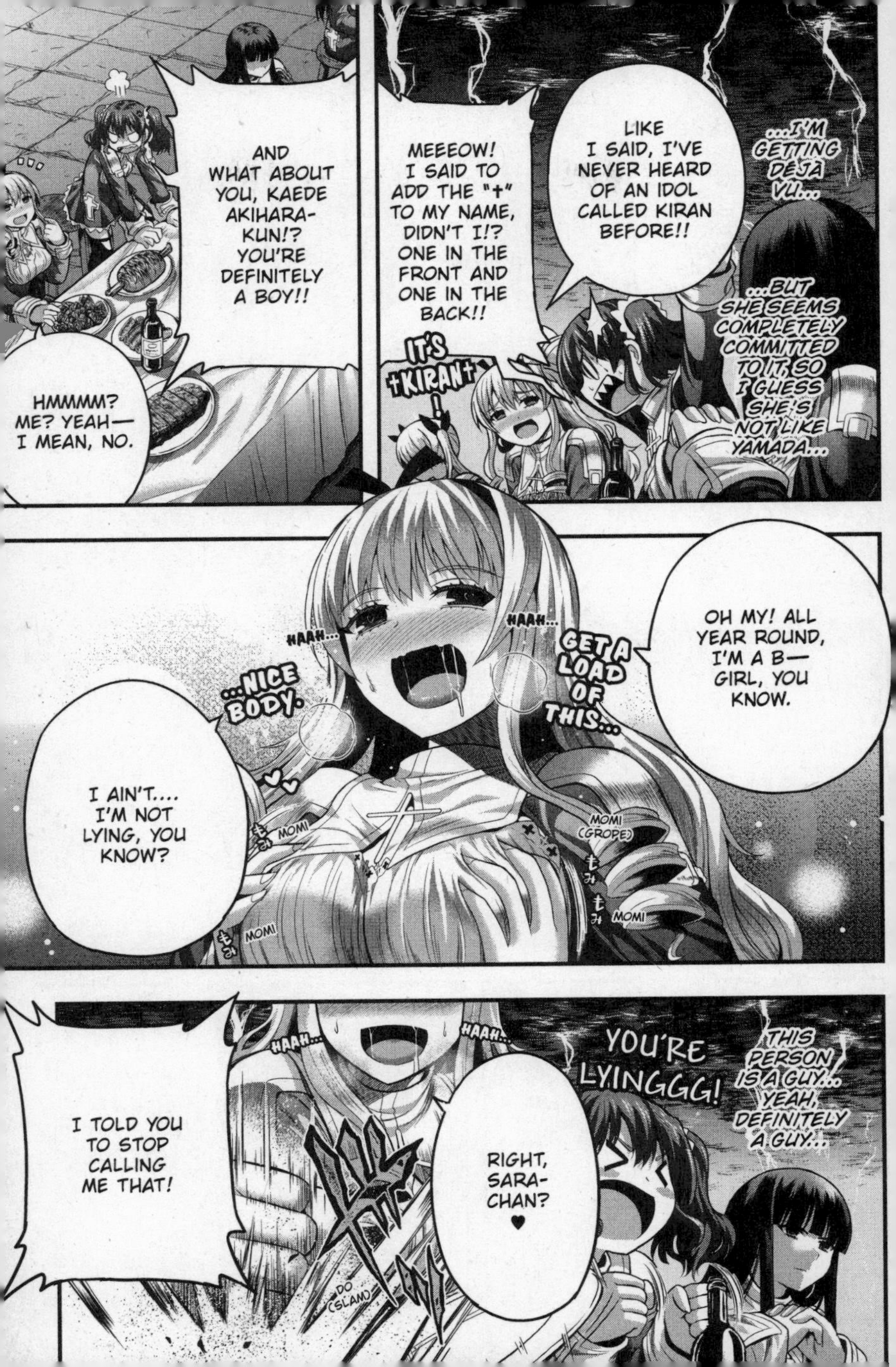

...I'M GETTING DEJA VU...
LIKE I SAID, I'VE NEVER HEARD OF AN IDOL CALLED KIRAN BEFORE!!
...BUT SHE SEEMS COMPLETELY COMMITTED TO IT, SO I GUESS SHE'S NOT LIKE YAMADA...
MEEEOW! I SAID TO ADD THE "†" TO MY NAME, DIDN'T I!? ONE IN THE FRONT AND ONE IN THE BACK!!
IT'S †KIRAN†!
AND WHAT ABOUT YOU, KAEDE AKIHARA-KUN!? YOU'RE DEFINITELY A BOY!!
HMMMMM? ME? YEAH— I MEAN, NO.
OH MY! ALL YEAR ROUND, I'M A B— GIRL, YOU KNOW.
GET A LOAD OF THIS...
HAAH...
HAAH...
...NICE BODY.
MOMI (GROPE)
MOMI
MOMI
MOMI
I AIN'T.... I'M NOT LYING, YOU KNOW?
THIS PERSON IS A GUY... YEAH, DEFINITELY A GUY...
YOU'RE LYINGGG!
HAAH...
HAAH...
RIGHT, SARA-CHAN? ♥
I TOLD YOU TO STOP CALLING ME THAT!
DO (SLAM)

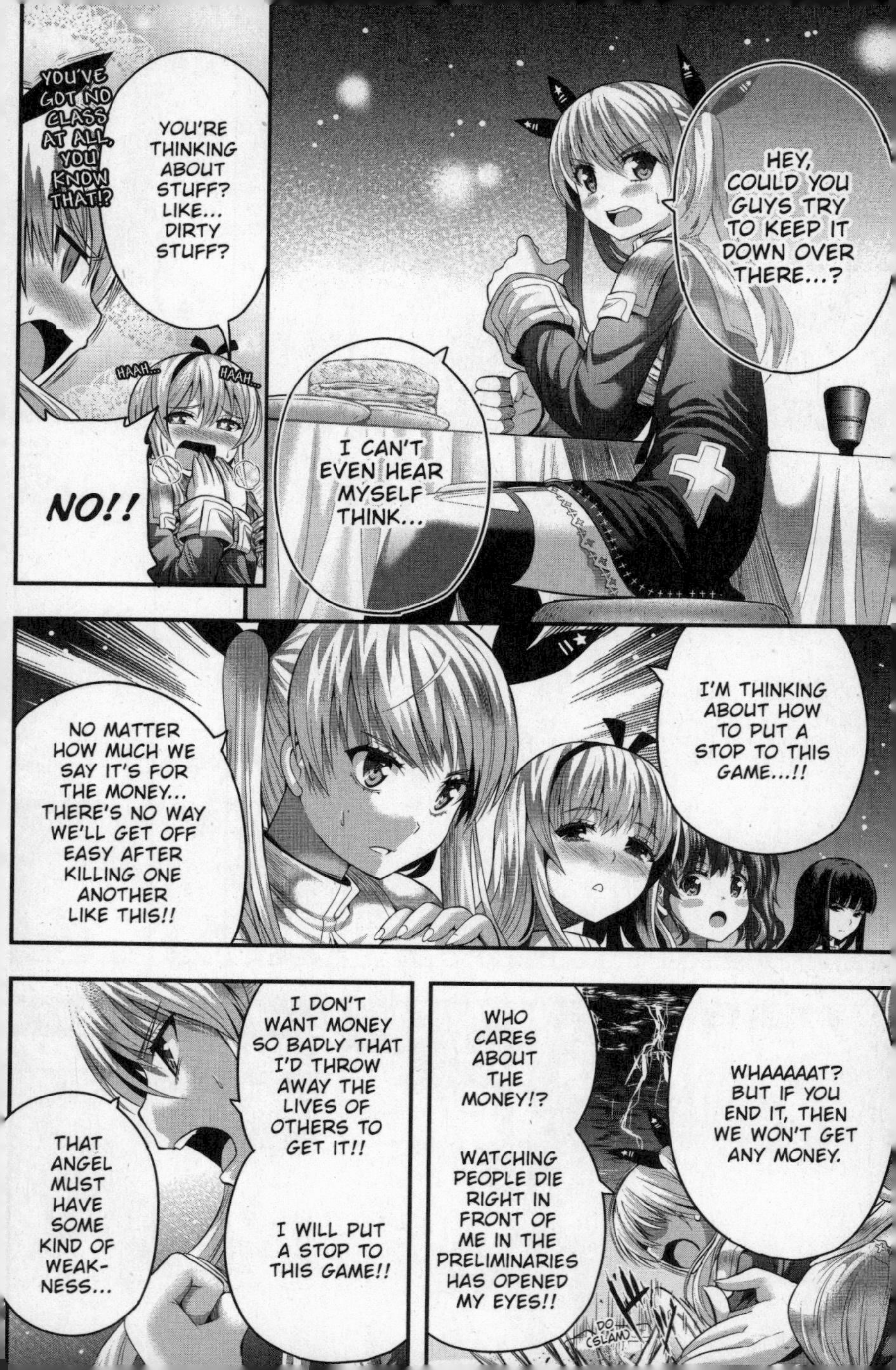
HEY, COULD YOU GUYS TRY TO KEEP IT DOWN OVER THERE...?
I CAN'T EVEN HEAR MYSELF THINK...
YOU'RE THINKING ABOUT STUFF? LIKE... DIRTY STUFF?
YOU'VE GOT NO CLASS AT ALL, YOU KNOW THAT!?
HAAH...
HAAH...
NO!!
I'M THINKING ABOUT HOW TO PUT A STOP TO THIS GAME...!!
NO MATTER HOW MUCH WE SAY IT'S FOR THE MONEY... THERE'S NO WAY WE'LL GET OFF EASY AFTER KILLING ONE ANOTHER LIKE THIS!!
WHAAAAAT? BUT IF YOU END IT, THEN WE WON'T GET ANY MONEY.
WHO CARES ABOUT THE MONEY!?
WATCHING PEOPLE DIE RIGHT IN FRONT OF ME IN THE PRELIMINARIES HAS OPENED MY EYES!!
DO (SLAM)
I DON'T WANT MONEY SO BADLY THAT I'D THROW AWAY THE LIVES OF OTHERS TO GET IT!!
I WILL PUT A STOP TO THIS GAME!!
THAT ANGEL MUST HAVE SOME KIND OF WEAK-NESS...

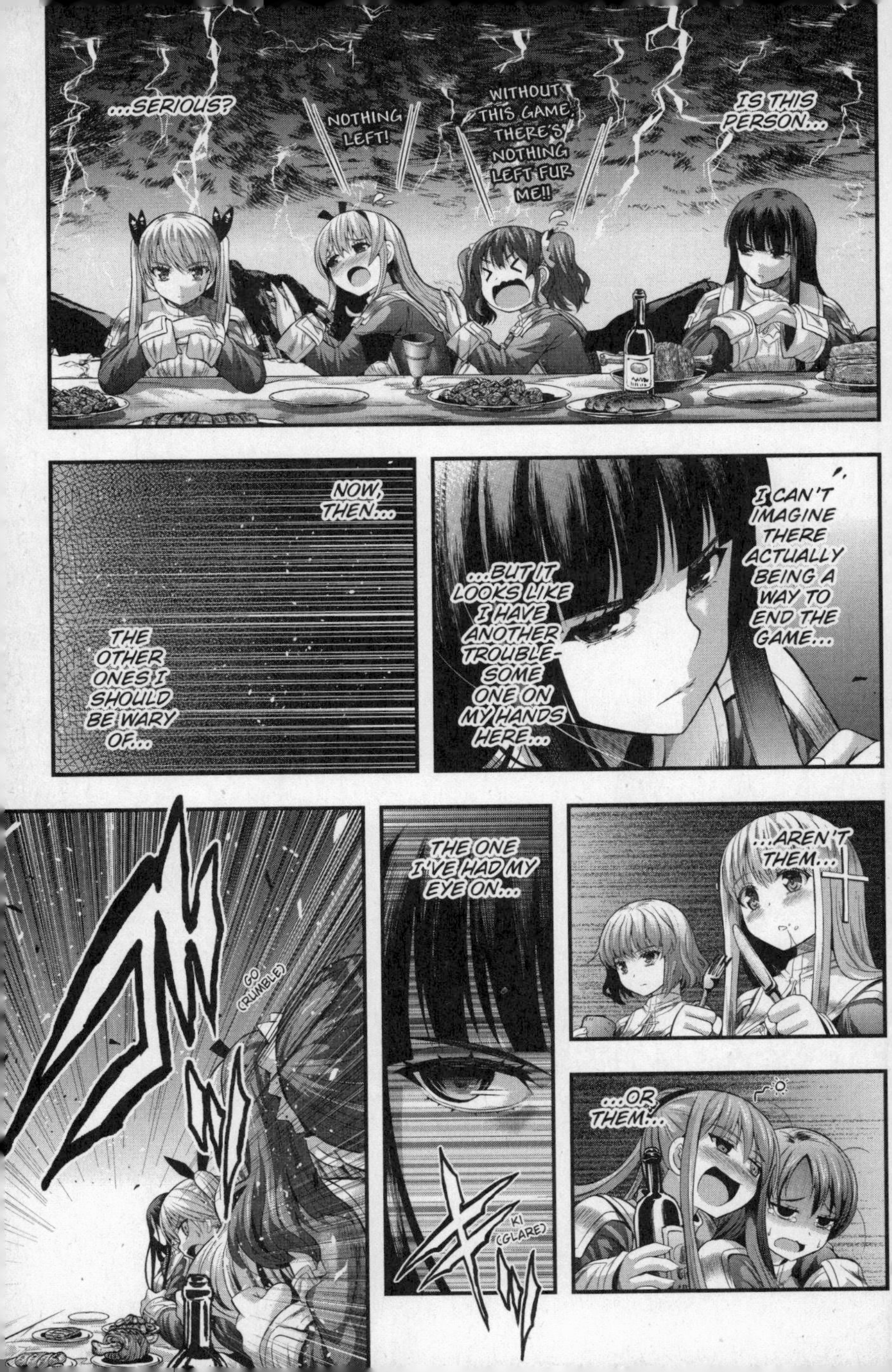
IS THIS PERSON...
WITHOUT THIS GAME, THERE'S NOTHING LEFT FUR ME!!
NOTHING LEFT!
...SERIOUS?
I CAN'T IMAGINE THERE ACTUALLY BEING A WAY TO END THE GAME...
...BUT IT LOOKS LIKE I HAVE ANOTHER TROUBLE-SOME ONE ON MY HANDS HERE...
NOW, THEN...
THE OTHER ONES I SHOULD BE WARY OF...
...AREN'T THEM...
...OR THEM...
THE ONE I'VE HAD MY EYE ON...
KI (GLARE)
GO (RUMBLE)

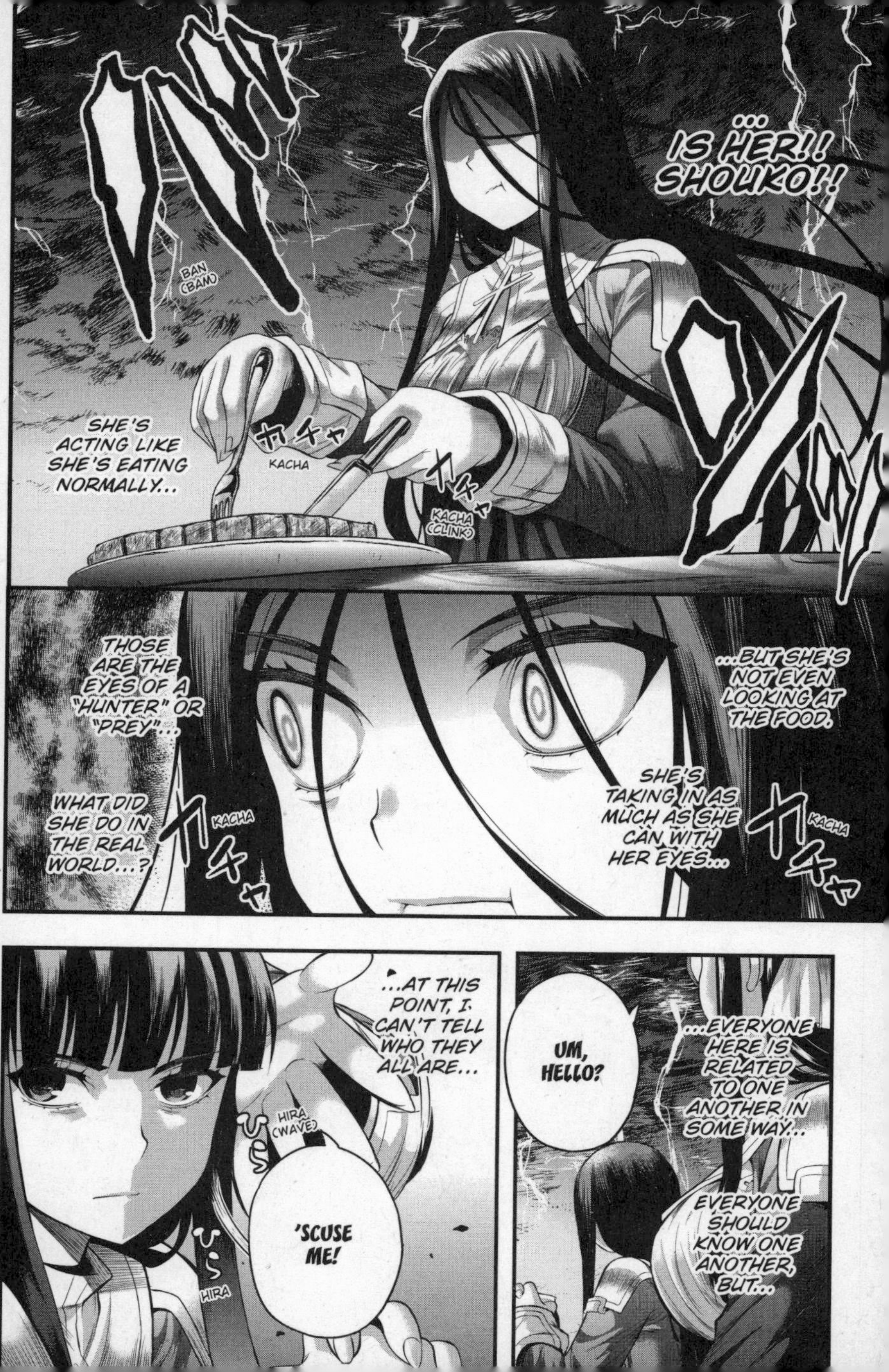
... IS HER!! SHOUKO!!
BAN (BAM)
SHE'S ACTING LIKE SHE'S EATING NORMALLY...
KACHA
KACHA (CLINK)
...BUT SHE'S NOT EVEN LOOKING AT THE FOOD.
SHE'S TAKING IN AS MUCH AS SHE CAN WITH HER EYES...
KACHA
THOSE ARE THE EYES OF A "HUNTER" OR "PREY"...
WHAT DID SHE DO IN THE REAL WORLD...?
KACHA
...EVERYONE HERE IS RELATED TO ONE ANOTHER IN SOME WAY...
UM, HELLO?
EVERYONE SHOULD KNOW ONE ANOTHER, BUT...
...AT THIS POINT, I CAN'T TELL WHO THEY ALL ARE...
HIRA (WAVE)
'SCUSE ME!
HIRA

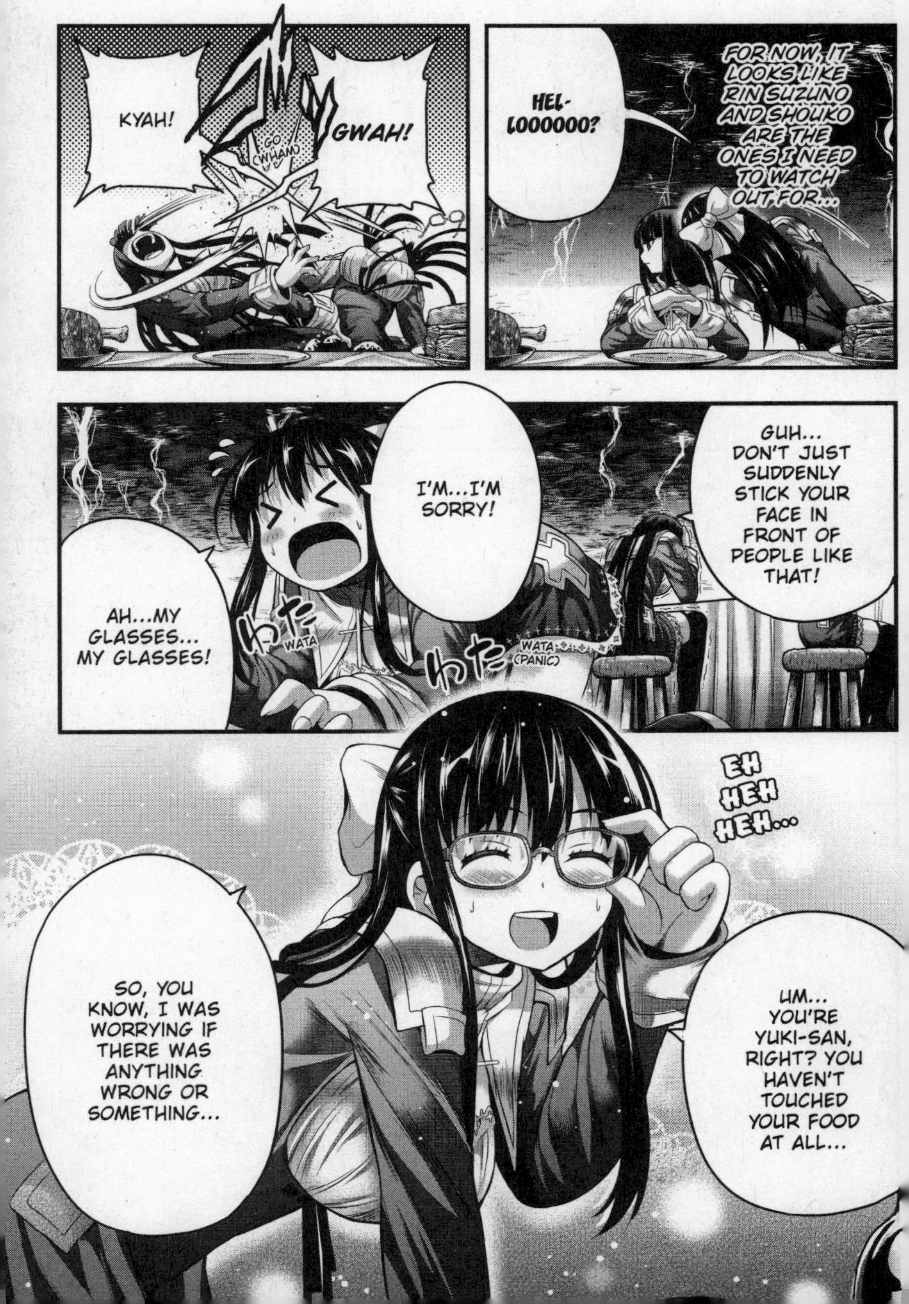
FOR NOW, IT LOOKS LIKE RIN SUZUNO AND SHOUKO ARE THE ONES I NEED TO WATCH OUT FOR...
HEL-LOOOOOO?
GWAH!
GO (WHAM)
KYAH!
GUH... DON'T JUST SUDDENLY STICK YOUR FACE IN FRONT OF PEOPLE LIKE THAT!
I'M...I'M SORRY!
WATA (PANIC)
WATA
AH...MY GLASSES... MY GLASSES!
EH HEH HEH...
UM... YOU'RE YUKI-SAN, RIGHT? YOU HAVEN'T TOUCHED YOUR FOOD AT ALL...
SO, YOU KNOW, I WAS WORRYING IF THERE WAS ANYTHING WRONG OR SOMETHING...

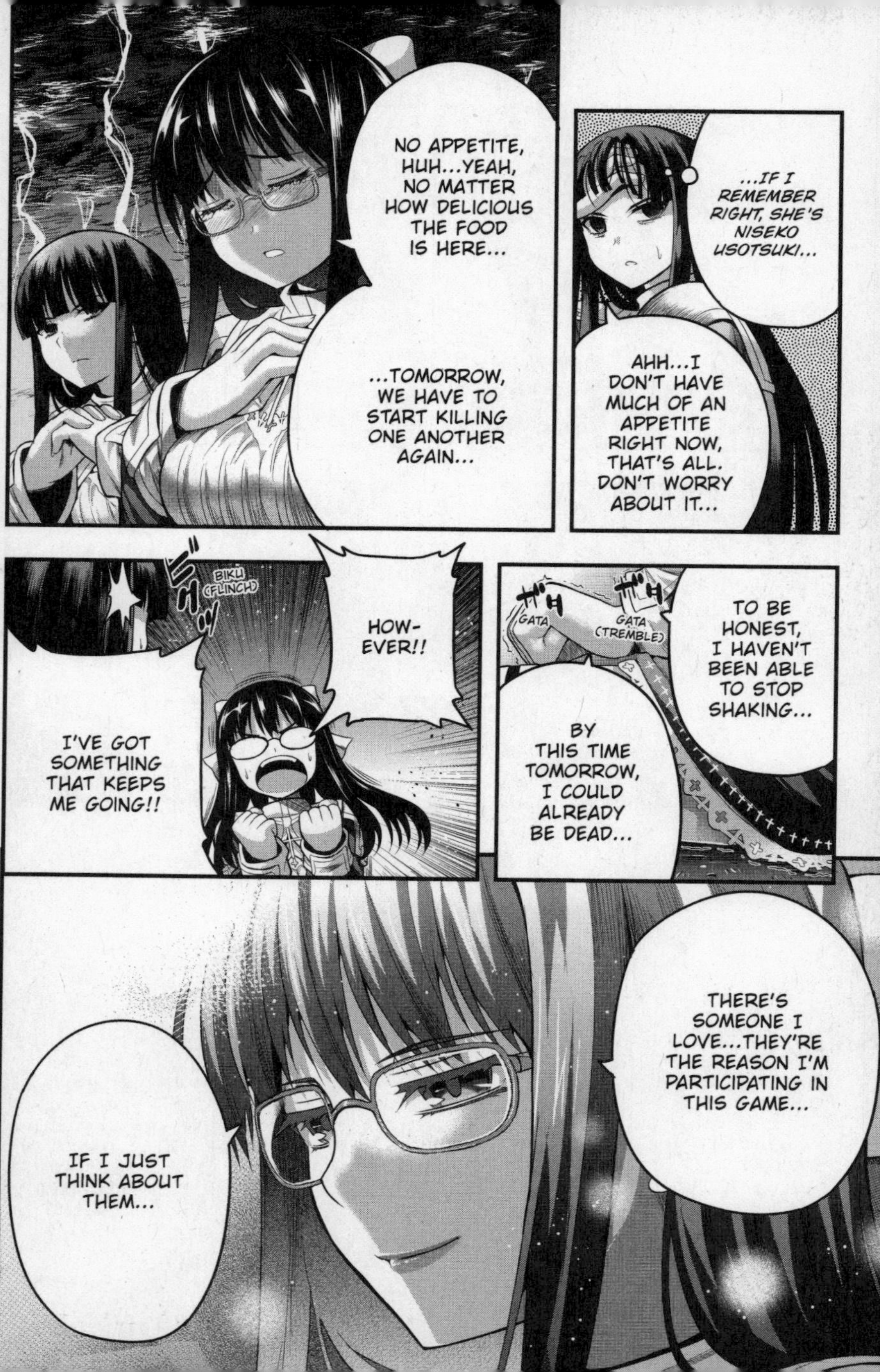
...IF I REMEMBER RIGHT, SHE'S NISEKO USOTSUKI...
AHH...I DON'T HAVE MUCH OF AN APPETITE RIGHT NOW, THAT'S ALL. DON'T WORRY ABOUT IT...
NO APPETITE, HUH...YEAH, NO MATTER HOW DELICIOUS THE FOOD IS HERE...
...TOMORROW, WE HAVE TO START KILLING ONE ANOTHER AGAIN...
GATA
GATA (TREMBLE)
TO BE HONEST, I HAVEN'T BEEN ABLE TO STOP SHAKING...
BY THIS TIME TOMORROW, I COULD ALREADY BE DEAD...
HOW-EVER!!
BIKU (FLINCH)
I'VE GOT SOMETHING THAT KEEPS ME GOING!!
THERE'S SOMEONE I LOVE...THEY'RE THE REASON I'M PARTICIPATING IN THIS GAME...
IF I JUST THINK ABOUT THEM...

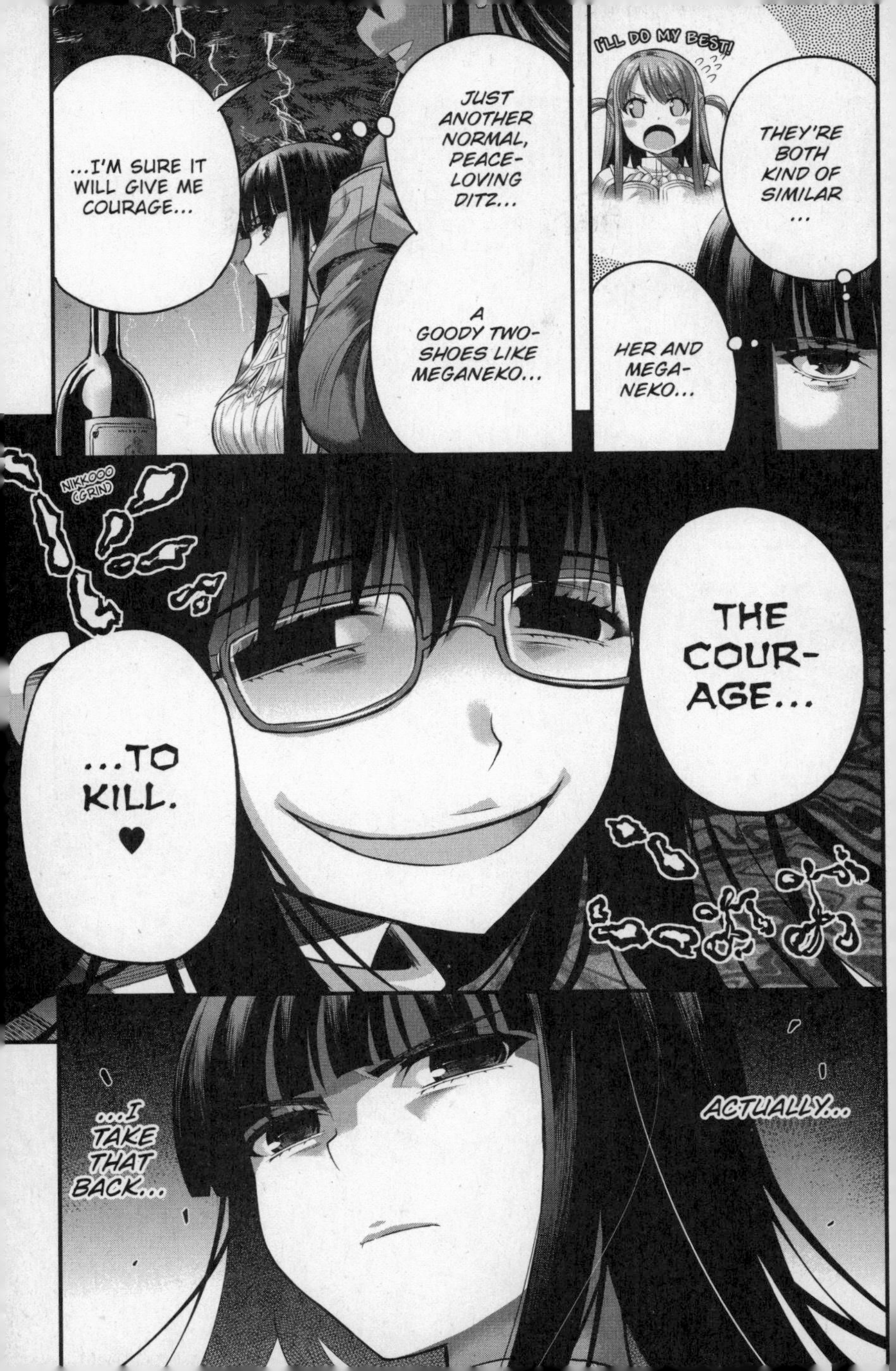
I'LL DO MY BEST!
THEY'RE BOTH KIND OF SIMILAR...
HER AND MEGA-NEKO...
JUST ANOTHER NORMAL, PEACE-LOVING DITZ...
A GOODY TWO-SHOES LIKE MEGANEKO...
...I'M SURE IT WILL GIVE ME COURAGE...
THE COUR-AGE...
NIKKOOO (GRIN)
...TO KILL. ♥
ACTUALLY...
...I TAKE THAT BACK...

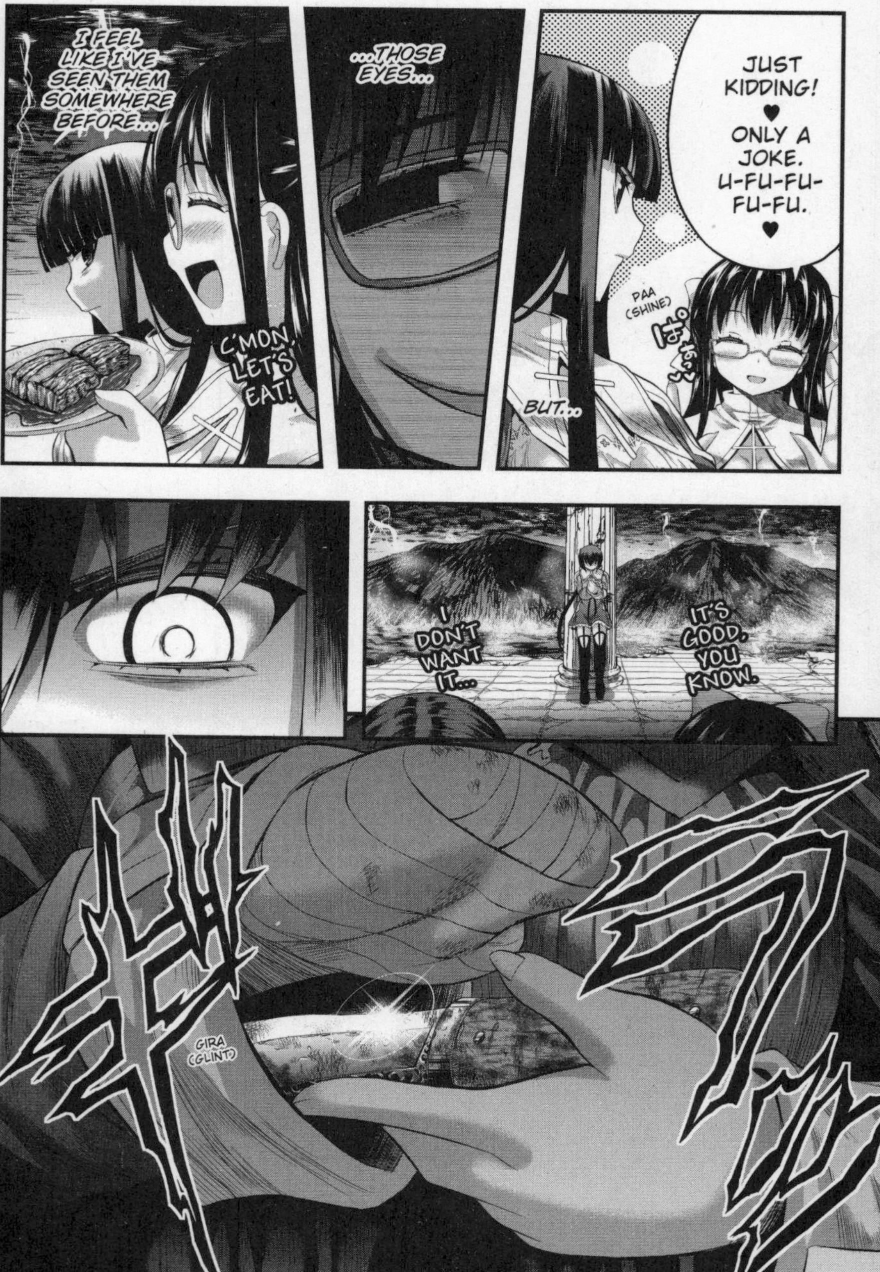
JUST KIDDING! ♥ ONLY A JOKE. U-FU-FU-FU-FU. ♥
PAA (SHINE)
BUT...
...THOSE EYES...
I FEEL LIKE I'VE SEEN THEM SOMEWHERE BEFORE...
C'MON, LET'S EAT!
IT'S GOOD, YOU KNOW.
I DON'T WANT IT...
GIRA (GLINT)

Though You May Burn to Ash

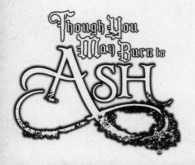

Though You May Burn to ASH

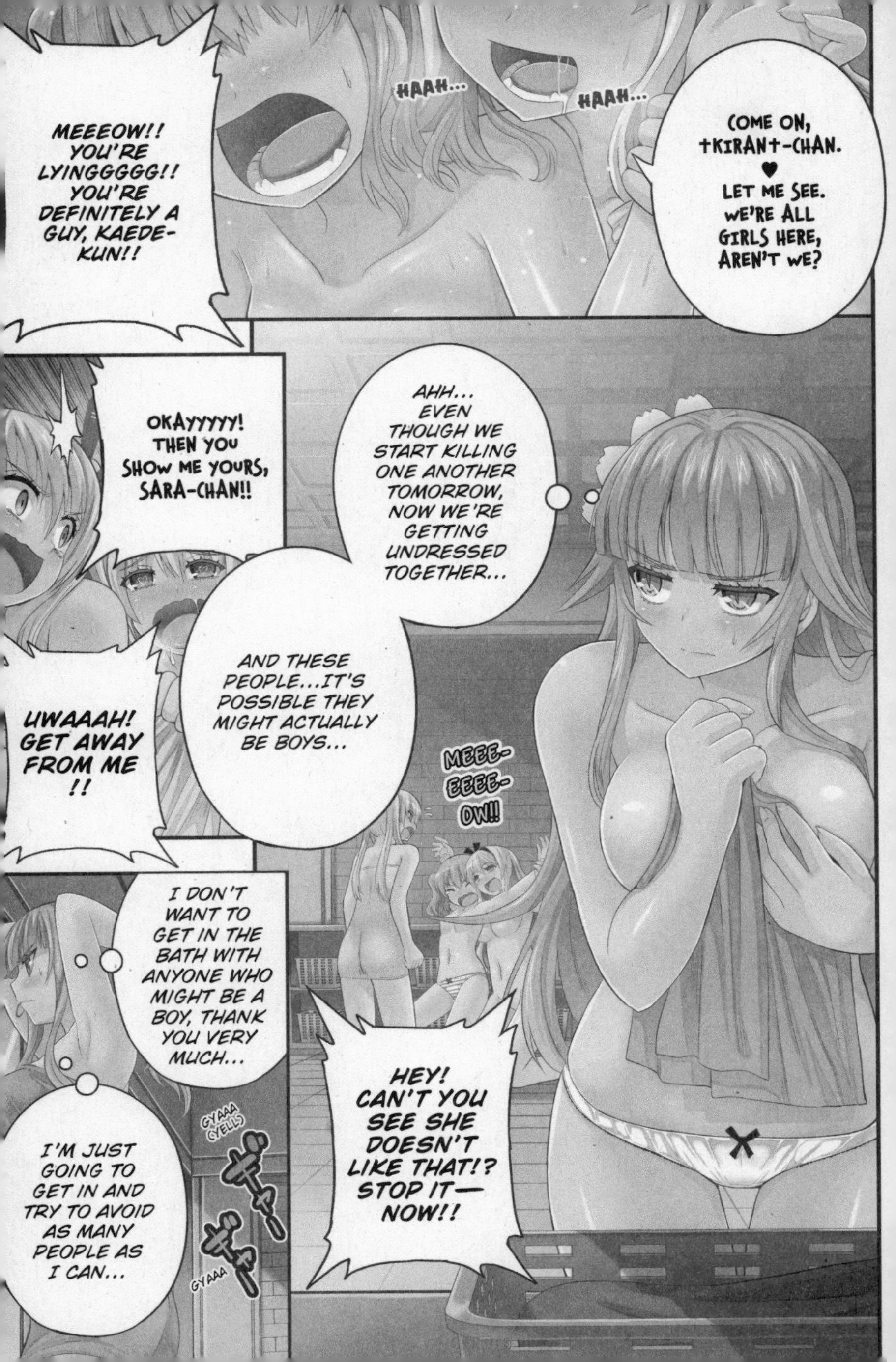
COME ON, †KIRAN†-CHAN. ♥ LET ME SEE. WE'RE ALL GIRLS HERE, AREN'T WE?
HAAH...
HAAH...
MEEEOW!! YOU'RE LYINGGGGG!! YOU'RE DEFINITELY A GUY, KAEDE-KUN!!
AHH... EVEN THOUGH WE START KILLING ONE ANOTHER TOMORROW, NOW WE'RE GETTING UNDRESSED TOGETHER...
AND THESE PEOPLE...IT'S POSSIBLE THEY MIGHT ACTUALLY BE BOYS...
MEEE-EEEE-OW!!
HEY! CAN'T YOU SEE SHE DOESN'T LIKE THAT!? STOP IT—NOW!!
OKAYYYYY! THEN YOU SHOW ME YOURS, SARA-CHAN!!
UWAAAH! GET AWAY FROM ME !!
I DON'T WANT TO GET IN THE BATH WITH ANYONE WHO MIGHT BE A BOY, THANK YOU VERY MUCH...
I'M JUST GOING TO GET IN AND TRY TO AVOID AS MANY PEOPLE AS I CAN...
GYAAA (YELLS)
GYAAA

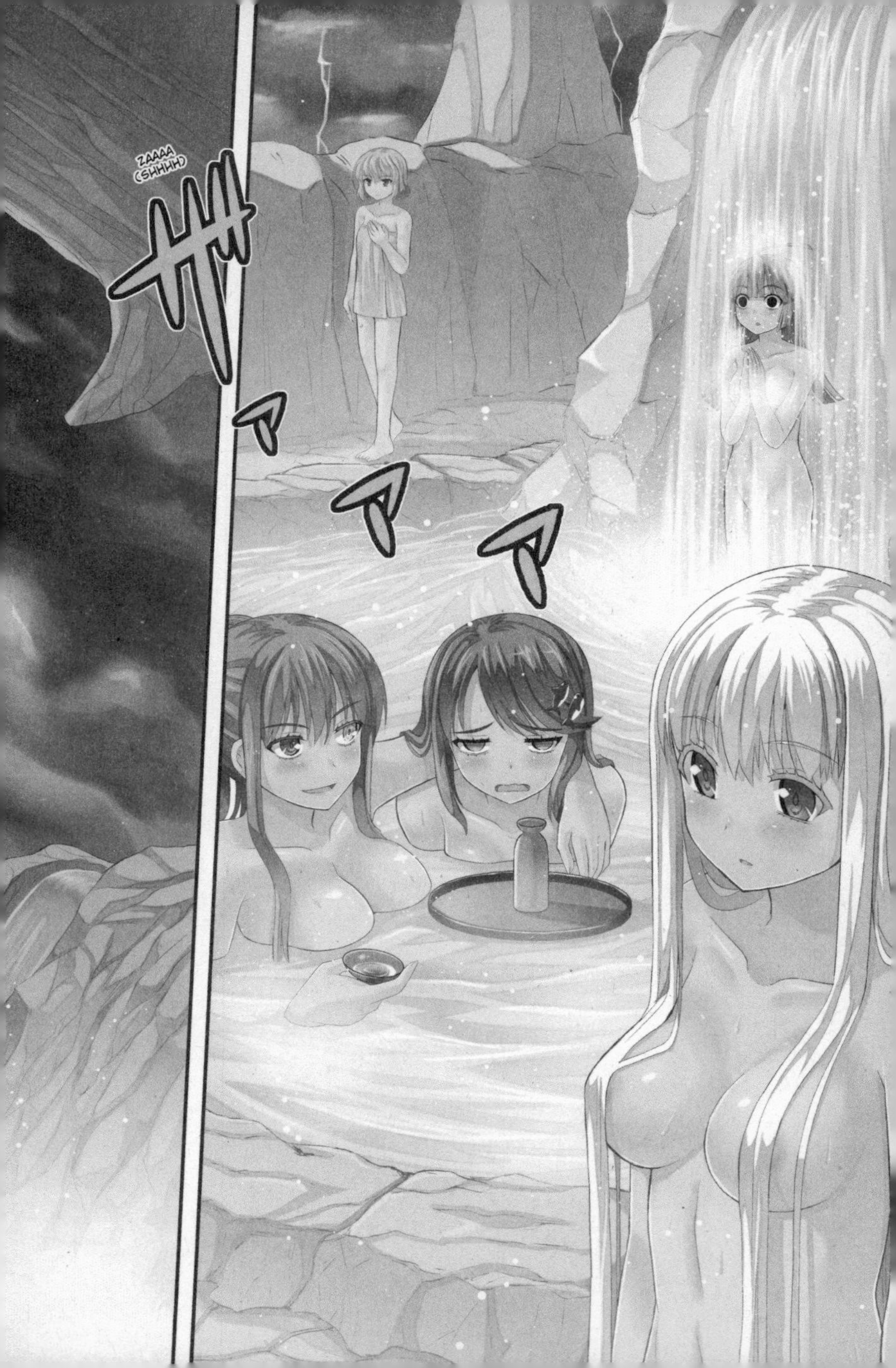
ZAAAA
(SHHHH)

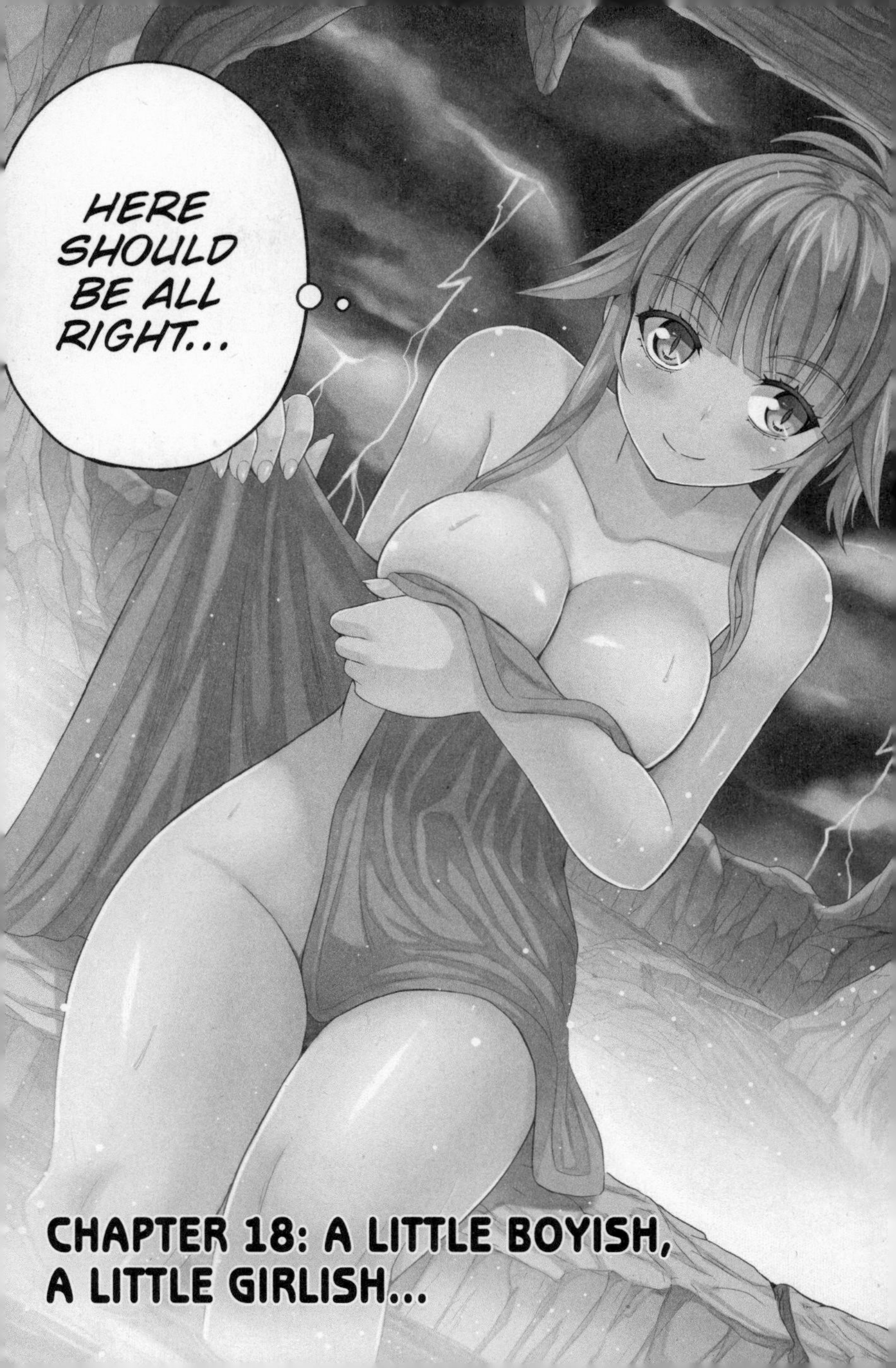
HERE SHOULD BE ALL RIGHT...

# CHAPTER 18: A LITTLE BOYISH, A LITTLE GIRLISH...

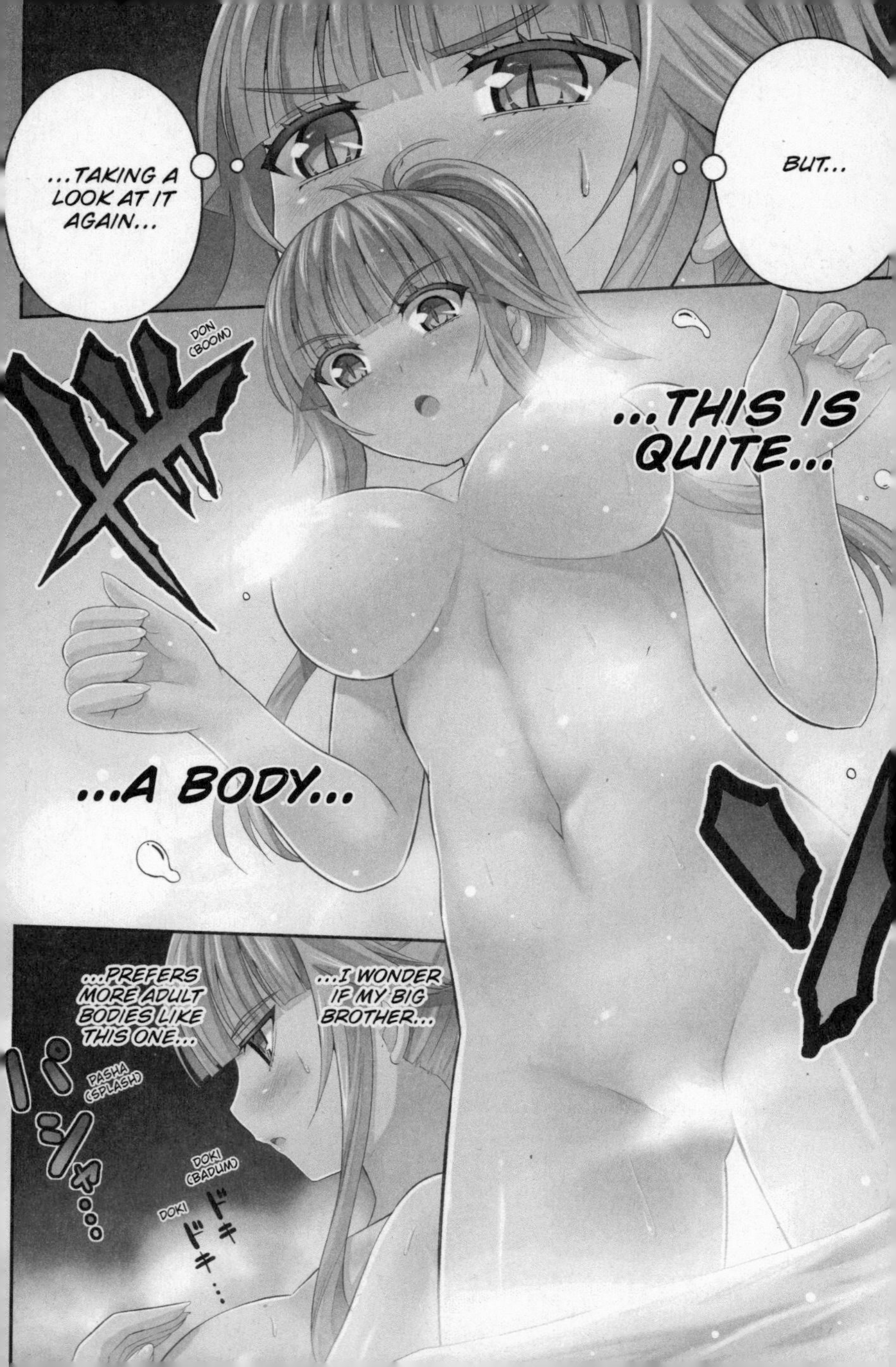
BUT...
...TAKING A LOOK AT IT AGAIN...
DON (BOOM)
...THIS IS QUITE...
...A BODY...
...I WONDER IF MY BIG BROTHER...
...PREFERS MORE ADULT BODIES LIKE THIS ONE...
PASHA (SPLASH)
パシャ...
DOKI (BADUM)
DOKI
ドキ
ドキ...

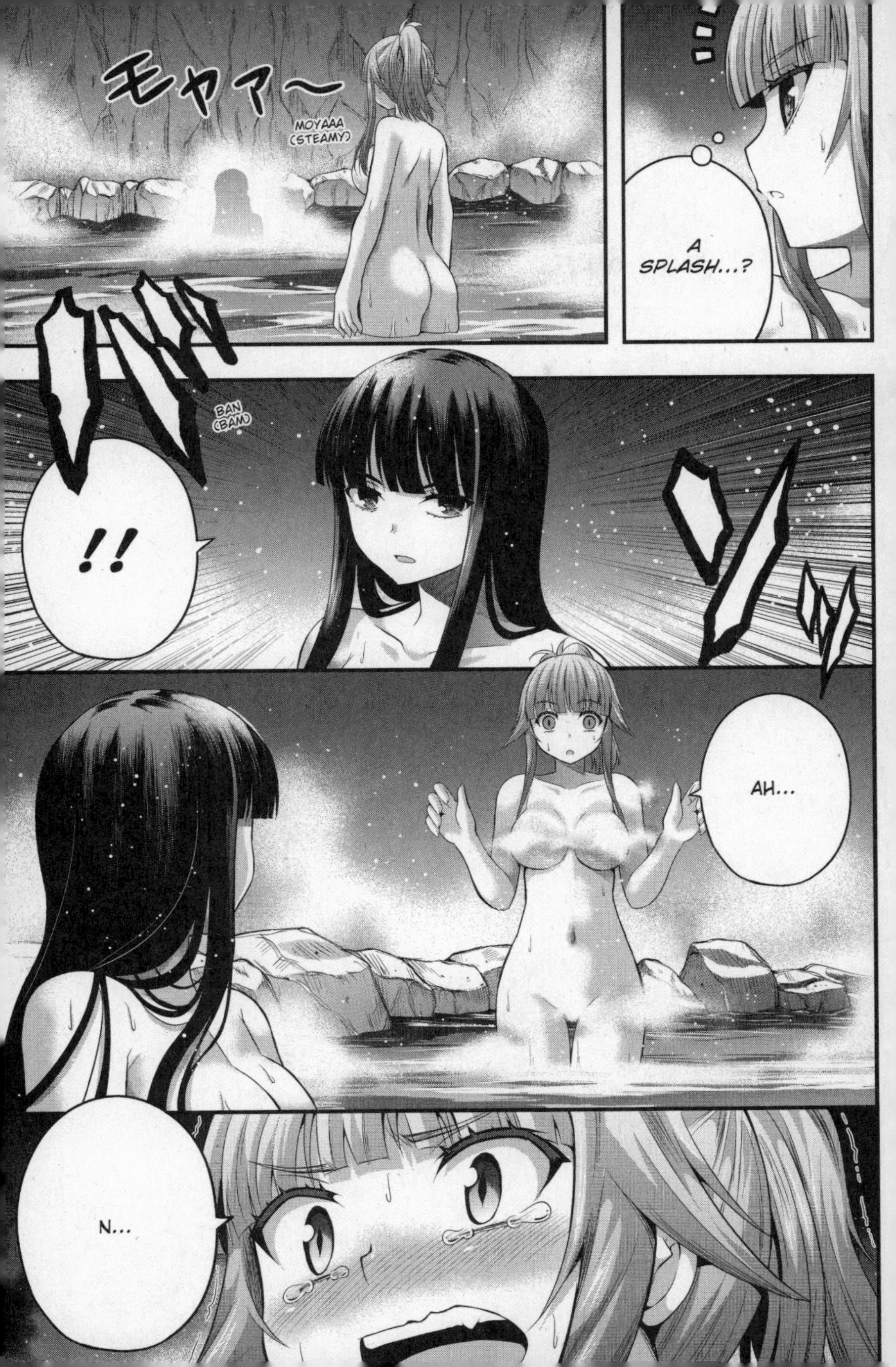
A SPLASH...?
モヤァ～
MOYAAA (STEAMY)
BAN (BAM)
!!
AH...
N...

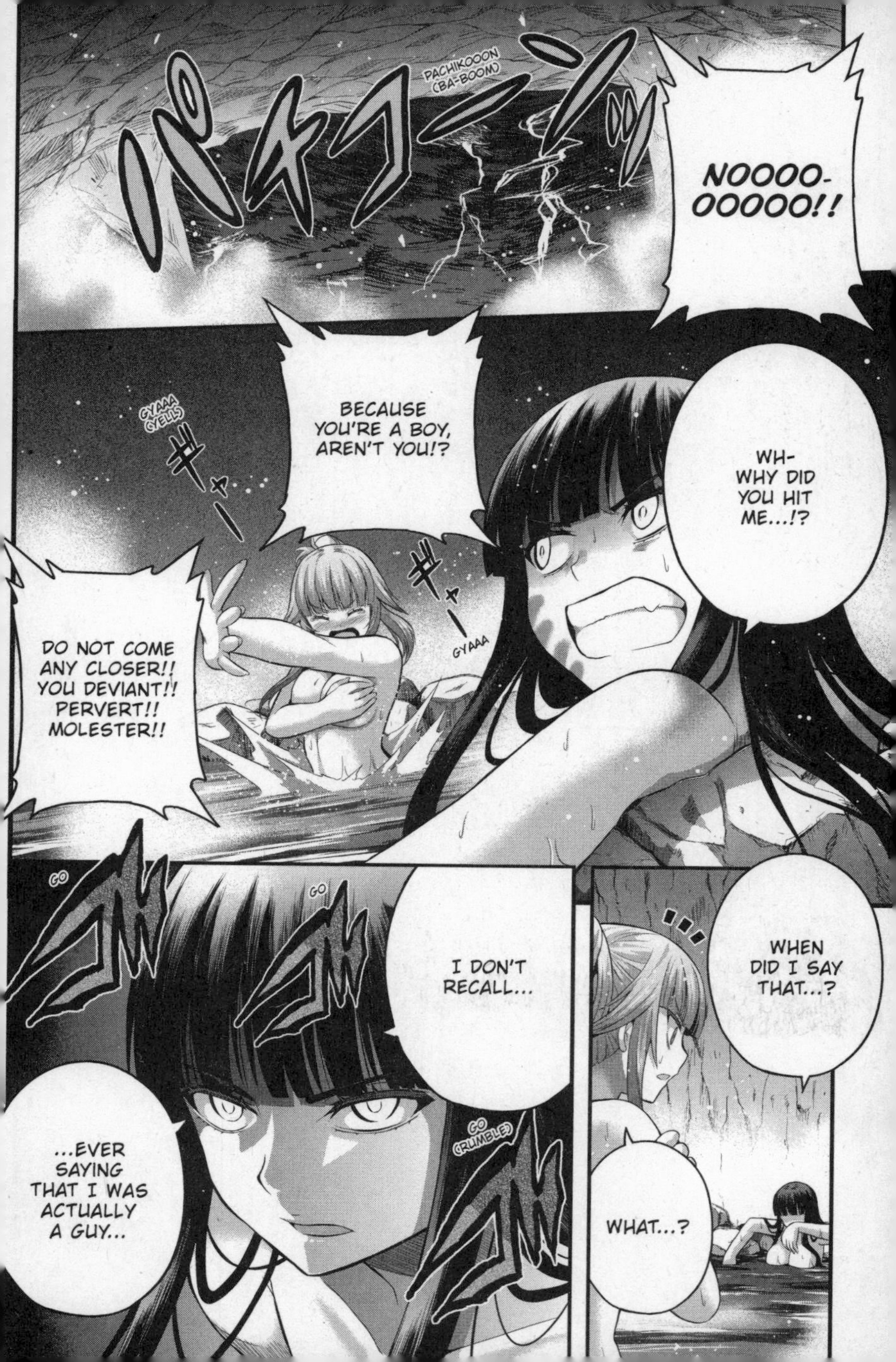
NOOOO-OOOOO!!
PACHIKOOON (BA-BOOM)
WH- WHY DID YOU HIT ME...!?
BECAUSE YOU'RE A BOY, AREN'T YOU!?
GYAAA (YELLS)
GYAAA
DO NOT COME ANY CLOSER!! YOU DEVIANT!! PERVERT!! MOLESTER!!
...
WHEN DID I SAY THAT...?
WHAT...?
GO
GO
I DON'T RECALL...
GO (RUMBLE)
...EVER SAYING THAT I WAS ACTUALLY A GUY...

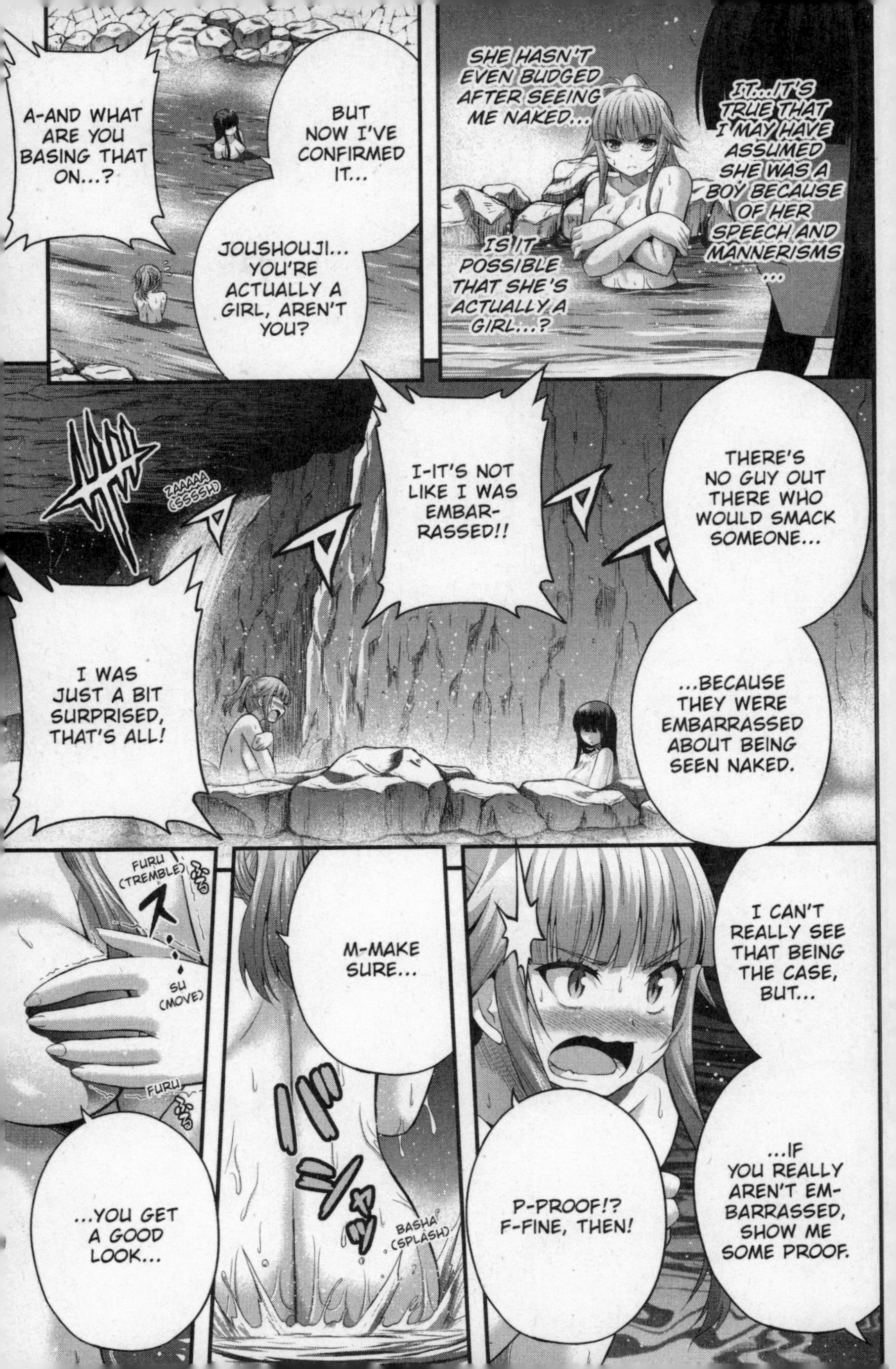
IT...IT'S TRUE THAT I MAY HAVE ASSUMED SHE WAS A BOY BECAUSE OF HER SPEECH AND MANNERISMS...
SHE HASN'T EVEN BUDGED AFTER SEEING ME NAKED...
IS IT POSSIBLE THAT SHE'S ACTUALLY A GIRL...?
BUT NOW I'VE CONFIRMED IT...
JOUSHOUJI... YOU'RE ACTUALLY A GIRL, AREN'T YOU?
A-AND WHAT ARE YOU BASING THAT ON...?
THERE'S NO GUY OUT THERE WHO WOULD SMACK SOMEONE...
...BECAUSE THEY WERE EMBARRASSED ABOUT BEING SEEN NAKED.
I-IT'S NOT LIKE I WAS EMBARRASSED!!
ZAAAAA (SSSSH)
I WAS JUST A BIT SURPRISED, THAT'S ALL!
I CAN'T REALLY SEE THAT BEING THE CASE, BUT...
...IF YOU REALLY AREN'T EM-BARRASSED, SHOW ME SOME PROOF.
P-PROOF!? F-FINE, THEN!
M-MAKE SURE...
BASHA (SPLASH)
FURU (TREMBLE)
SU (MOVE)
FURU
...YOU GET A GOOD LOOK...

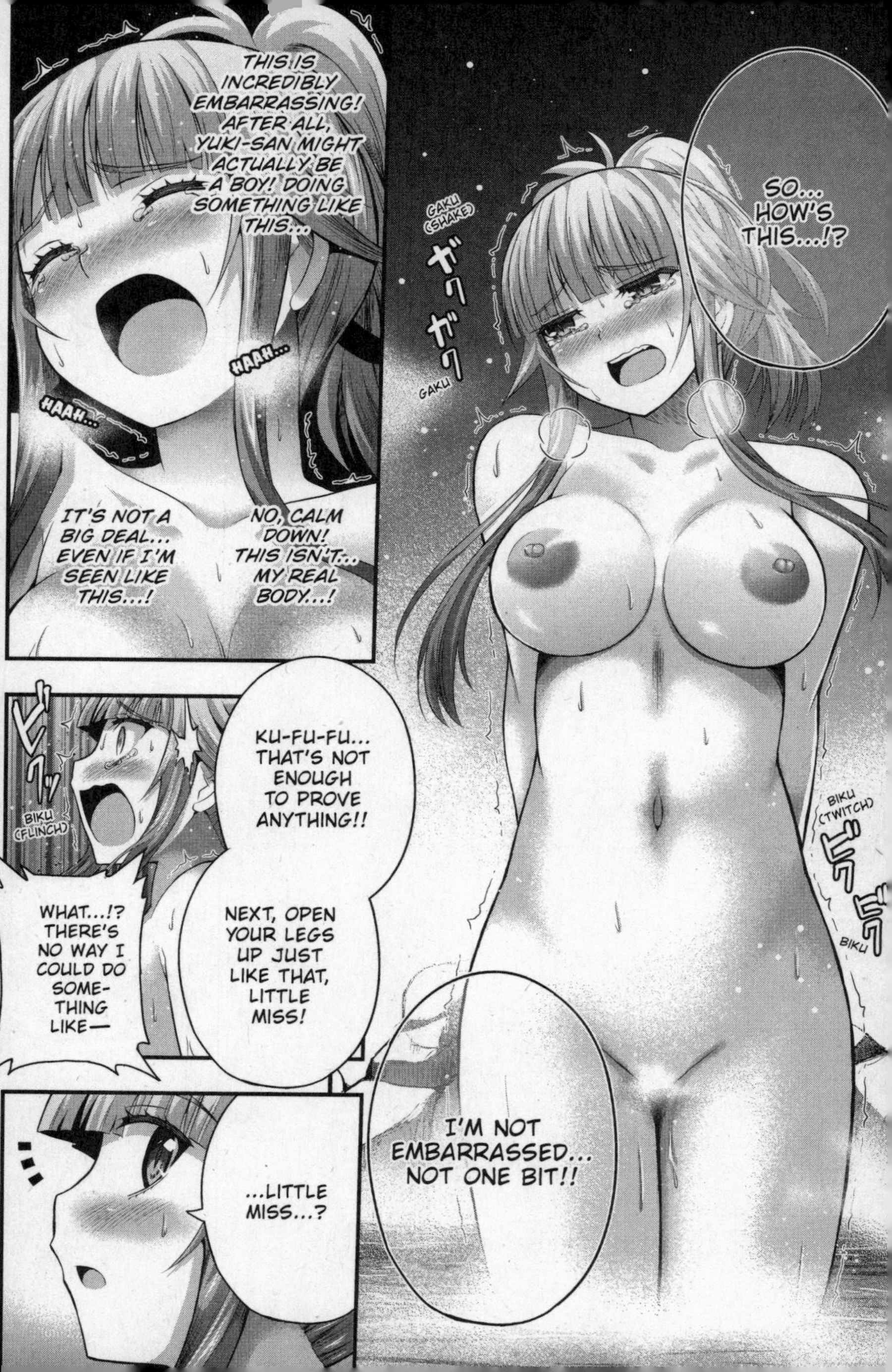
SO... HOW'S THIS...!?
GAKU (SHAKE)
GAKU
BIKU (TWITCH)
BIKU
I'M NOT EMBARRASSED... NOT ONE BIT!!
THIS IS INCREDIBLY EMBARRASSING! AFTER ALL, YUKI-SAN MIGHT ACTUALLY BE A BOY! DOING SOMETHING LIKE THIS...
HAAH...
HAAH...
NO, CALM DOWN! THIS ISN'T... MY REAL BODY...!
IT'S NOT A BIG DEAL... EVEN IF I'M SEEN LIKE THIS...!
KU-FU-FU... THAT'S NOT ENOUGH TO PROVE ANYTHING!!
BIKU (FLINCH)
NEXT, OPEN YOUR LEGS UP JUST LIKE THAT, LITTLE MISS!
WHAT...!? THERE'S NO WAY I COULD DO SOME-THING LIKE—
...LITTLE MISS...?
...

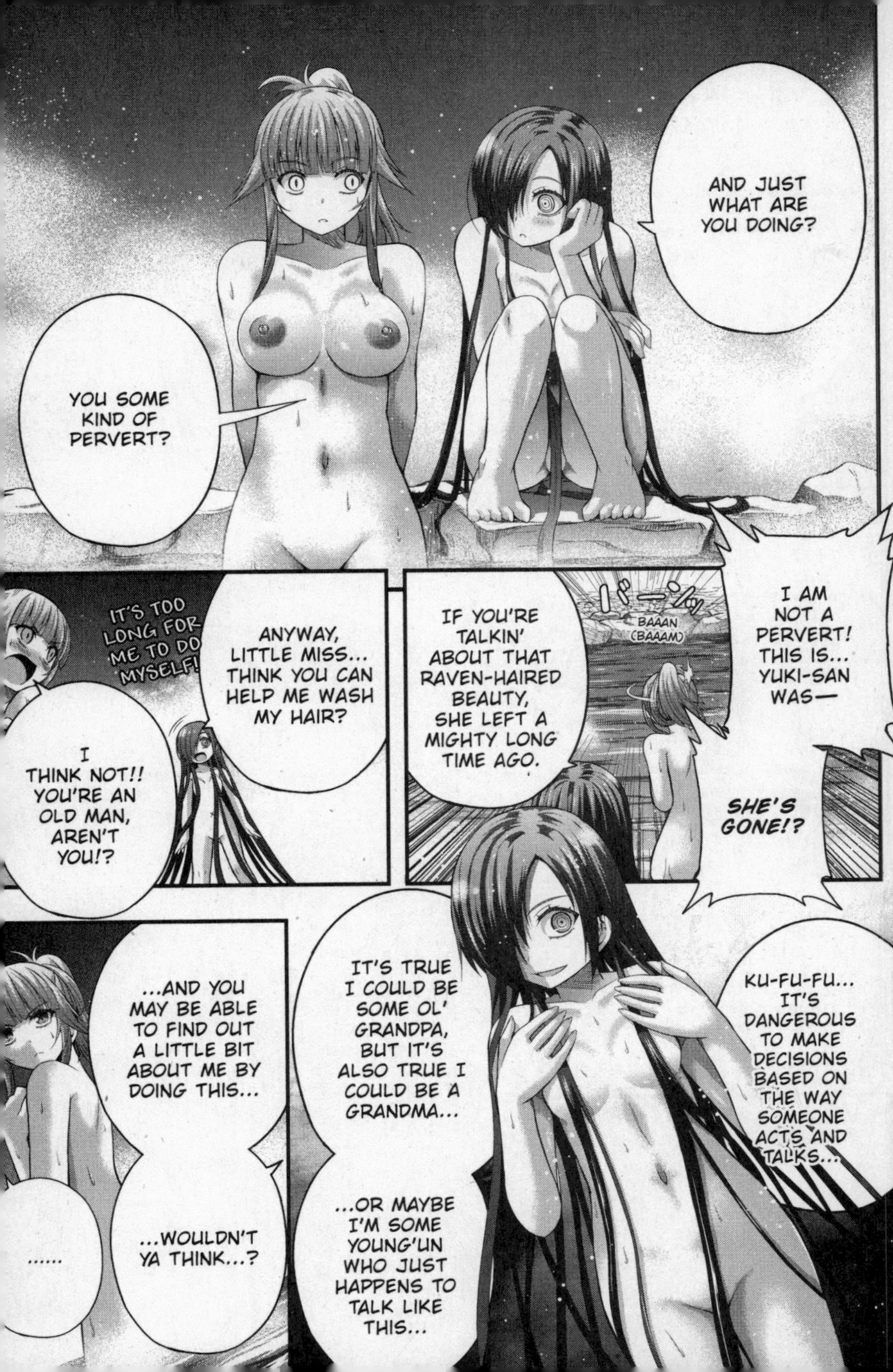
AND JUST WHAT ARE YOU DOING?
YOU SOME KIND OF PERVERT?
I AM NOT A PERVERT! THIS IS... YUKI-SAN WAS—
SHE'S GONE!?
BAAAN (BAAAM)
IF YOU'RE TALKIN' ABOUT THAT RAVEN-HAIRED BEAUTY, SHE LEFT A MIGHTY LONG TIME AGO.
ANYWAY, LITTLE MISS... THINK YOU CAN HELP ME WASH MY HAIR?
IT'S TOO LONG FOR ME TO DO MYSELF!
I THINK NOT!! YOU'RE AN OLD MAN, AREN'T YOU!?
KU-FU-FU... IT'S DANGEROUS TO MAKE DECISIONS BASED ON THE WAY SOMEONE ACTS AND TALKS...
IT'S TRUE I COULD BE SOME OL' GRANDPA, BUT IT'S ALSO TRUE I COULD BE A GRANDMA...
...OR MAYBE I'M SOME YOUNG'UN WHO JUST HAPPENS TO TALK LIKE THIS...
...AND YOU MAY BE ABLE TO FIND OUT A LITTLE BIT ABOUT ME BY DOING THIS...
...WOULDN'T YA THINK...?
......

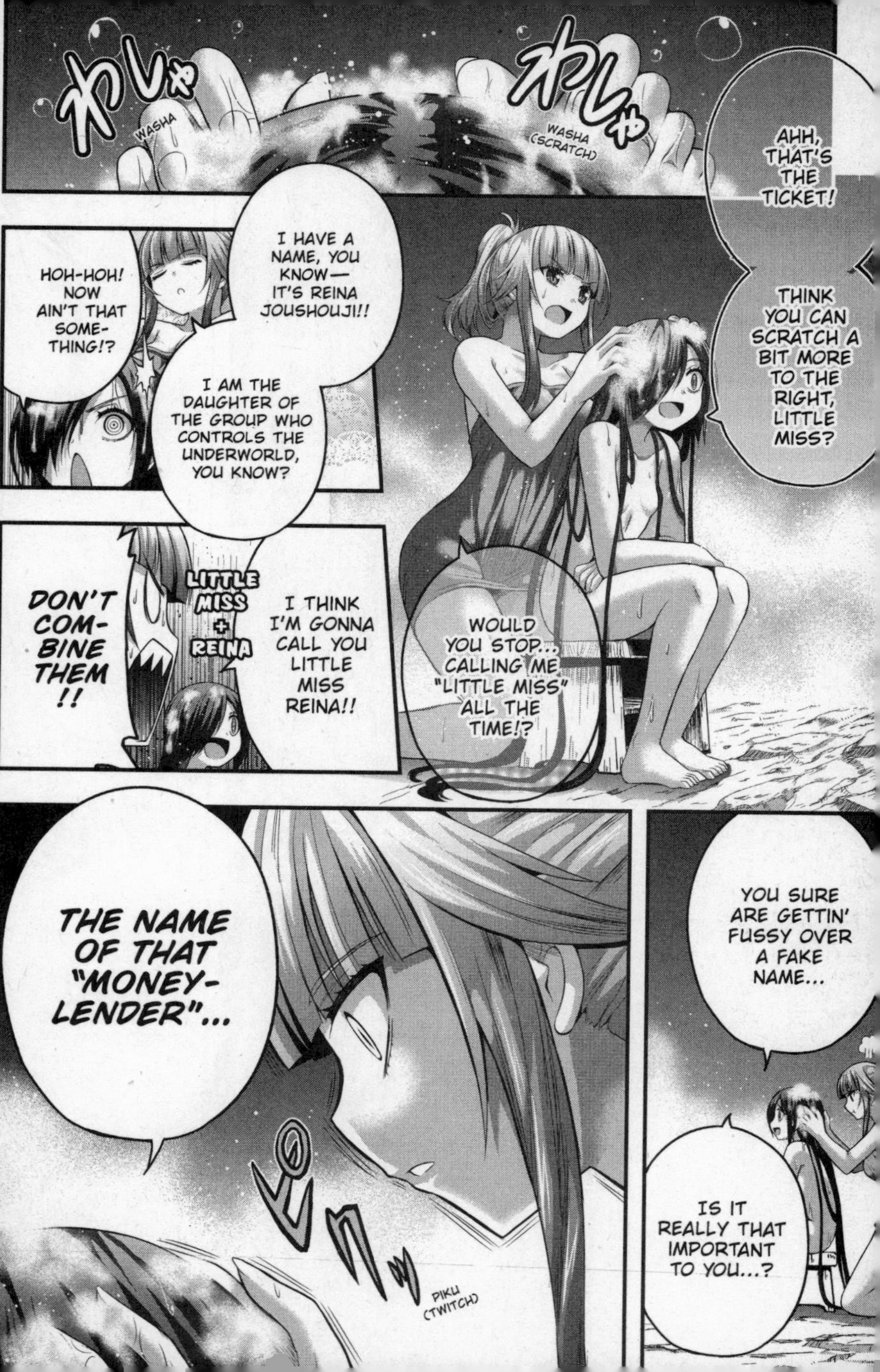
わしゃ
WASHA (SCRATCH)
わしゃ
WASHA
AHH, THAT'S THE TICKET!
THINK YOU CAN SCRATCH A BIT MORE TO THE RIGHT, LITTLE MISS?
WOULD YOU STOP... CALLING ME "LITTLE MISS" ALL THE TIME!?
I HAVE A NAME, YOU KNOW— IT'S REINA JOUSHOUJI!!
I AM THE DAUGHTER OF THE GROUP WHO CONTROLS THE UNDERWORLD, YOU KNOW?
HOH-HOH! NOW AIN'T THAT SOME-THING!?
I THINK I'M GONNA CALL YOU LITTLE MISS REINA!!
LITTLE MISS + REINA
DON'T COM-BINE THEM!!
YOU SURE ARE GETTIN' FUSSY OVER A FAKE NAME...
IS IT REALLY THAT IMPORTANT TO YOU...?
THE NAME OF THAT "MONEY-LENDER"...
PIKU (TWITCH)

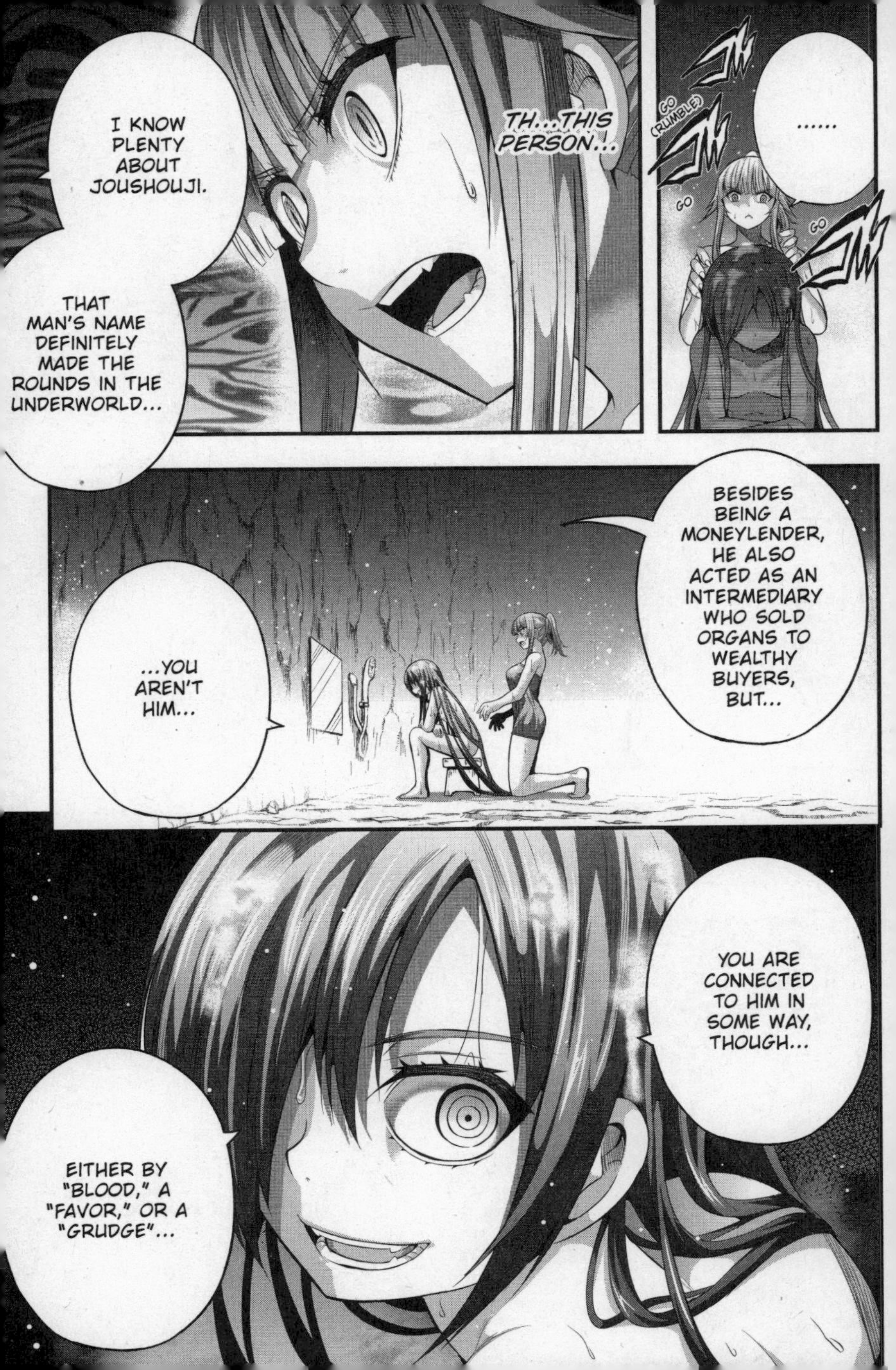
GO (RUMBLE)
......
GO
GO
TH...THIS PERSON..!
I KNOW PLENTY ABOUT JOUSHOUJI.
THAT MAN'S NAME DEFINITELY MADE THE ROUNDS IN THE UNDERWORLD...
BESIDES BEING A MONEYLENDER, HE ALSO ACTED AS AN INTERMEDIARY WHO SOLD ORGANS TO WEALTHY BUYERS, BUT...
...YOU AREN'T HIM...
YOU ARE CONNECTED TO HIM IN SOME WAY, THOUGH...
EITHER BY "BLOOD," A "FAVOR," OR A "GRUDGE"...

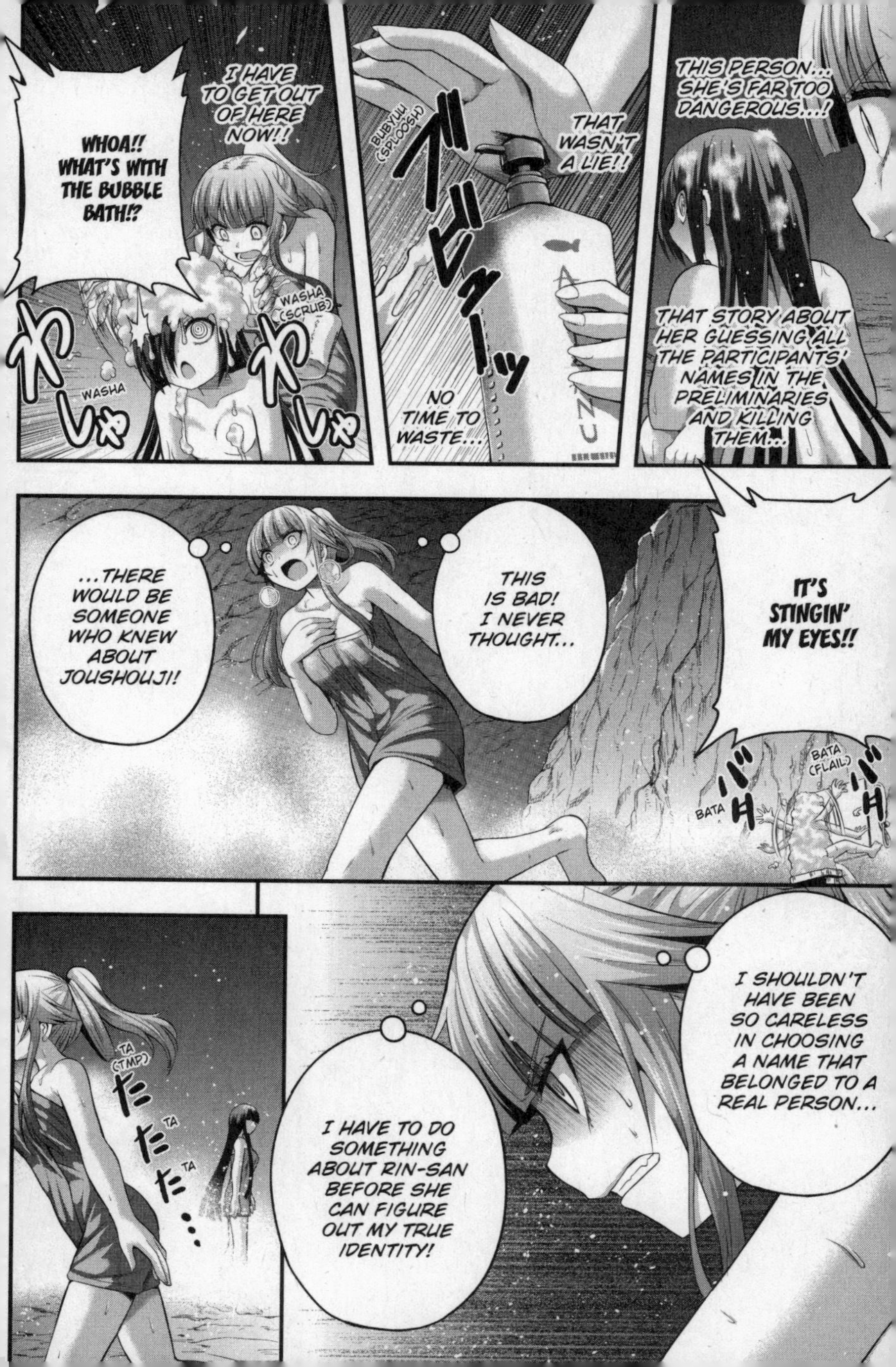
THIS PERSON... SHE'S FAR TOO DANGEROUS...!
THAT STORY ABOUT HER GUESSING ALL THE PARTICIPANTS' NAMES IN THE PRELIMINARIES AND KILLING THEM...
THAT WASN'T A LIE!!
BUBYUU (SPLOOSH)
NO TIME TO WASTE...
I HAVE TO GET OUT OF HERE NOW!!
WHOA!! WHAT'S WITH THE BUBBLE BATH!?
WASHA (SCRUB)
WASHA
IT'S STINGIN' MY EYES!!
BATA (FLAIL)
BATA
THIS IS BAD! I NEVER THOUGHT...
...THERE WOULD BE SOMEONE WHO KNEW ABOUT JOUSHOUJI!
I SHOULDN'T HAVE BEEN SO CARELESS IN CHOOSING A NAME THAT BELONGED TO A REAL PERSON...
I HAVE TO DO SOMETHING ABOUT RIN-SAN BEFORE SHE CAN FIGURE OUT MY TRUE IDENTITY!
TA (TMP)
TA
TA

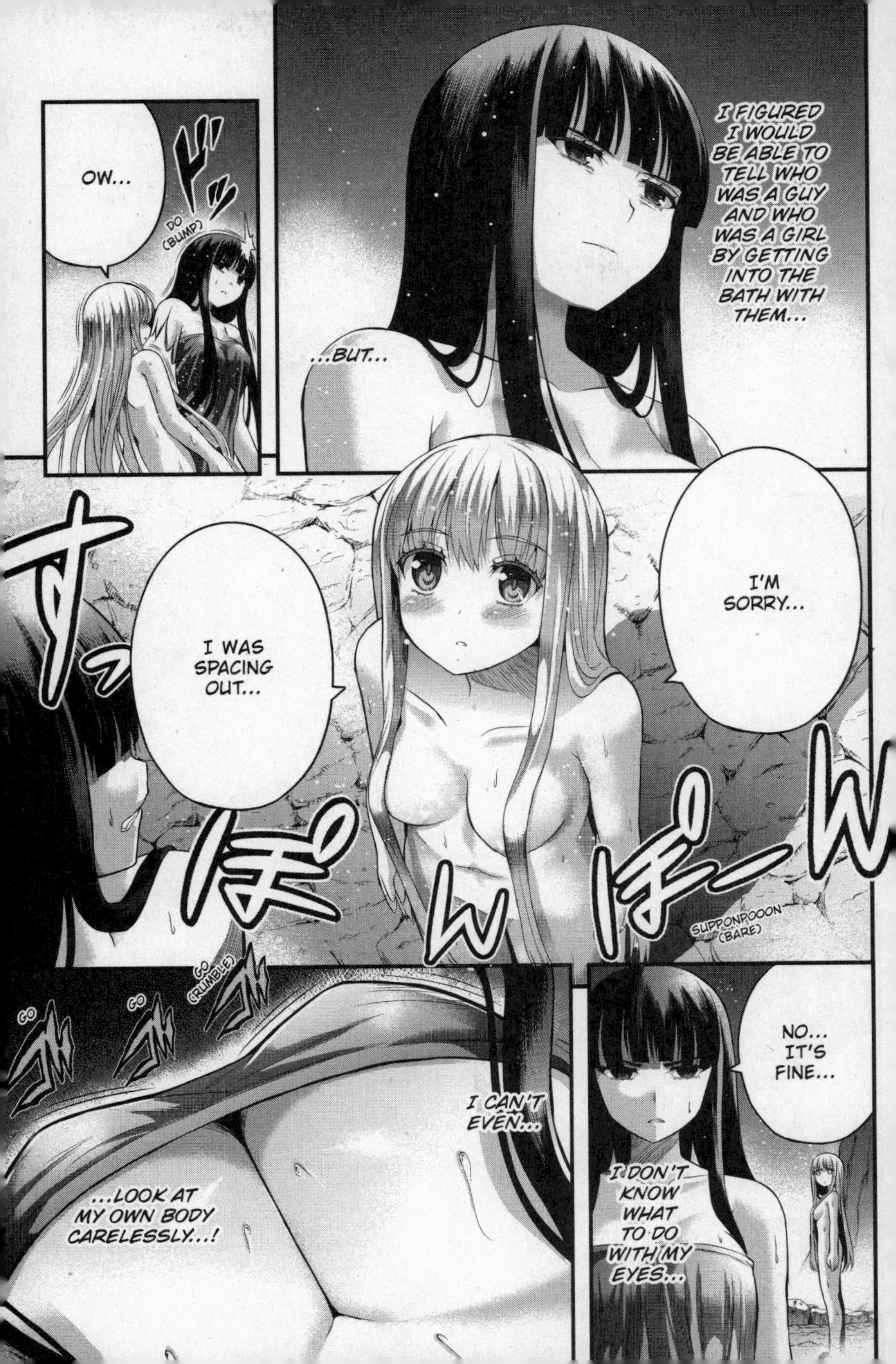
I FIGURED I WOULD BE ABLE TO TELL WHO WAS A GUY AND WHO WAS A GIRL BY GETTING INTO THE BATH WITH THEM...
...BUT...
DO (BUMP)
OW...
I'M SORRY...
I WAS SPACING OUT...
SUPPONPOOON (BARE)
NO... IT'S FINE...
I DON'T KNOW WHAT TO DO WITH MY EYES...
I CAN'T EVEN...
...LOOK AT MY OWN BODY CARELESSLY...!
GO (RUMBLE)
GO
GO

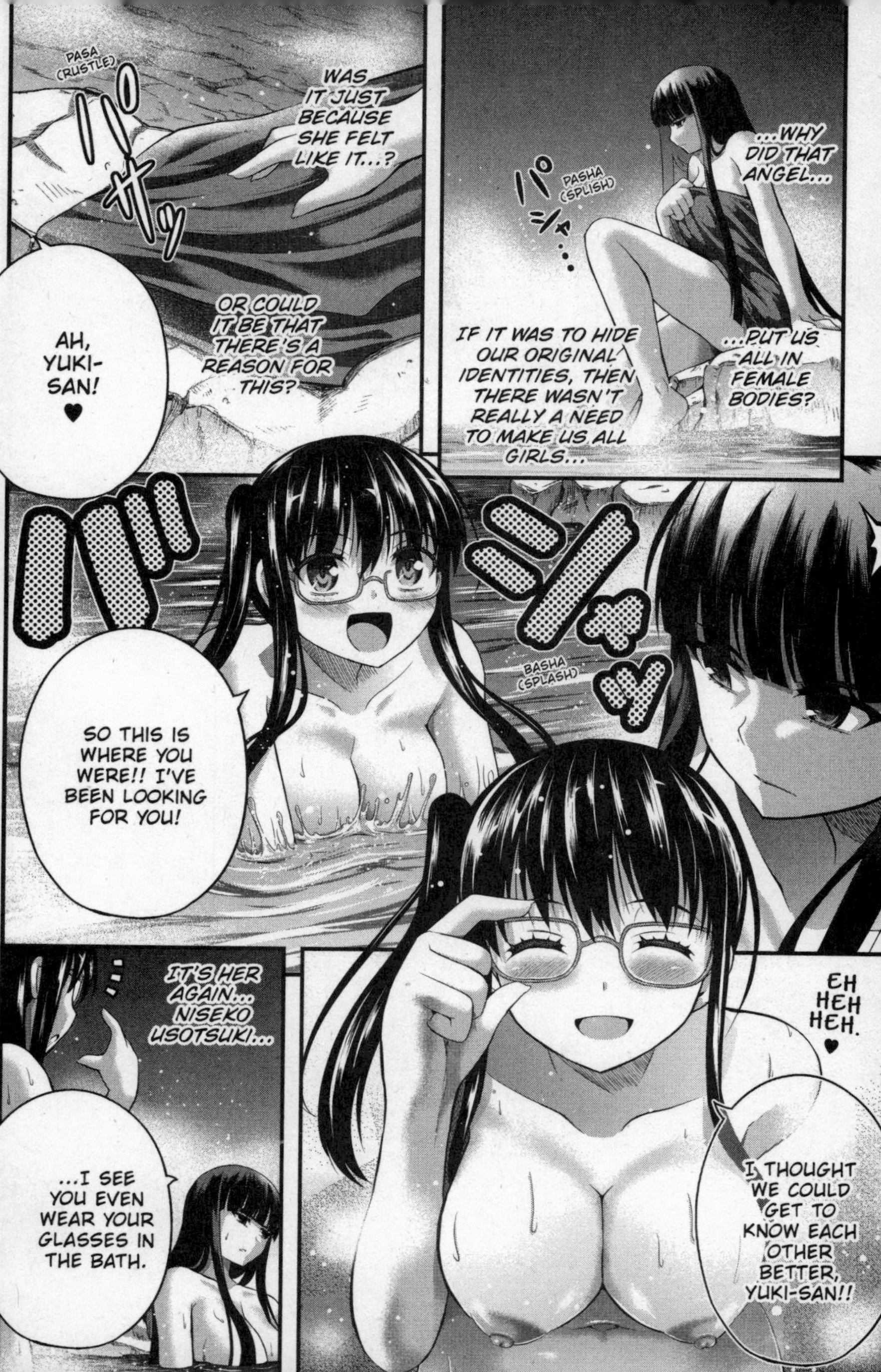
...WHY DID THAT ANGEL...
PASHA (SPLISH)
...PUT US ALL IN FEMALE BODIES?
IF IT WAS TO HIDE OUR ORIGINAL IDENTITIES, THEN THERE WASN'T REALLY A NEED TO MAKE US ALL GIRLS...
WAS IT JUST BECAUSE SHE FELT LIKE IT...?
PASA (RUSTLE)
OR COULD IT BE THAT THERE'S A REASON FOR THIS?
AH, YUKI-SAN! ♥
BASHA (SPLASH)
SO THIS IS WHERE YOU WERE!! I'VE BEEN LOOKING FOR YOU!
EH HEH HEH. ♥
I THOUGHT WE COULD GET TO KNOW EACH OTHER BETTER, YUKI-SAN!!
...
IT'S HER AGAIN... NISEKO USOTSUKI...
...I SEE YOU EVEN WEAR YOUR GLASSES IN THE BATH.

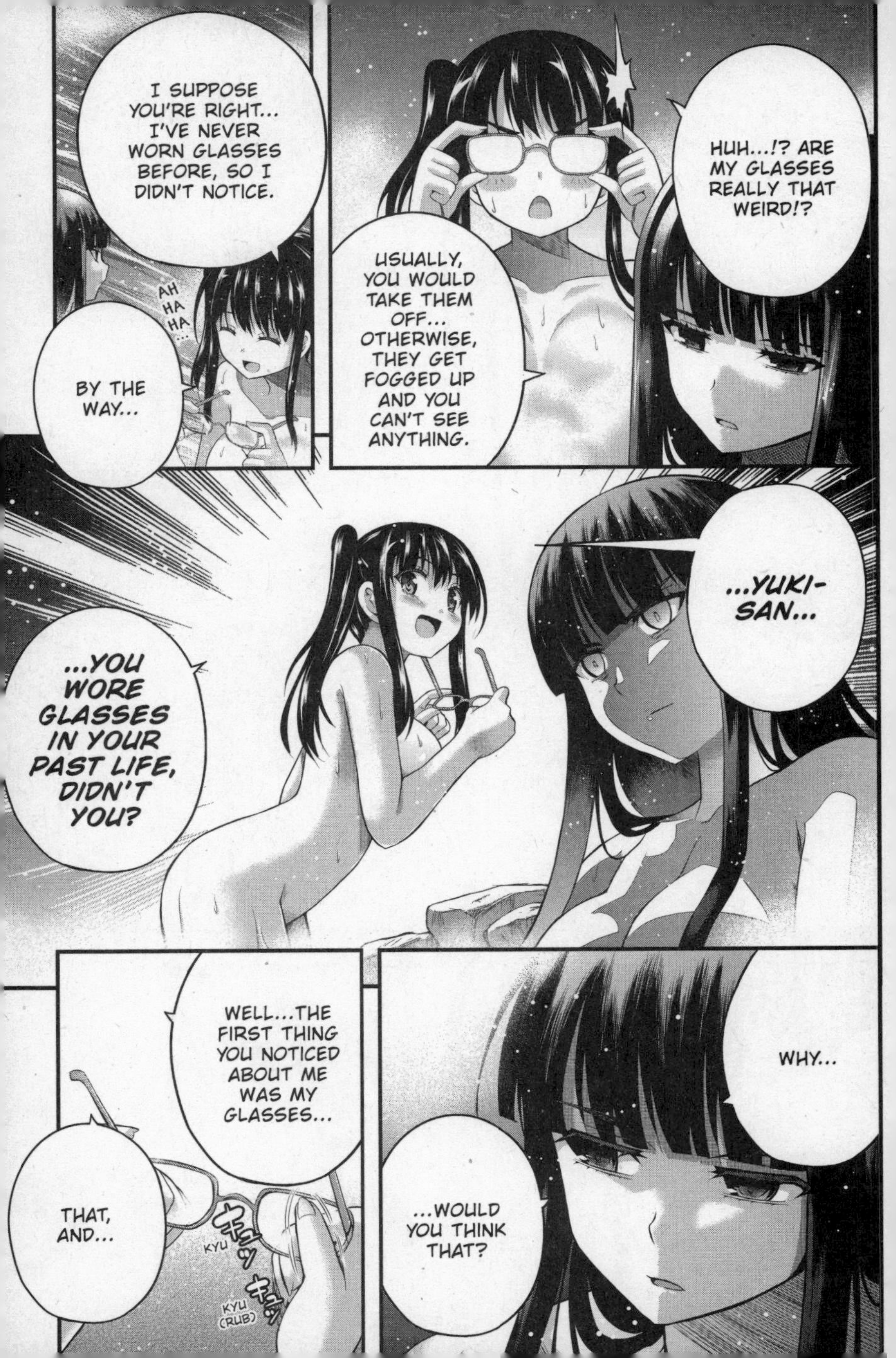
HUH...!? ARE MY GLASSES REALLY THAT WEIRD!?
USUALLY, YOU WOULD TAKE THEM OFF... OTHERWISE, THEY GET FOGGED UP AND YOU CAN'T SEE ANYTHING.
I SUPPOSE YOU'RE RIGHT... I'VE NEVER WORN GLASSES BEFORE, SO I DIDN'T NOTICE.
AH HA HA...
BY THE WAY...
...YUKI-SAN...
...YOU WORE GLASSES IN YOUR PAST LIFE, DIDN'T YOU?
WHY...
...WOULD YOU THINK THAT?
WELL...THE FIRST THING YOU NOTICED ABOUT ME WAS MY GLASSES...
THAT, AND...
KYU
KYU (RUB)

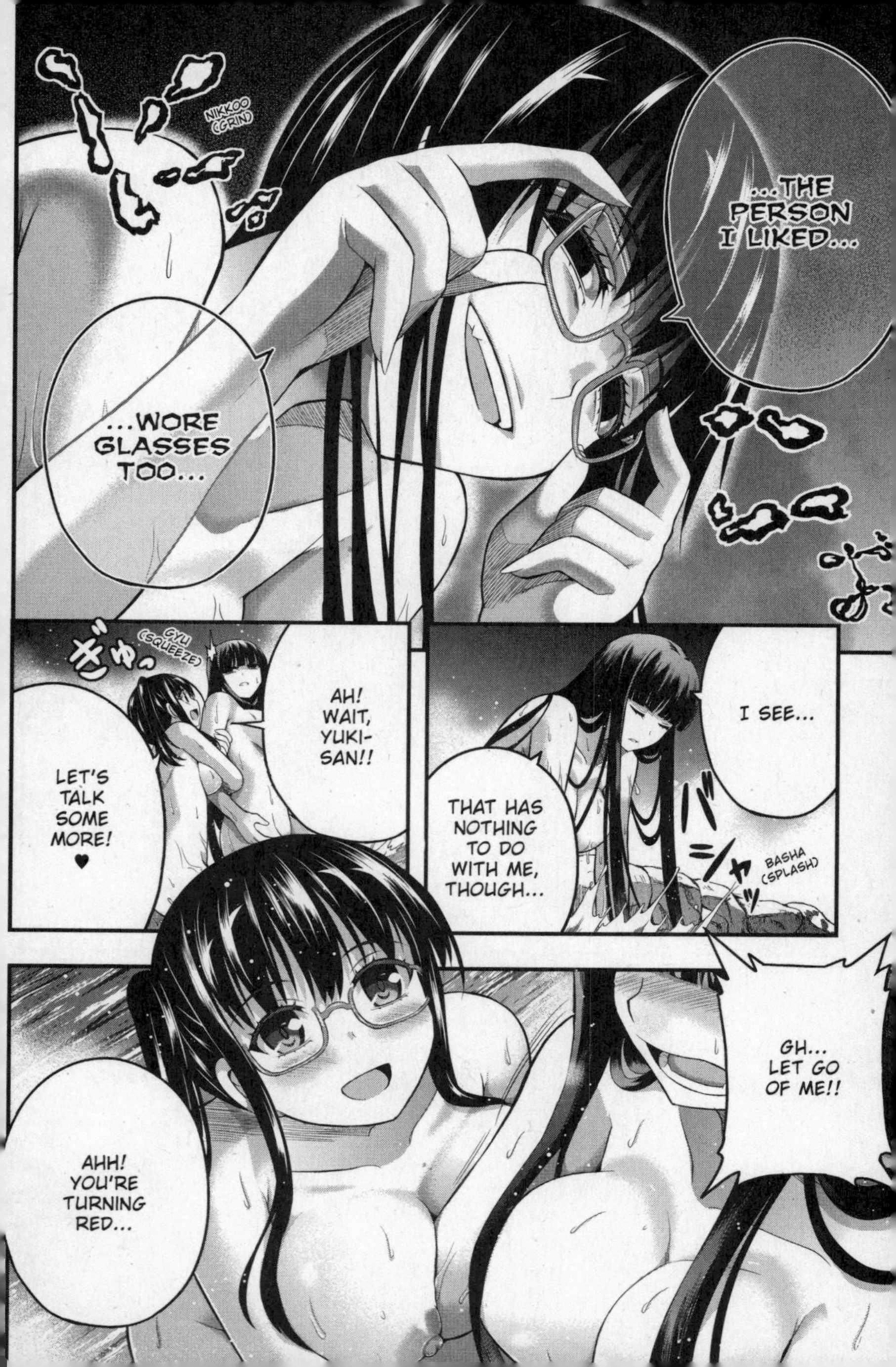
...THE PERSON I LIKED...
NIKKOO (GRIN)
...WORE GLASSES TOO...
I SEE...
THAT HAS NOTHING TO DO WITH ME, THOUGH...
BASHA (SPLASH)
AH! WAIT, YUKI-SAN!!
GYU (SQUEEZE)
LET'S TALK SOME MORE! ♥
GH... LET GO OF ME!!
AHH! YOU'RE TURNING RED...

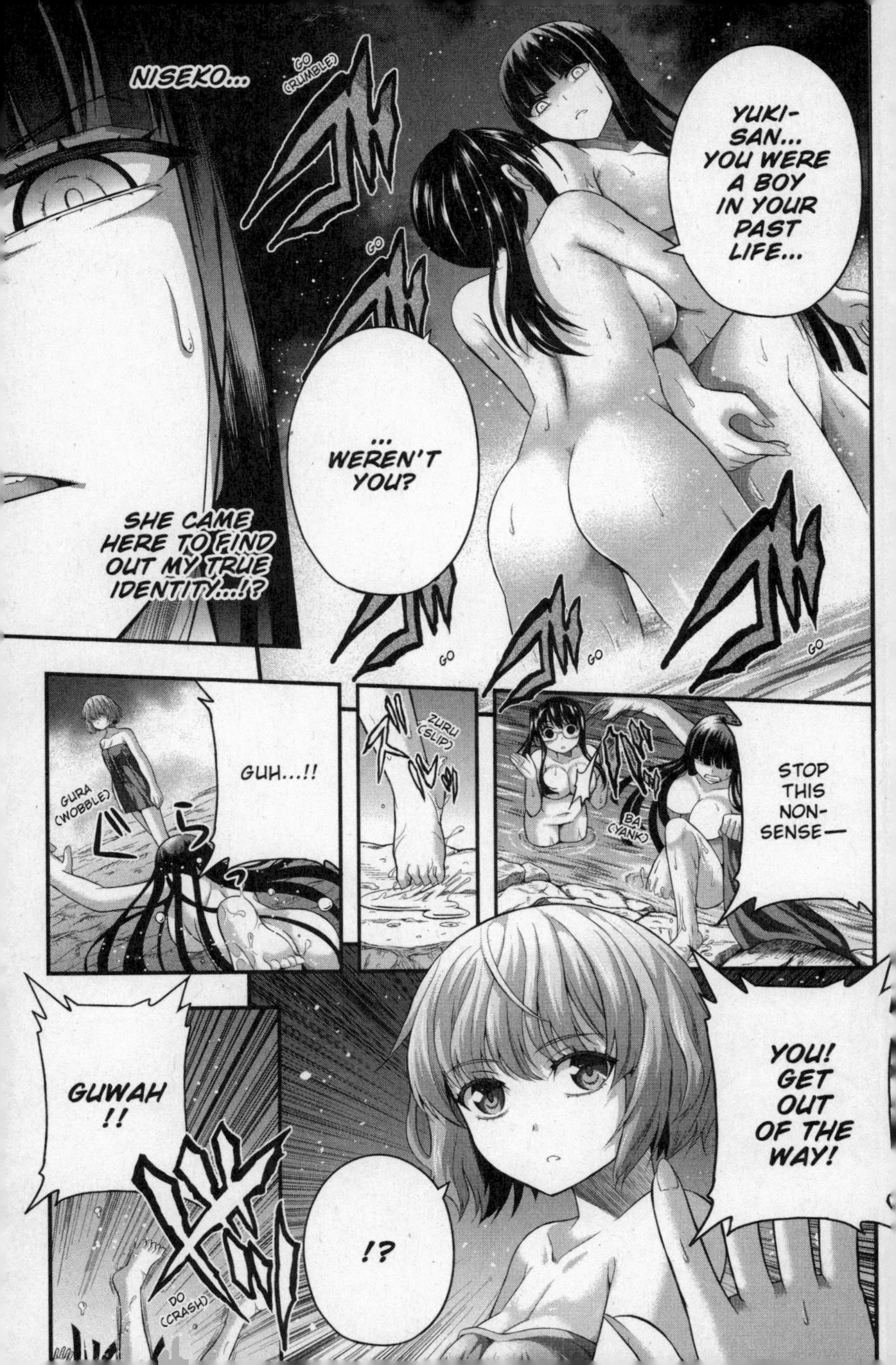
YUKI-SAN... YOU WERE A BOY IN YOUR PAST LIFE...
GO (RUMBLE)
GO
... WEREN'T YOU?
NISEKO...
SHE CAME HERE TO FIND OUT MY TRUE IDENTITY...!?
GO
GO
GO
STOP THIS NON-SENSE—
BA (YANK)
ZURU (SLIP)
GUH...!!
GURA (WOBBLE)
YOU! GET OUT OF THE WAY!
!?
GUWAH !!
DO (CRASH)

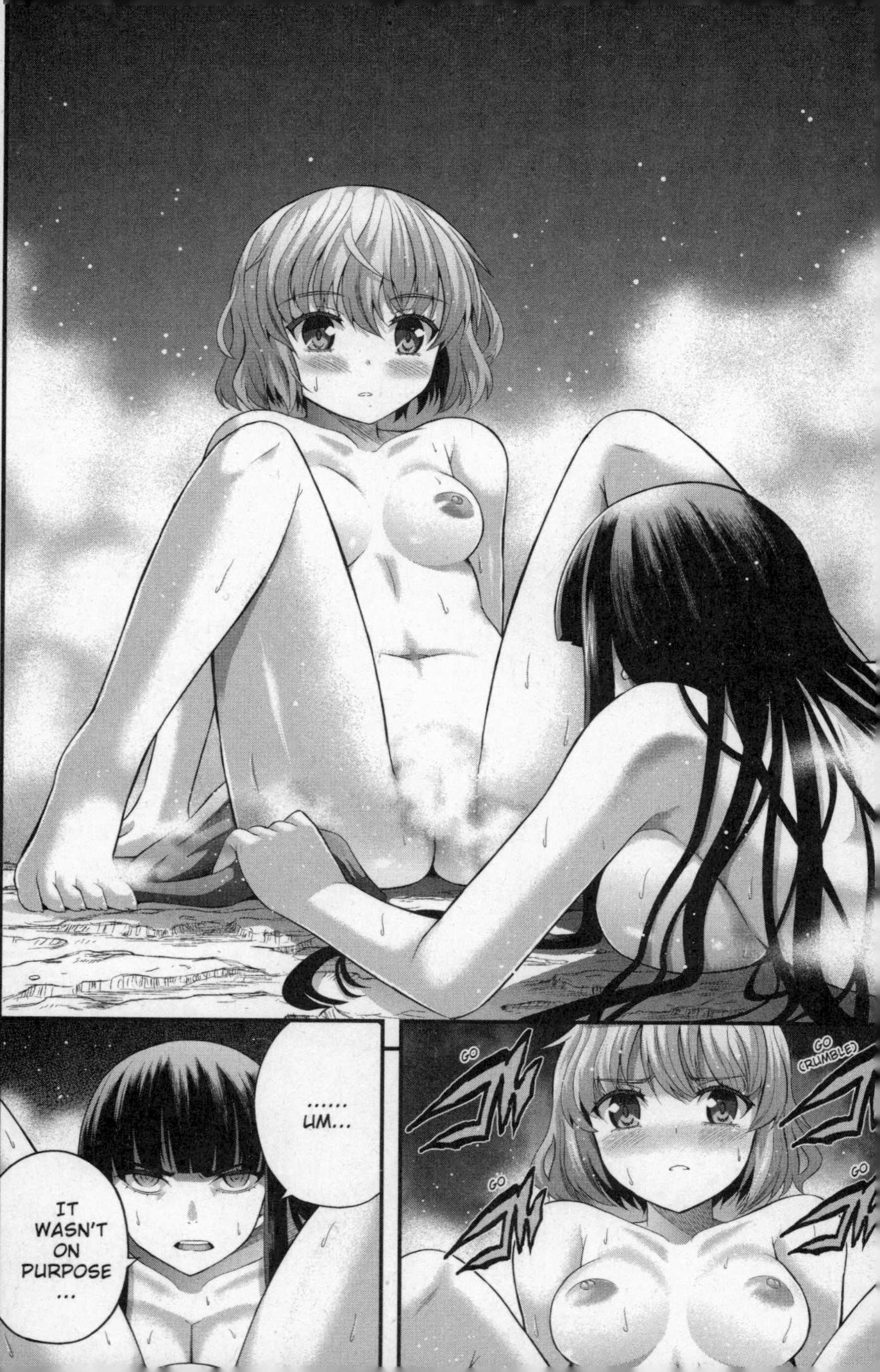
GO (RUMBLE)
GO
GO
GO
...... UM...
IT WASN'T ON PURPOSE ...

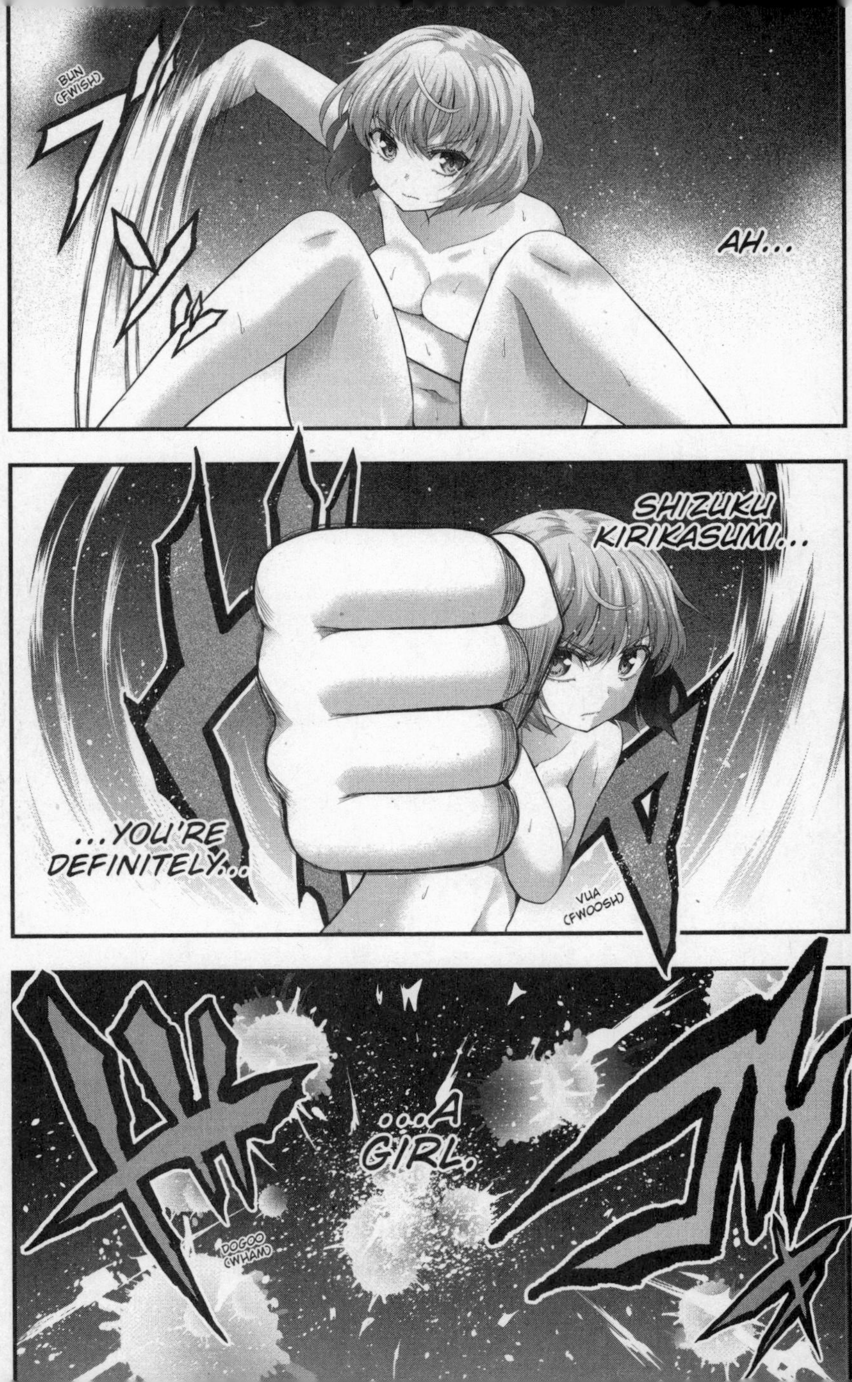

AH...
BUN (FWISH)
SHIZUKU KIRIKASUMI...
...YOU'RE DEFINITELY...
VUA (FWOOSH)
...A GIRL.
DOGOO (WHAM)

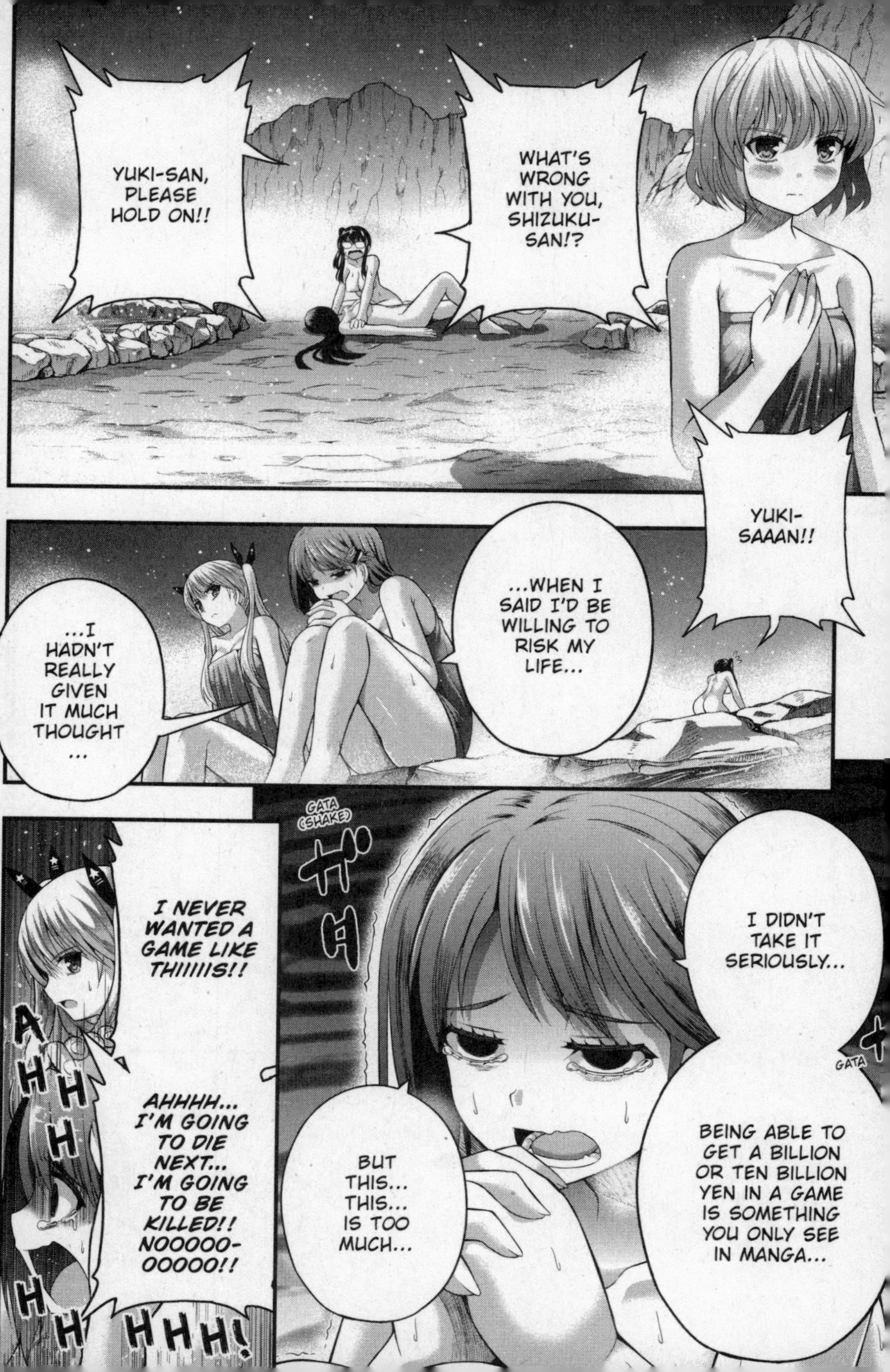
WHAT'S WRONG WITH YOU, SHIZUKU-SAN!?
YUKI-SAN, PLEASE HOLD ON!!
YUKI-SAAAN!!
...WHEN I SAID I'D BE WILLING TO RISK MY LIFE...
...I HADN'T REALLY GIVEN IT MUCH THOUGHT...
I DIDN'T TAKE IT SERIOUSLY...
GATA
BEING ABLE TO GET A BILLION OR TEN BILLION YEN IN A GAME IS SOMETHING YOU ONLY SEE IN MANGA...
GATA (SHAKE)
BUT THIS... THIS... IS TOO MUCH...
I NEVER WANTED A GAME LIKE THIIIIIS!!
AHHHH... I'M GOING TO DIE NEXT... I'M GOING TO BE KILLED!! NOOOOO-OOOOO!!
AHHHHHHHH!

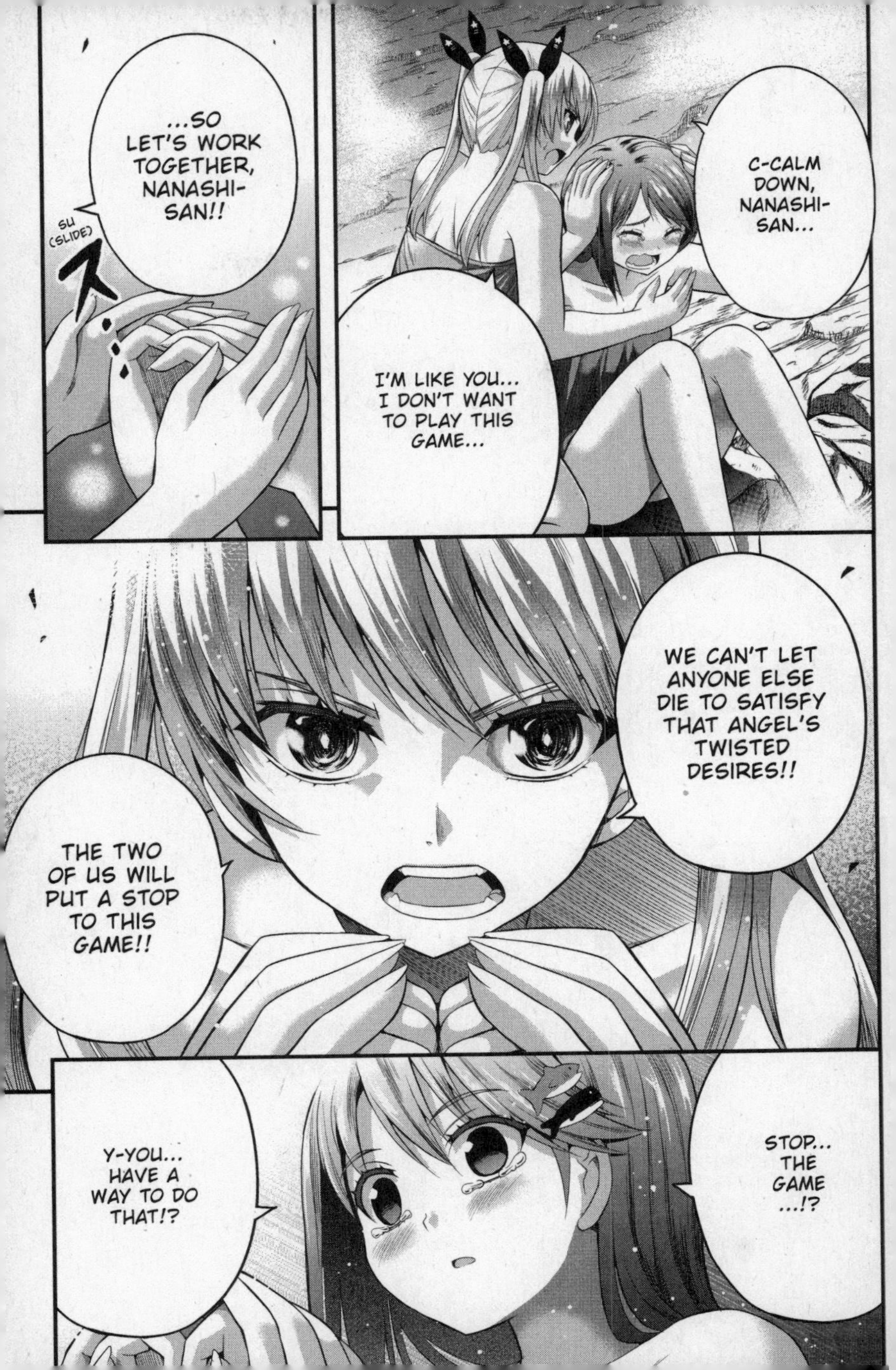
C-CALM DOWN, NANASHI-SAN...
I'M LIKE YOU... I DON'T WANT TO PLAY THIS GAME...
...SO LET'S WORK TOGETHER, NANASHI-SAN!!
SU (SLIDE)
ス
WE CAN'T LET ANYONE ELSE DIE TO SATISFY THAT ANGEL'S TWISTED DESIRES!!
THE TWO OF US WILL PUT A STOP TO THIS GAME!!
STOP... THE GAME ...!?
Y-YOU... HAVE A WAY TO DO THAT!?

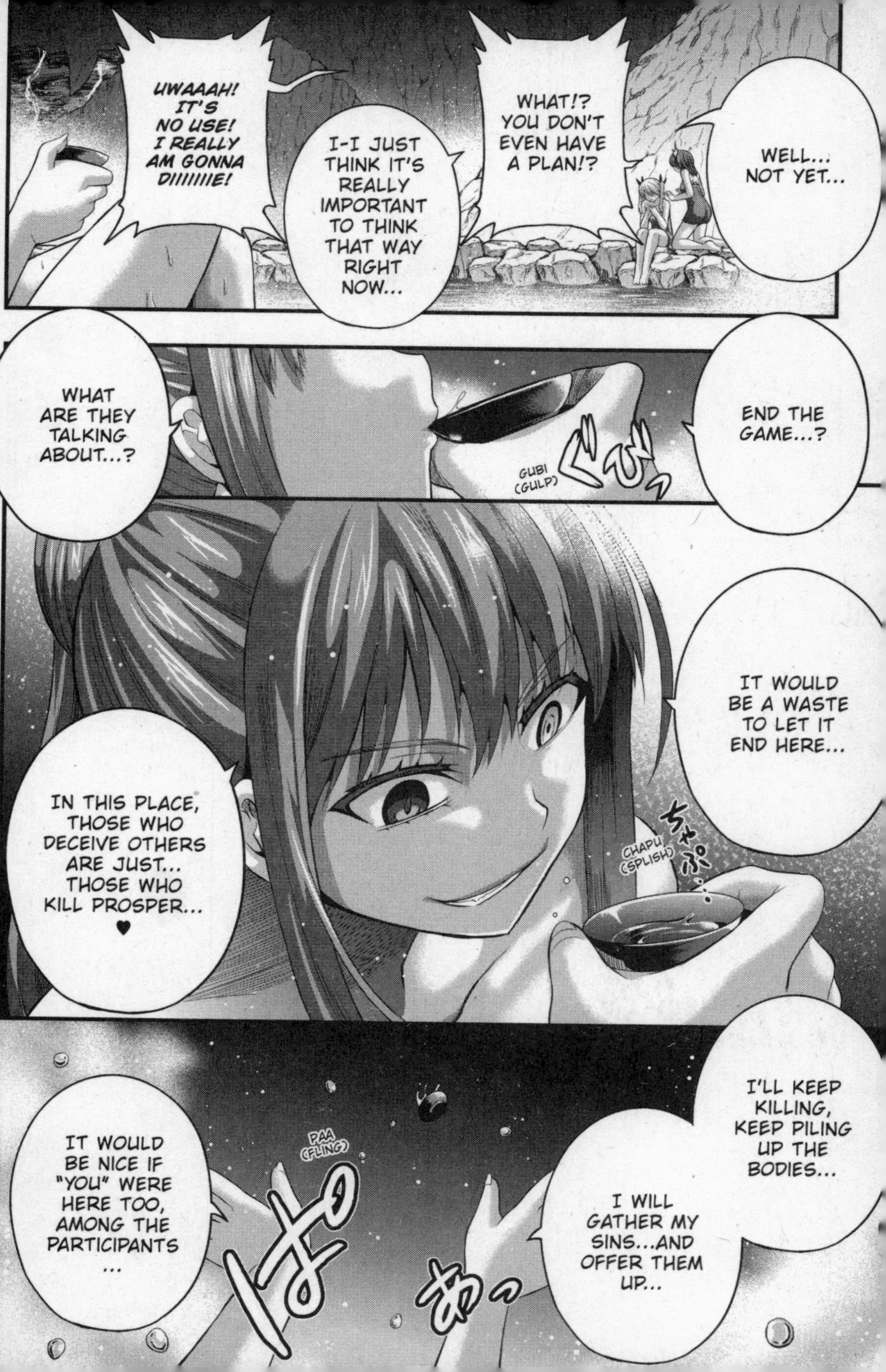
WHAT!? YOU DON'T EVEN HAVE A PLAN!?
WELL... NOT YET...
I-I JUST THINK IT'S REALLY IMPORTANT TO THINK THAT WAY RIGHT NOW...
UWAAAH! IT'S NO USE! I REALLY AM GONNA DIIIIIIIE!
END THE GAME...?
ぐびっ
GUBI (GULP)
WHAT ARE THEY TALKING ABOUT...?
IT WOULD BE A WASTE TO LET IT END HERE...
ちゃぷ
CHAPU (SPLISH)
IN THIS PLACE, THOSE WHO DECEIVE OTHERS ARE JUST... THOSE WHO KILL PROSPER... ♥
I'LL KEEP KILLING, KEEP PILING UP THE BODIES...
I WILL GATHER MY SINS...AND OFFER THEM UP...
ぱあっ
PAA (FLING)
IT WOULD BE NICE IF "YOU" WERE HERE TOO, AMONG THE PARTICIPANTS ...

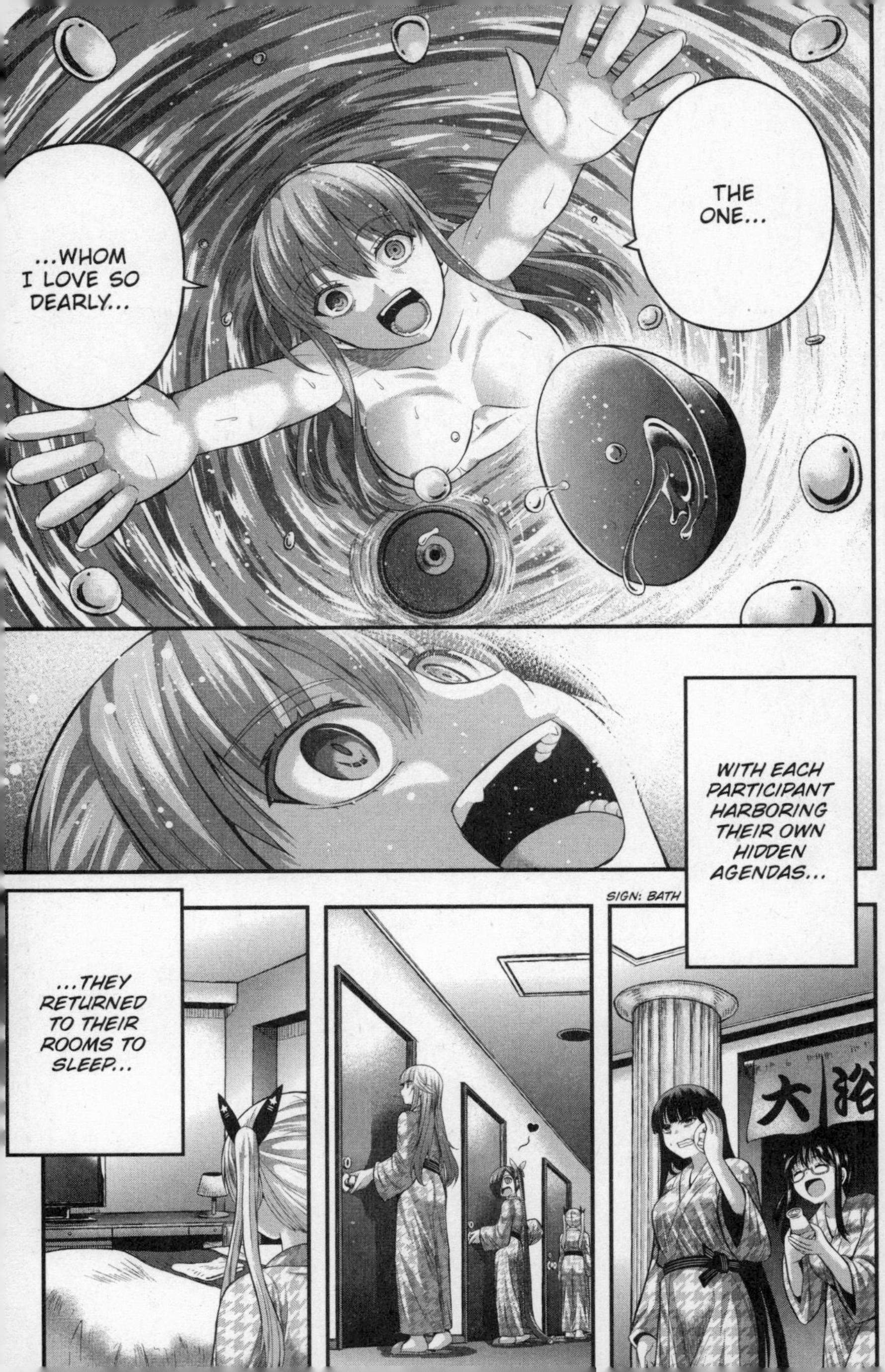
THE ONE...
...WHOM I LOVE SO DEARLY...
WITH EACH PARTICIPANT HARBORING THEIR OWN HIDDEN AGENDAS...
SIGN: BATH
...THEY RETURNED TO THEIR ROOMS TO SLEEP...

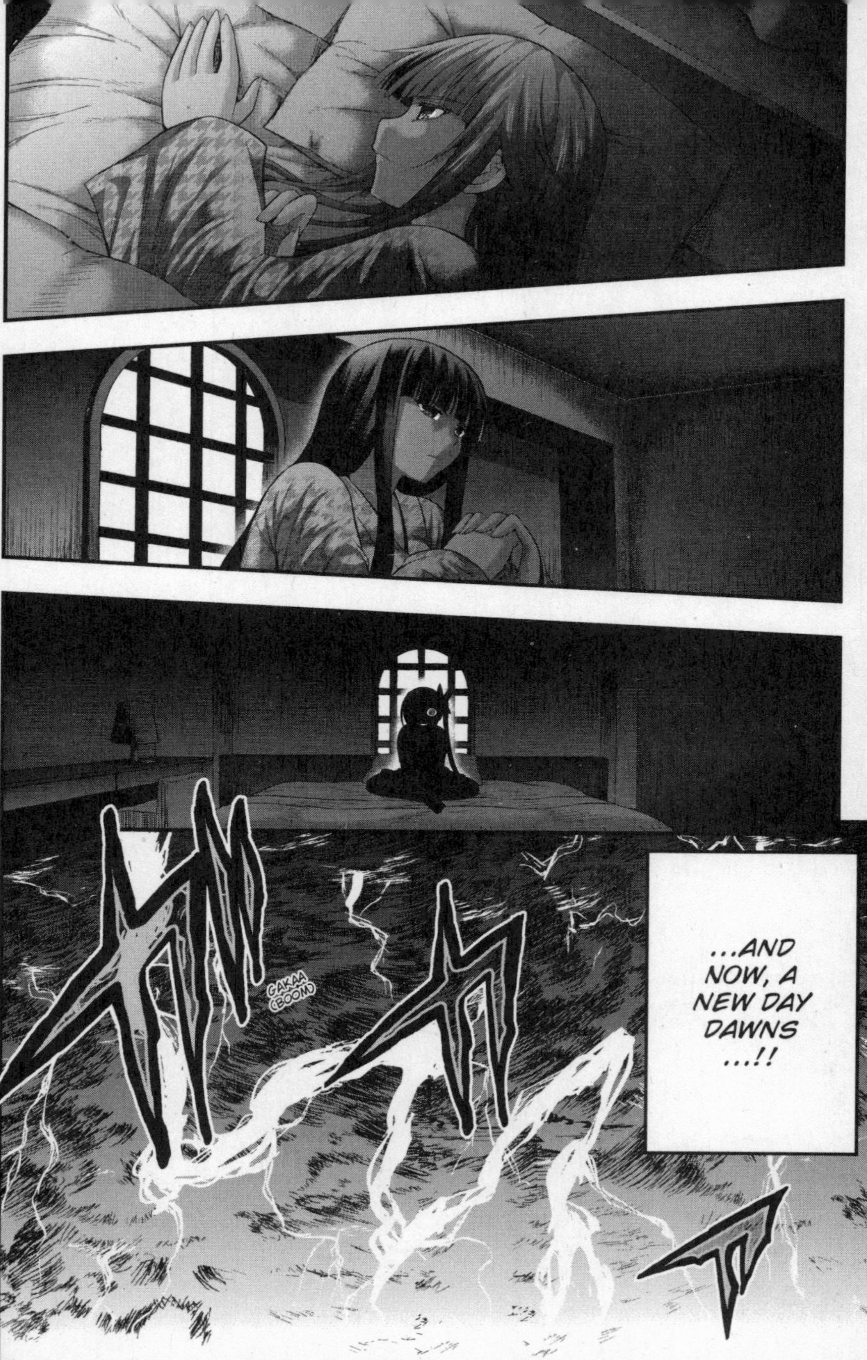
GAKAA (BOOM)
...AND NOW, A NEW DAY DAWNS ...!!

Though You May Burn to ASH

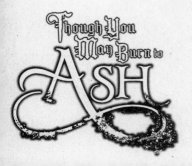

# Though You May Burn to Ash

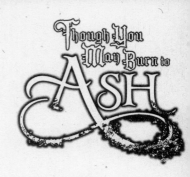

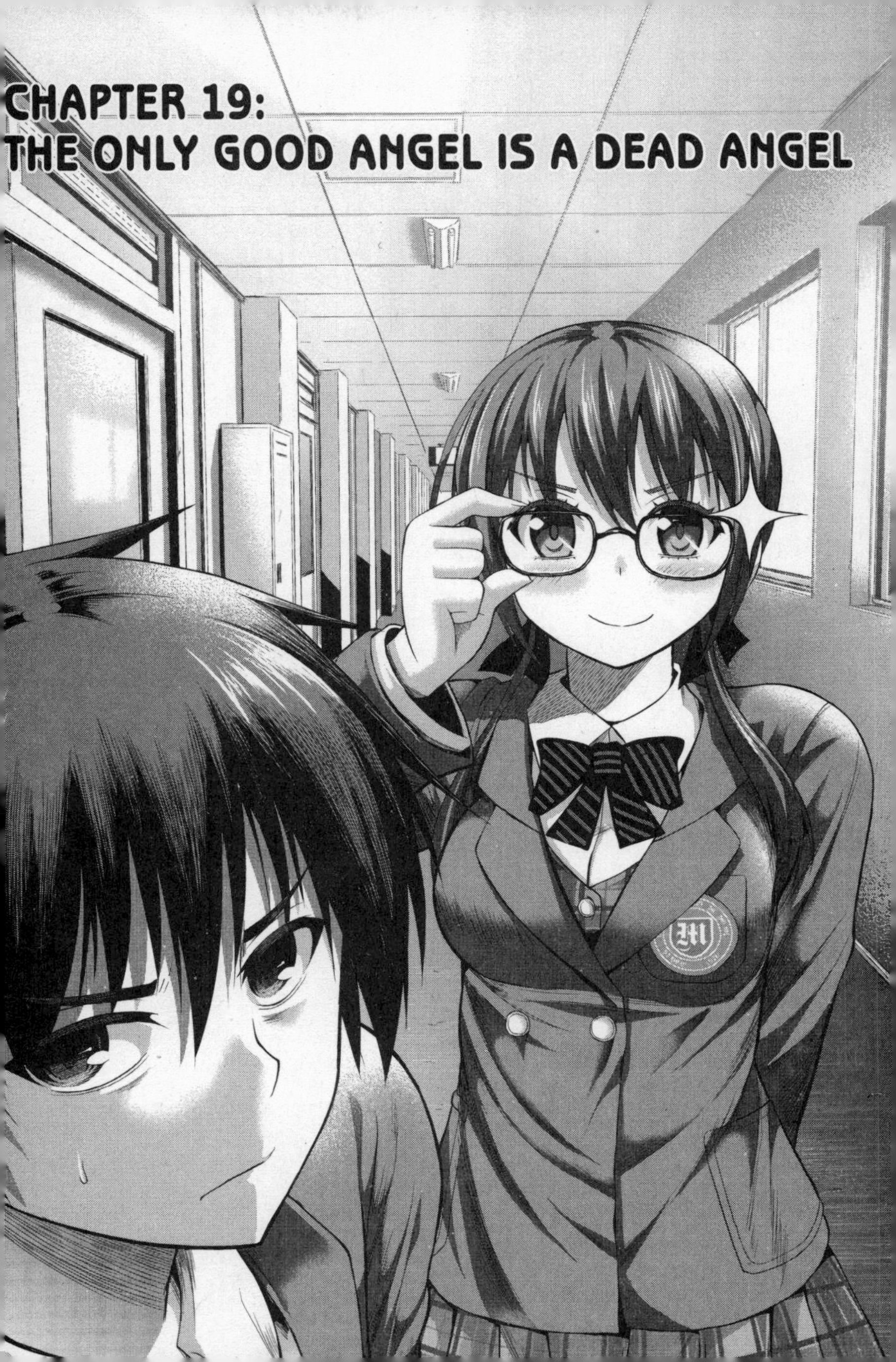
CHAPTER 19:
THE ONLY GOOD ANGEL IS A DEAD ANGEL

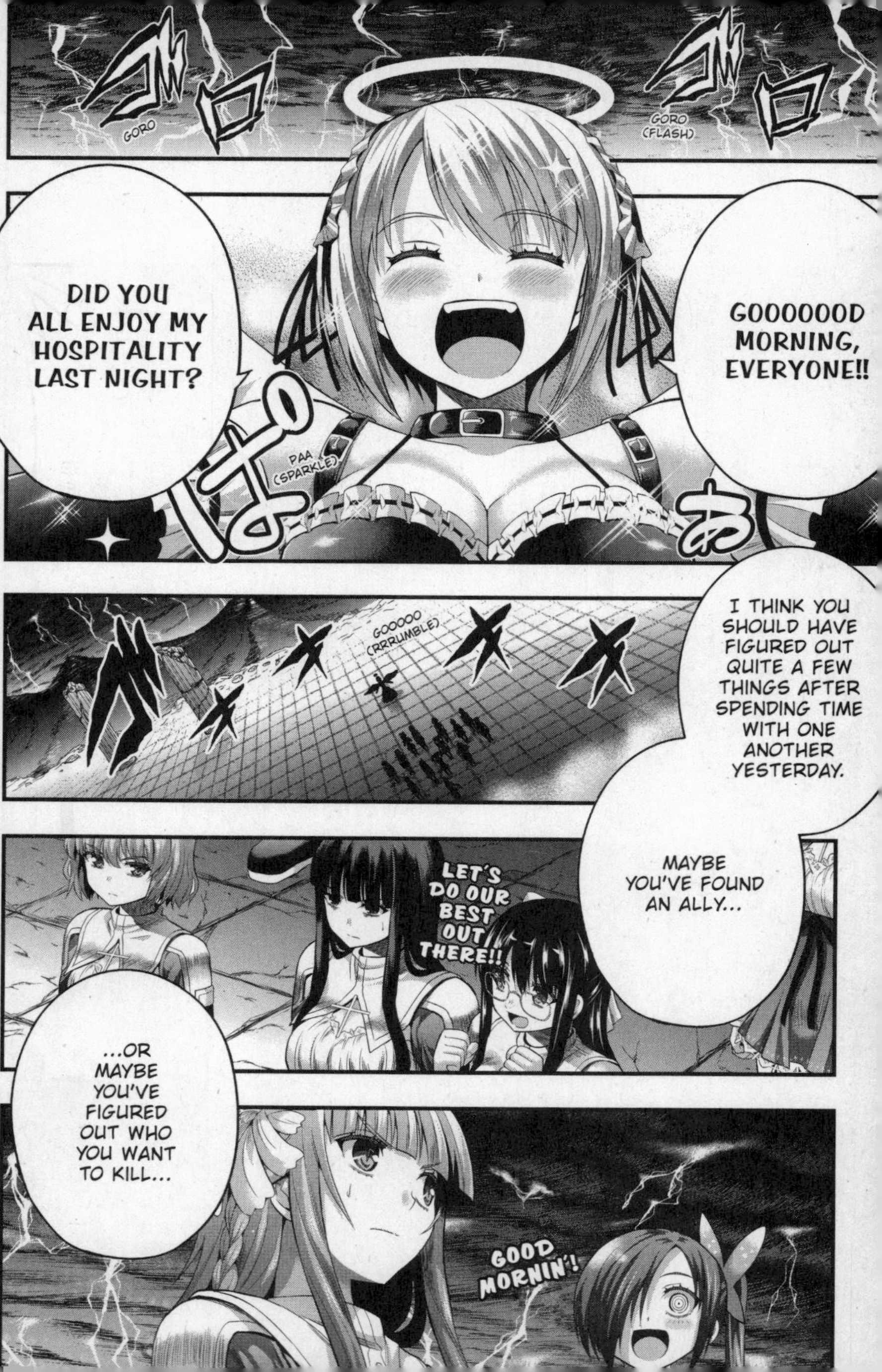
GORO (FLASH)
GORO
GOOOOOOD MORNING, EVERYONE!!
DID YOU ALL ENJOY MY HOSPITALITY LAST NIGHT?
PAA (SPARKLE)
I THINK YOU SHOULD HAVE FIGURED OUT QUITE A FEW THINGS AFTER SPENDING TIME WITH ONE ANOTHER YESTERDAY.
GOOOOO (RRRUMBLE)
MAYBE YOU'VE FOUND AN ALLY...
LET'S DO OUR BEST OUT THERE!!
...OR MAYBE YOU'VE FIGURED OUT WHO YOU WANT TO KILL...
GOOD MORNIN'!

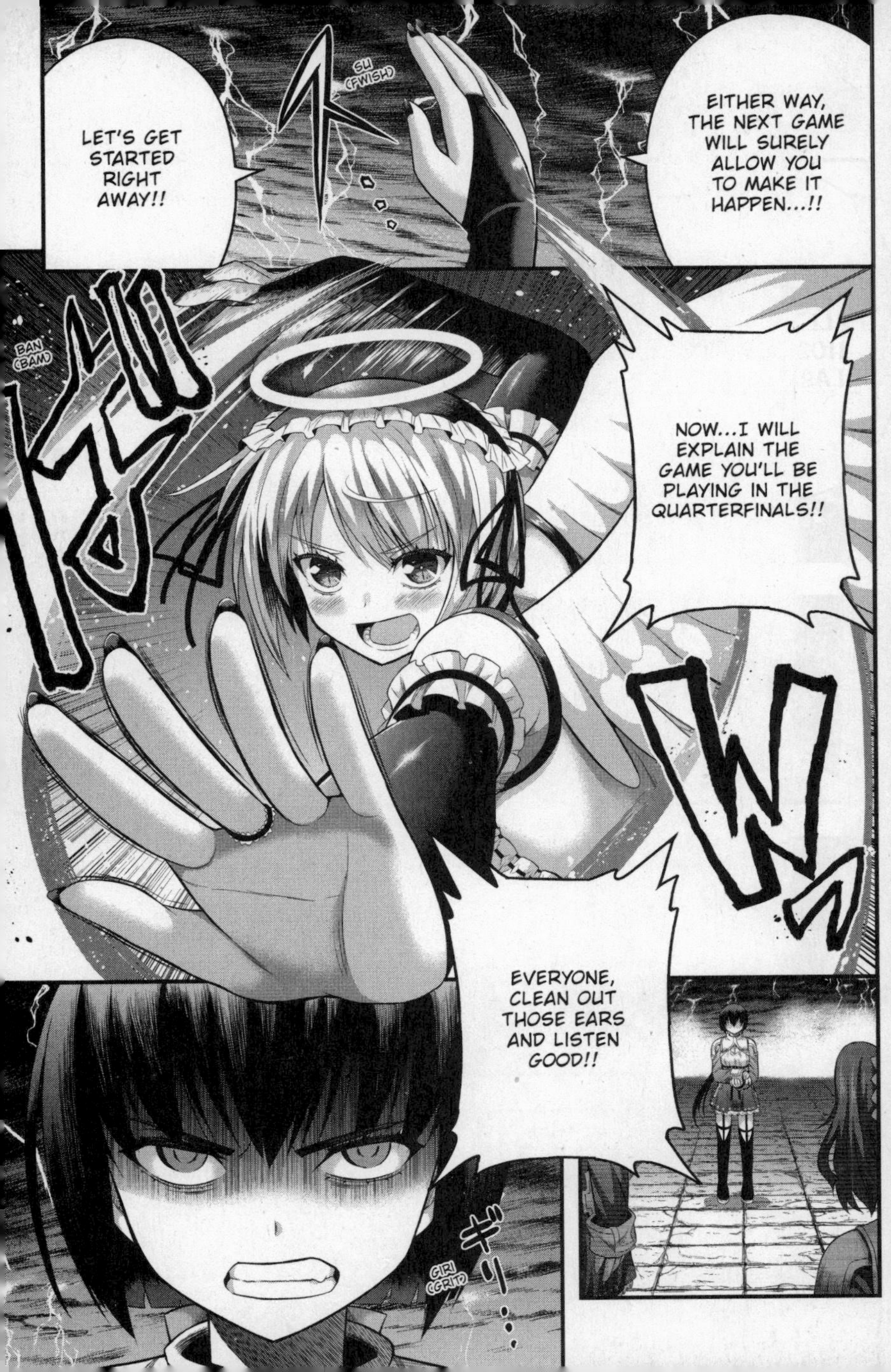
EITHER WAY, THE NEXT GAME WILL SURELY ALLOW YOU TO MAKE IT HAPPEN...!!
SU (FWISH)
LET'S GET STARTED RIGHT AWAY!!
NOW...I WILL EXPLAIN THE GAME YOU'LL BE PLAYING IN THE QUARTERFINALS!!
BAN (BAM)
EVERYONE, CLEAN OUT THOSE EARS AND LISTEN GOOD!!
ギリ…
GIRI (GRIT)

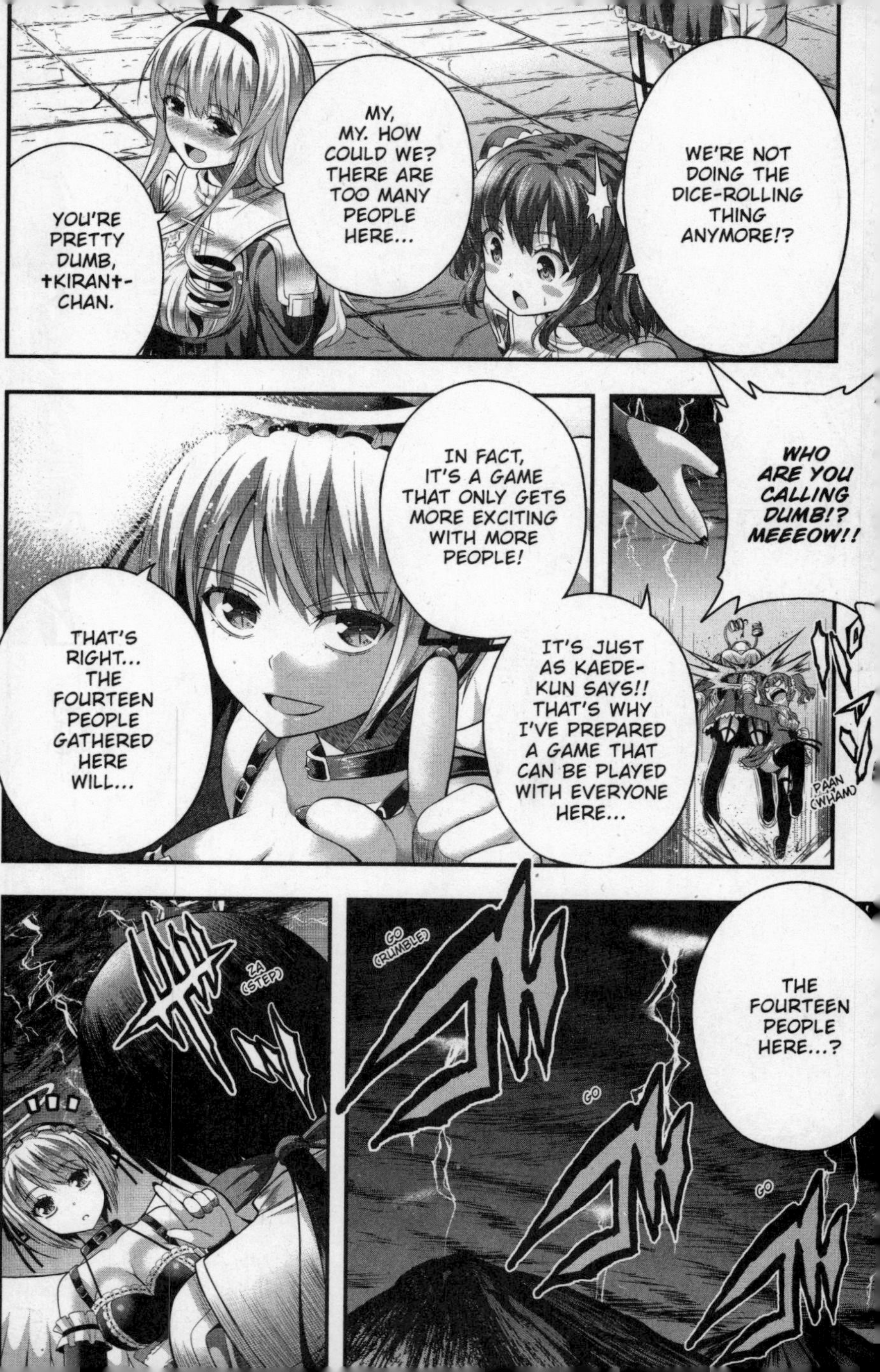
WE'RE NOT DOING THE DICE-ROLLING THING ANYMORE!?
MY, MY. HOW COULD WE? THERE ARE TOO MANY PEOPLE HERE...
YOU'RE PRETTY DUMB, †KIRAN†-CHAN.
WHO ARE YOU CALLING DUMB!? MEEEOW!!
PAAN (WHAM)
IN FACT, IT'S A GAME THAT ONLY GETS MORE EXCITING WITH MORE PEOPLE!
IT'S JUST AS KAEDE-KUN SAYS!! THAT'S WHY I'VE PREPARED A GAME THAT CAN BE PLAYED WITH EVERYONE HERE...
THAT'S RIGHT... THE FOURTEEN PEOPLE GATHERED HERE WILL...
THE FOURTEEN PEOPLE HERE...?
GO (RUMBLE)
GO
GO
ZA (STEP)

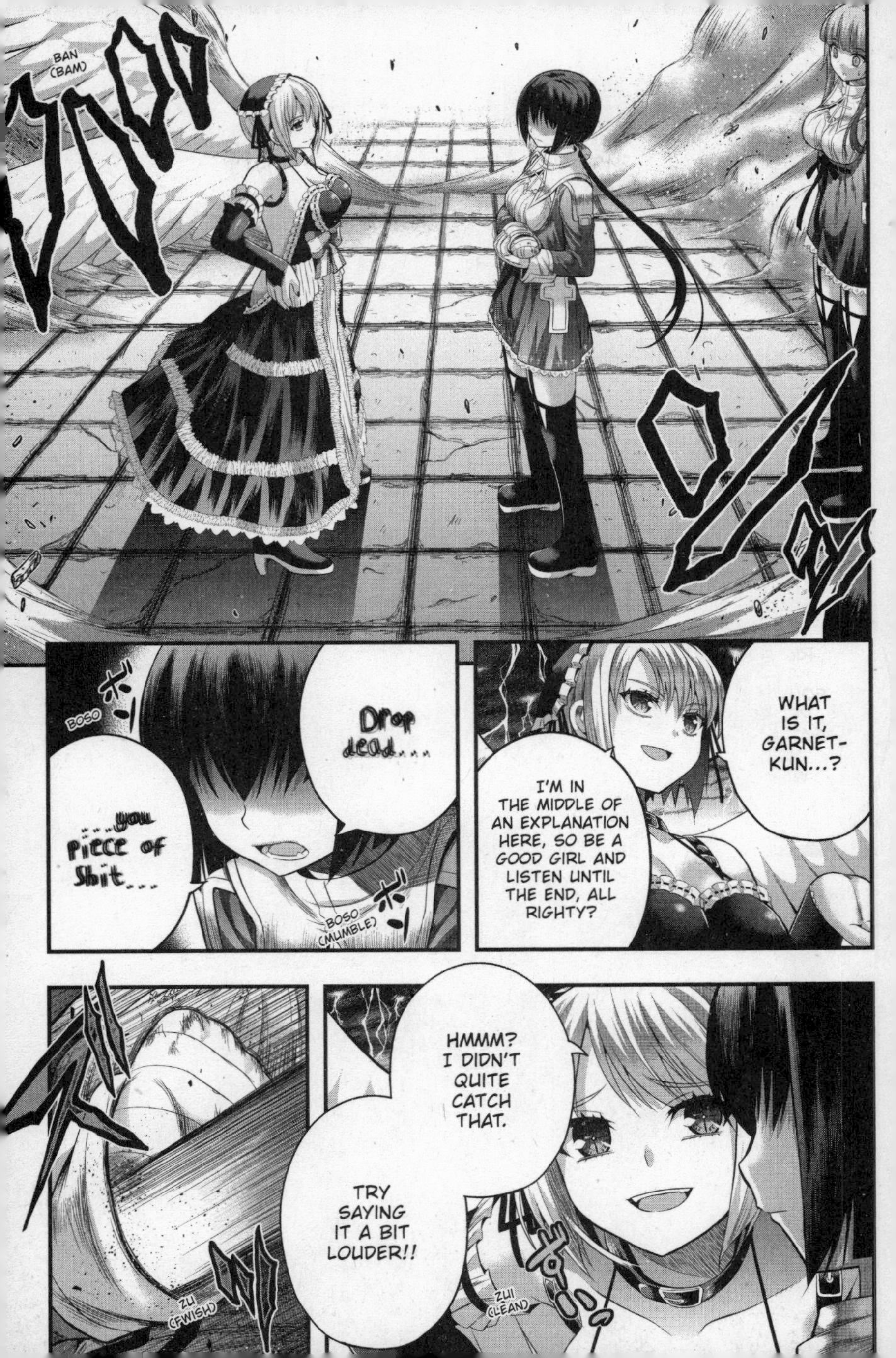
BAN (BAM)
WHAT IS IT, GARNET-KUN...?
I'M IN THE MIDDLE OF AN EXPLANATION HERE, SO BE A GOOD GIRL AND LISTEN UNTIL THE END, ALL RIGHTY?
BOSO
Drop dead...
...you piece of shit...
BOSO (MUMBLE)
HMMM? I DIDN'T QUITE CATCH THAT.
TRY SAYING IT A BIT LOUDER!!
ZUI (LEAN)
ZU (FWISH)

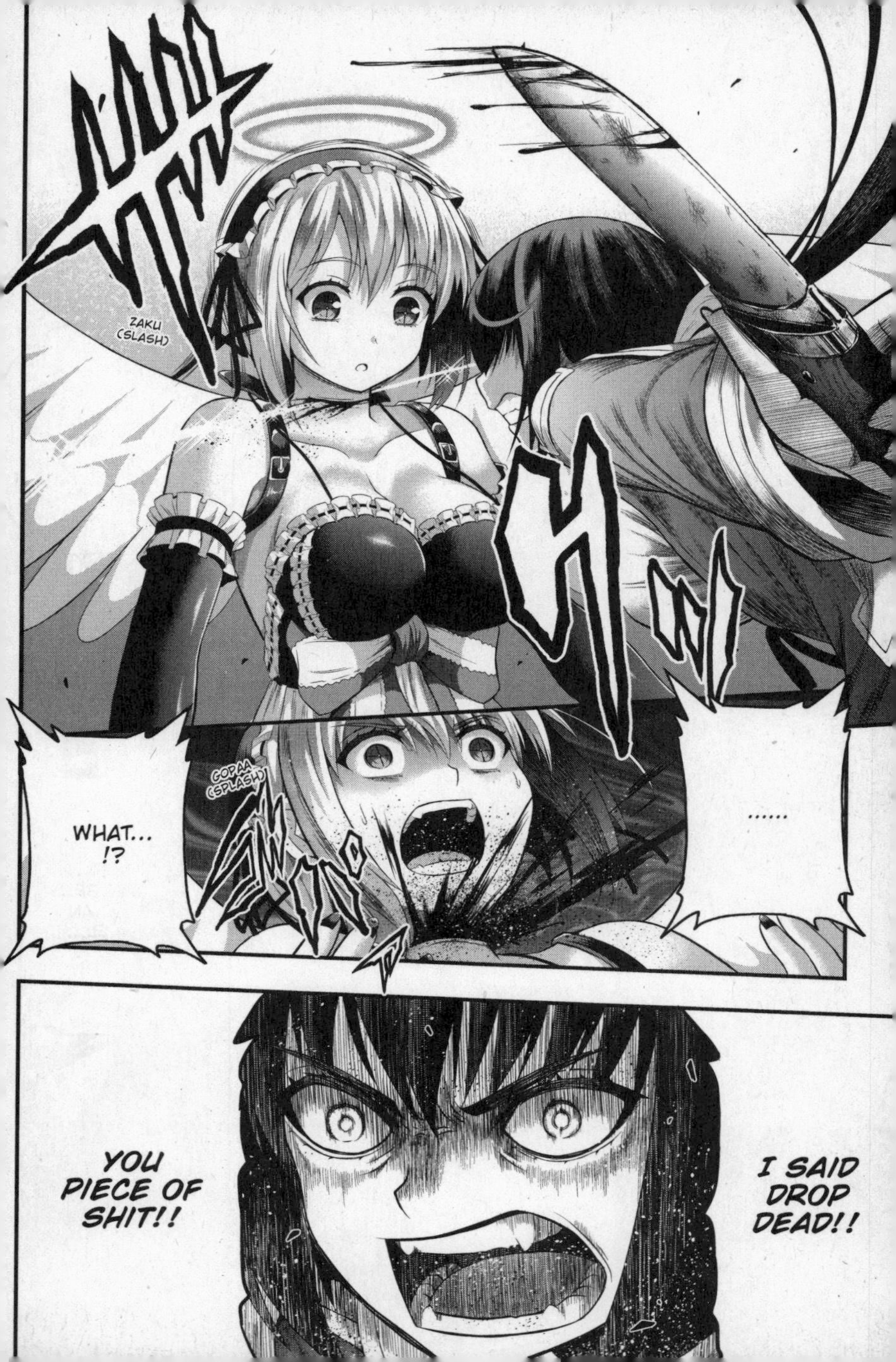
ZAKU (SLASH)
......
GOPAA (SPLASH)
WHAT... !?
I SAID DROP DEAD!!
YOU PIECE OF SHIT!!

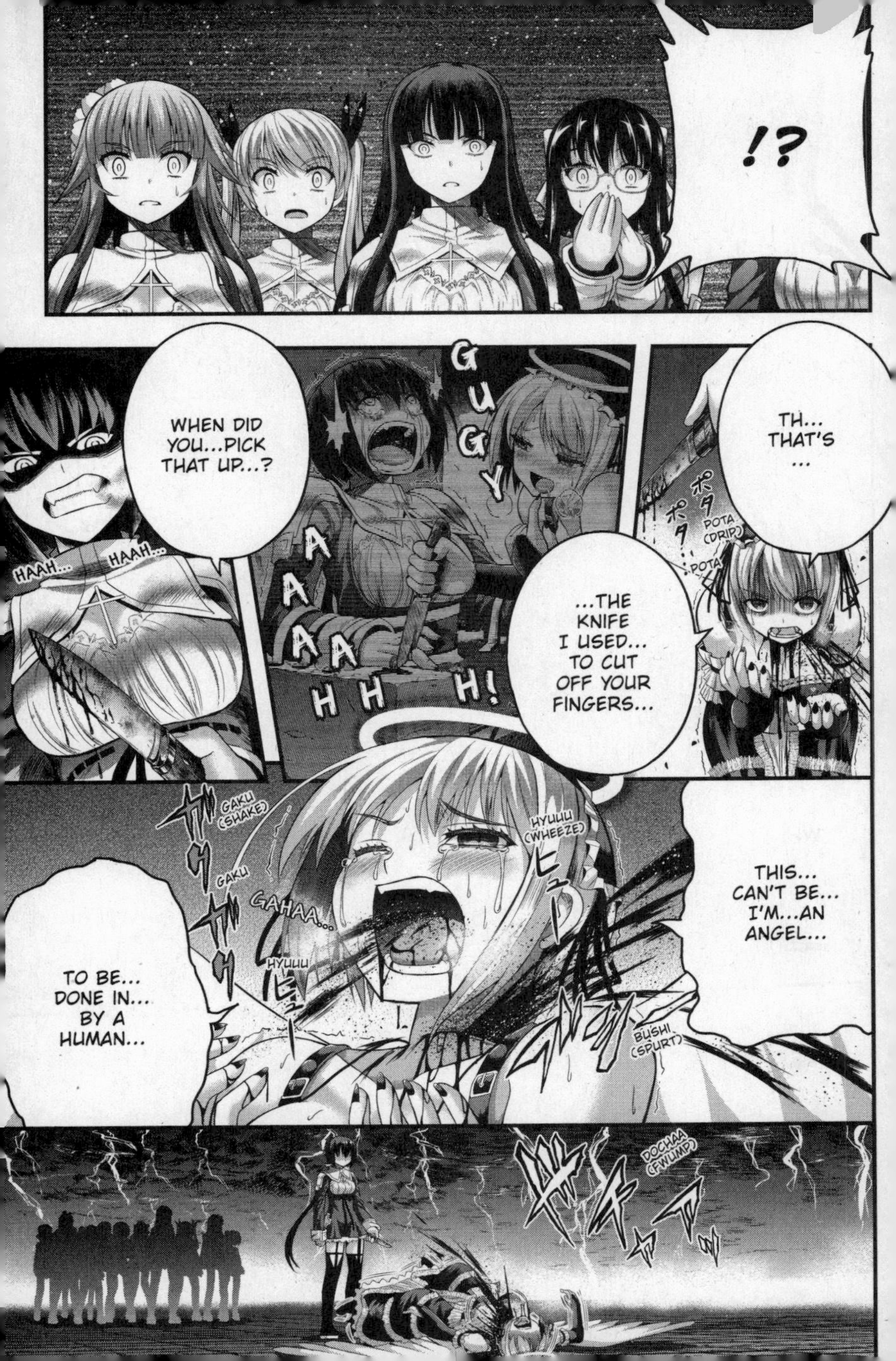
!?
TH... THAT'S ...
POTA (DRIP)
POTA
...THE KNIFE I USED... TO CUT OFF YOUR FINGERS...
GUGYAAAAHHH!
WHEN DID YOU...PICK THAT UP...?
HAAH... HAAH...
THIS... CAN'T BE... I'M...AN ANGEL...
HYUUU (WHEEZE)
BUSHI (SPURT)
GAHAA...
HYUUU
GAKU (SHAKE)
GAKU
TO BE... DONE IN... BY A HUMAN...
DOCHAA (FWUMP)

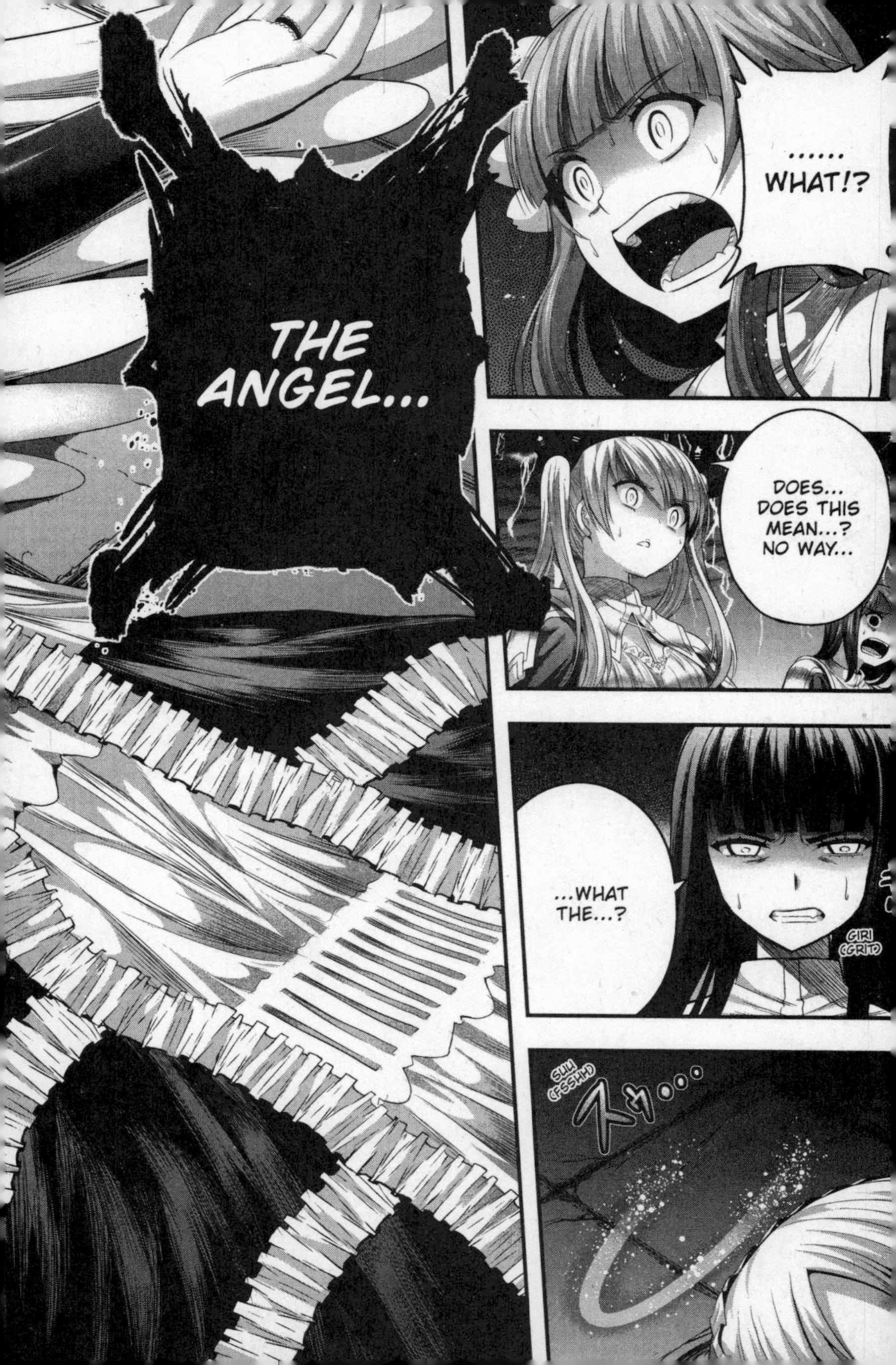

...... WHAT!?
DOES... DOES THIS MEAN...? NO WAY...
...WHAT THE...?
GIRI (GRIT)
SUU (FSSHH)
THE ANGEL...

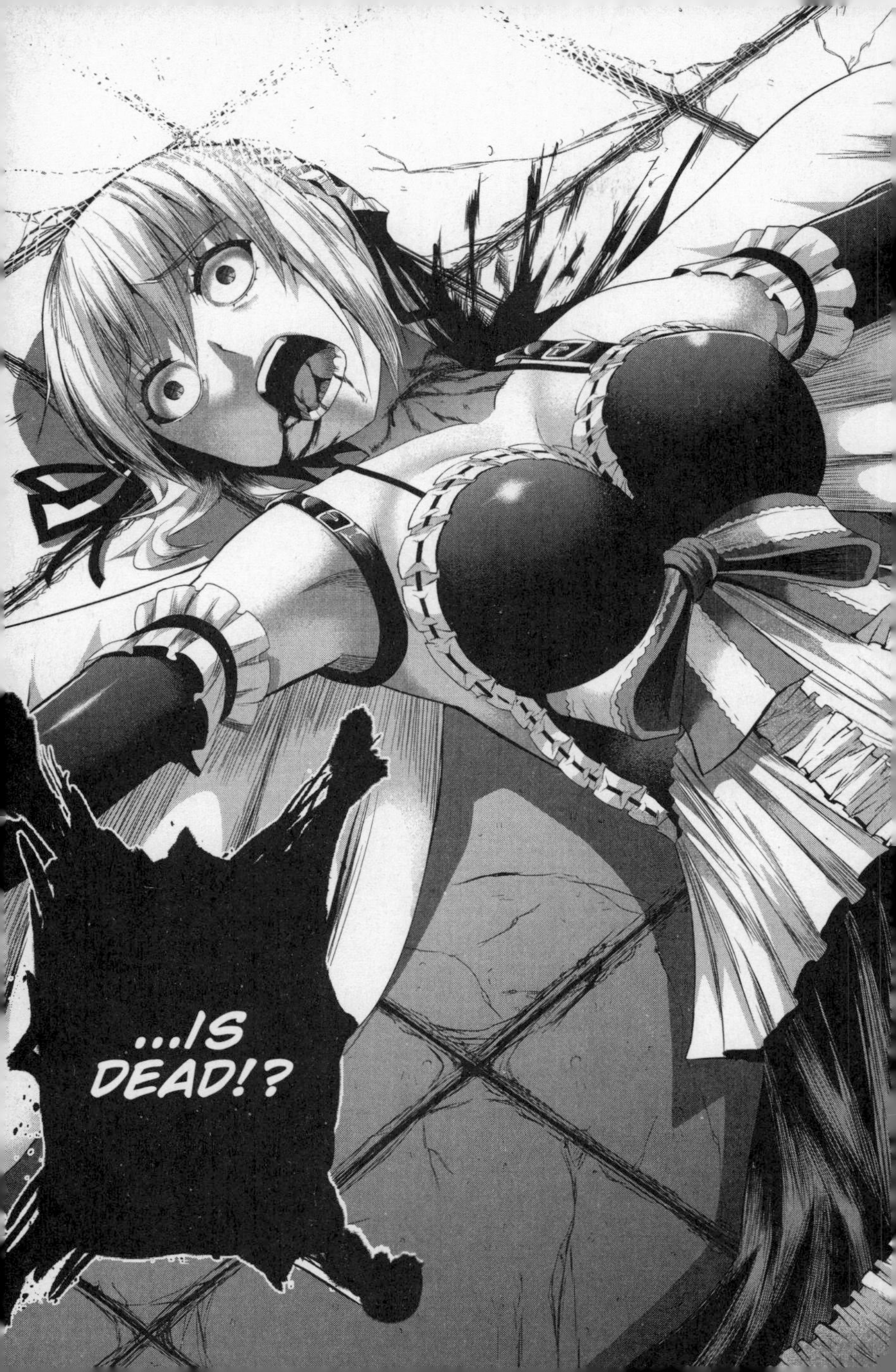
...IS
DEAD!?

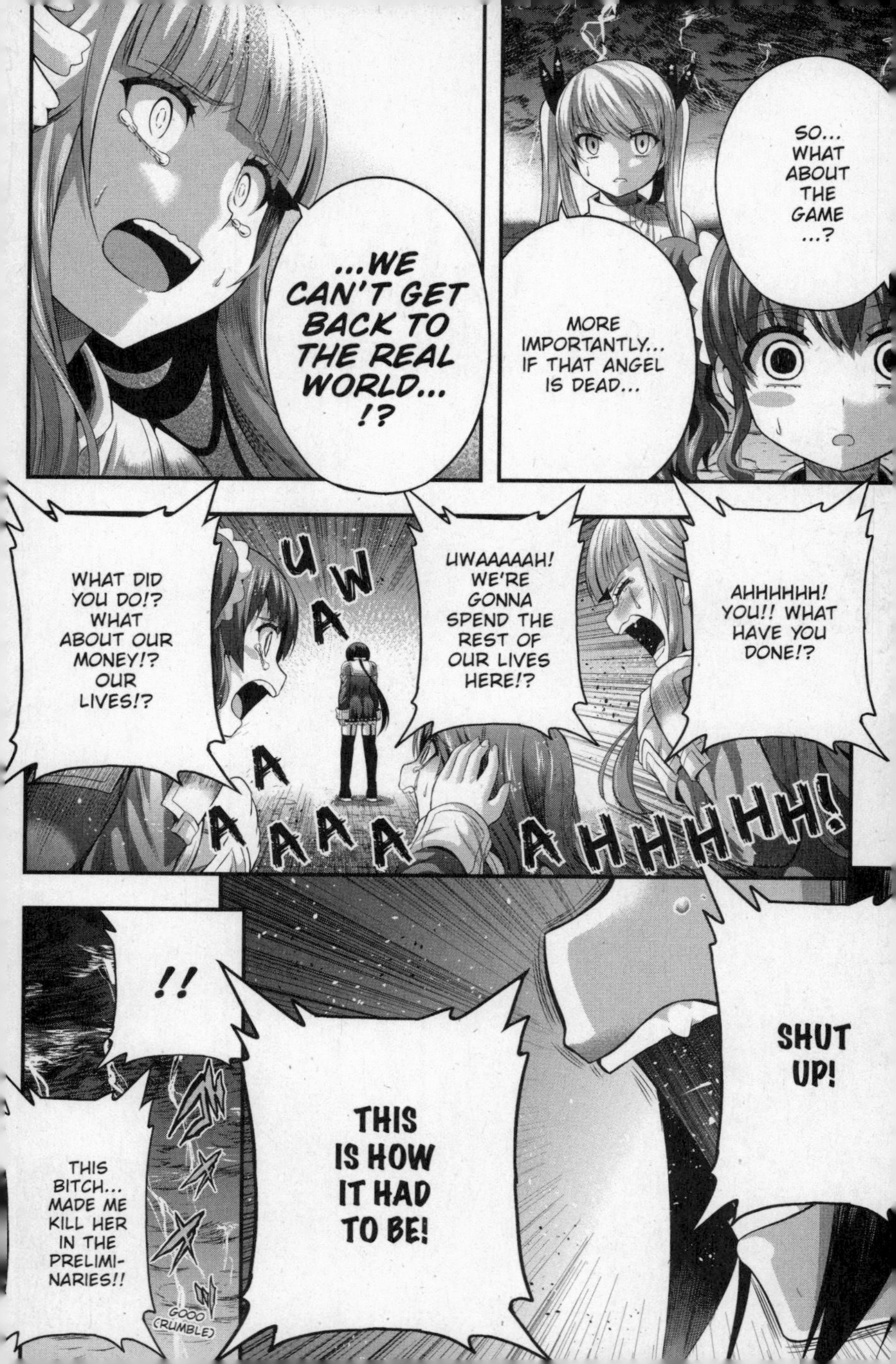
SO... WHAT ABOUT THE GAME ...?
MORE IMPORTANTLY... IF THAT ANGEL IS DEAD...
...WE CAN'T GET BACK TO THE REAL WORLD... !?
AHHHHHH! YOU!! WHAT HAVE YOU DONE!?
UWAAAAAH! WE'RE GONNA SPEND THE REST OF OUR LIVES HERE!?
WHAT DID YOU DO!? WHAT ABOUT OUR MONEY!? OUR LIVES!?
UWAAAAAAAHHHHHH!
SHUT UP!
THIS IS HOW IT HAD TO BE!
!!
THIS BITCH... MADE ME KILL HER IN THE PRELIMI-NARIES!!
GOOO (RUMBLE)

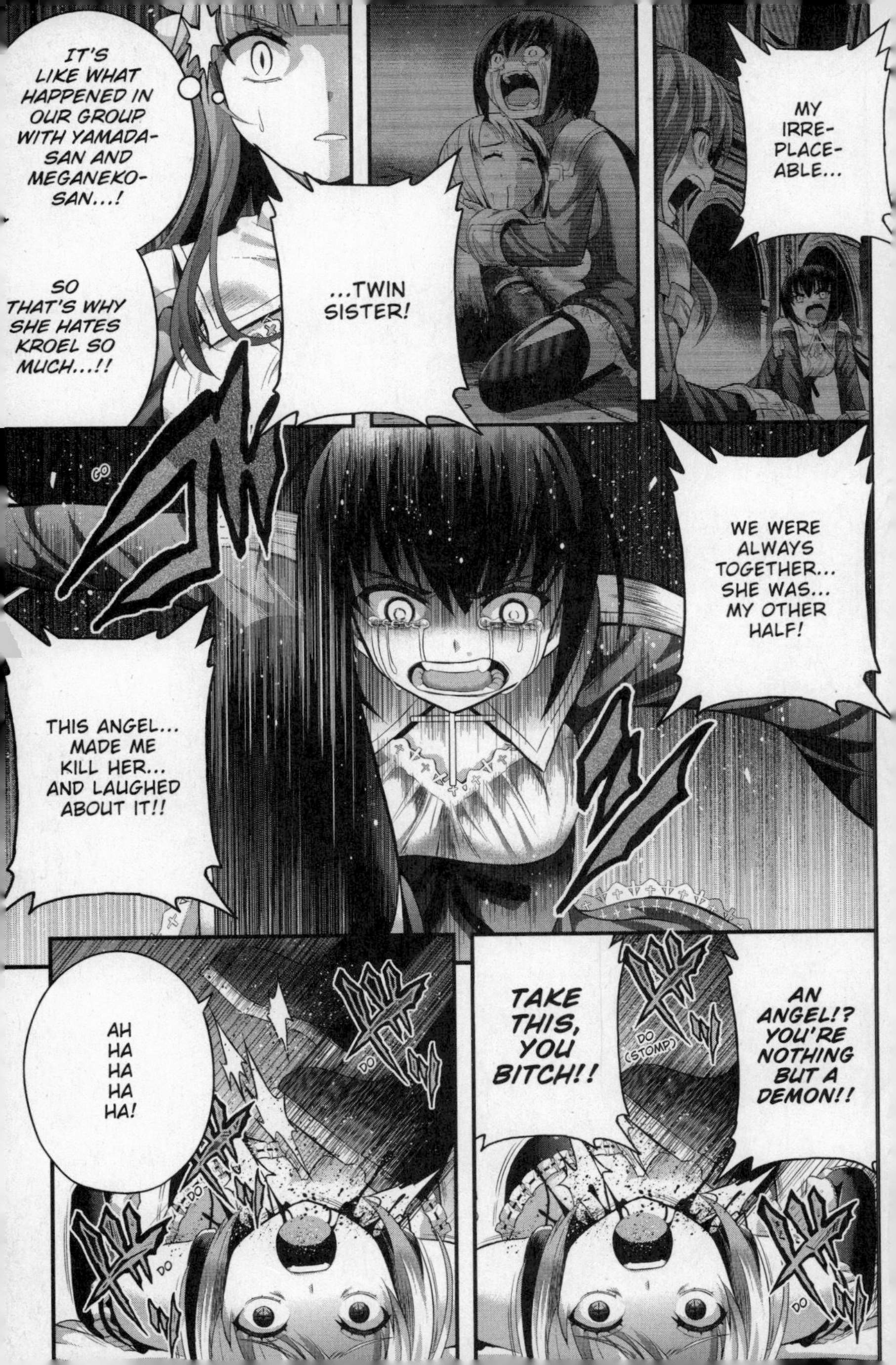
MY IRRE-PLACE-ABLE...
...TWIN SISTER!
IT'S LIKE WHAT HAPPENED IN OUR GROUP WITH YAMADA-SAN AND MEGANEKO-SAN...!
SO THAT'S WHY SHE HATES KROEL SO MUCH...!!
WE WERE ALWAYS TOGETHER... SHE WAS... MY OTHER HALF!
GO
THIS ANGEL... MADE ME KILL HER... AND LAUGHED ABOUT IT!!
AN ANGEL!? YOU'RE NOTHING BUT A DEMON!!
DO (STOMP)
TAKE THIS, YOU BITCH!!
DO
DO
AH HA HA HA HA!
DO
DO
DO

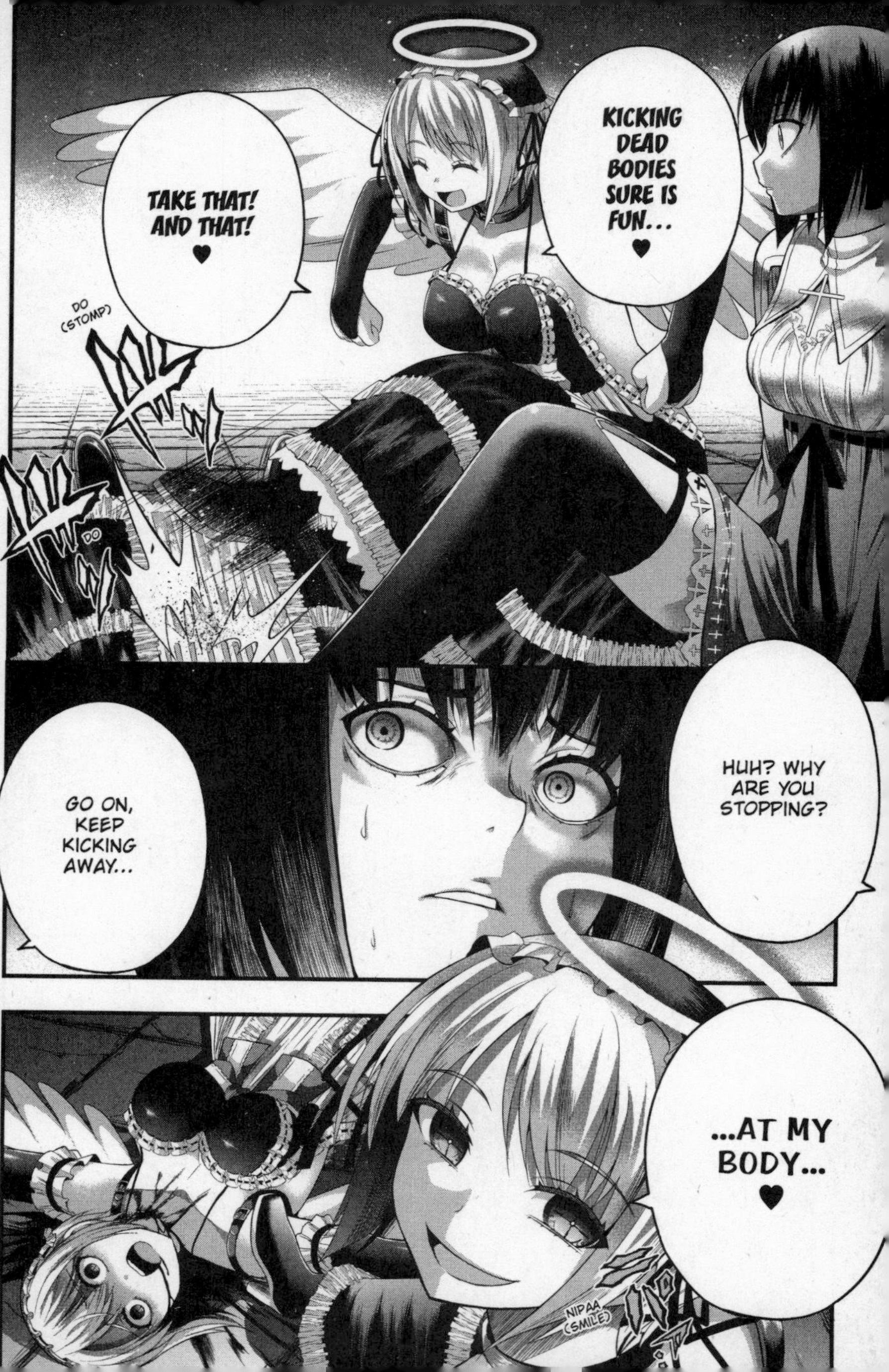
KICKING DEAD BODIES SURE IS FUN... ♥
TAKE THAT! AND THAT! ♥
DO (STOMP)
DO
HUH? WHY ARE YOU STOPPING?
GO ON, KEEP KICKING AWAY...
...AT MY BODY... ♥
NIPAA (SMILE)

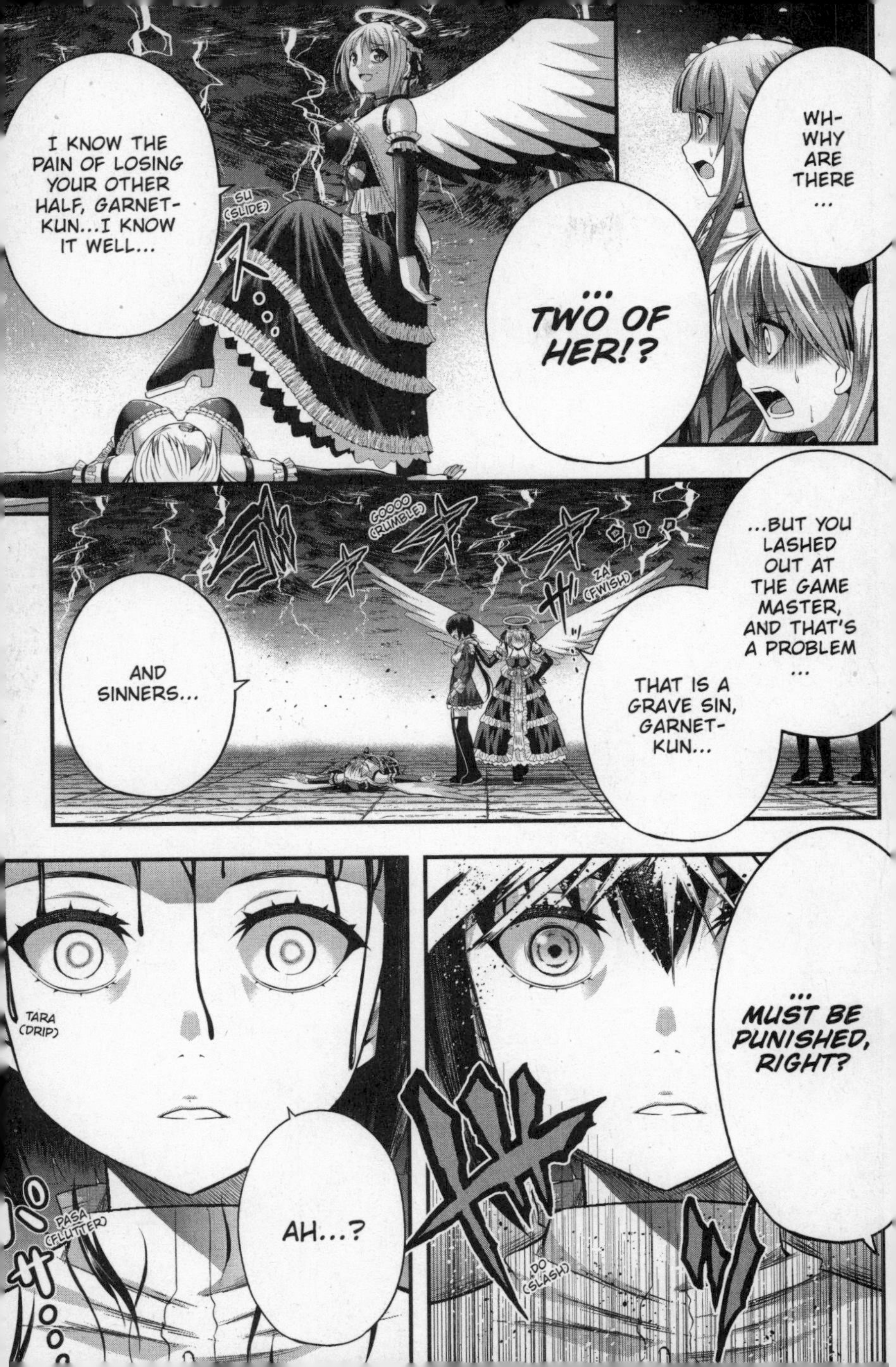
WH- WHY ARE THERE ...
... TWO OF HER!?
I KNOW THE PAIN OF LOSING YOUR OTHER HALF, GARNET-KUN...I KNOW IT WELL...
SU (SLIDE)
...BUT YOU LASHED OUT AT THE GAME MASTER, AND THAT'S A PROBLEM ...
THAT IS A GRAVE SIN, GARNET-KUN...
ZA (FWISH)
GOOOO (RUMBLE)
AND SINNERS...
... MUST BE PUNISHED, RIGHT?
DO (SLASH)
AH...?
TARA (DRIP)
PASA (FLUTTER)

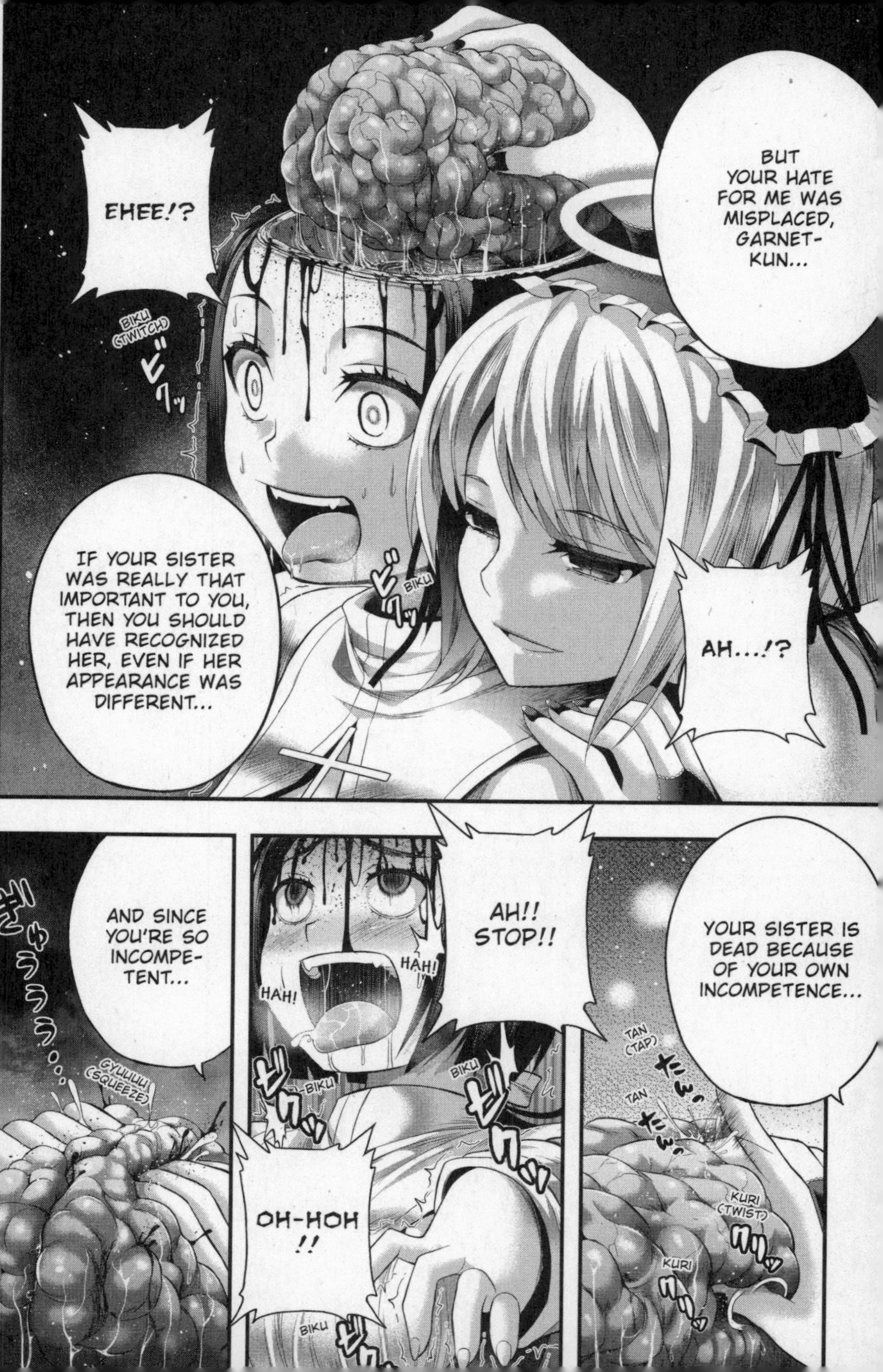
BUT YOUR HATE FOR ME WAS MISPLACED, GARNET-KUN...
EHEE!?
BIKU (TWITCH)
AH...!?
IF YOUR SISTER WAS REALLY THAT IMPORTANT TO YOU, THEN YOU SHOULD HAVE RECOGNIZED HER, EVEN IF HER APPEARANCE WAS DIFFERENT...
BIKU
YOUR SISTER IS DEAD BECAUSE OF YOUR OWN INCOMPETENCE...
TAN (TAP)
TAN
KURI (TWIST)
KURI
AH!! STOP!!
HAH!
HAH!
BIKU
BIKU
OH-HOH !!
BIKU
AND SINCE YOU'RE SO INCOMPE-TENT...
GYUUUU! (SQUEEZE)

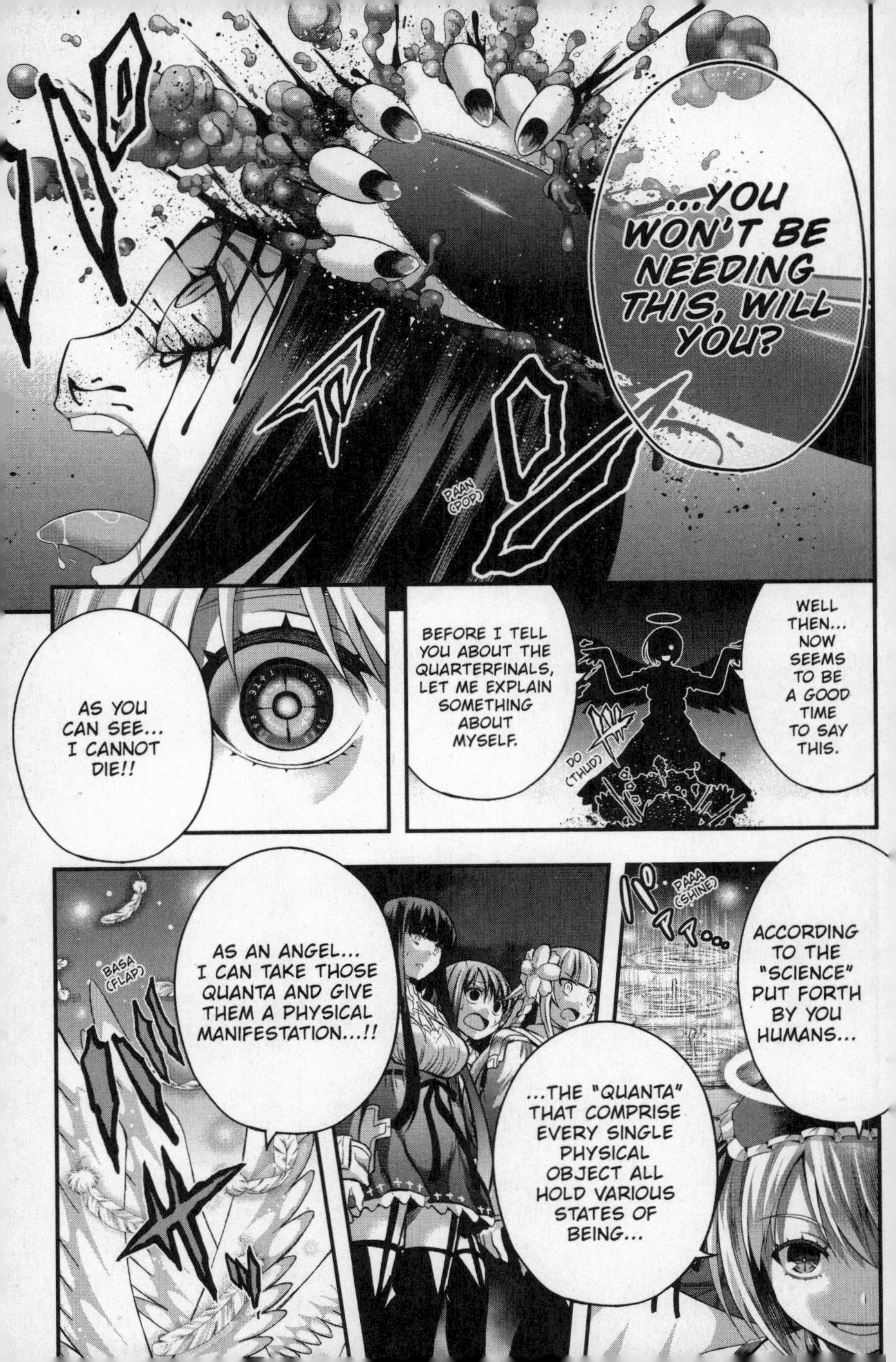
...YOU WON'T BE NEEDING THIS, WILL YOU?
PAAN (POP)
WELL THEN... NOW SEEMS TO BE A GOOD TIME TO SAY THIS.
BEFORE I TELL YOU ABOUT THE QUARTERFINALS, LET ME EXPLAIN SOMETHING ABOUT MYSELF.
DO (THUD)
AS YOU CAN SEE... I CANNOT DIE!!
PAAA (SHINE)
ACCORDING TO THE "SCIENCE" PUT FORTH BY YOU HUMANS...
...THE "QUANTA" THAT COMPRISE EVERY SINGLE PHYSICAL OBJECT ALL HOLD VARIOUS STATES OF BEING...
BASA (FLAP)
AS AN ANGEL... I CAN TAKE THOSE QUANTA AND GIVE THEM A PHYSICAL MANIFESTATION...!!

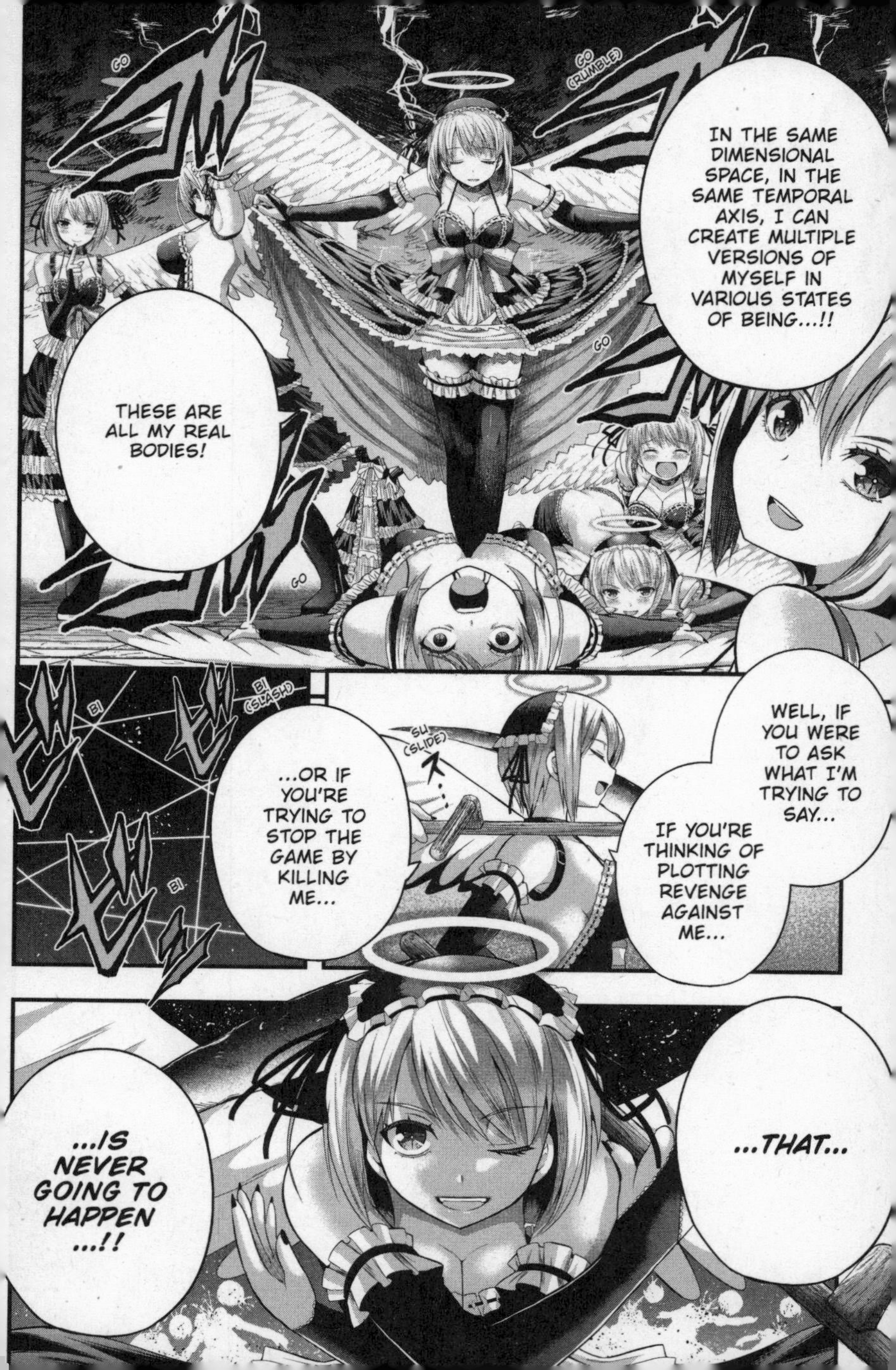
GO (RUMBLE)
GO
IN THE SAME DIMENSIONAL SPACE, IN THE SAME TEMPORAL AXIS, I CAN CREATE MULTIPLE VERSIONS OF MYSELF IN VARIOUS STATES OF BEING...!!
GO
THESE ARE ALL MY REAL BODIES!
GO
WELL, IF YOU WERE TO ASK WHAT I'M TRYING TO SAY...
IF YOU'RE THINKING OF PLOTTING REVENGE AGAINST ME...
SU (SLIDE)
...OR IF YOU'RE TRYING TO STOP THE GAME BY KILLING ME...
BI (SLASH)
BI
BI
...THAT...
...IS NEVER GOING TO HAPPEN ...!!

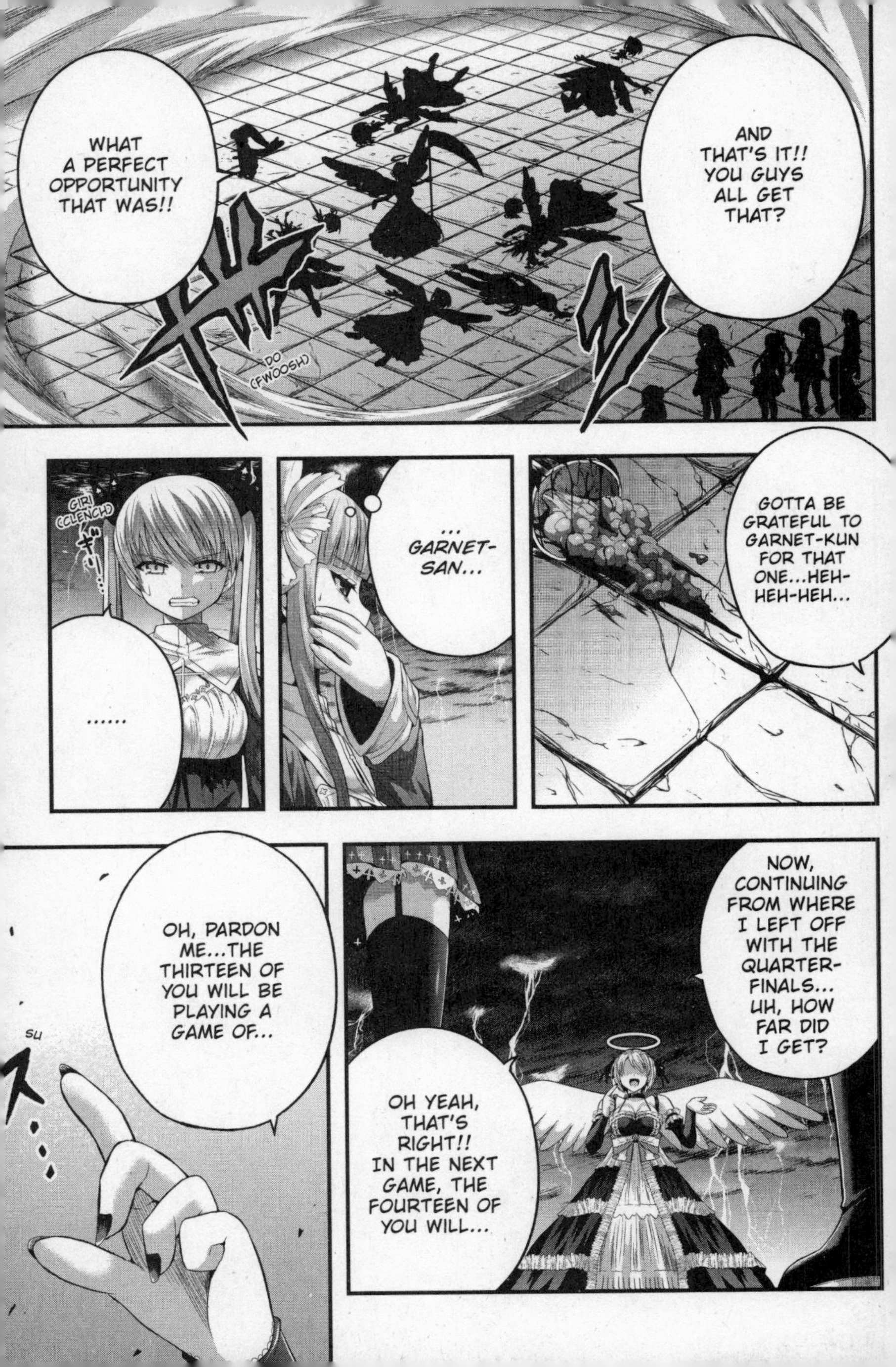
AND THAT'S IT!! YOU GUYS ALL GET THAT?
WHAT A PERFECT OPPORTUNITY THAT WAS!!
DO (FWOOSH)
GOTTA BE GRATEFUL TO GARNET-KUN FOR THAT ONE...HEH-HEH-HEH...
...GARNET-SAN...
GIRI (CLENCH)
......
NOW, CONTINUING FROM WHERE I LEFT OFF WITH THE QUARTER-FINALS... UH, HOW FAR DID I GET?
OH YEAH, THAT'S RIGHT!! IN THE NEXT GAME, THE FOURTEEN OF YOU WILL...
OH, PARDON ME...THE THIRTEEN OF YOU WILL BE PLAYING A GAME OF...
SU

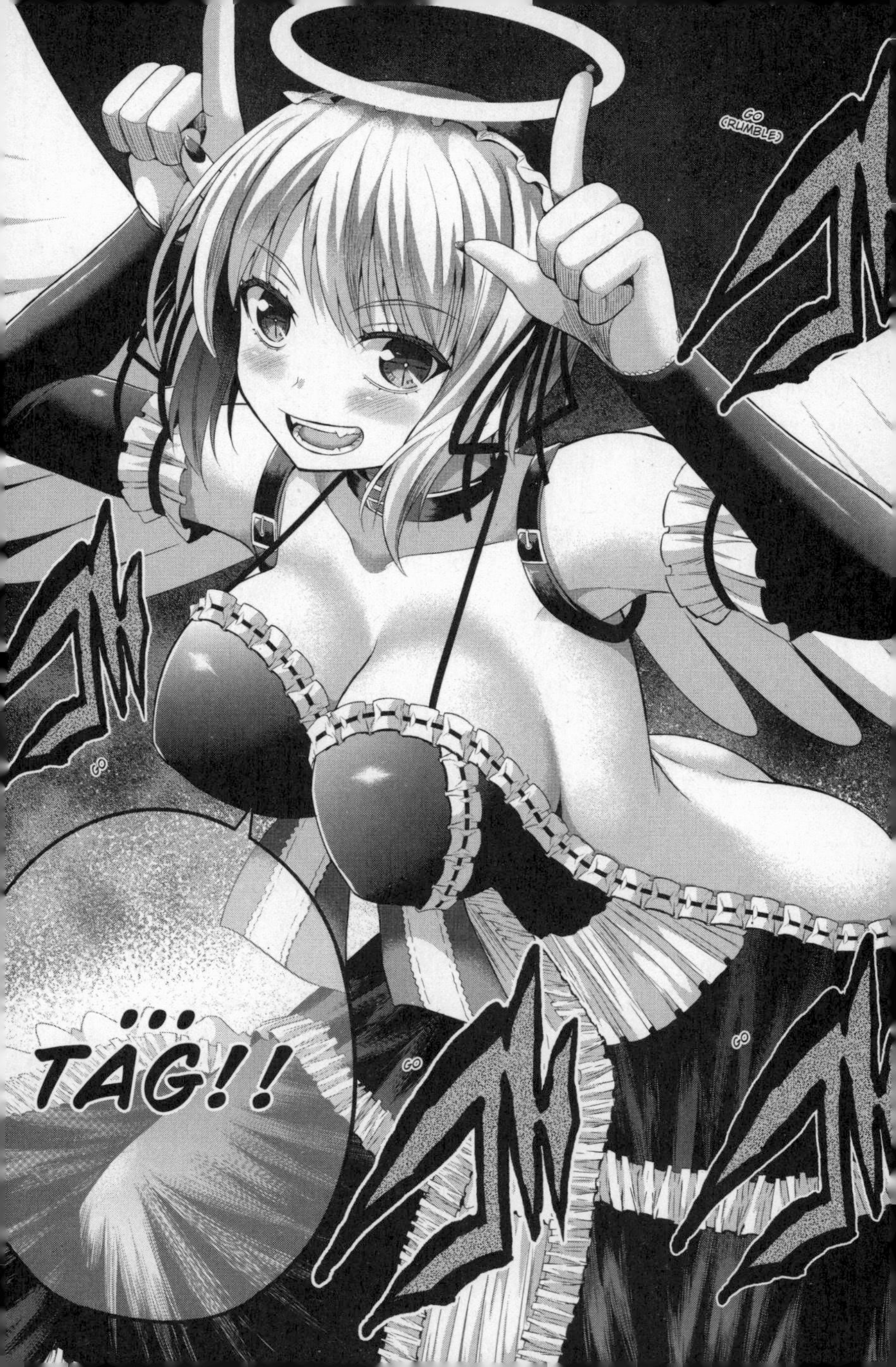
GO
(RUMBLE)
GO
GO
GO
...TÄG!!

Though You May Burn to ASH

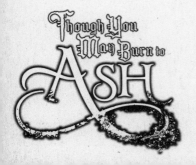

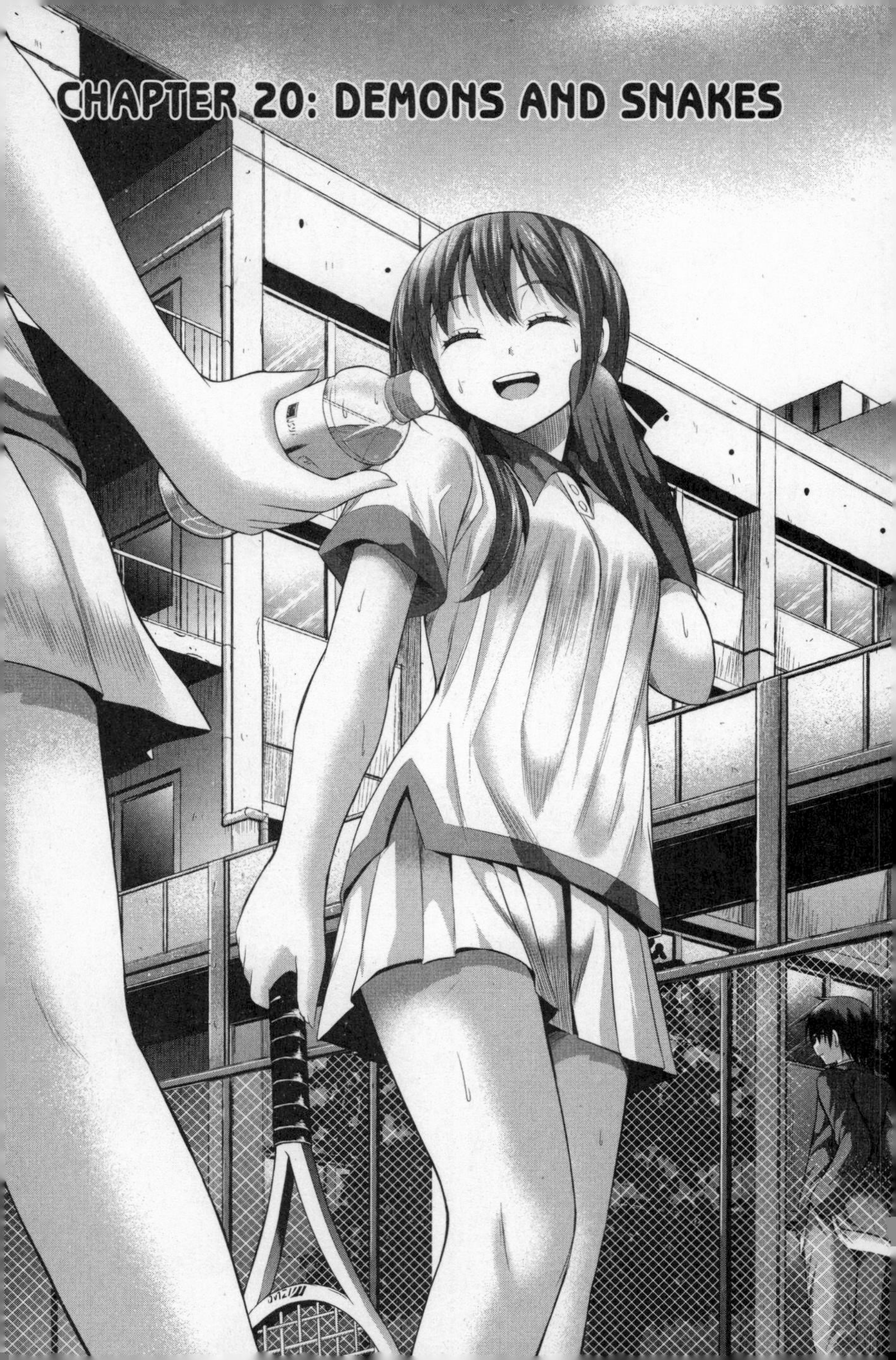
CHAPTER 20: DEMONS AND SNAKES

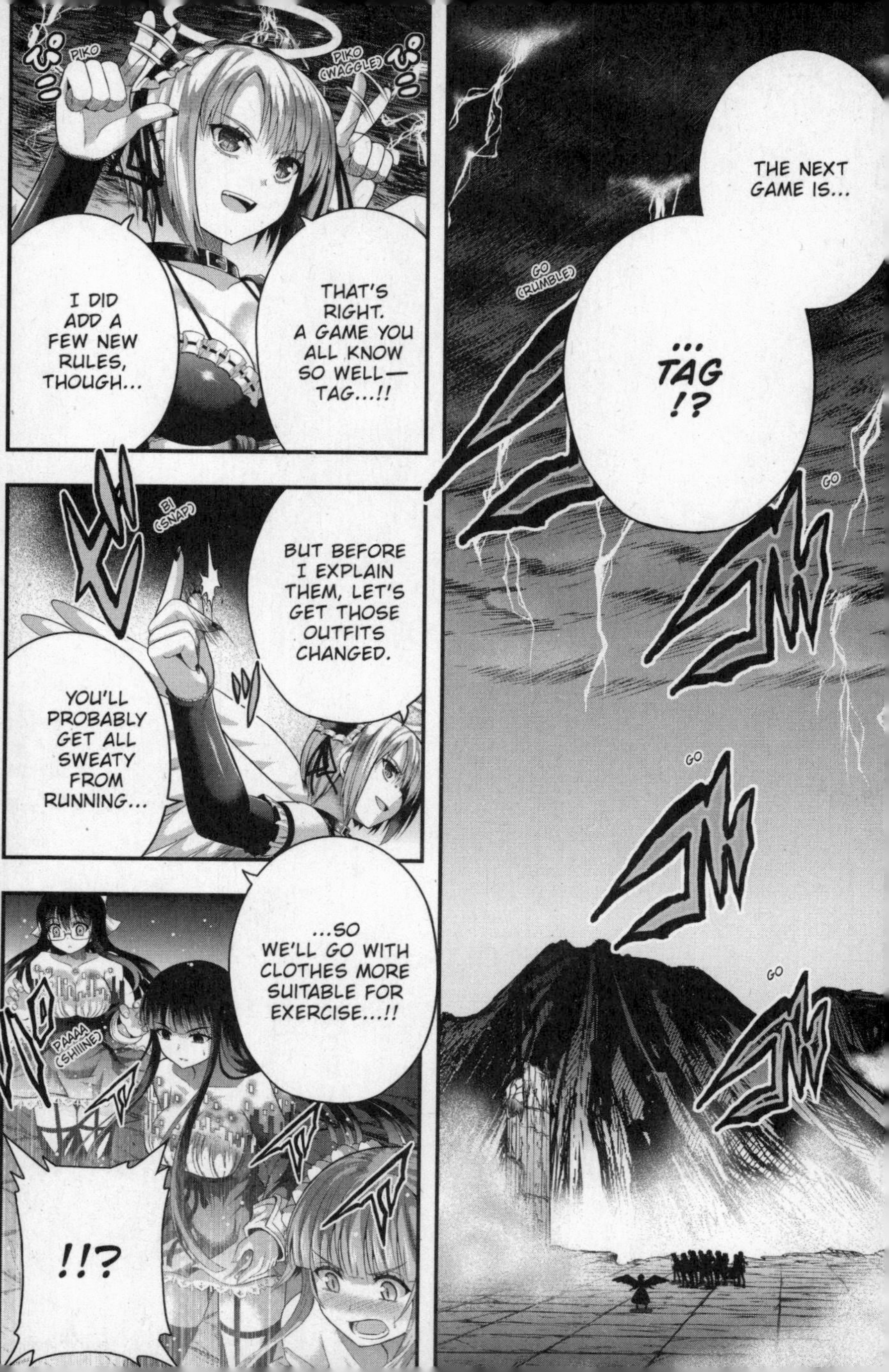
THE NEXT GAME IS...
GO (RUMBLE)
...TAG!?
GO
GO
GO
PIKO (WAGGLE)
PIKO
THAT'S RIGHT. A GAME YOU ALL KNOW SO WELL—TAG...!!
I DID ADD A FEW NEW RULES, THOUGH...
BI (SNAP)
BUT BEFORE I EXPLAIN THEM, LET'S GET THOSE OUTFITS CHANGED.
YOU'LL PROBABLY GET ALL SWEATY FROM RUNNING...
...SO WE'LL GO WITH CLOTHES MORE SUITABLE FOR EXERCISE...!!
PAAAA (SHIIINE)
!!?

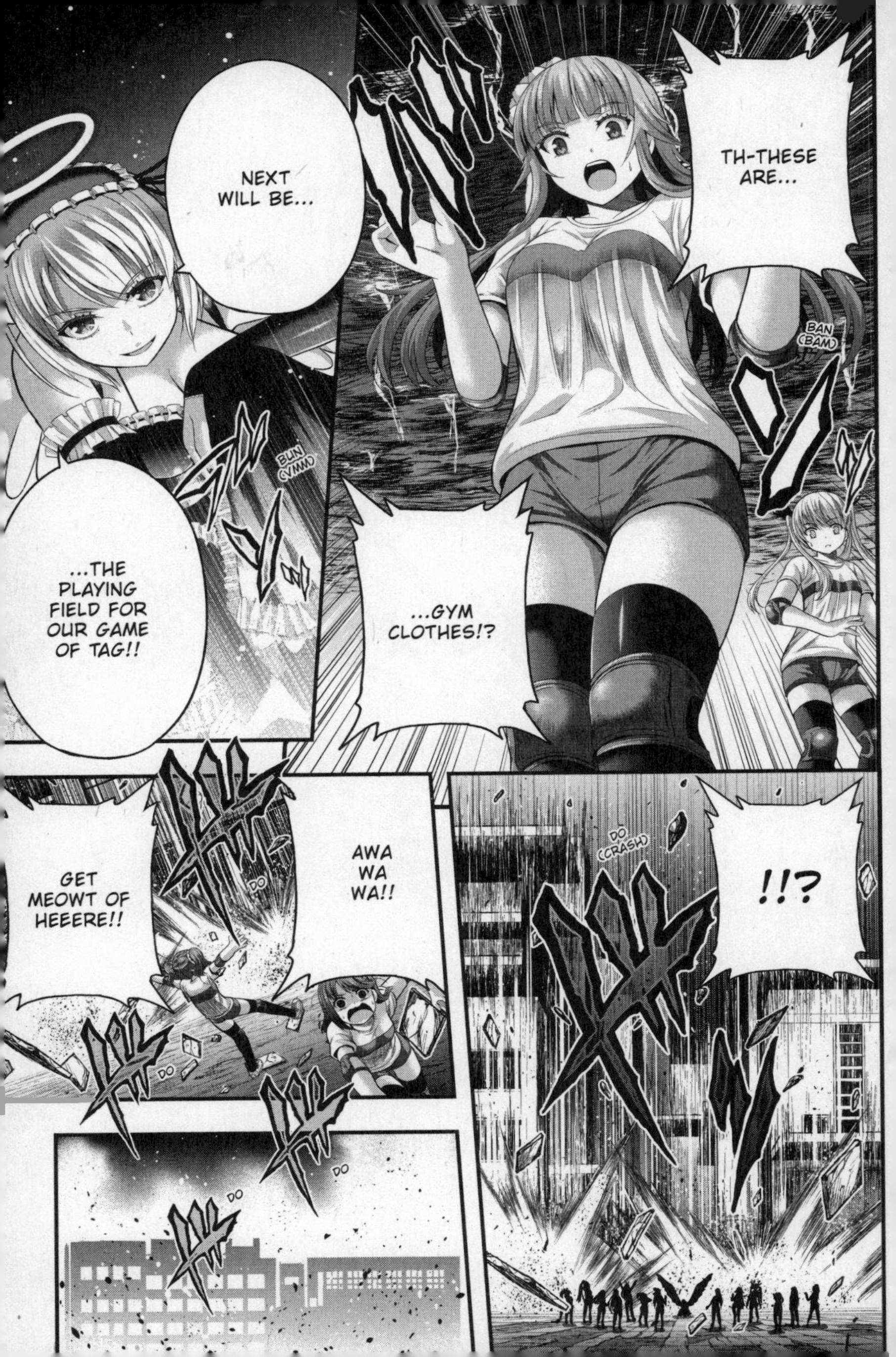

TH-THESE ARE...
BAN (BAM)
...GYM CLOTHES!?
NEXT WILL BE...
BUN (VMM)
...THE PLAYING FIELD FOR OUR GAME OF TAG!!
!!?
DO (CRASH)
AWA WA WA!!
GET MEOWT OF HEEERE!!
DO
DO
DO
DO

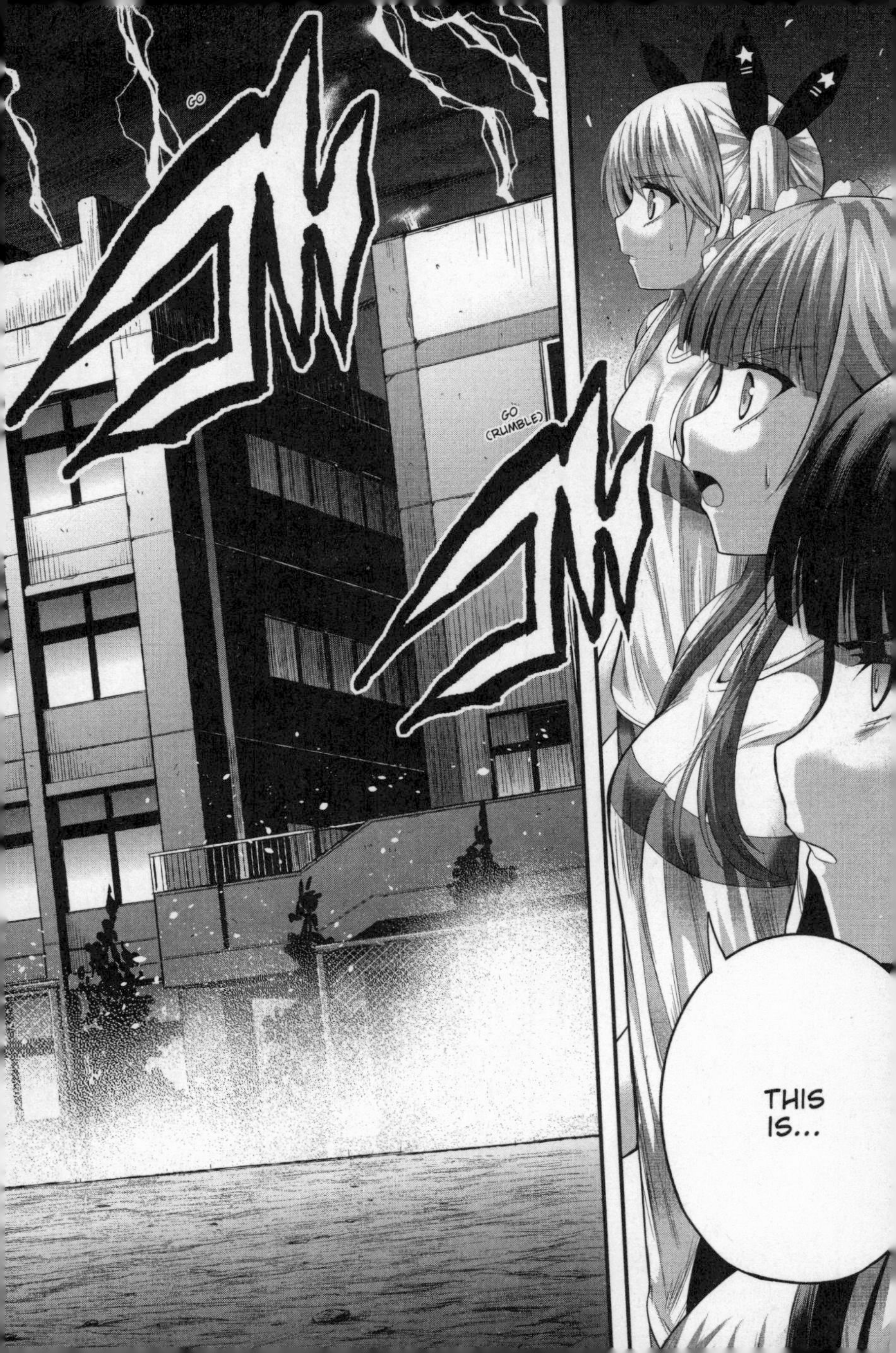
THIS IS...
GO
GO (RUMBLE)

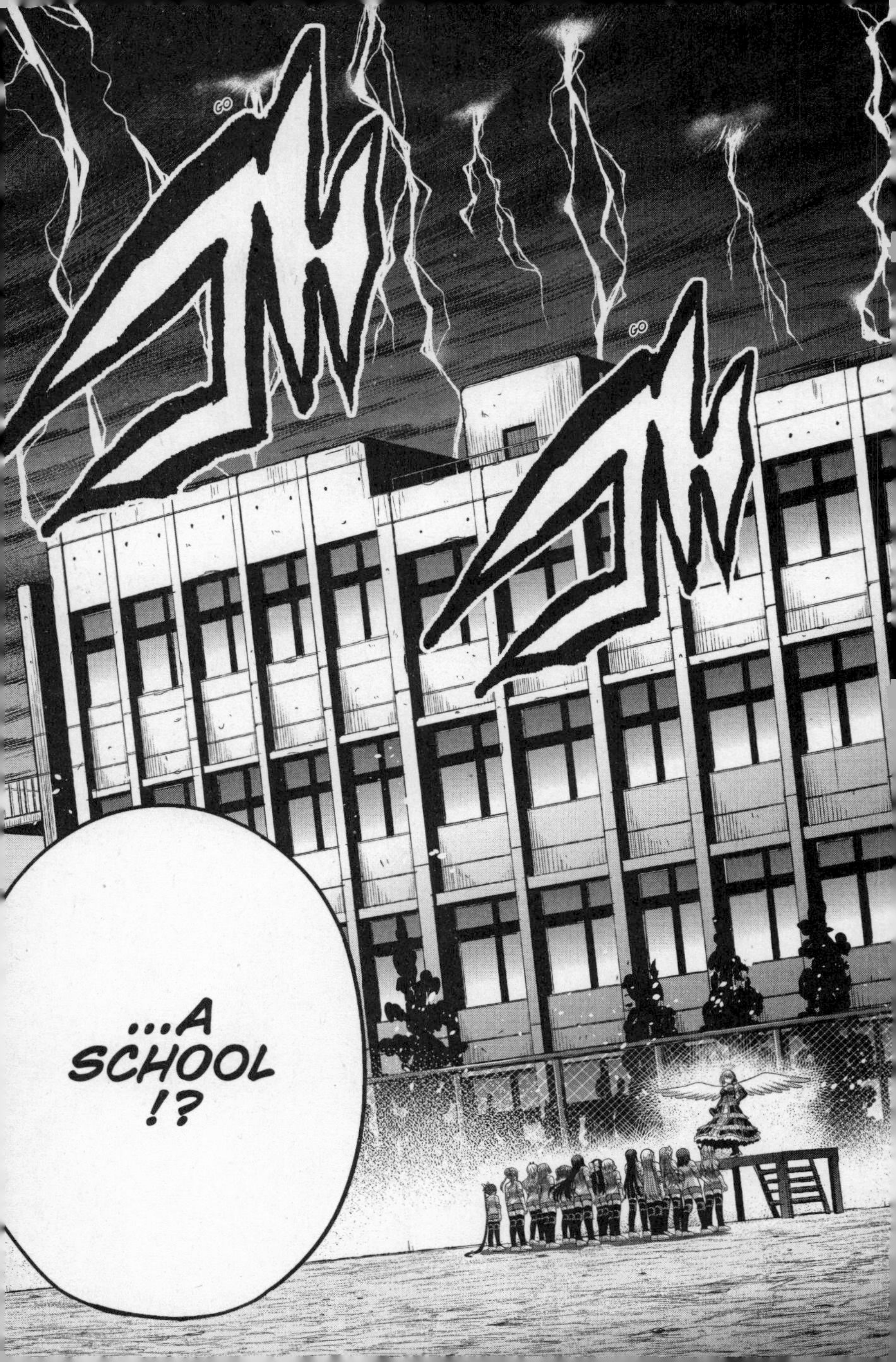
GO
GO
...A SCHOOL !?

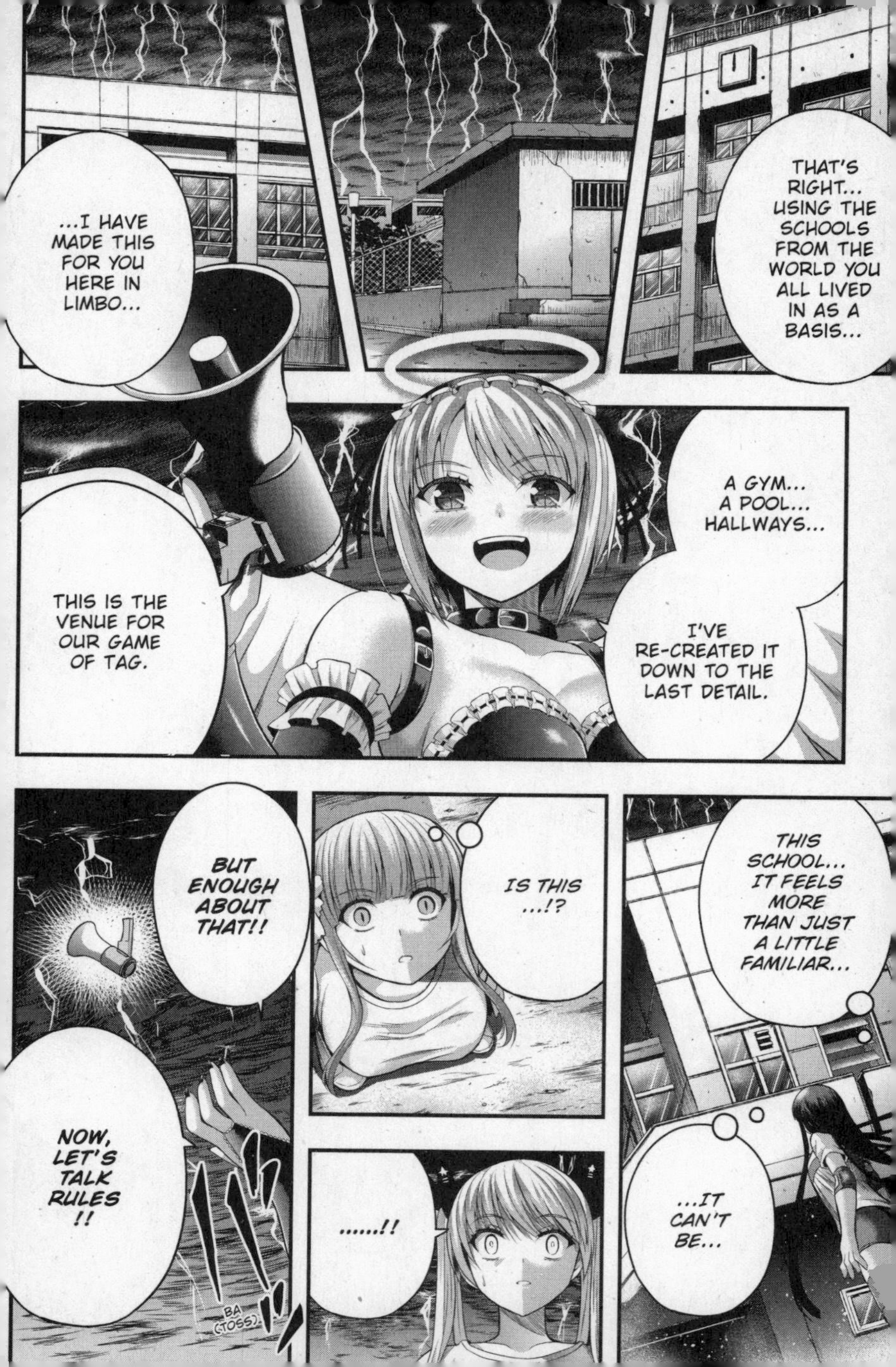
THAT'S RIGHT... USING THE SCHOOLS FROM THE WORLD YOU ALL LIVED IN AS A BASIS...
...I HAVE MADE THIS FOR YOU HERE IN LIMBO...
A GYM... A POOL... HALLWAYS...
I'VE RE-CREATED IT DOWN TO THE LAST DETAIL.
THIS IS THE VENUE FOR OUR GAME OF TAG.
THIS SCHOOL... IT FEELS MORE THAN JUST A LITTLE FAMILIAR...
...IT CAN'T BE...
IS THIS ...!?
......!!
BUT ENOUGH ABOUT THAT!!
NOW, LET'S TALK RULES!!
BA (TOSS)

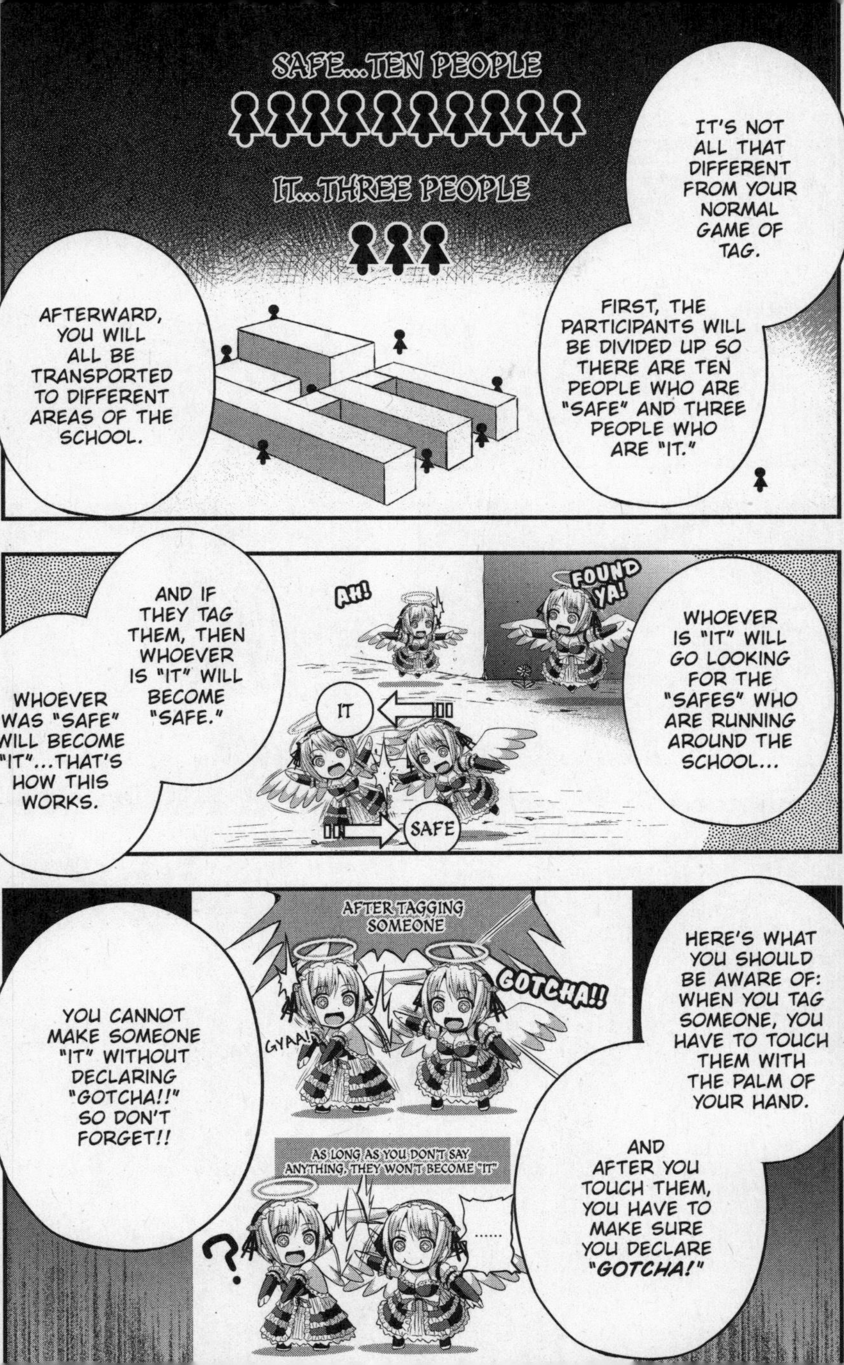

IT'S NOT ALL THAT DIFFERENT FROM YOUR NORMAL GAME OF TAG.
FIRST, THE PARTICIPANTS WILL BE DIVIDED UP SO THERE ARE TEN PEOPLE WHO ARE "SAFE" AND THREE PEOPLE WHO ARE "IT."
SAFE...TEN PEOPLE
IT...THREE PEOPLE
AFTERWARD, YOU WILL ALL BE TRANSPORTED TO DIFFERENT AREAS OF THE SCHOOL.
WHOEVER IS "IT" WILL GO LOOKING FOR THE "SAFES" WHO ARE RUNNING AROUND THE SCHOOL...
FOUND YA!
AH!
IT
SAFE
AND IF THEY TAG THEM, THEN WHOEVER IS "IT" WILL BECOME "SAFE."
WHOEVER WAS "SAFE" WILL BECOME "IT"...THAT'S HOW THIS WORKS.
HERE'S WHAT YOU SHOULD BE AWARE OF: WHEN YOU TAG SOMEONE, YOU HAVE TO TOUCH THEM WITH THE PALM OF YOUR HAND.
AND AFTER YOU TOUCH THEM, YOU HAVE TO MAKE SURE YOU DECLARE "GOTCHA!"
AFTER TAGGING SOMEONE
GOTCHA!!
GYAA!
AS LONG AS YOU DON'T SAY ANYTHING, THEY WON'T BECOME "IT"
......
?
YOU CANNOT MAKE SOMEONE "IT" WITHOUT DECLARING "GOTCHA!!" SO DON'T FORGET!!

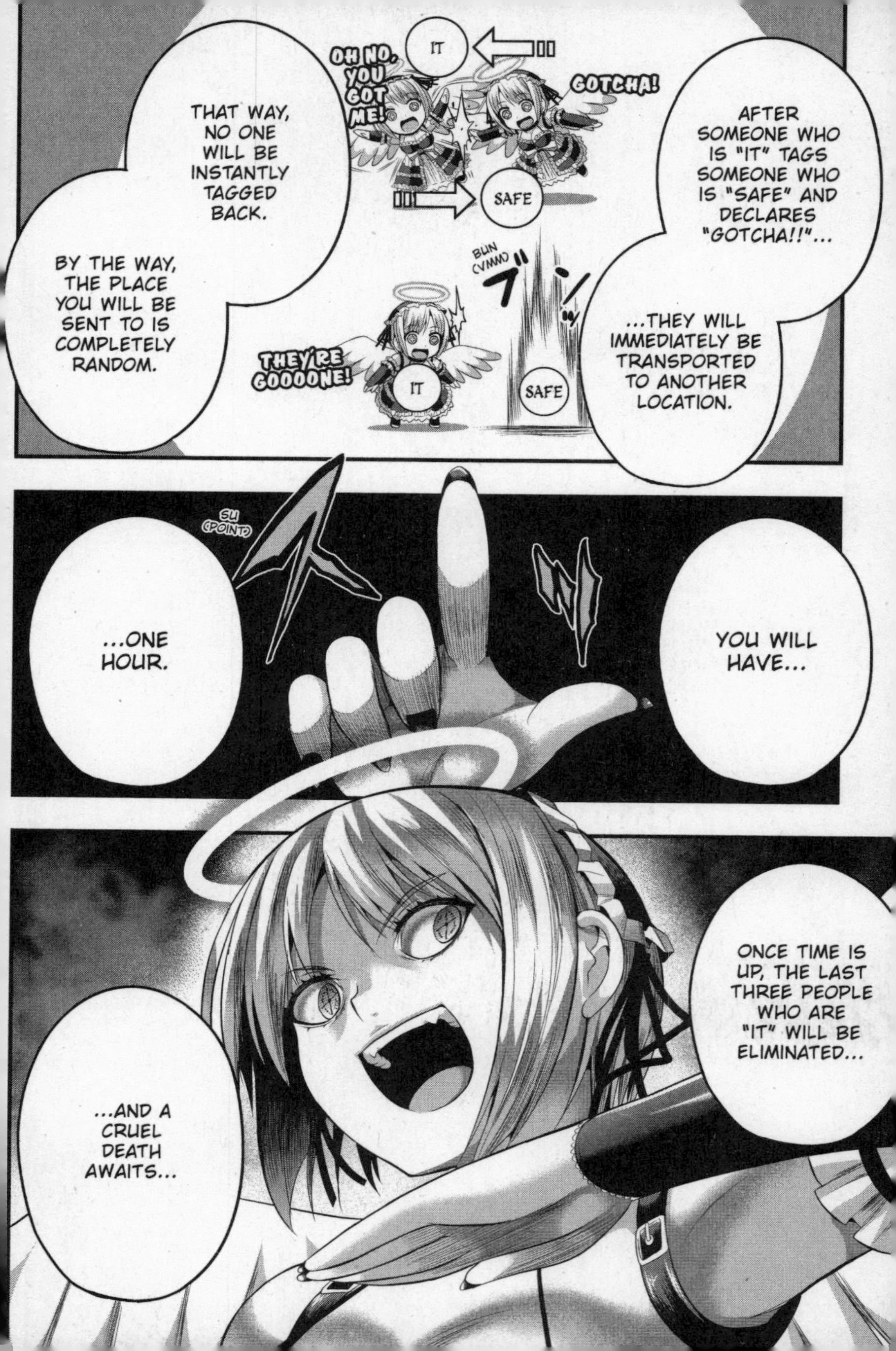
AFTER SOMEONE WHO IS "IT" TAGS SOMEONE WHO IS "SAFE" AND DECLARES "GOTCHA!!"...
IT
GOTCHA!
OH NO, YOU GOT ME!
SAFE
...THEY WILL IMMEDIATELY BE TRANSPORTED TO ANOTHER LOCATION.
BUN (VMM)
SAFE
THEY'RE GOOOONE!
IT
THAT WAY, NO ONE WILL BE INSTANTLY TAGGED BACK.
BY THE WAY, THE PLACE YOU WILL BE SENT TO IS COMPLETELY RANDOM.
YOU WILL HAVE...
SU (POINT)
...ONE HOUR.
ONCE TIME IS UP, THE LAST THREE PEOPLE WHO ARE "IT" WILL BE ELIMINATED...
...AND A CRUEL DEATH AWAITS...

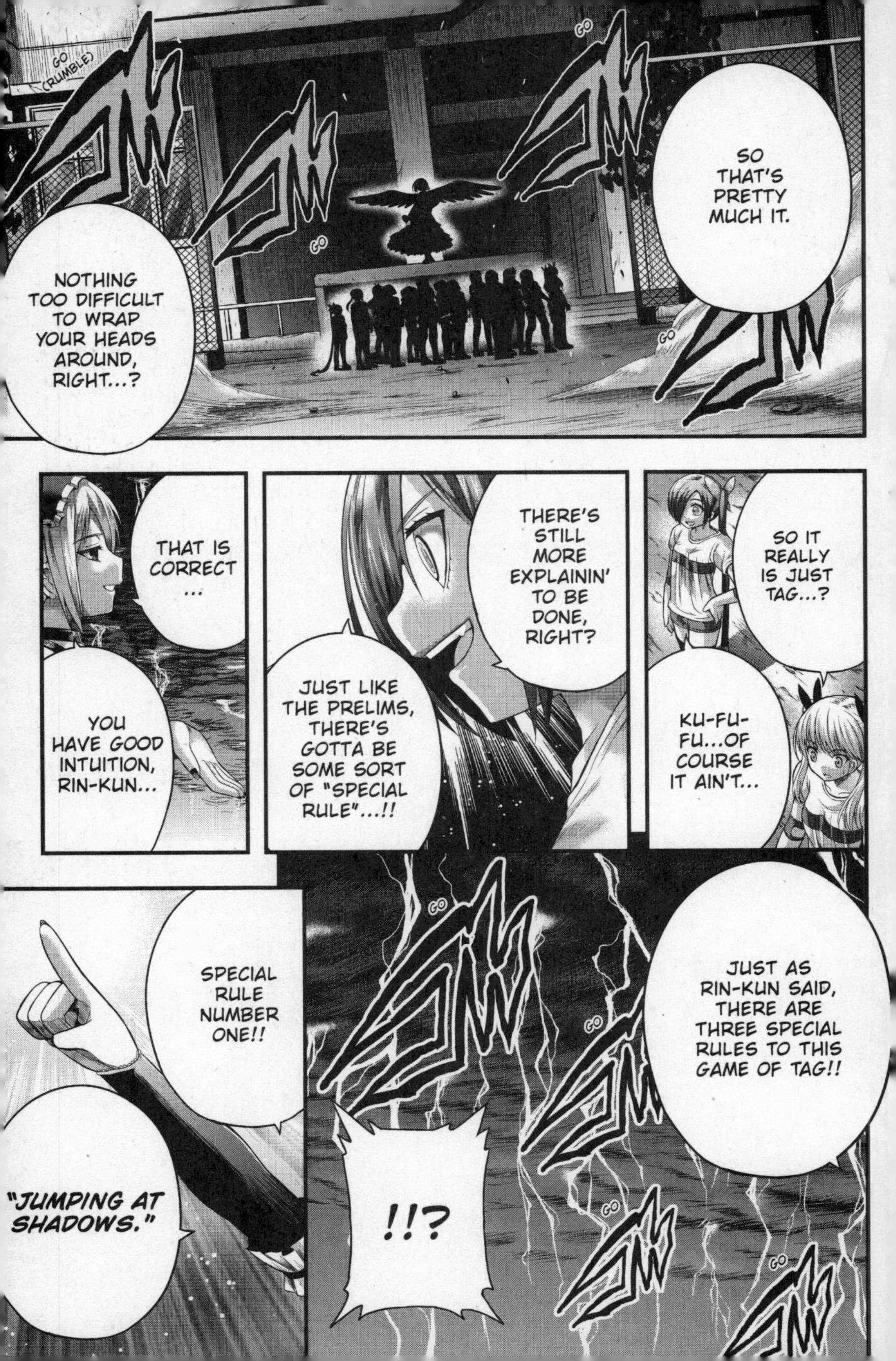

GO
SO THAT'S PRETTY MUCH IT.
GO
GO
GO (RUMBLE)
NOTHING TOO DIFFICULT TO WRAP YOUR HEADS AROUND, RIGHT...?
SO IT REALLY IS JUST TAG...?
KU-FU-FU...OF COURSE IT AIN'T...
THERE'S STILL MORE EXPLAININ' TO BE DONE, RIGHT?
JUST LIKE THE PRELIMS, THERE'S GOTTA BE SOME SORT OF "SPECIAL RULE"...!!
THAT IS CORRECT...
YOU HAVE GOOD INTUITION, RIN-KUN...
JUST AS RIN-KUN SAID, THERE ARE THREE SPECIAL RULES TO THIS GAME OF TAG!!
GO
GO
GO
GO
!!?
SPECIAL RULE NUMBER ONE!!
"JUMPING AT SHADOWS."

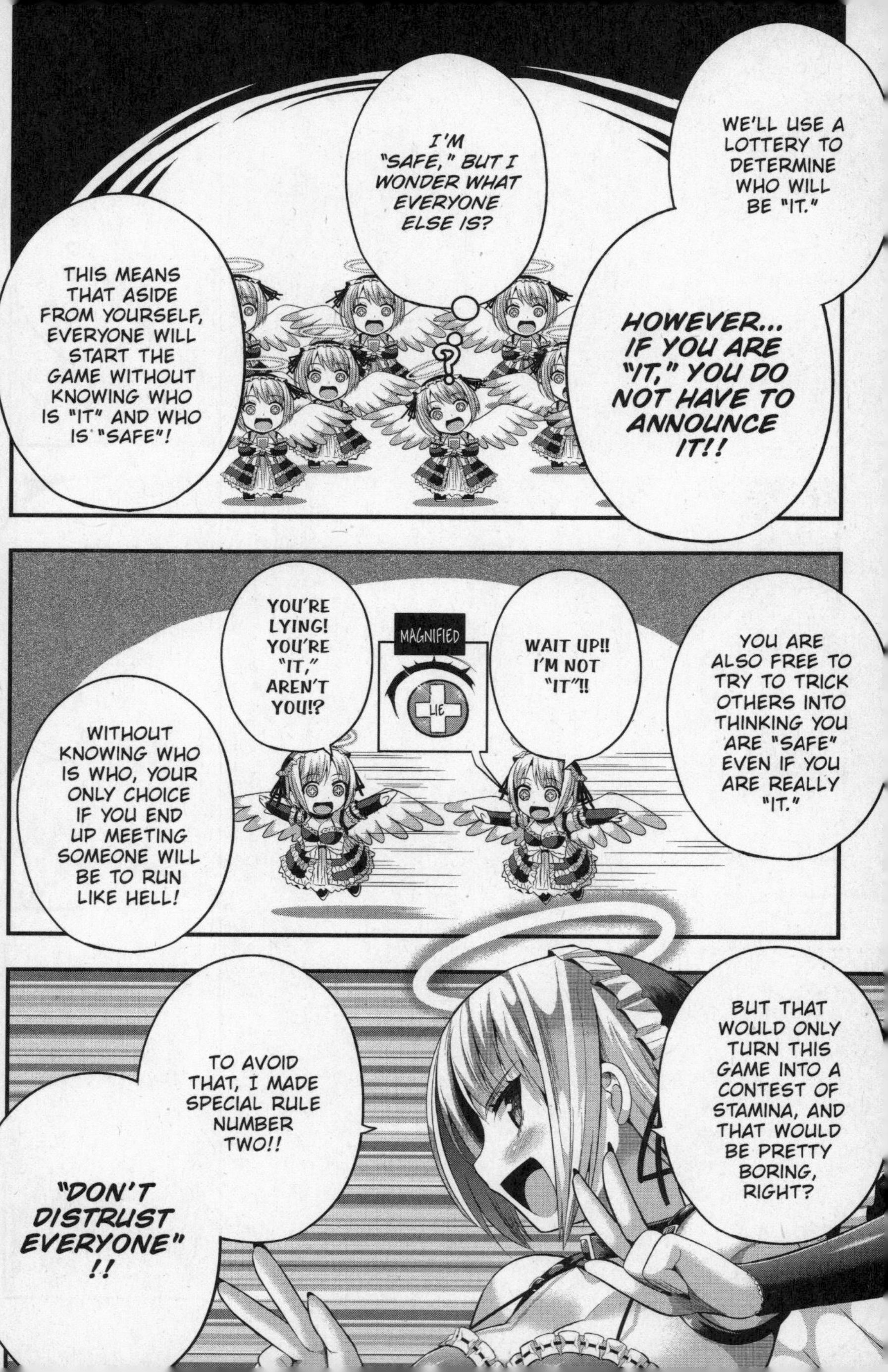
WE'LL USE A LOTTERY TO DETERMINE WHO WILL BE "IT."
HOWEVER... IF YOU ARE "IT," YOU DO NOT HAVE TO ANNOUNCE IT!!
THIS MEANS THAT ASIDE FROM YOURSELF, EVERYONE WILL START THE GAME WITHOUT KNOWING WHO IS "IT" AND WHO IS "SAFE"!
I'M "SAFE," BUT I WONDER WHAT EVERYONE ELSE IS?
YOU ARE ALSO FREE TO TRY TO TRICK OTHERS INTO THINKING YOU ARE "SAFE" EVEN IF YOU ARE REALLY "IT."
WAIT UP!! I'M NOT "IT"!!
MAGNIFIED
LIE
YOU'RE LYING! YOU'RE "IT," AREN'T YOU!?
WITHOUT KNOWING WHO IS WHO, YOUR ONLY CHOICE IF YOU END UP MEETING SOMEONE WILL BE TO RUN LIKE HELL!
BUT THAT WOULD ONLY TURN THIS GAME INTO A CONTEST OF STAMINA, AND THAT WOULD BE PRETTY BORING, RIGHT?
TO AVOID THAT, I MADE SPECIAL RULE NUMBER TWO!!
"DON'T DISTRUST EVERYONE" !!

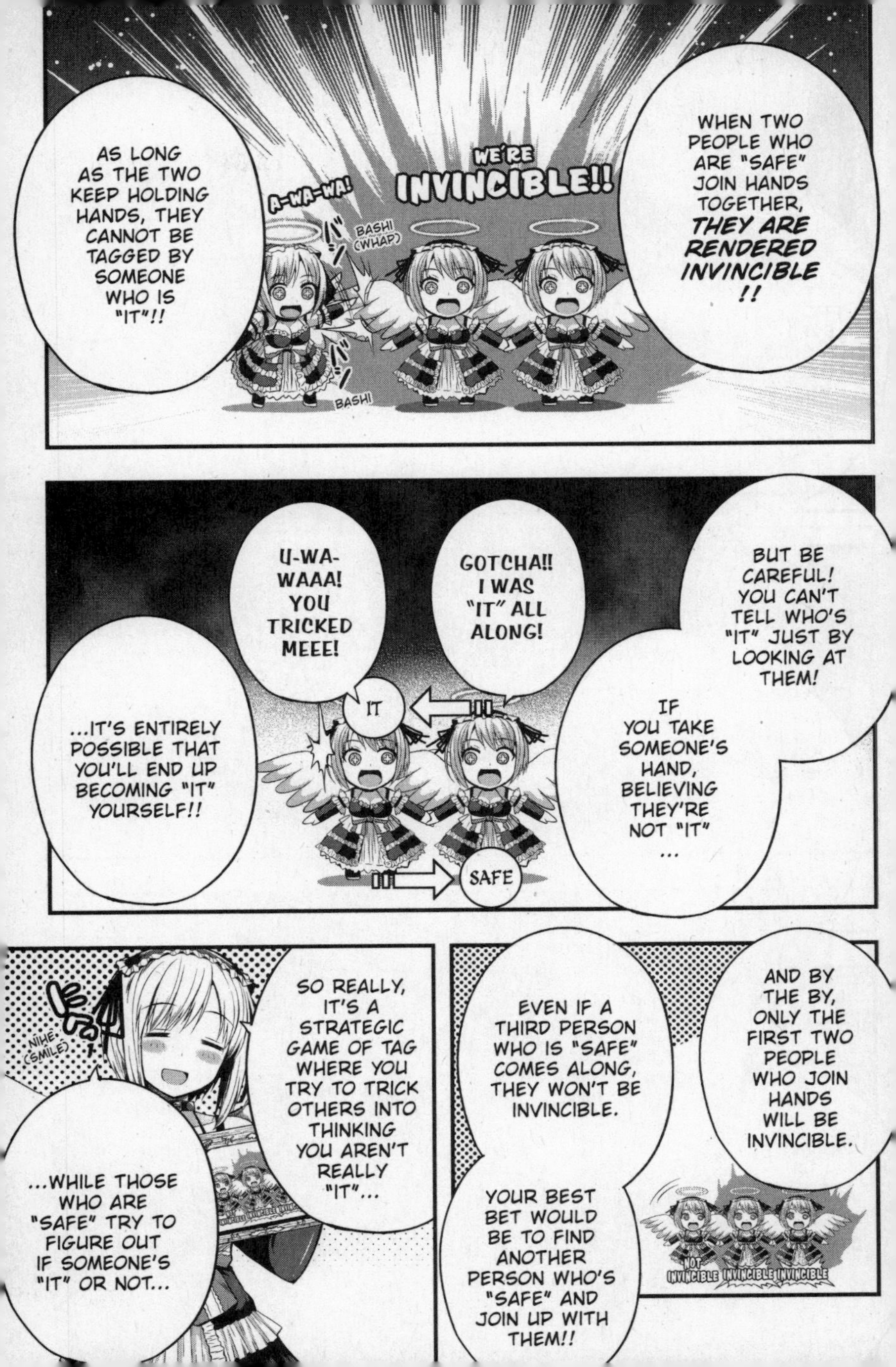
WHEN TWO PEOPLE WHO ARE "SAFE" JOIN HANDS TOGETHER, ***THEY ARE RENDERED INVINCIBLE!!***
WE'RE INVINCIBLE!!
BASHI (WHAP)
A-WA-WA!
BASHI
AS LONG AS THE TWO KEEP HOLDING HANDS, THEY CANNOT BE TAGGED BY SOMEONE WHO IS "IT"!!
BUT BE CAREFUL! YOU CAN'T TELL WHO'S "IT" JUST BY LOOKING AT THEM!
IF YOU TAKE SOMEONE'S HAND, BELIEVING THEY'RE NOT "IT"...
GOTCHA!! I WAS "IT" ALL ALONG!
U-WA-WAAA! YOU TRICKED MEEE!
IT
SAFE
...IT'S ENTIRELY POSSIBLE THAT YOU'LL END UP BECOMING "IT" YOURSELF!!
AND BY THE BY, ONLY THE FIRST TWO PEOPLE WHO JOIN HANDS WILL BE INVINCIBLE.
EVEN IF A THIRD PERSON WHO IS "SAFE" COMES ALONG, THEY WON'T BE INVINCIBLE.
YOUR BEST BET WOULD BE TO FIND ANOTHER PERSON WHO'S "SAFE" AND JOIN UP WITH THEM!!
NOT INVINCIBLE
INVINCIBLE
INVINCIBLE
SO REALLY, IT'S A STRATEGIC GAME OF TAG WHERE YOU TRY TO TRICK OTHERS INTO THINKING YOU AREN'T REALLY "IT"...
NIHE (SMILE)
...WHILE THOSE WHO ARE "SAFE" TRY TO FIGURE OUT IF SOMEONE'S "IT" OR NOT...

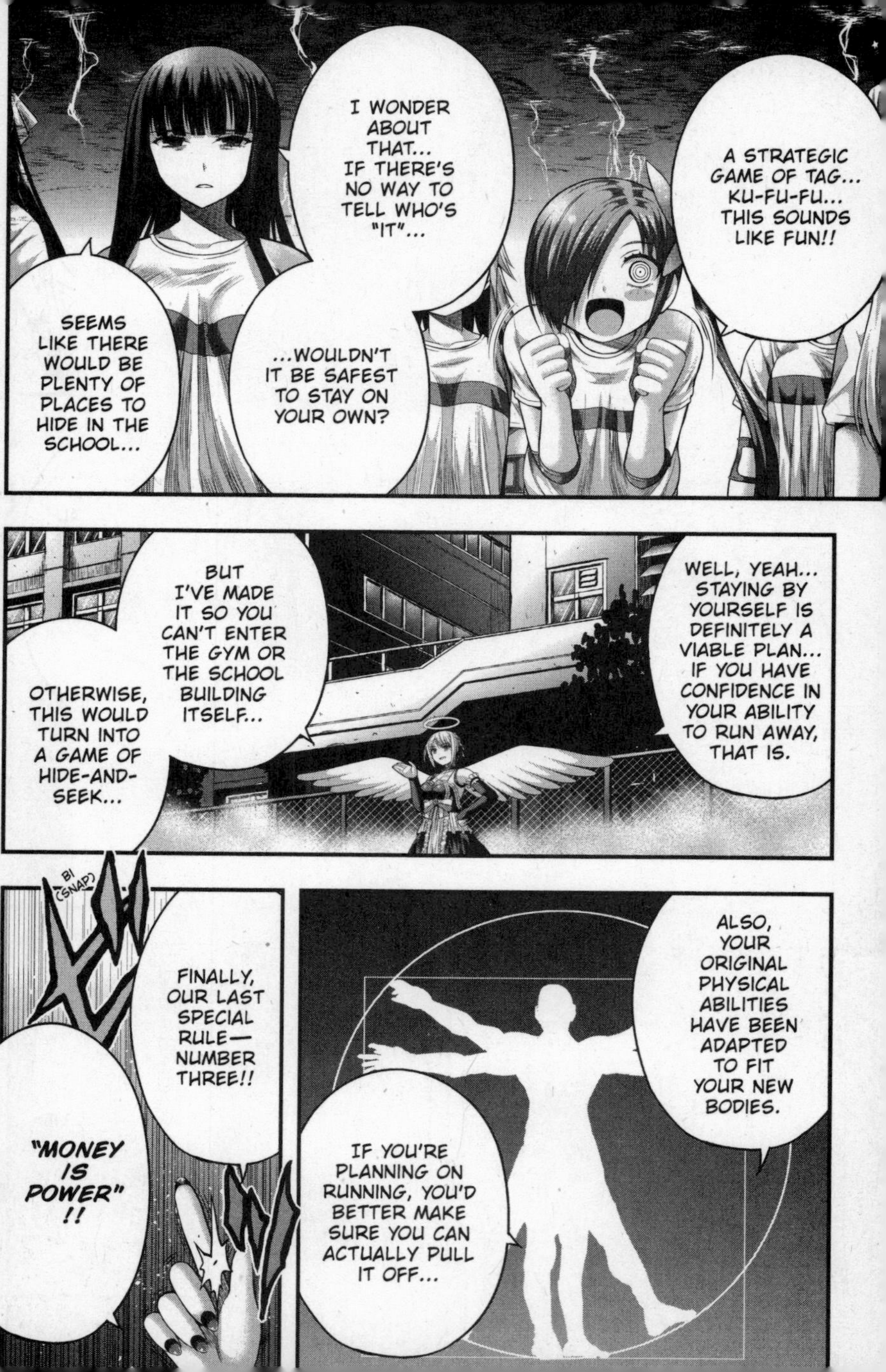
A STRATEGIC GAME OF TAG... KU-FU-FU... THIS SOUNDS LIKE FUN!!
I WONDER ABOUT THAT... IF THERE'S NO WAY TO TELL WHO'S "IT"...
...WOULDN'T IT BE SAFEST TO STAY ON YOUR OWN?
SEEMS LIKE THERE WOULD BE PLENTY OF PLACES TO HIDE IN THE SCHOOL...
WELL, YEAH... STAYING BY YOURSELF IS DEFINITELY A VIABLE PLAN... IF YOU HAVE CONFIDENCE IN YOUR ABILITY TO RUN AWAY, THAT IS.
BUT I'VE MADE IT SO YOU CAN'T ENTER THE GYM OR THE SCHOOL BUILDING ITSELF...
OTHERWISE, THIS WOULD TURN INTO A GAME OF HIDE-AND-SEEK...
ALSO, YOUR ORIGINAL PHYSICAL ABILITIES HAVE BEEN ADAPTED TO FIT YOUR NEW BODIES.
IF YOU'RE PLANNING ON RUNNING, YOU'D BETTER MAKE SURE YOU CAN ACTUALLY PULL IT OFF...
BI (SNAP)
FINALLY, OUR LAST SPECIAL RULE—NUMBER THREE!!
"MONEY IS POWER" !!

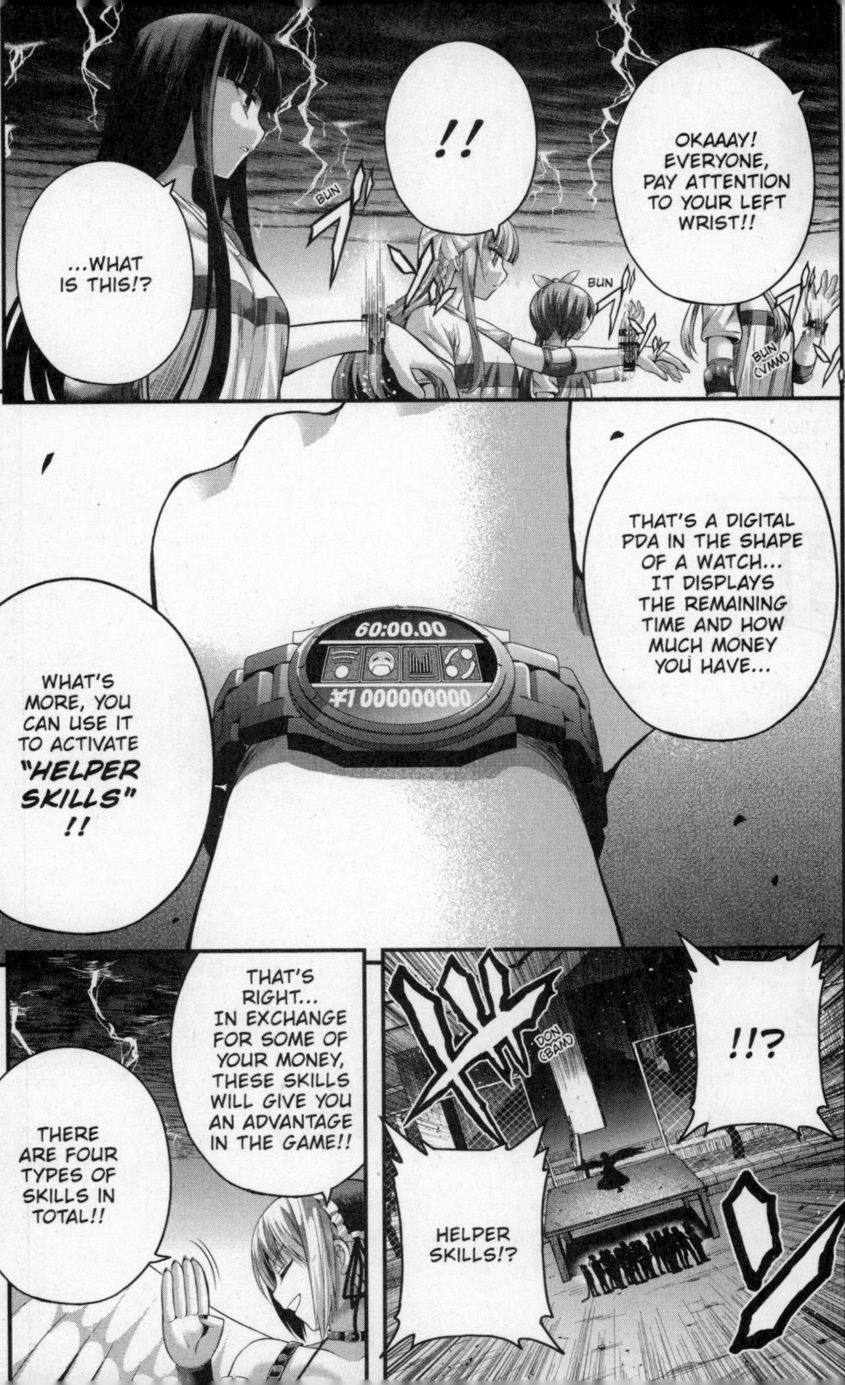
OKAAAY! EVERYONE, PAY ATTENTION TO YOUR LEFT WRIST!!
BUN (VMM)
BUN
!!
BUN
...WHAT IS THIS!?
THAT'S A DIGITAL PDA IN THE SHAPE OF A WATCH... IT DISPLAYS THE REMAINING TIME AND HOW MUCH MONEY YOU HAVE...
60:00.00
¥1 000000000
WHAT'S MORE, YOU CAN USE IT TO ACTIVATE "HELPER SKILLS"!!
!!?
DON (BAM)
HELPER SKILLS!?
THAT'S RIGHT... IN EXCHANGE FOR SOME OF YOUR MONEY, THESE SKILLS WILL GIVE YOU AN ADVANTAGE IN THE GAME!!
THERE ARE FOUR TYPES OF SKILLS IN TOTAL!!

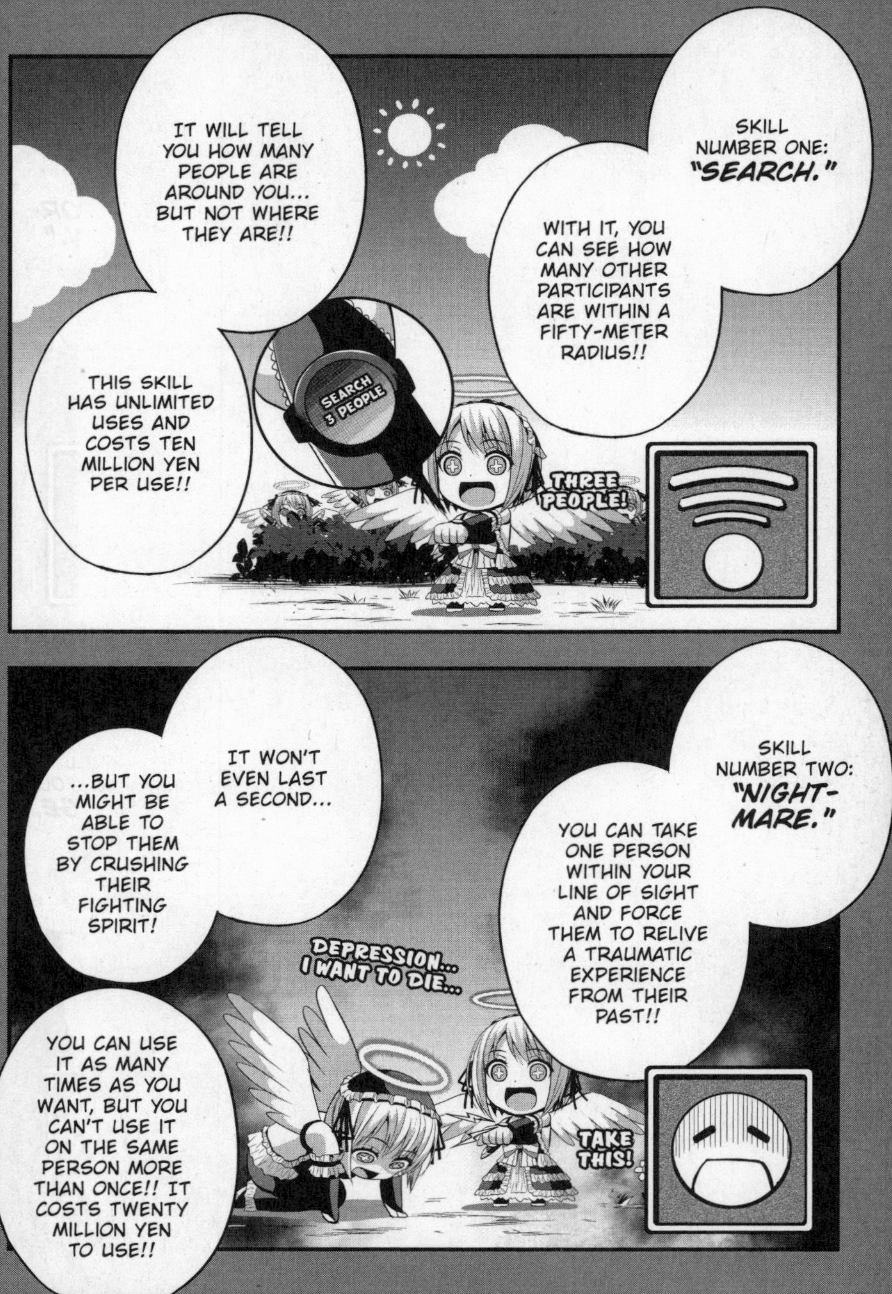

SKILL NUMBER ONE: **"SEARCH."**
WITH IT, YOU CAN SEE HOW MANY OTHER PARTICIPANTS ARE WITHIN A FIFTY-METER RADIUS!!
IT WILL TELL YOU HOW MANY PEOPLE ARE AROUND YOU... BUT NOT WHERE THEY ARE!!
SEARCH 3 PEOPLE
THIS SKILL HAS UNLIMITED USES AND COSTS TEN MILLION YEN PER USE!!
THREE PEOPLE!
SKILL NUMBER TWO: **"NIGHT-MARE."**
YOU CAN TAKE ONE PERSON WITHIN YOUR LINE OF SIGHT AND FORCE THEM TO RELIVE A TRAUMATIC EXPERIENCE FROM THEIR PAST!!
IT WON'T EVEN LAST A SECOND...
...BUT YOU MIGHT BE ABLE TO STOP THEM BY CRUSHING THEIR FIGHTING SPIRIT!
DEPRESSION... I WANT TO DIE...
TAKE THIS!
YOU CAN USE IT AS MANY TIMES AS YOU WANT, BUT YOU CAN'T USE IT ON THE SAME PERSON MORE THAN ONCE!! IT COSTS TWENTY MILLION YEN TO USE!!

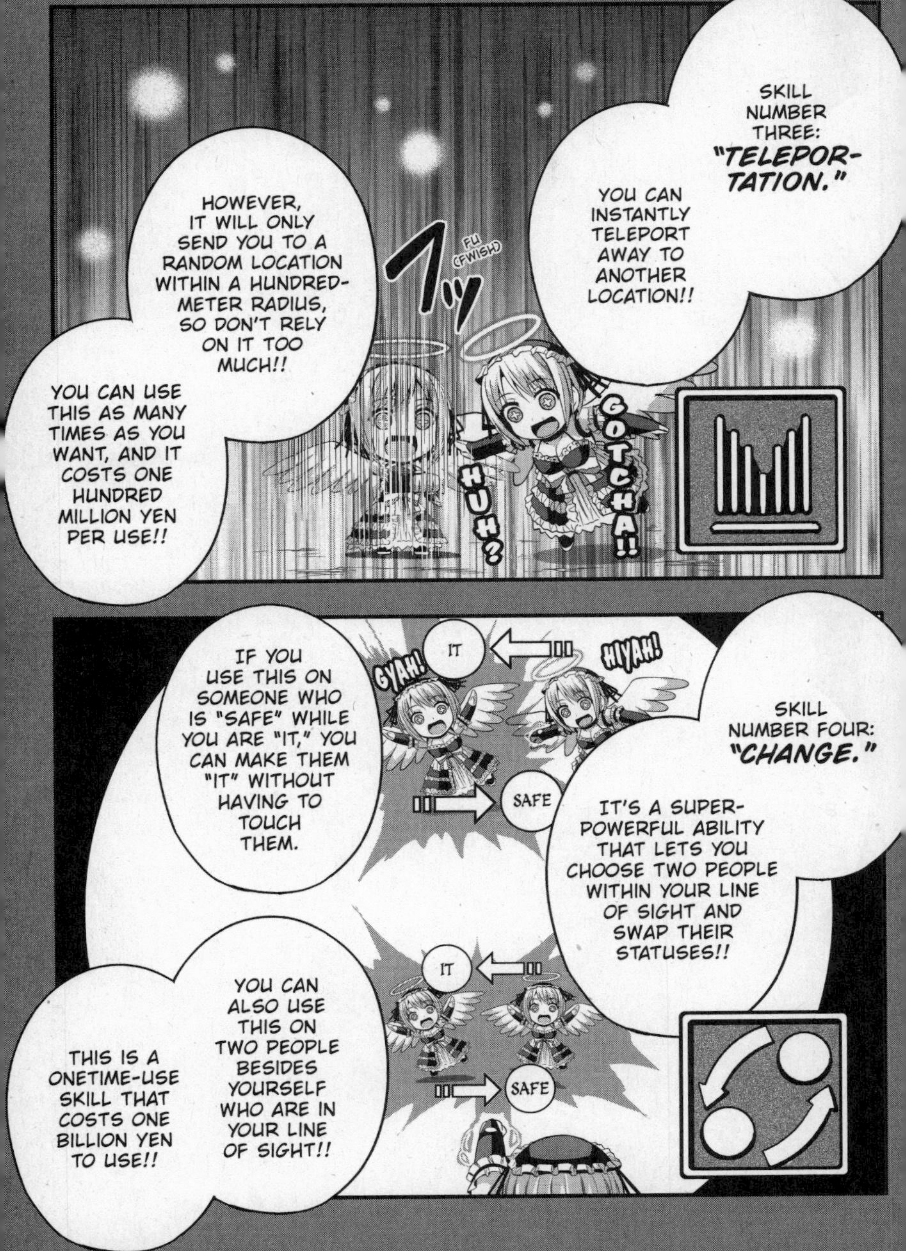
SKILL NUMBER THREE: "TELEPORTATION."
YOU CAN INSTANTLY TELEPORT AWAY TO ANOTHER LOCATION!!
FU (FWISH)
GOTCHA!!
HUH?
HOWEVER, IT WILL ONLY SEND YOU TO A RANDOM LOCATION WITHIN A HUNDRED-METER RADIUS, SO DON'T RELY ON IT TOO MUCH!!
YOU CAN USE THIS AS MANY TIMES AS YOU WANT, AND IT COSTS ONE HUNDRED MILLION YEN PER USE!!
SKILL NUMBER FOUR: "CHANGE."
IT'S A SUPER-POWERFUL ABILITY THAT LETS YOU CHOOSE TWO PEOPLE WITHIN YOUR LINE OF SIGHT AND SWAP THEIR STATUSES!!
HIYAH!
IT
GYAH!
SAFE
IF YOU USE THIS ON SOMEONE WHO IS "SAFE" WHILE YOU ARE "IT," YOU CAN MAKE THEM "IT" WITHOUT HAVING TO TOUCH THEM.
IT
SAFE
YOU CAN ALSO USE THIS ON TWO PEOPLE BESIDES YOURSELF WHO ARE IN YOUR LINE OF SIGHT!!
THIS IS A ONETIME-USE SKILL THAT COSTS ONE BILLION YEN TO USE!!

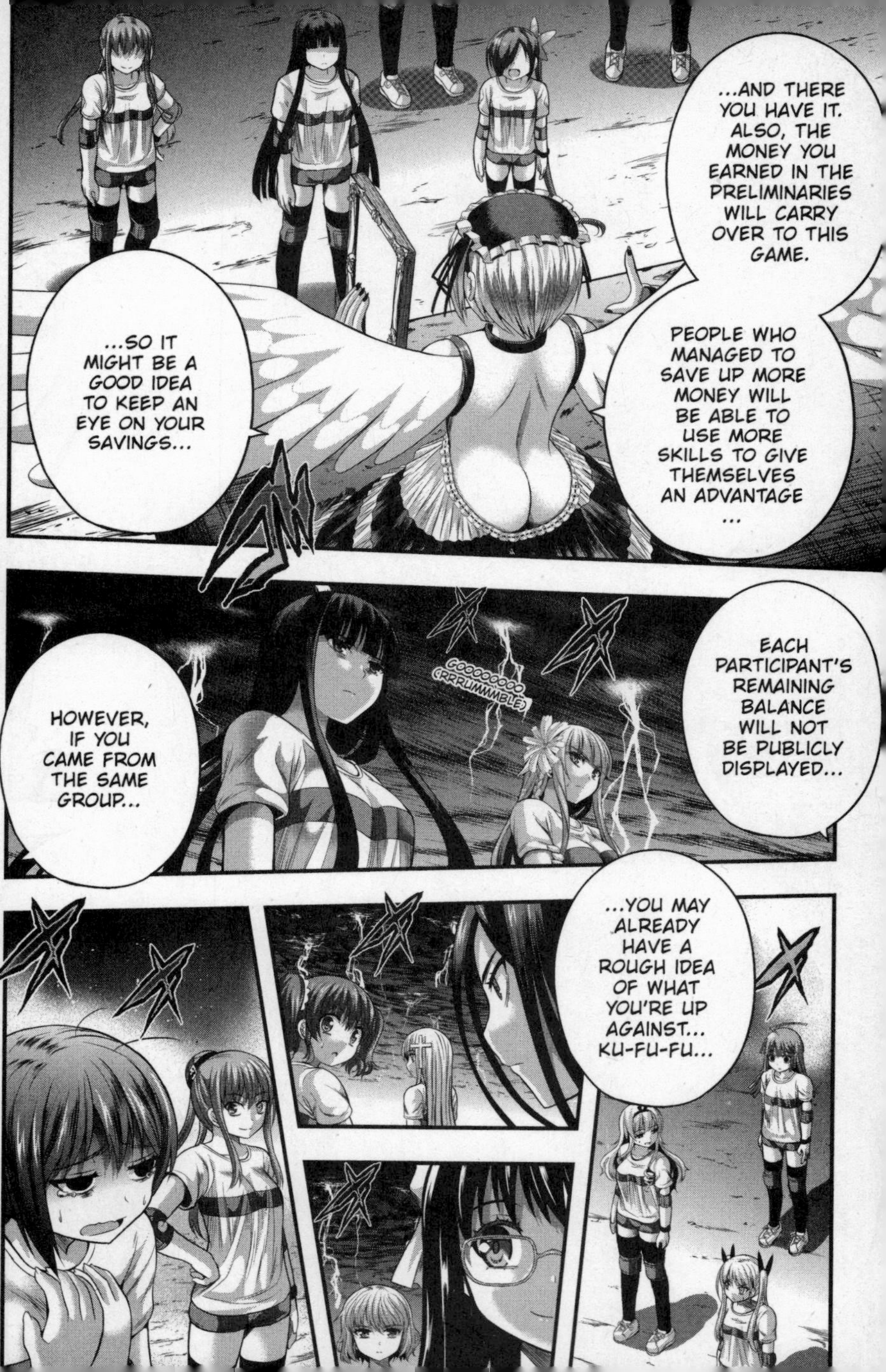
...AND THERE YOU HAVE IT. ALSO, THE MONEY YOU EARNED IN THE PRELIMINARIES WILL CARRY OVER TO THIS GAME.
PEOPLE WHO MANAGED TO SAVE UP MORE MONEY WILL BE ABLE TO USE MORE SKILLS TO GIVE THEMSELVES AN ADVANTAGE...
...SO IT MIGHT BE A GOOD IDEA TO KEEP AN EYE ON YOUR SAVINGS...
EACH PARTICIPANT'S REMAINING BALANCE WILL NOT BE PUBLICLY DISPLAYED...
GOOOOOOOO (RRRUMMMBLE)
HOWEVER, IF YOU CAME FROM THE SAME GROUP...
...YOU MAY ALREADY HAVE A ROUGH IDEA OF WHAT YOU'RE UP AGAINST... KU-FU-FU...

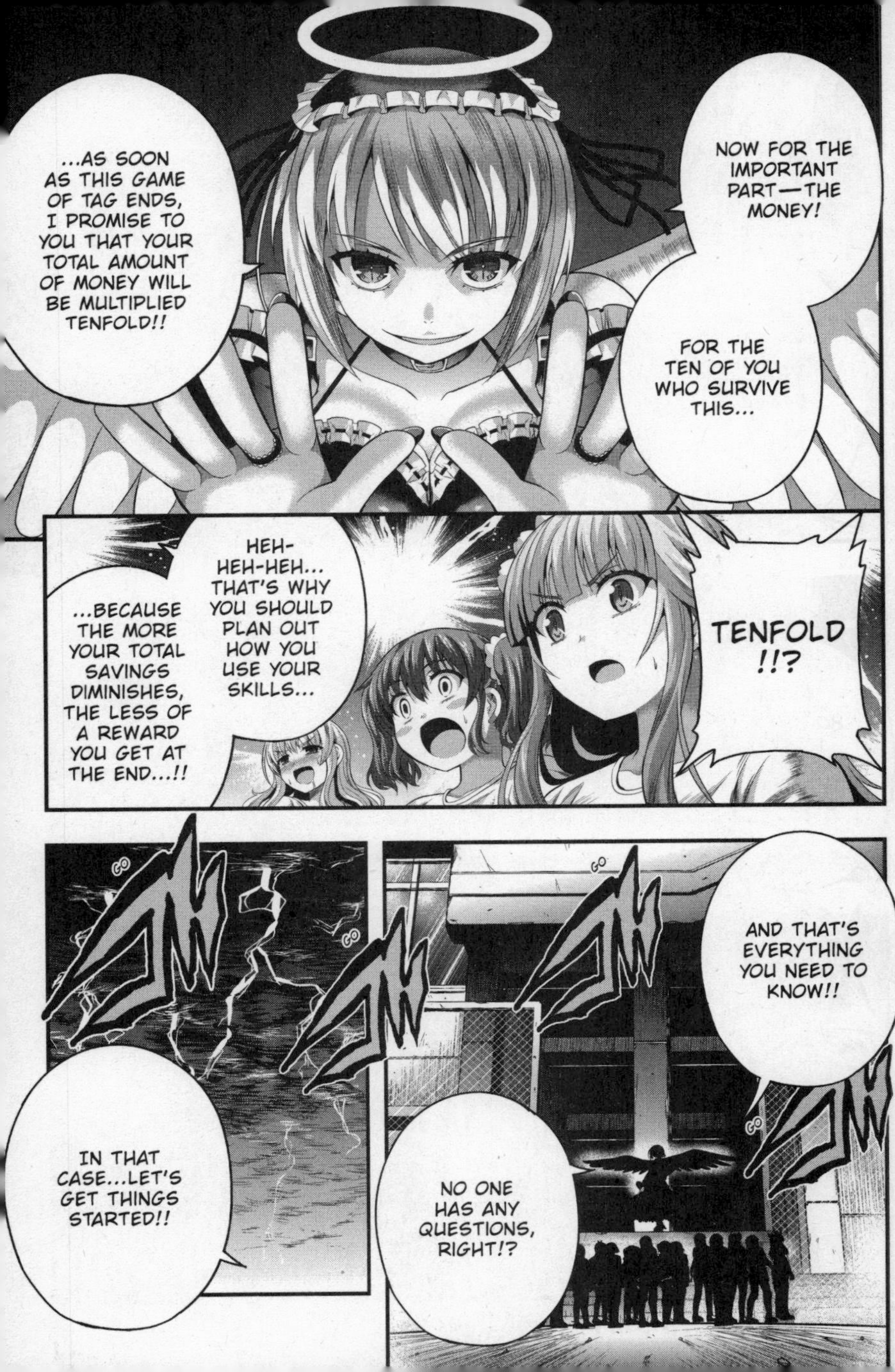
NOW FOR THE IMPORTANT PART—THE MONEY!
FOR THE TEN OF YOU WHO SURVIVE THIS...
...AS SOON AS THIS GAME OF TAG ENDS, I PROMISE TO YOU THAT YOUR TOTAL AMOUNT OF MONEY WILL BE MULTIPLIED TENFOLD!!
TENFOLD!!?
HEH-HEH-HEH... THAT'S WHY YOU SHOULD PLAN OUT HOW YOU USE YOUR SKILLS...
...BECAUSE THE MORE YOUR TOTAL SAVINGS DIMINISHES, THE LESS OF A REWARD YOU GET AT THE END...!!
GO
AND THAT'S EVERYTHING YOU NEED TO KNOW!!
GO
NO ONE HAS ANY QUESTIONS, RIGHT!?
GO
GO
IN THAT CASE...LET'S GET THINGS STARTED!!

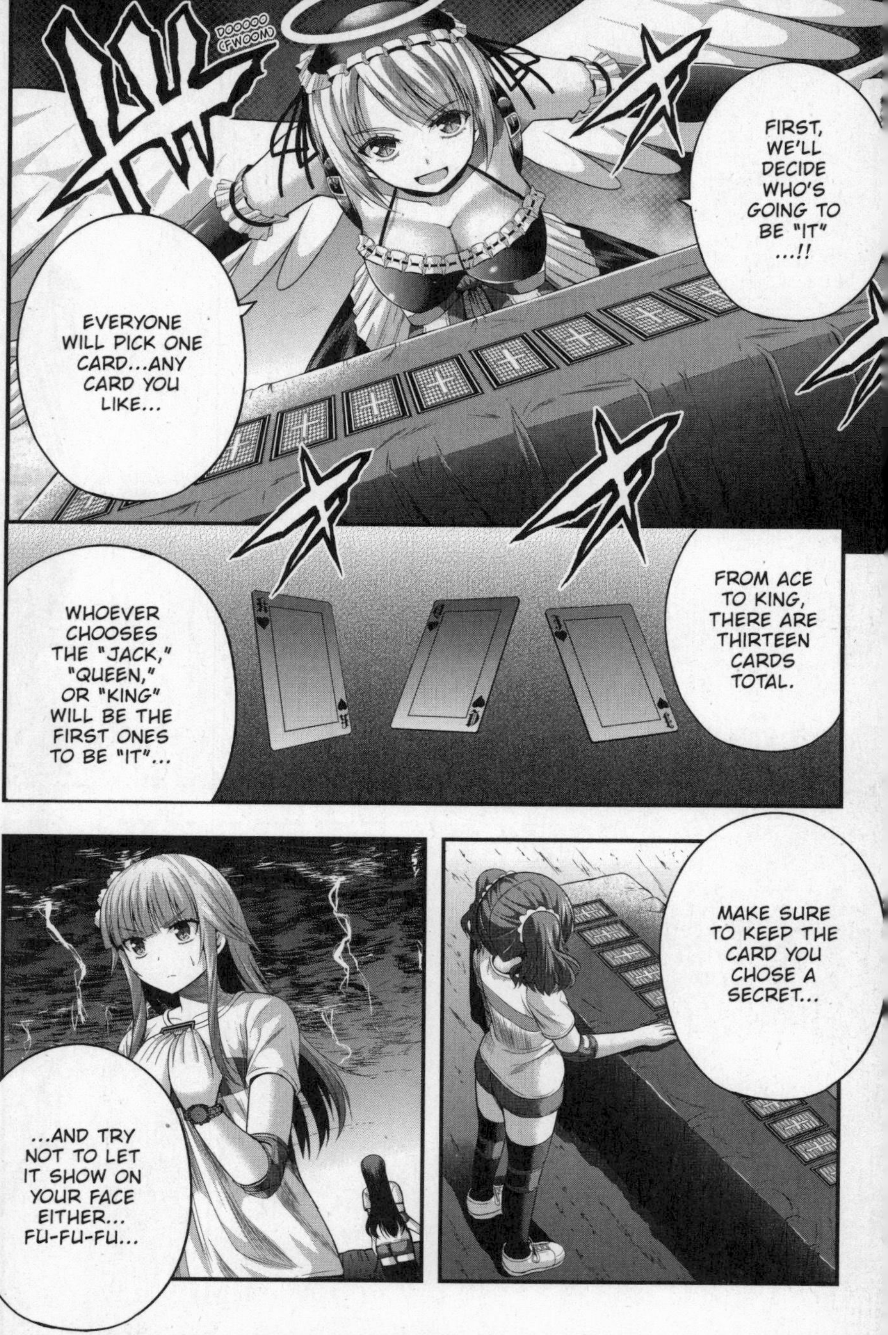
DOOOOO (FWOOM)
FIRST, WE'LL DECIDE WHO'S GOING TO BE "IT" ...!!
EVERYONE WILL PICK ONE CARD...ANY CARD YOU LIKE...
FROM ACE TO KING, THERE ARE THIRTEEN CARDS TOTAL.
WHOEVER CHOOSES THE "JACK," "QUEEN," OR "KING" WILL BE THE FIRST ONES TO BE "IT"...
MAKE SURE TO KEEP THE CARD YOU CHOSE A SECRET...
...AND TRY NOT TO LET IT SHOW ON YOUR FACE EITHER... FU-FU-FU...

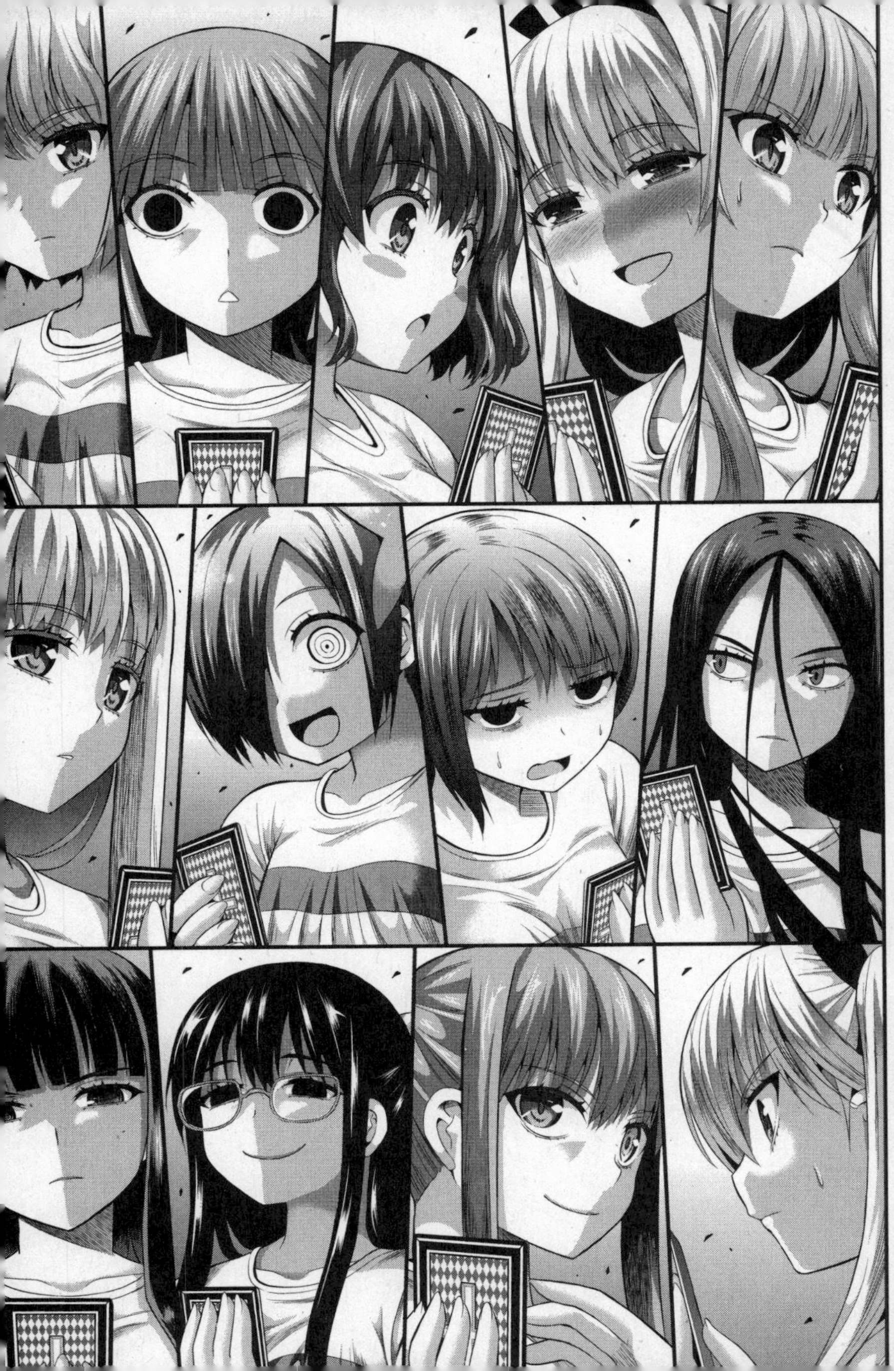

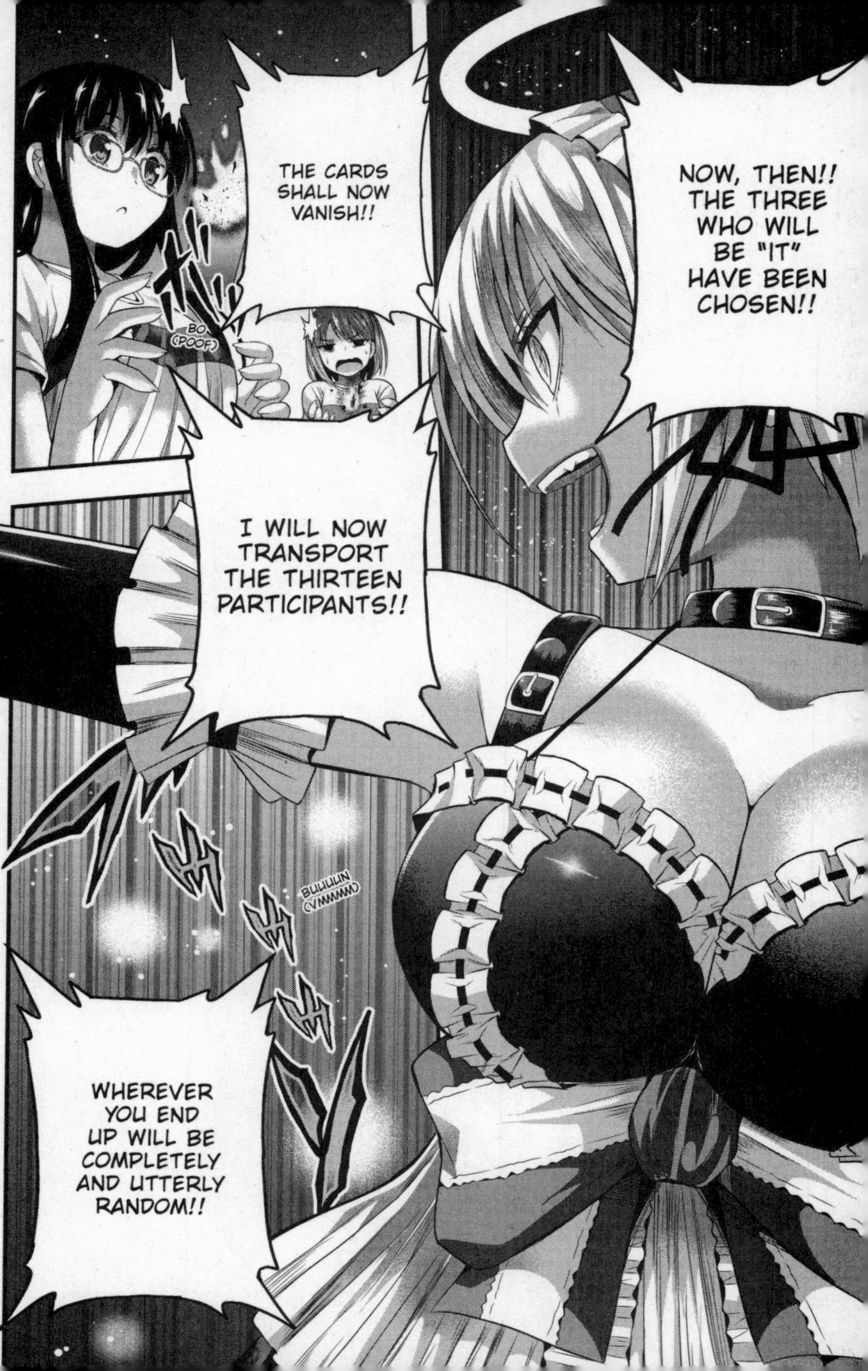
NOW, THEN!! THE THREE WHO WILL BE "IT" HAVE BEEN CHOSEN!!
THE CARDS SHALL NOW VANISH!!
BO (POOF)
I WILL NOW TRANSPORT THE THIRTEEN PARTICIPANTS!!
BUUUUN (VMMMMM)
WHEREVER YOU END UP WILL BE COMPLETELY AND UTTERLY RANDOM!!

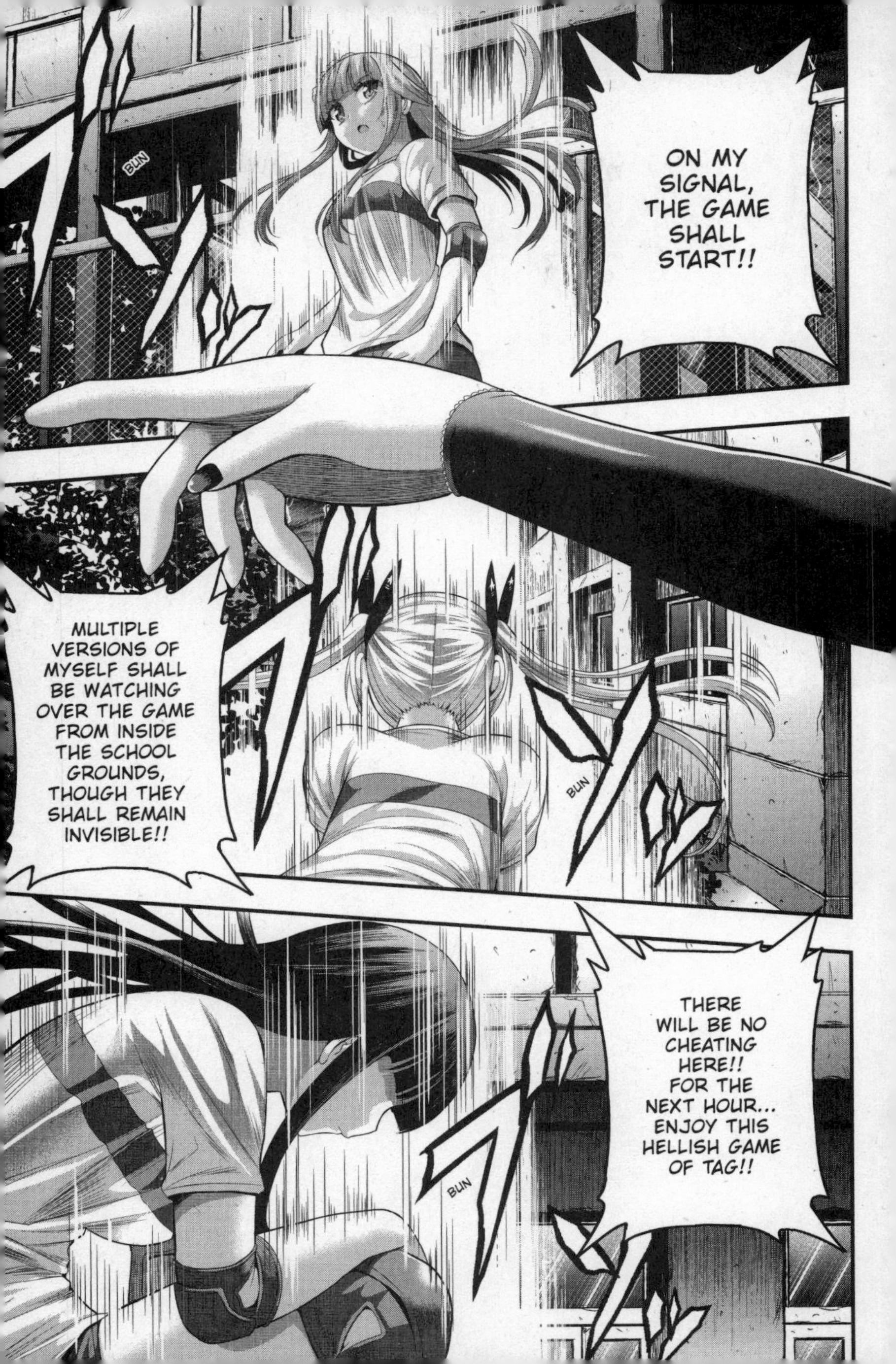
ON MY SIGNAL, THE GAME SHALL START!!
BUN
MULTIPLE VERSIONS OF MYSELF SHALL BE WATCHING OVER THE GAME FROM INSIDE THE SCHOOL GROUNDS, THOUGH THEY SHALL REMAIN INVISIBLE!!
BUN
THERE WILL BE NO CHEATING HERE!! FOR THE NEXT HOUR... ENJOY THIS HELLISH GAME OF TAG!!
BUN

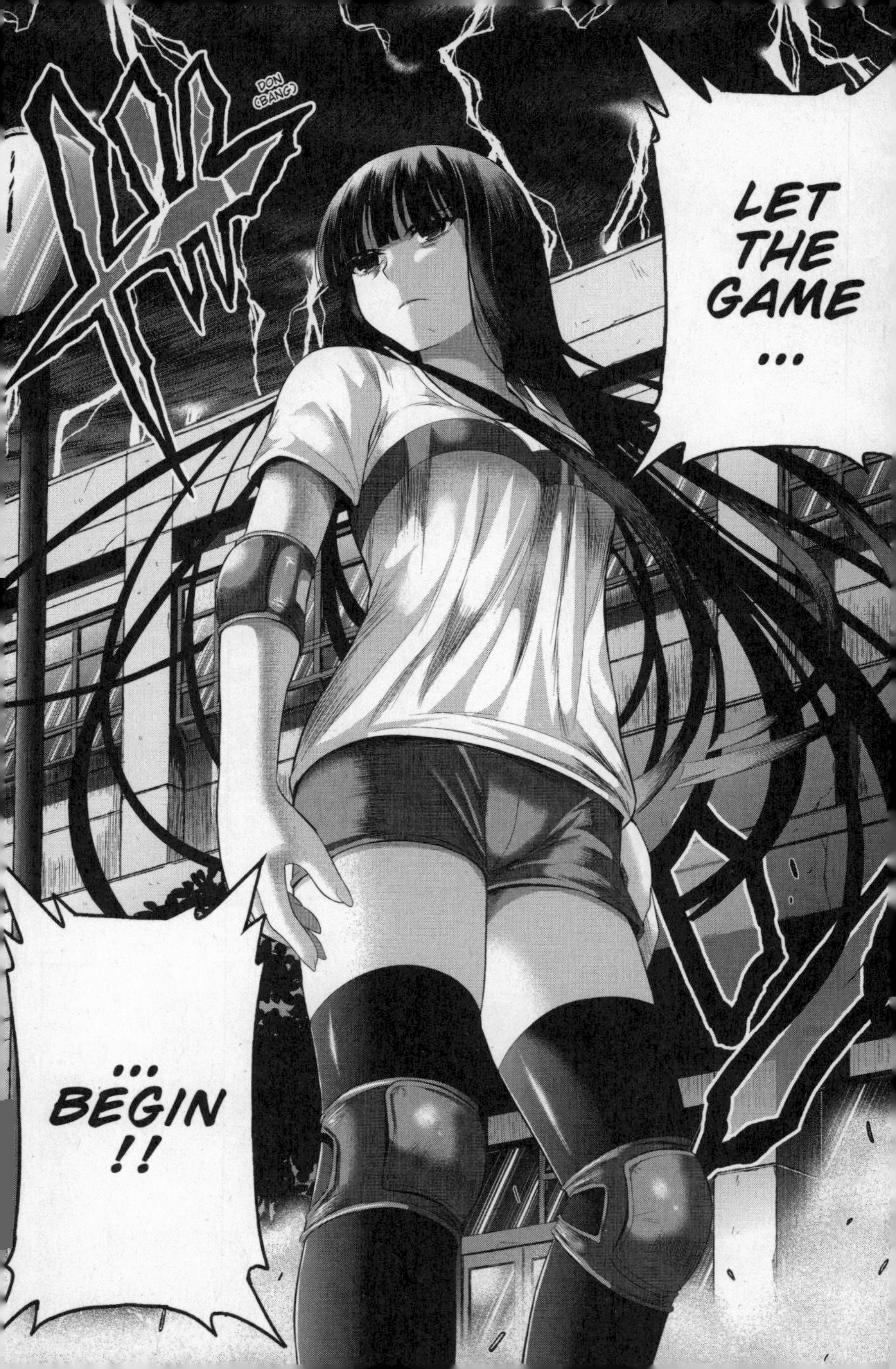
LET THE GAME ...
DON (BANG)
... BEGIN !!

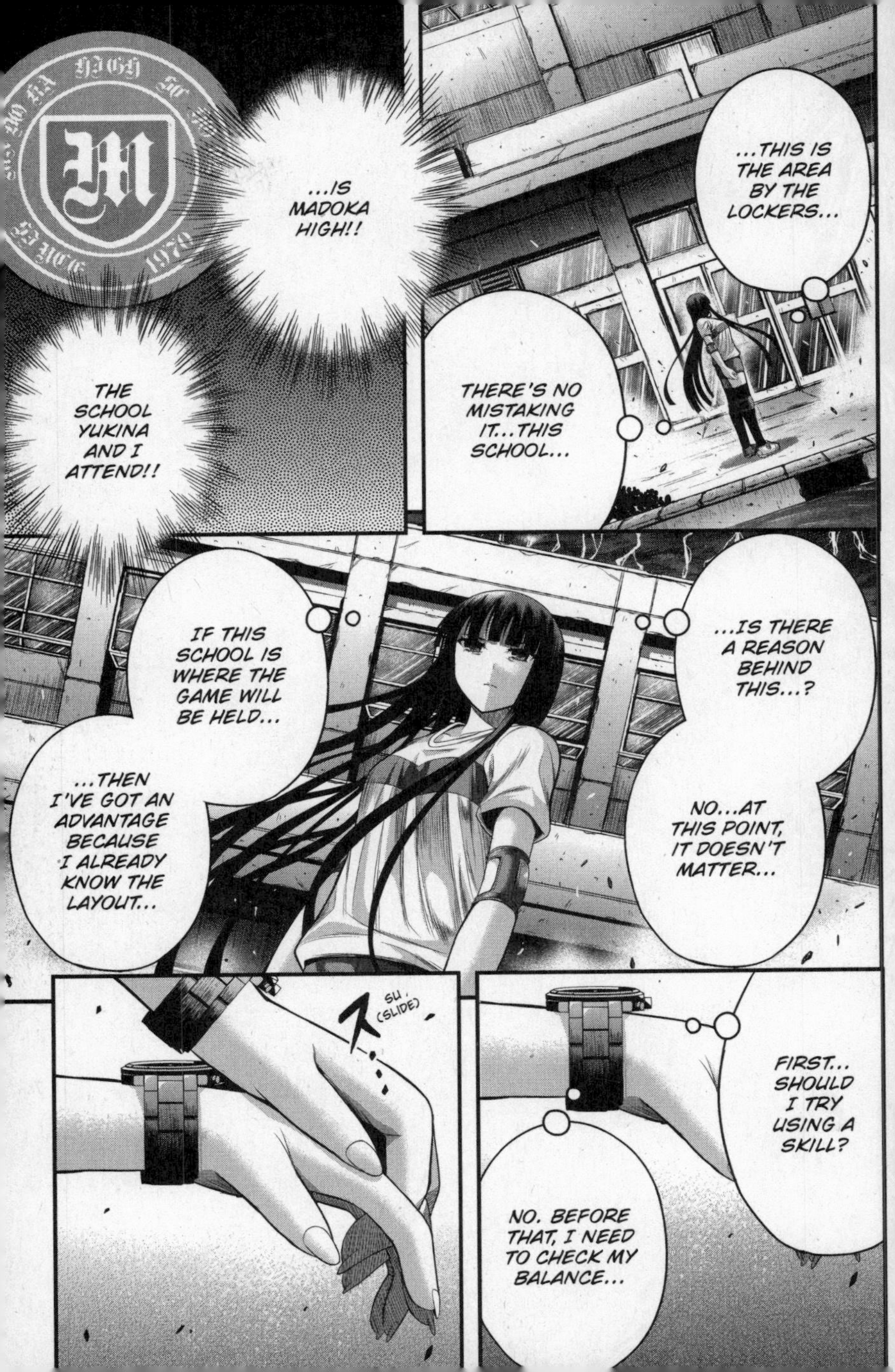
...THIS IS THE AREA BY THE LOCKERS...
THERE'S NO MISTAKING IT...THIS SCHOOL...
...IS MADOKA HIGH!!
THE SCHOOL YUKINA AND I ATTEND!!
...IS THERE A REASON BEHIND THIS...?
NO...AT THIS POINT, IT DOESN'T MATTER...
IF THIS SCHOOL IS WHERE THE GAME WILL BE HELD...
...THEN I'VE GOT AN ADVANTAGE BECAUSE I ALREADY KNOW THE LAYOUT...
FIRST... SHOULD I TRY USING A SKILL?
NO. BEFORE THAT, I NEED TO CHECK MY BALANCE...
SU (SLIDE)

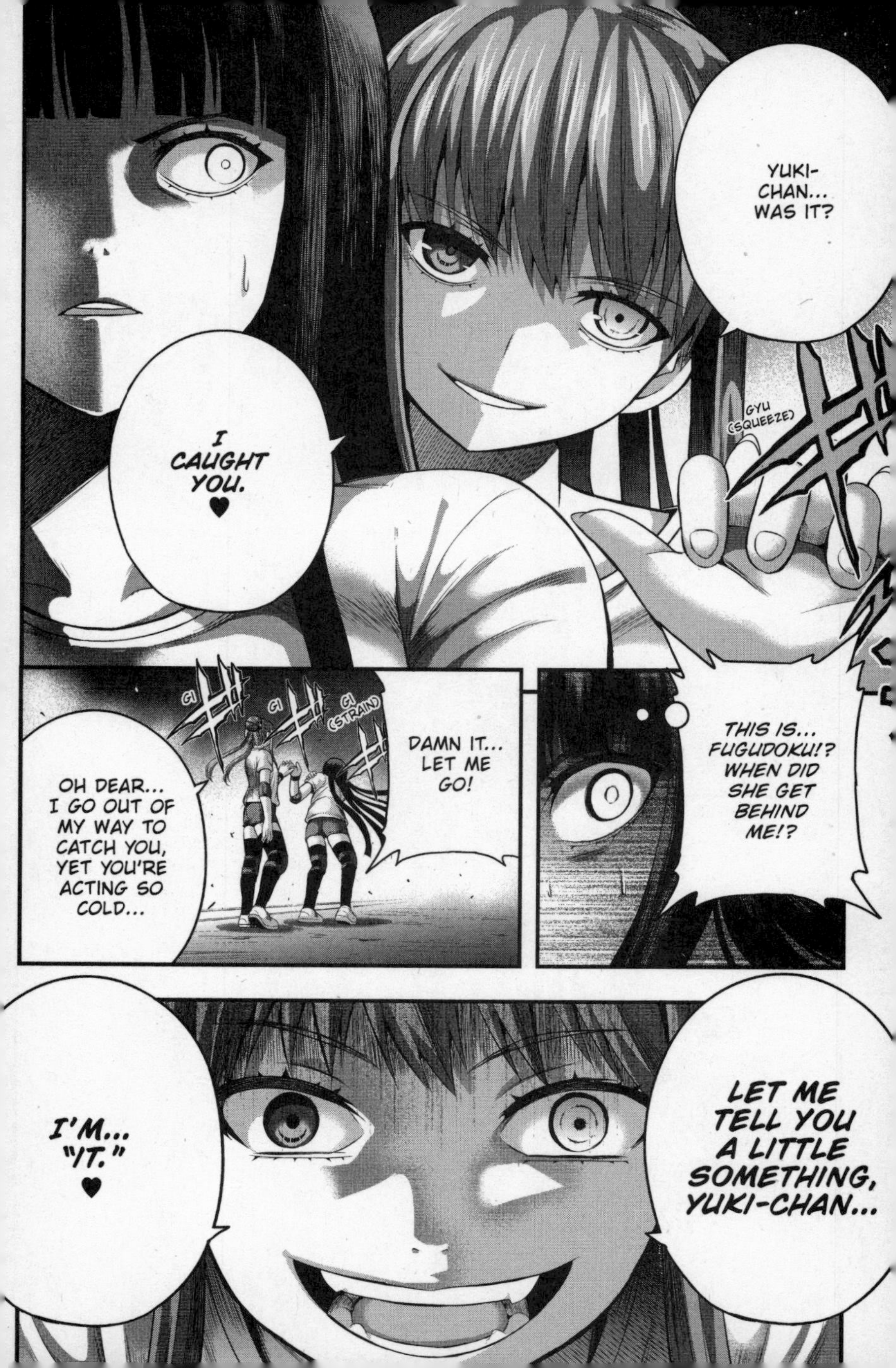

YUKI-CHAN... WAS IT?
GYU (SQUEEZE)
I CAUGHT YOU. ♥
THIS IS... FUGUDOKU!? WHEN DID SHE GET BEHIND ME!?
GI (STRAIN)
DAMN IT... LET ME GO!
GI
GI
OH DEAR... I GO OUT OF MY WAY TO CATCH YOU, YET YOU'RE ACTING SO COLD...
LET ME TELL YOU A LITTLE SOMETHING, YUKI-CHAN...
I'M... "IT." ♥

Though You May Burn to Ash

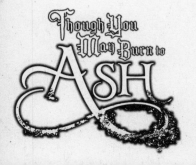

# Though You May Burn to Ash

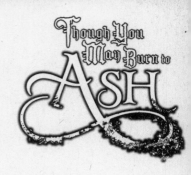

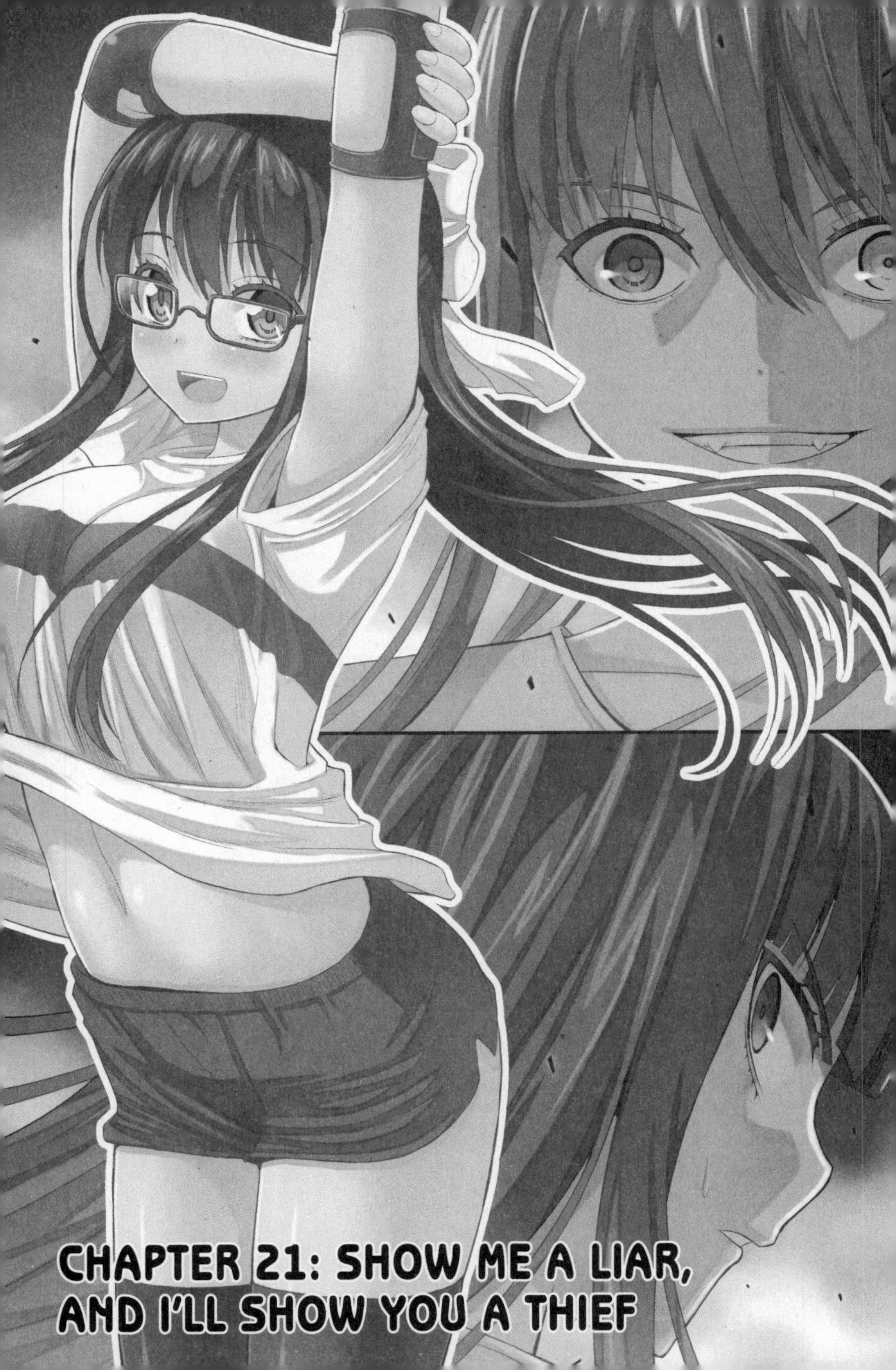
CHAPTER 21: SHOW ME A LIAR,
AND I'LL SHOW YOU A THIEF

Though You May Burn to ASH

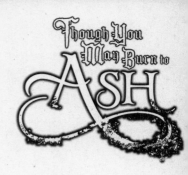

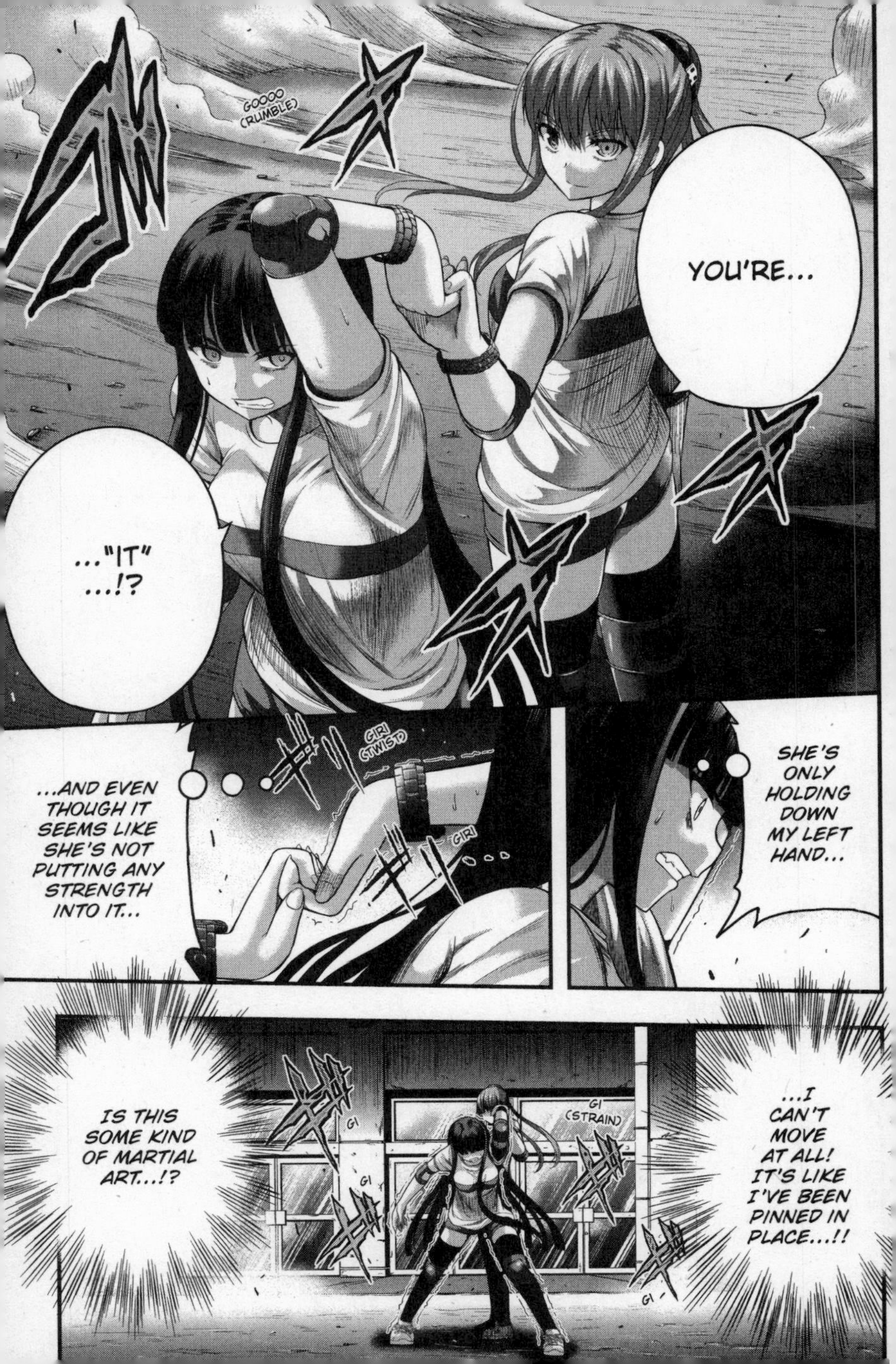
GOOOO (RUMBLE)
YOU'RE...
..."IT" ...!?
SHE'S ONLY HOLDING DOWN MY LEFT HAND...
GIRI (TWIST)
GIRI
...AND EVEN THOUGH IT SEEMS LIKE SHE'S NOT PUTTING ANY STRENGTH INTO IT...
...I CAN'T MOVE AT ALL! IT'S LIKE I'VE BEEN PINNED IN PLACE...!!
GI (STRAIN)
GI
GI
GI
IS THIS SOME KIND OF MARTIAL ART...!?

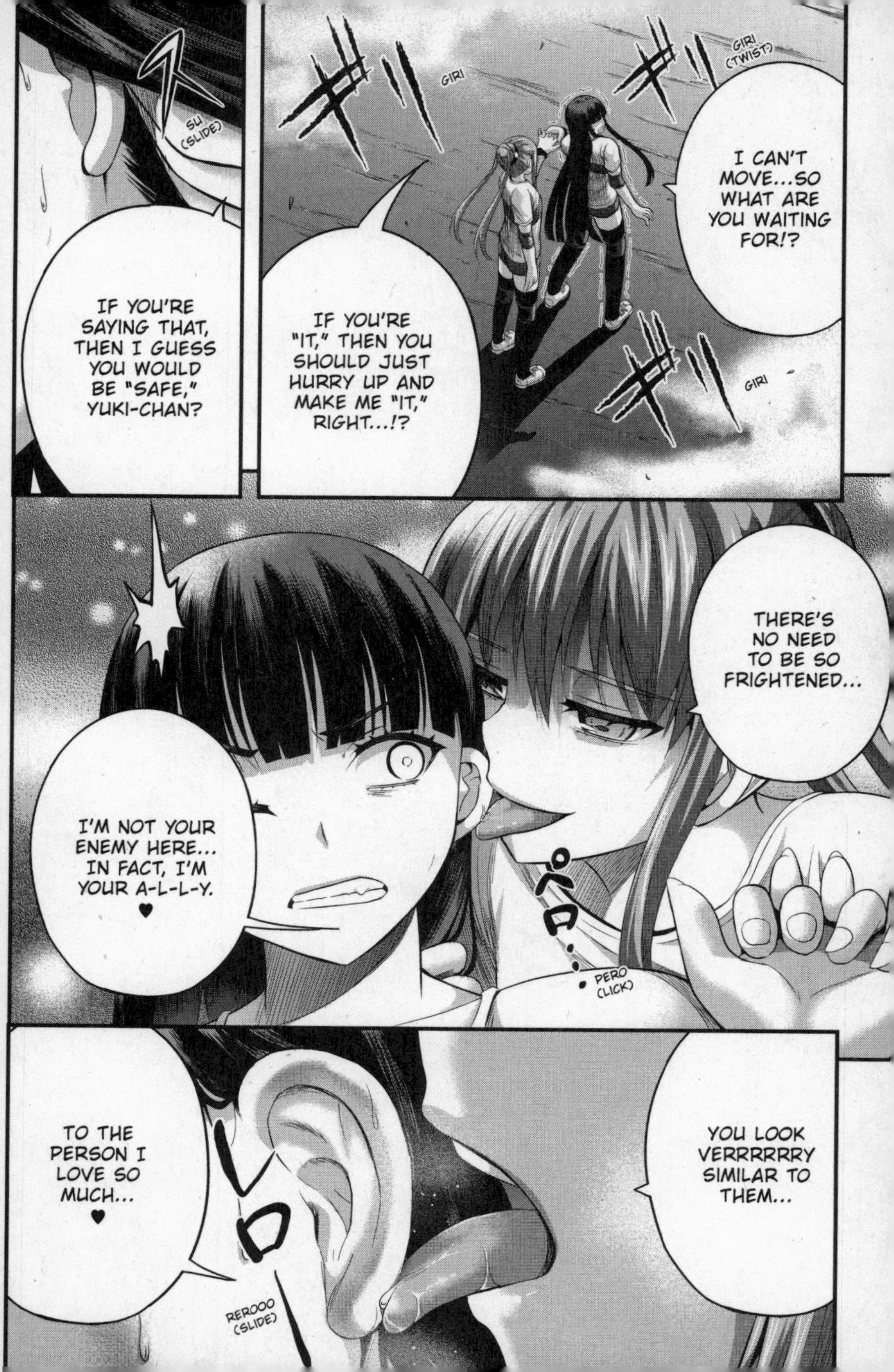
GIRI (TWIST)
GIRI
I CAN'T MOVE...SO WHAT ARE YOU WAITING FOR!?
GIRI
IF YOU'RE "IT," THEN YOU SHOULD JUST HURRY UP AND MAKE ME "IT," RIGHT...!?
SU (SLIDE)
IF YOU'RE SAYING THAT, THEN I GUESS YOU WOULD BE "SAFE," YUKI-CHAN?
THERE'S NO NEED TO BE SO FRIGHTENED...
I'M NOT YOUR ENEMY HERE... IN FACT, I'M YOUR A-L-L-Y. ♥
PERO (LICK)
YOU LOOK VERRRRRRY SIMILAR TO THEM...
TO THE PERSON I LOVE SO MUCH... ♥
REROOO (SLIDE)

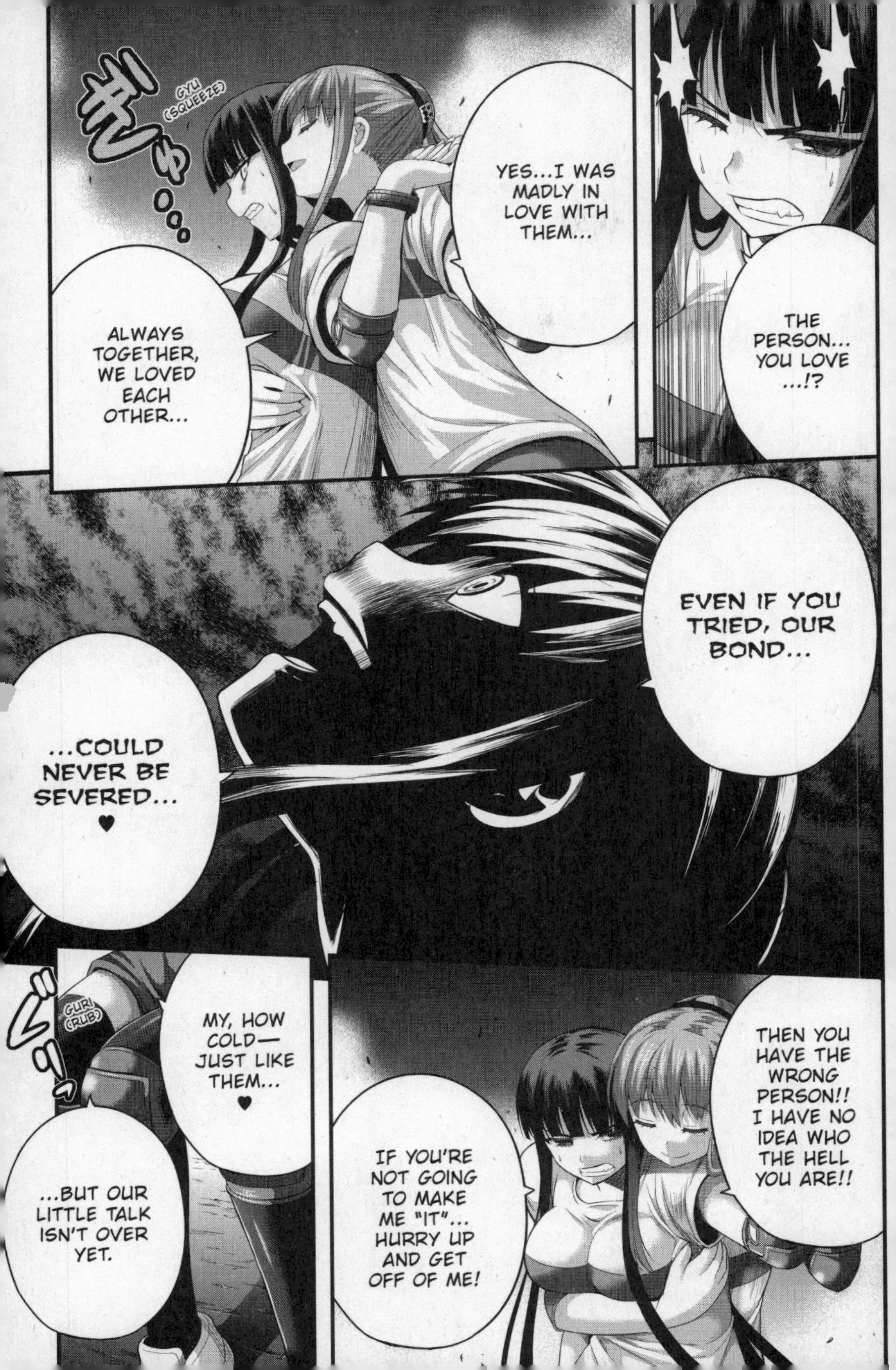
THE PERSON... YOU LOVE ...!?
YES...I WAS MADLY IN LOVE WITH THEM...
GYU (SQUEEZE)
ALWAYS TOGETHER, WE LOVED EACH OTHER...
EVEN IF YOU TRIED, OUR BOND...
...COULD NEVER BE SEVERED... ♥
THEN YOU HAVE THE WRONG PERSON!! I HAVE NO IDEA WHO THE HELL YOU ARE!!
IF YOU'RE NOT GOING TO MAKE ME "IT"... HURRY UP AND GET OFF OF ME!
MY, HOW COLD— JUST LIKE THEM... ♥
GURI (RUB)
...BUT OUR LITTLE TALK ISN'T OVER YET.

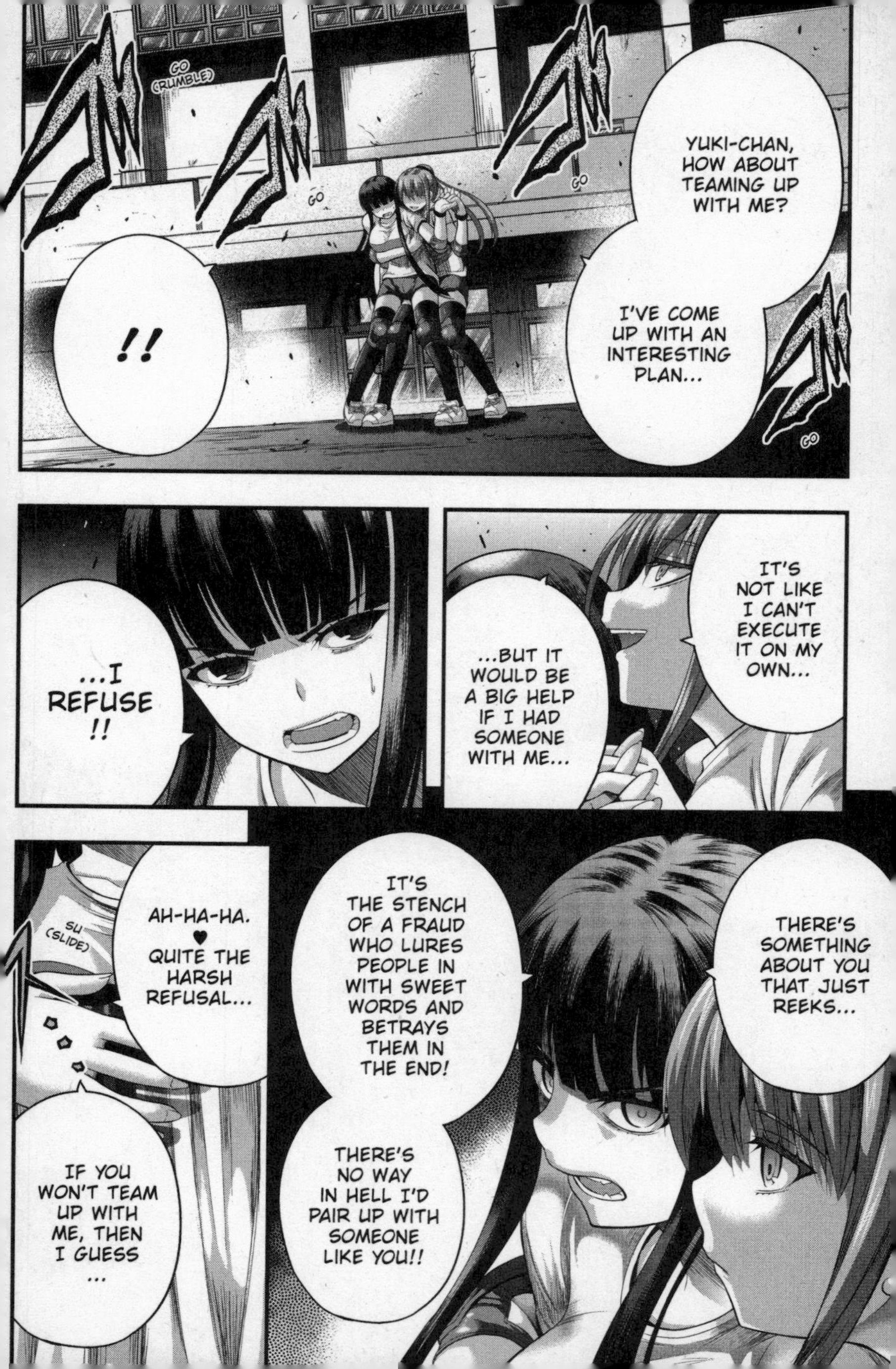
GO (RUMBLE)
GO
GO
YUKI-CHAN, HOW ABOUT TEAMING UP WITH ME?
I'VE COME UP WITH AN INTERESTING PLAN...
GO
!!
IT'S NOT LIKE I CAN'T EXECUTE IT ON MY OWN...
...BUT IT WOULD BE A BIG HELP IF I HAD SOMEONE WITH ME...
...I REFUSE!!
THERE'S SOMETHING ABOUT YOU THAT JUST REEKS...
IT'S THE STENCH OF A FRAUD WHO LURES PEOPLE IN WITH SWEET WORDS AND BETRAYS THEM IN THE END!
THERE'S NO WAY IN HELL I'D PAIR UP WITH SOMEONE LIKE YOU!!
AH-HA-HA. ♥ QUITE THE HARSH REFUSAL...
SU (SLIDE)
IF YOU WON'T TEAM UP WITH ME, THEN I GUESS ...

...I'LL JUST MAKE YOU "IT." ♥

!!

TON (TAP)

ONE...!!

NGH...

THREE...

TWO...

I'LL GIVE YOU THREE SECONDS...

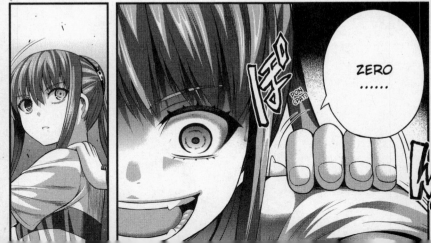

ZERO ......

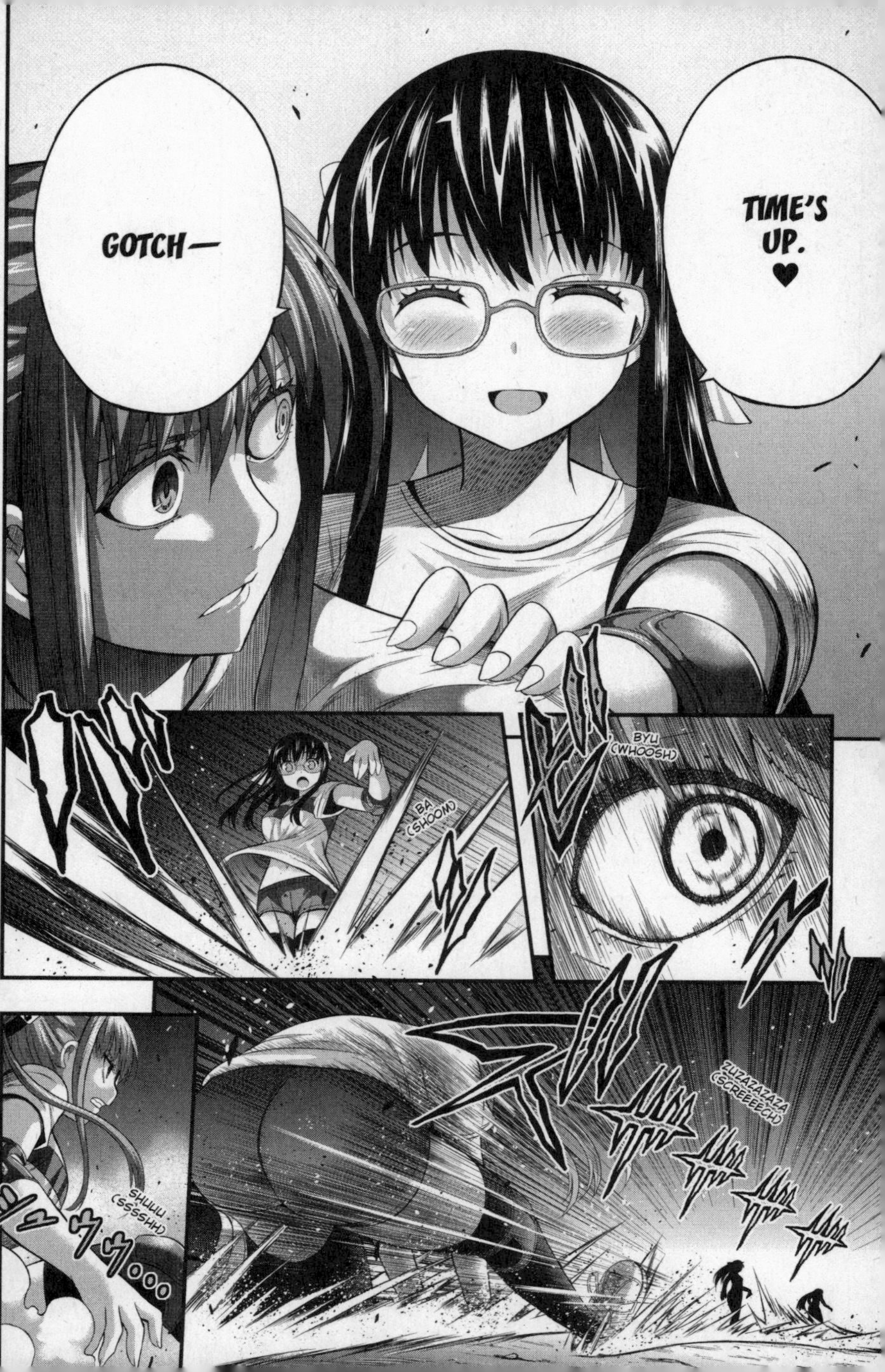
TIME'S UP. ♥
GOTCH—
BYU (WHOOSH)
BA (SHOOM)
ZUZAZAZAZA (SCREEEECH)
SHUUU (HSSSSHH)

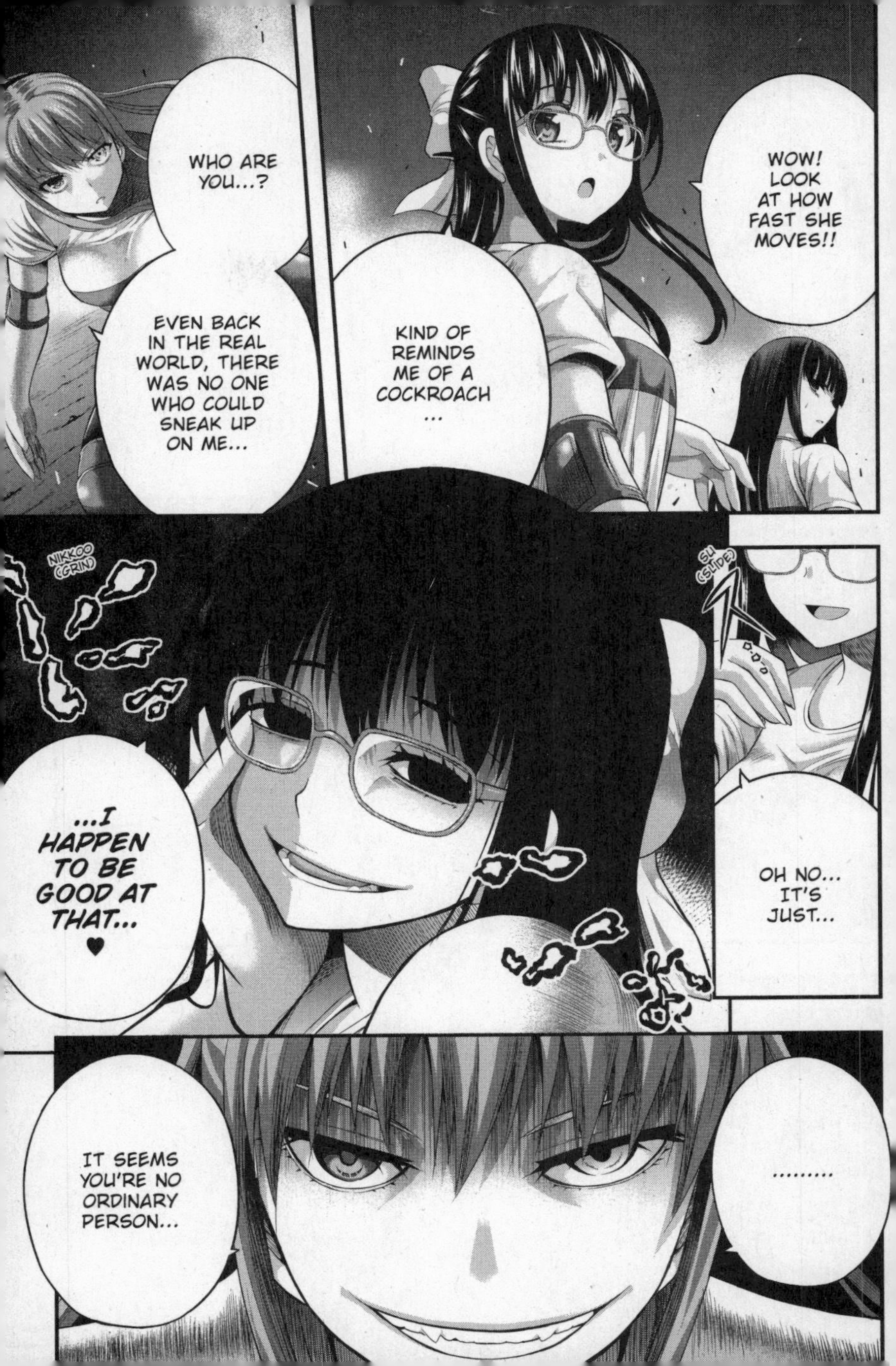
WOW! LOOK AT HOW FAST SHE MOVES!!
KIND OF REMINDS ME OF A COCKROACH...
WHO ARE YOU...?
EVEN BACK IN THE REAL WORLD, THERE WAS NO ONE WHO COULD SNEAK UP ON ME...
SU (SLIDE)
OH NO... IT'S JUST...
NIKKOO (GRIN)
...I HAPPEN TO BE GOOD AT THAT... ♥
.........
IT SEEMS YOU'RE NO ORDINARY PERSON...

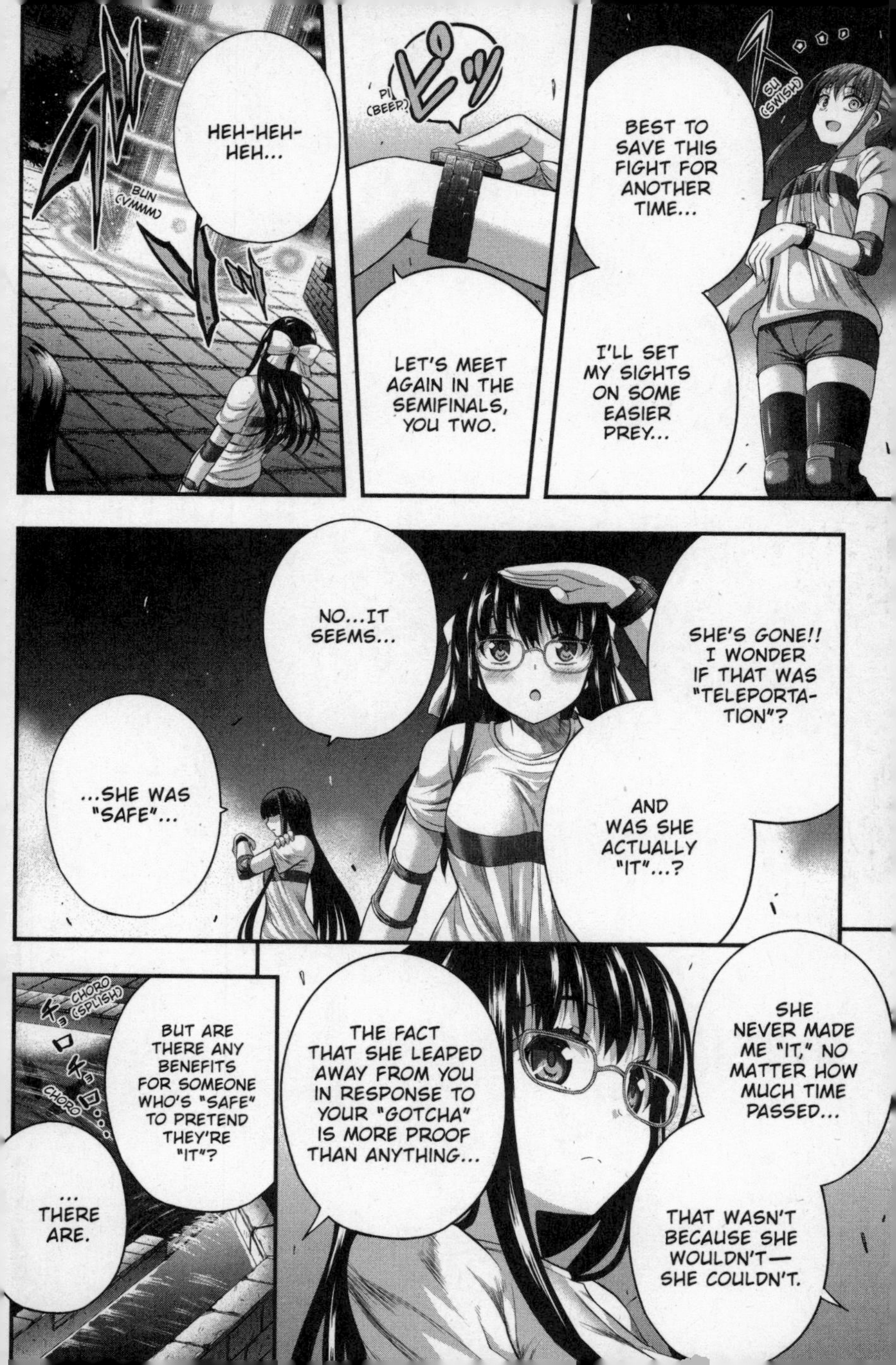
SU (SWISH)
BEST TO SAVE THIS FIGHT FOR ANOTHER TIME...
I'LL SET MY SIGHTS ON SOME EASIER PREY...
PI (BEEP)
LET'S MEET AGAIN IN THE SEMIFINALS, YOU TWO.
HEH-HEH-HEH...
BUN (VMMM)
SHE'S GONE!! I WONDER IF THAT WAS "TELEPORTATION"?
AND WAS SHE ACTUALLY "IT"...?
NO...IT SEEMS...
...SHE WAS "SAFE"...
SHE NEVER MADE ME "IT," NO MATTER HOW MUCH TIME PASSED...
THAT WASN'T BECAUSE SHE WOULDN'T—SHE COULDN'T.
THE FACT THAT SHE LEAPED AWAY FROM YOU IN RESPONSE TO YOUR "GOTCHA" IS MORE PROOF THAN ANYTHING...
CHORO (SPLISH)
CHORO
BUT ARE THERE ANY BENEFITS FOR SOMEONE WHO'S "SAFE" TO PRETEND THEY'RE "IT"?
... THERE ARE.

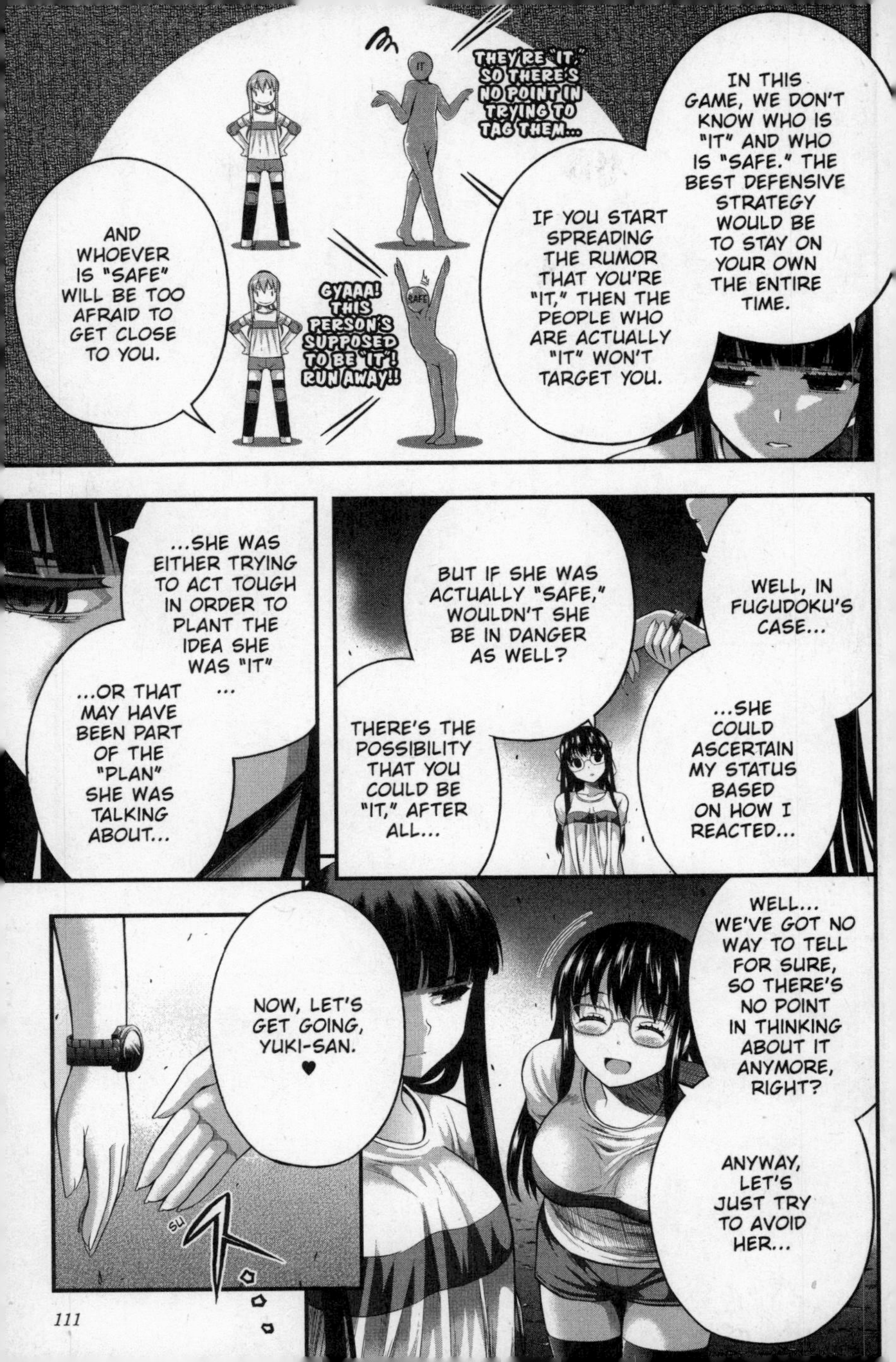

IN THIS GAME, WE DON'T KNOW WHO IS "IT" AND WHO IS "SAFE." THE BEST DEFENSIVE STRATEGY WOULD BE TO STAY ON YOUR OWN THE ENTIRE TIME.
IF YOU START SPREADING THE RUMOR THAT YOU'RE "IT," THEN THE PEOPLE WHO ARE ACTUALLY "IT" WON'T TARGET YOU.
IT
THEY'RE "IT," SO THERE'S NO POINT IN TRYING TO TAG THEM...
AND WHOEVER IS "SAFE" WILL BE TOO AFRAID TO GET CLOSE TO YOU.
SAFE
GYAAA! THIS PERSON'S SUPPOSED TO BE "IT"! RUN AWAY!!
WELL, IN FUGUDOKU'S CASE...
...SHE COULD ASCERTAIN MY STATUS BASED ON HOW I REACTED...
BUT IF SHE WAS ACTUALLY "SAFE," WOULDN'T SHE BE IN DANGER AS WELL?
THERE'S THE POSSIBILITY THAT YOU COULD BE "IT," AFTER ALL...
...SHE WAS EITHER TRYING TO ACT TOUGH IN ORDER TO PLANT THE IDEA SHE WAS "IT" ...
...OR THAT MAY HAVE BEEN PART OF THE "PLAN" SHE WAS TALKING ABOUT...
WELL... WE'VE GOT NO WAY TO TELL FOR SURE, SO THERE'S NO POINT IN THINKING ABOUT IT ANYMORE, RIGHT?
ANYWAY, LET'S JUST TRY TO AVOID HER...
NOW, LET'S GET GOING, YUKI-SAN. ♥
SU

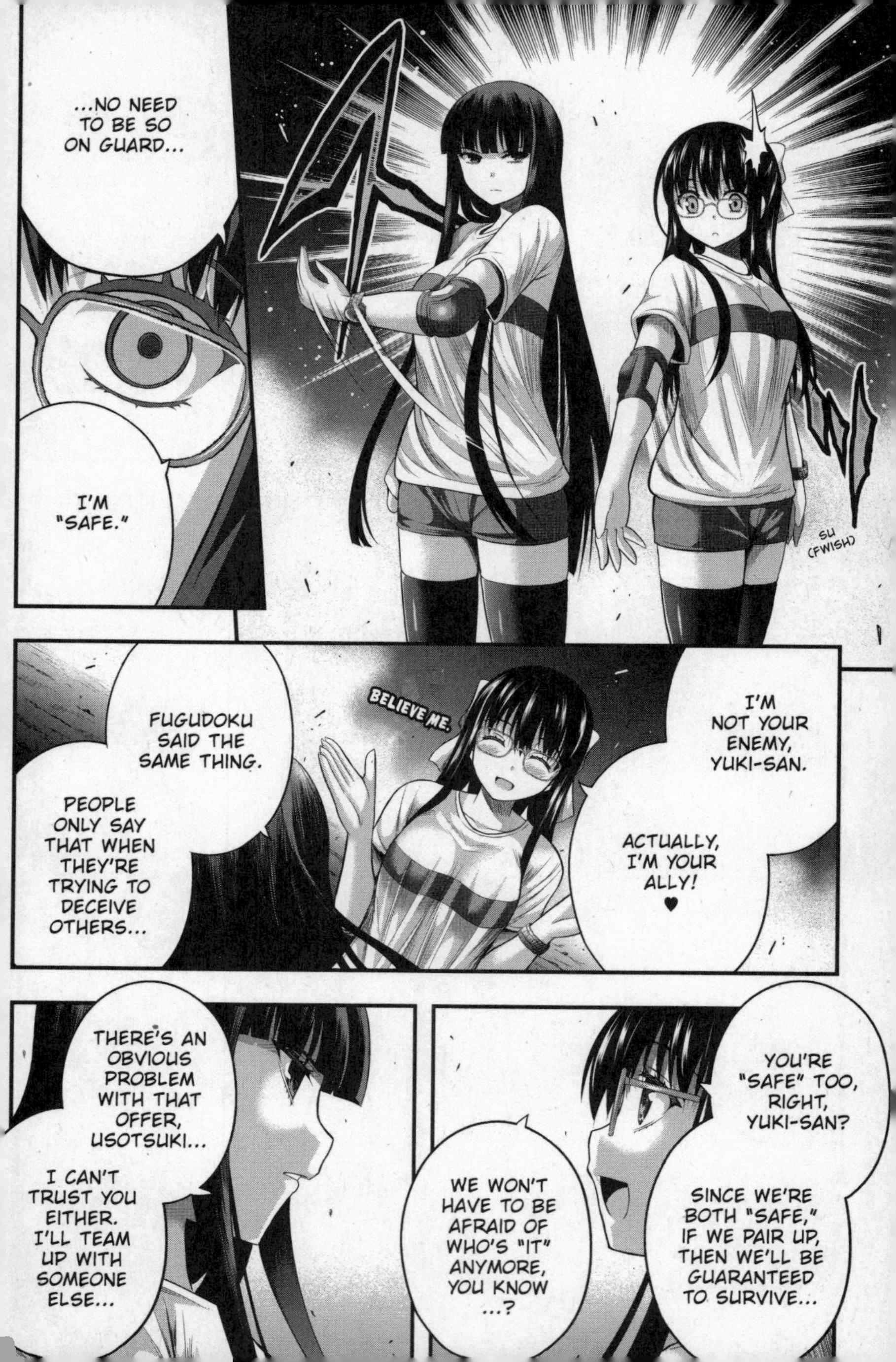
SU (FWISH)
…NO NEED TO BE SO ON GUARD…
I'M "SAFE."
I'M NOT YOUR ENEMY, YUKI-SAN.
ACTUALLY, I'M YOUR ALLY! ♥
BELIEVE ME.
FUGUDOKU SAID THE SAME THING.
PEOPLE ONLY SAY THAT WHEN THEY'RE TRYING TO DECEIVE OTHERS…
YOU'RE "SAFE" TOO, RIGHT, YUKI-SAN?
SINCE WE'RE BOTH "SAFE," IF WE PAIR UP, THEN WE'LL BE GUARANTEED TO SURVIVE…
WE WON'T HAVE TO BE AFRAID OF WHO'S "IT" ANYMORE, YOU KNOW …?
THERE'S AN OBVIOUS PROBLEM WITH THAT OFFER, USOTSUKI…
I CAN'T TRUST YOU EITHER. I'LL TEAM UP WITH SOMEONE ELSE…

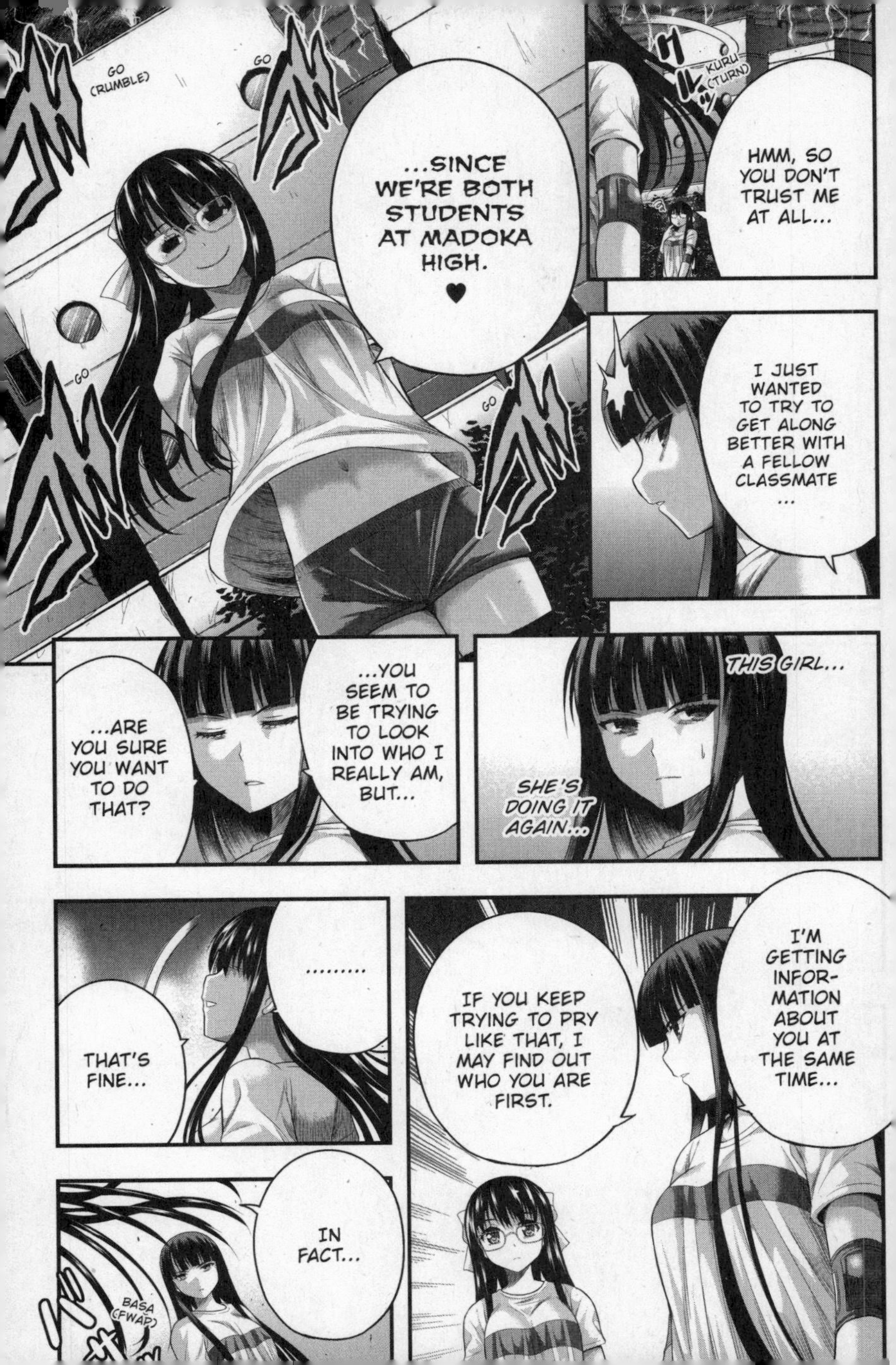
KURU (TURN)
HMM, SO YOU DON'T TRUST ME AT ALL...
I JUST WANTED TO TRY TO GET ALONG BETTER WITH A FELLOW CLASSMATE ...
GO
GO (RUMBLE)
...SINCE WE'RE BOTH STUDENTS AT MADOKA HIGH. ♥
GO
GO
THIS GIRL...
SHE'S DOING IT AGAIN...
...YOU SEEM TO BE TRYING TO LOOK INTO WHO I REALLY AM, BUT...
...ARE YOU SURE YOU WANT TO DO THAT?
I'M GETTING INFOR-MATION ABOUT YOU AT THE SAME TIME...
IF YOU KEEP TRYING TO PRY LIKE THAT, I MAY FIND OUT WHO YOU ARE FIRST.
.........
THAT'S FINE...
IN FACT...
BASA (FWAP)

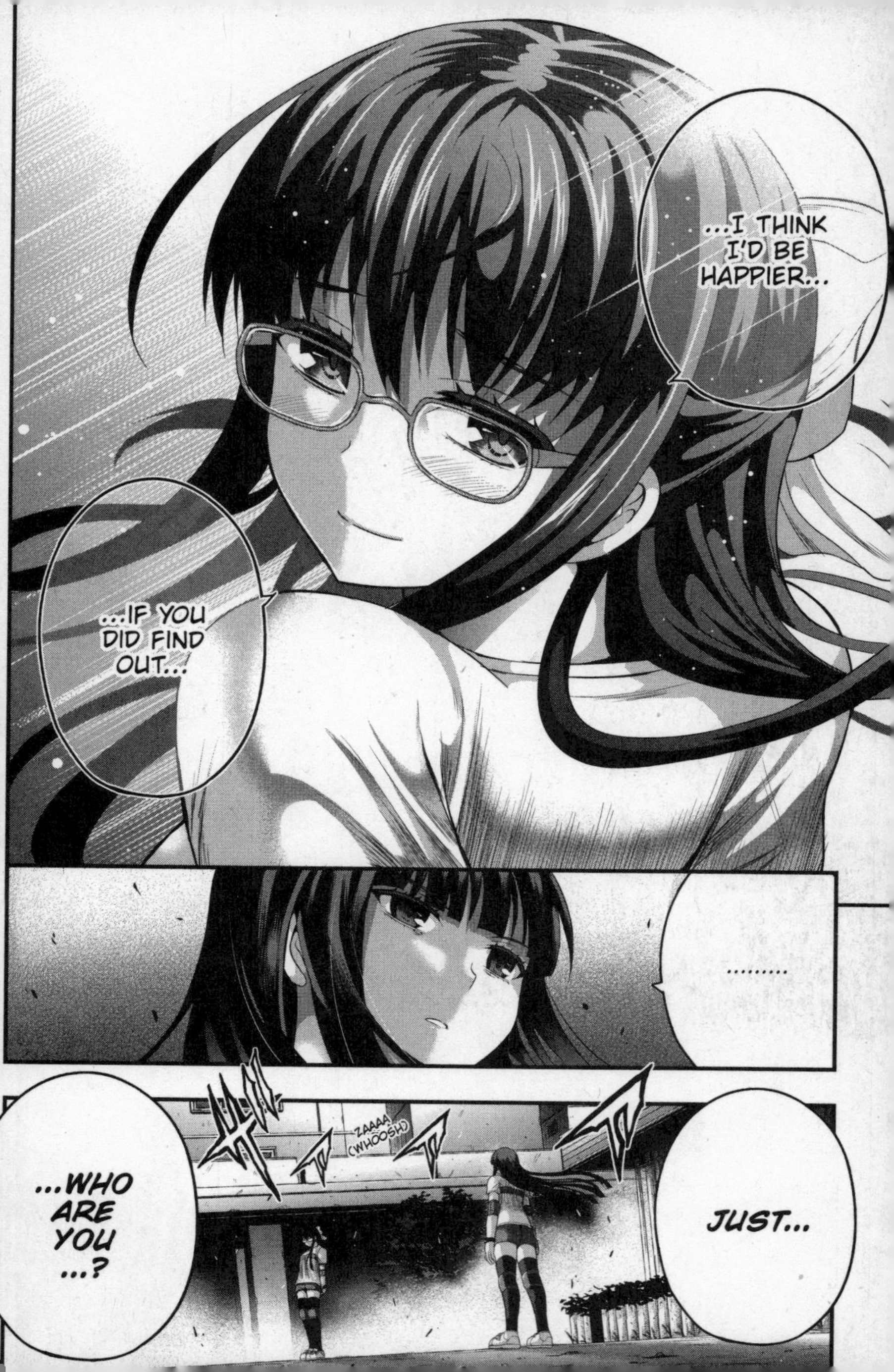
...I THINK I'D BE HAPPIER...
...IF YOU DID FIND OUT...
........
JUST...
ZAAAA (WHOOSH)
...WHO ARE YOU ...?

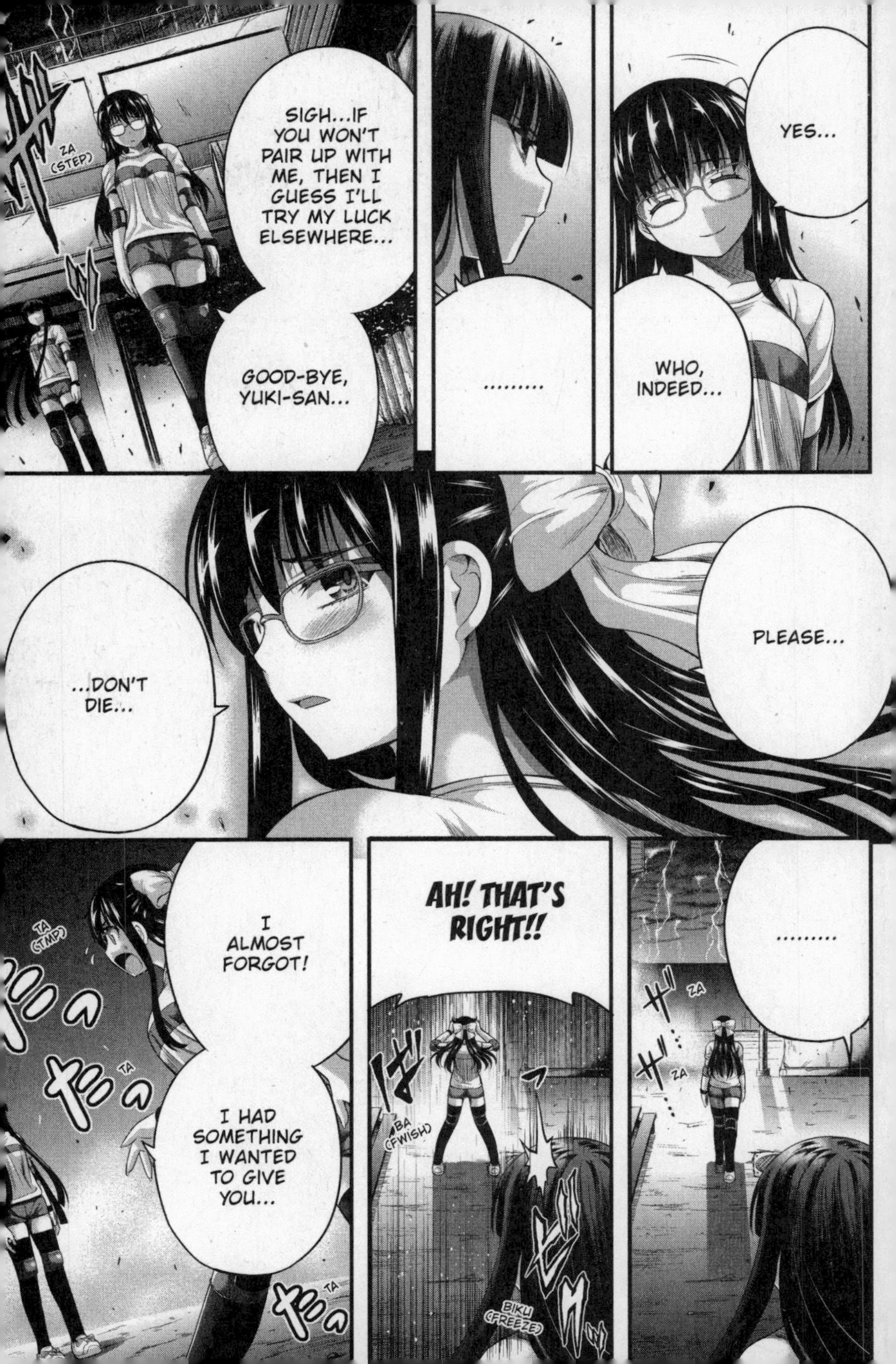
YES...
WHO, INDEED...
.........
SIGH...IF YOU WON'T PAIR UP WITH ME, THEN I GUESS I'LL TRY MY LUCK ELSEWHERE...
GOOD-BYE, YUKI-SAN...
ZA (STEP)
PLEASE...
...DON'T DIE...
.........
ZA
ZA
AH! THAT'S RIGHT!!
BA (FWISH)
BIKU (FREEZE)
I ALMOST FORGOT!
I HAD SOMETHING I WANTED TO GIVE YOU...
TA (TMP)
TA
TA

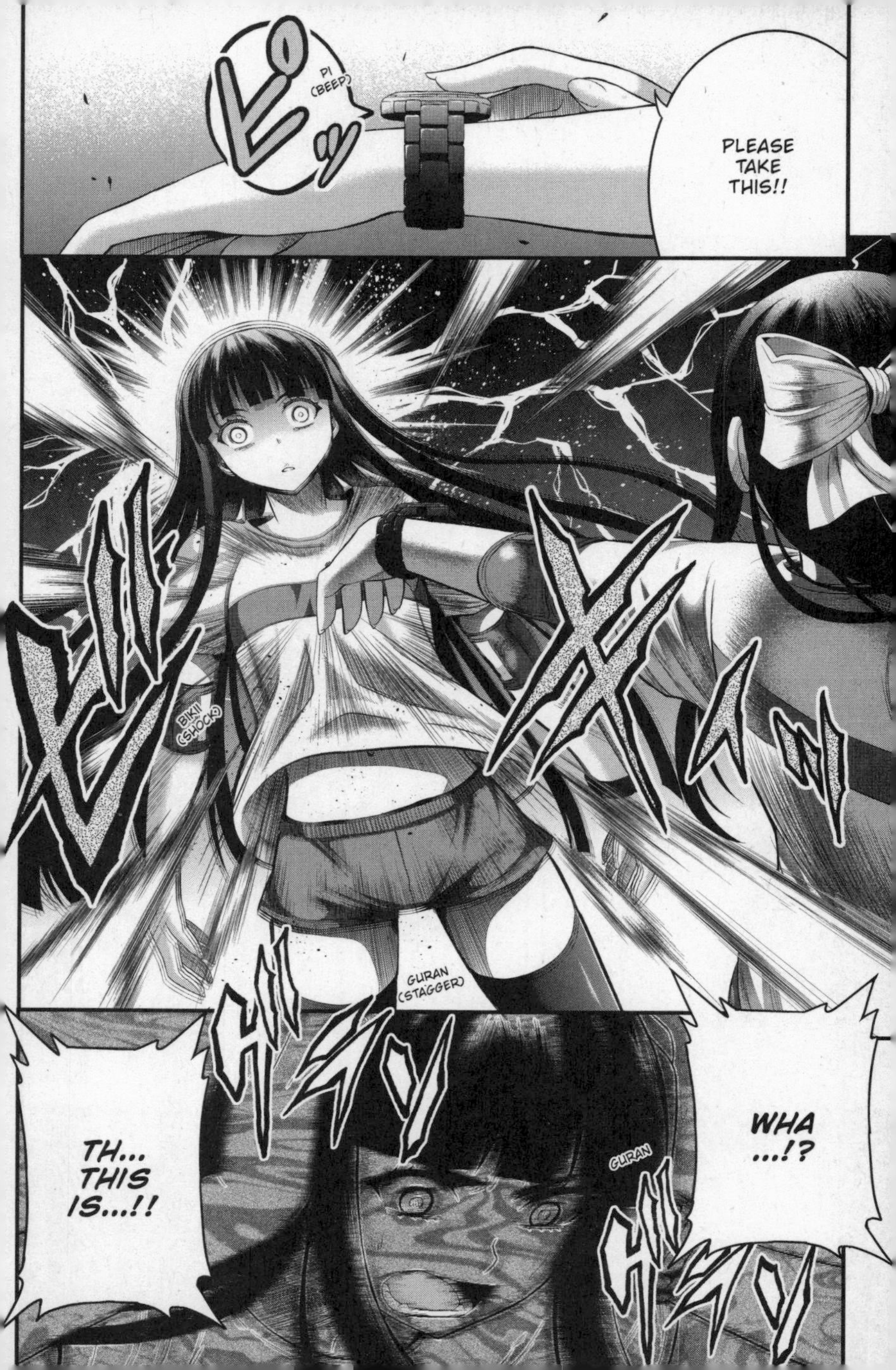
PLEASE TAKE THIS!!
PI (BEEP)
BIKI (SHOCK)
GURAN (STAGGER)
WHA ...!?
GURAN
TH... THIS IS...!!

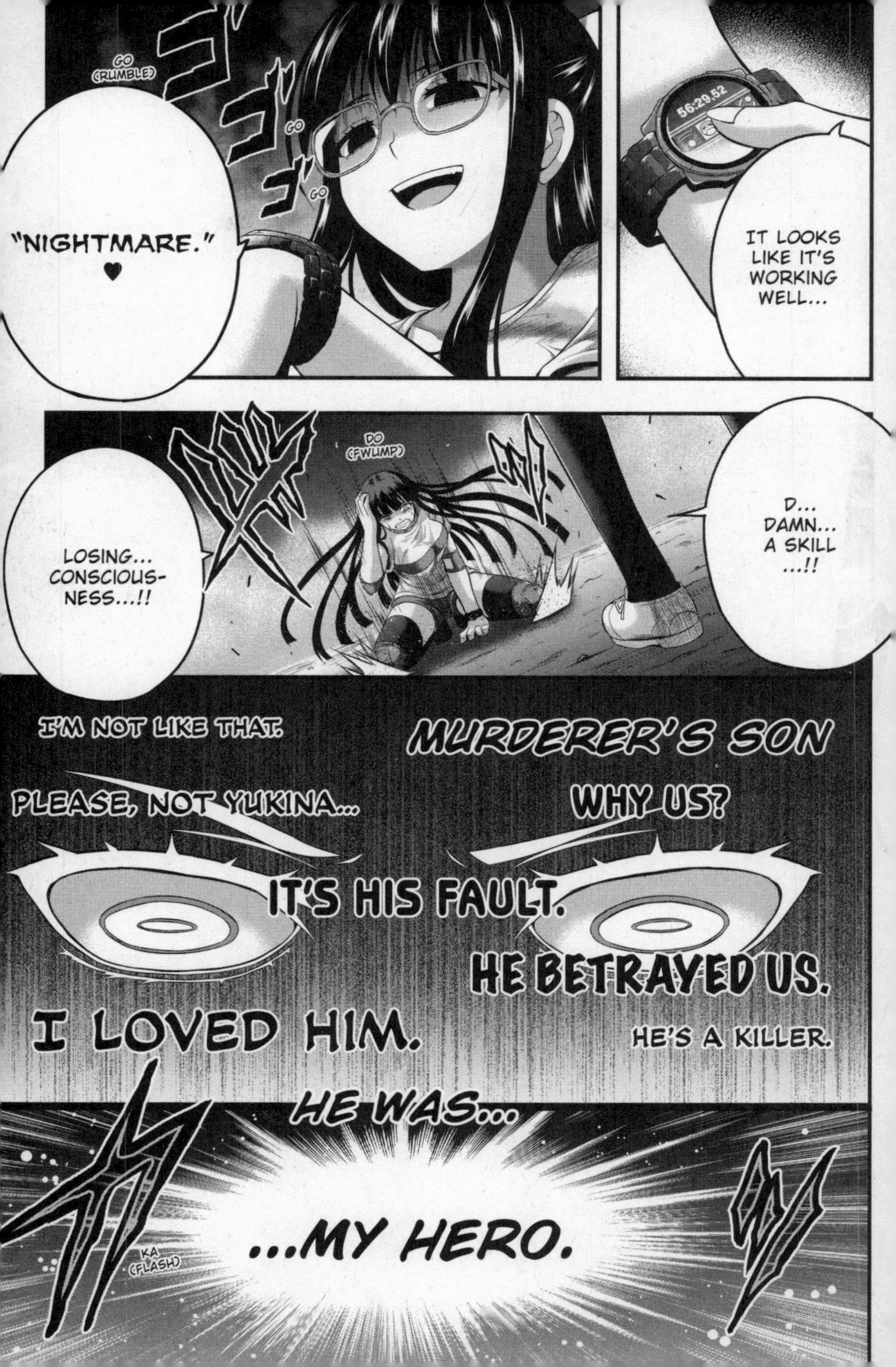
56:29.52
IT LOOKS LIKE IT'S WORKING WELL...
GO (RUMBLE)
GO
GO
"NIGHTMARE." ♥
D... DAMN... A SKILL ...!!
DO (FWUMP)
LOSING... CONSCIOUS-NESS...!!
MURDERER'S SON
I'M NOT LIKE THAT.
WHY US?
PLEASE, NOT YUKINA...
IT'S HIS FAULT.
HE BETRAYED US.
HE'S A KILLER.
I LOVED HIM.
HE WAS...
...MY HERO.
KA (FLASH)

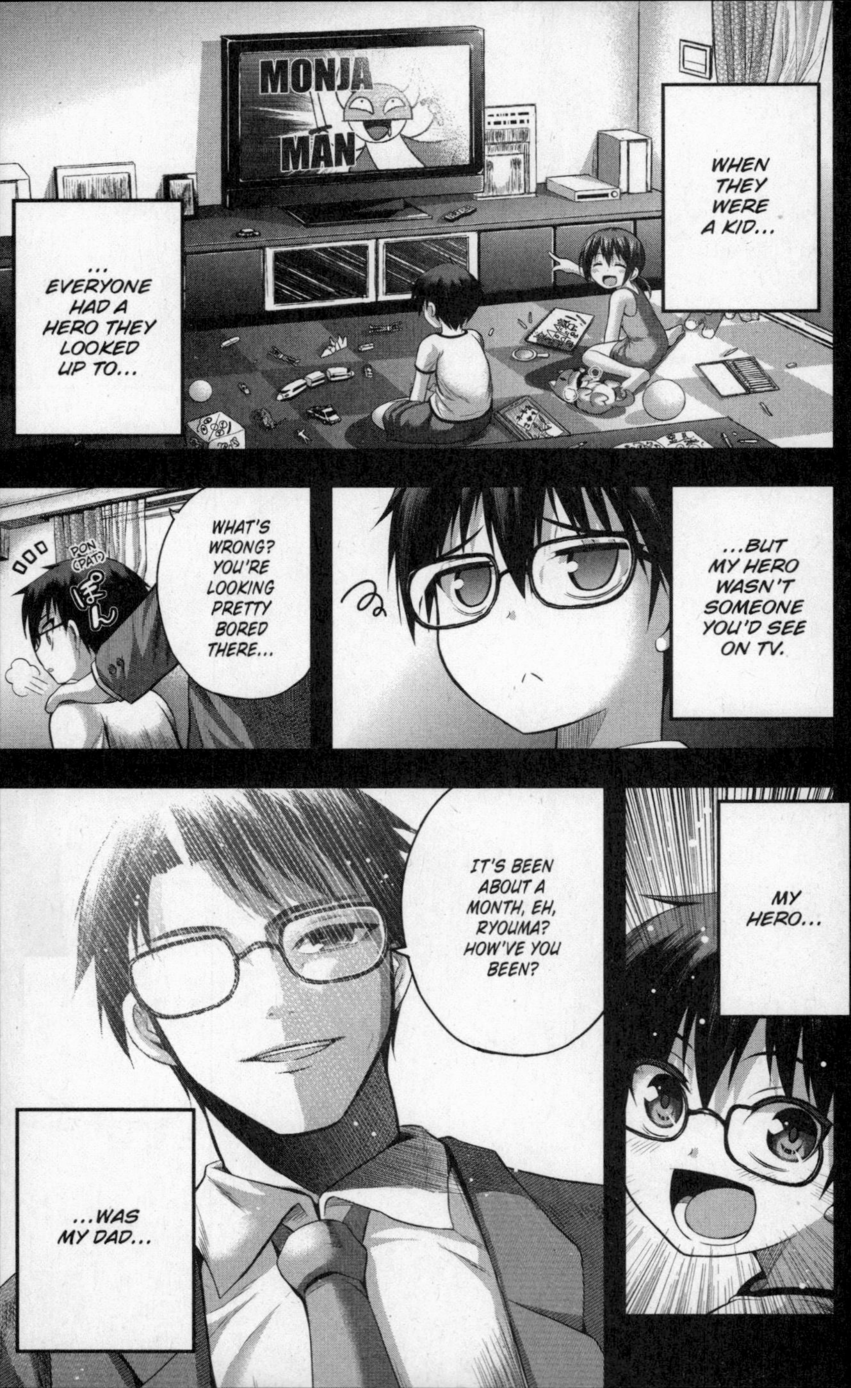
WHEN THEY WERE A KID...
MONJA MAN
...EVERYONE HAD A HERO THEY LOOKED UP TO...
...BUT MY HERO WASN'T SOMEONE YOU'D SEE ON TV.
WHAT'S WRONG? YOU'RE LOOKING PRETTY BORED THERE...
PON (PAT)
ぽん
MY HERO...
IT'S BEEN ABOUT A MONTH, EH, RYOUMA? HOW'VE YOU BEEN?
...WAS MY DAD...

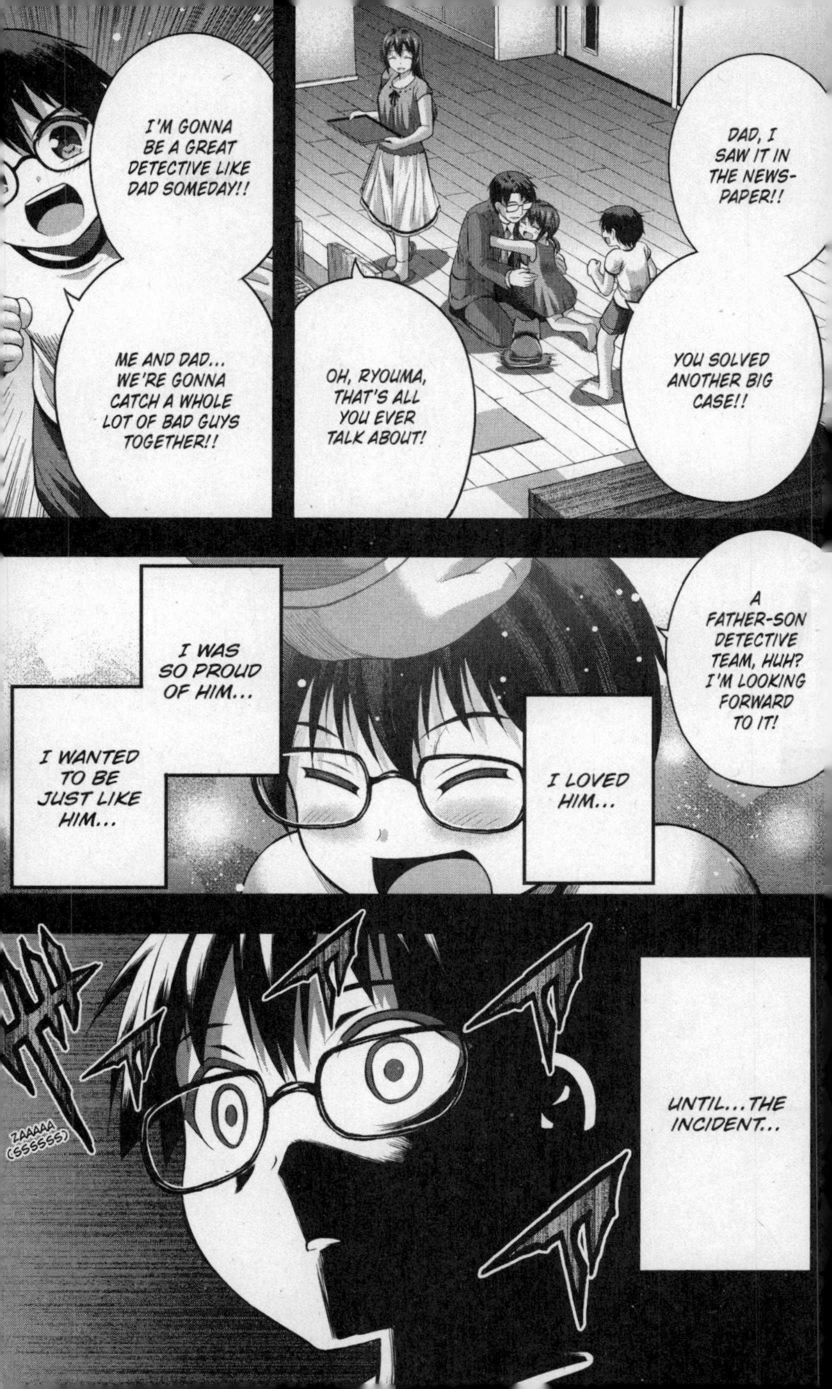
DAD, I SAW IT IN THE NEWS-PAPER!!
YOU SOLVED ANOTHER BIG CASE!!
OH, RYOUMA, THAT'S ALL YOU EVER TALK ABOUT!
I'M GONNA BE A GREAT DETECTIVE LIKE DAD SOMEDAY!!
ME AND DAD... WE'RE GONNA CATCH A WHOLE LOT OF BAD GUYS TOGETHER!!
A FATHER-SON DETECTIVE TEAM, HUH? I'M LOOKING FORWARD TO IT!
I LOVED HIM...
I WAS SO PROUD OF HIM...
I WANTED TO BE JUST LIKE HIM...
UNTIL...THE INCIDENT...
ZAAAAA (SSSSSS)

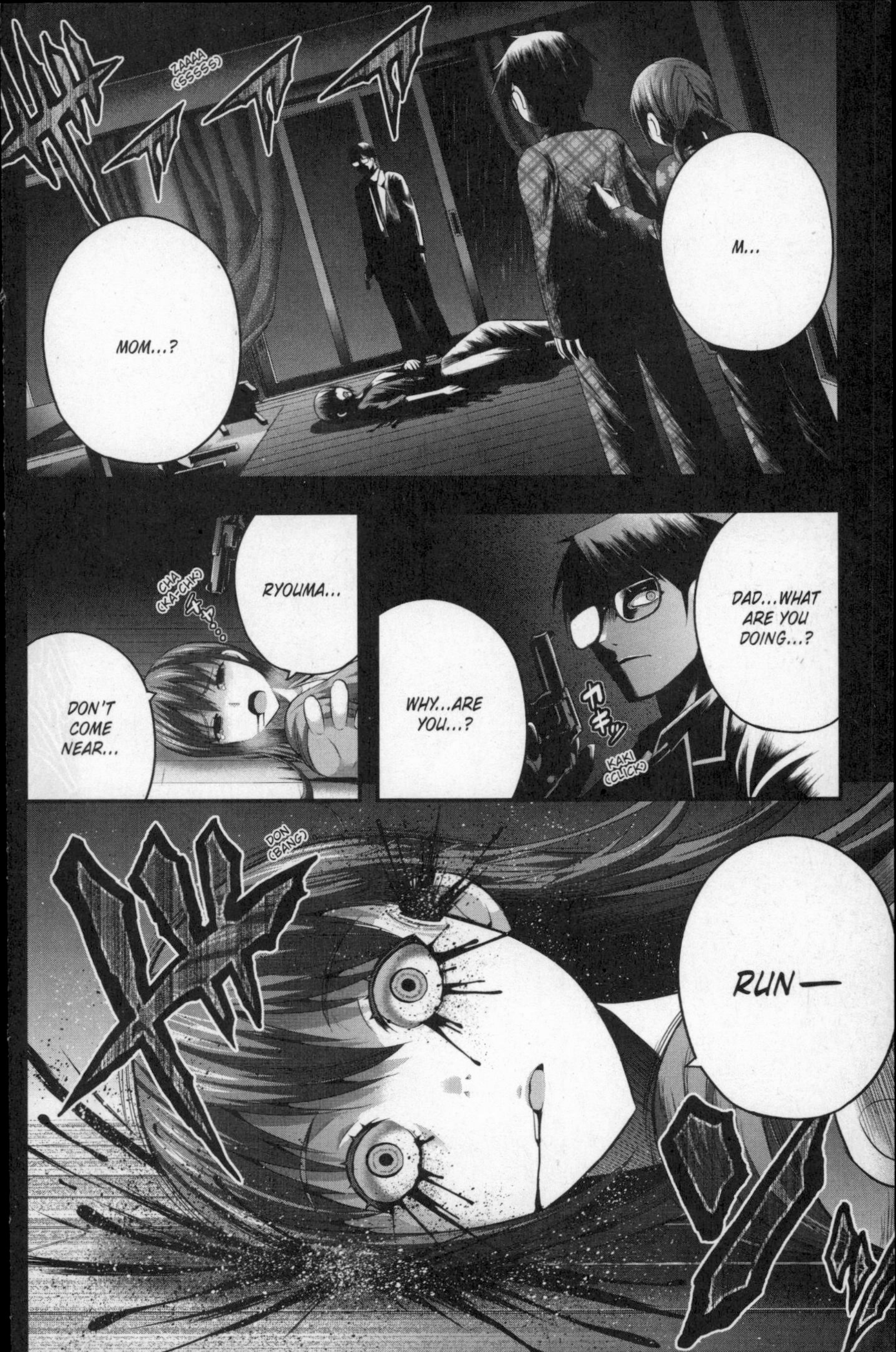
ZAAAA (SSSSS)
M...
MOM...?
DAD...WHAT ARE YOU DOING...?
KAKI (CLICK)
WHY...ARE YOU...?
RYOUMA...
CHA (KA-CHK)
DON'T COME NEAR...
DON (BANG)
RUN—

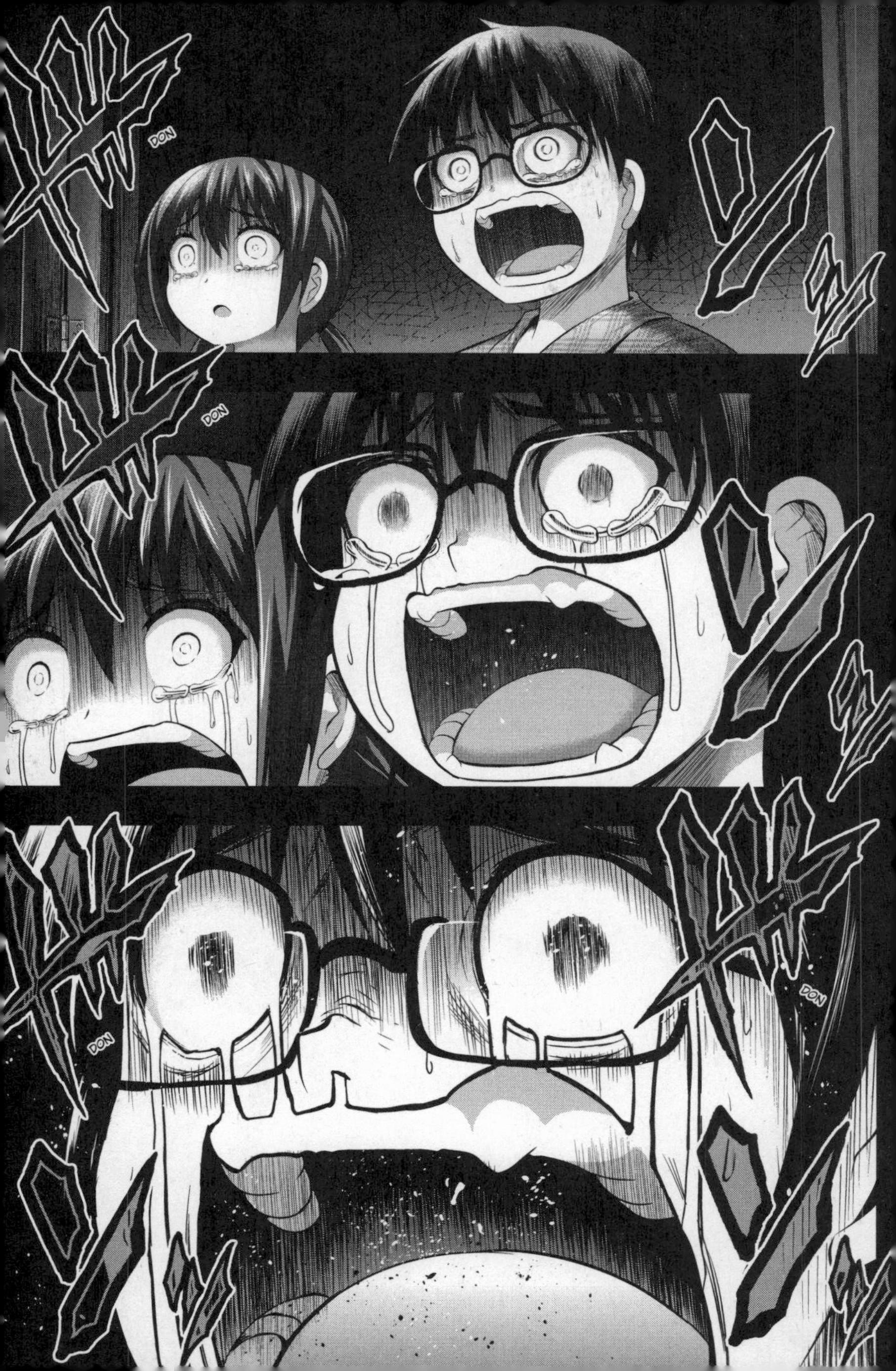
DON
DON
DON
DON

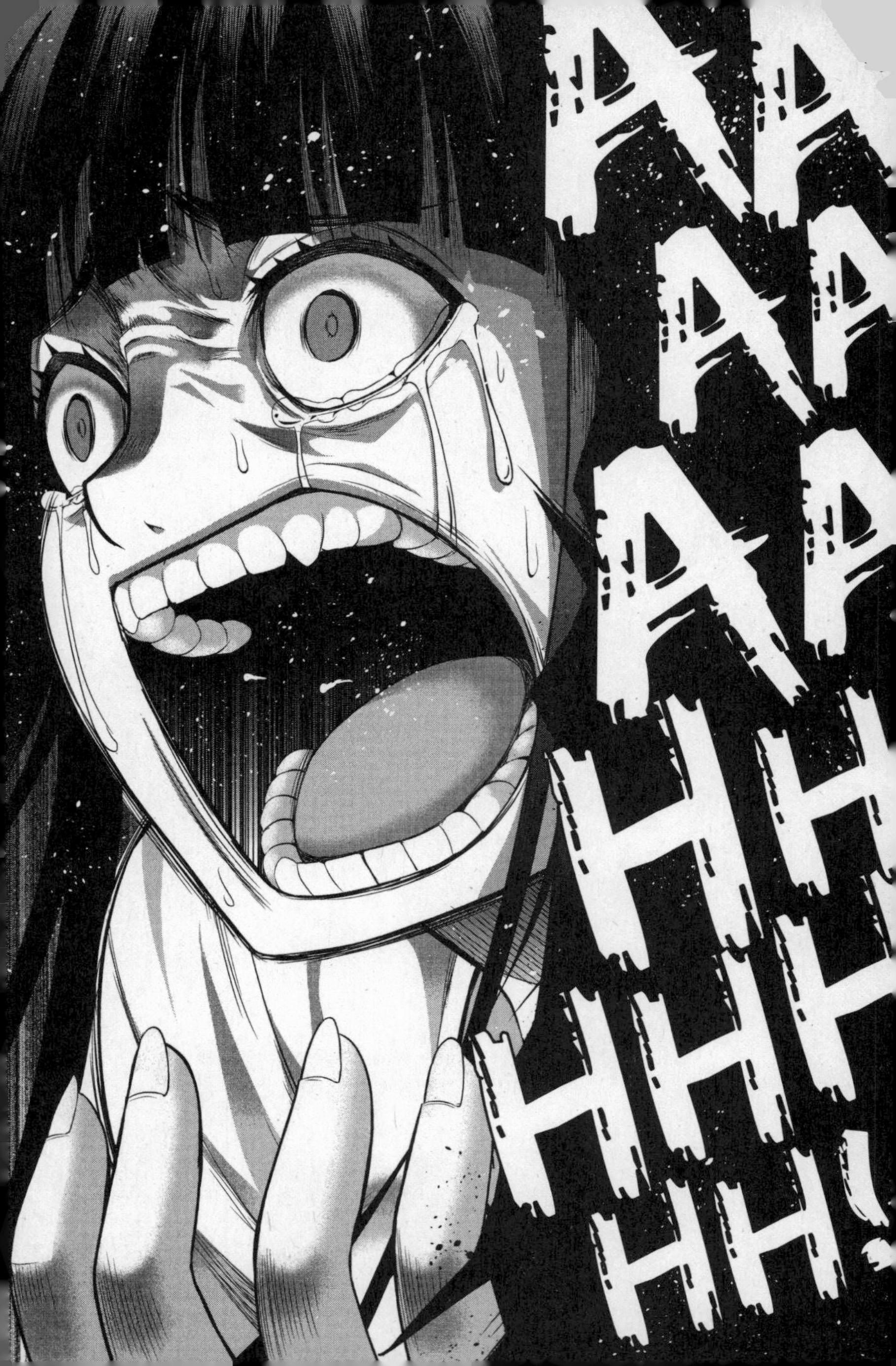
AA
AA
AA
HH
HH
HH
HH!

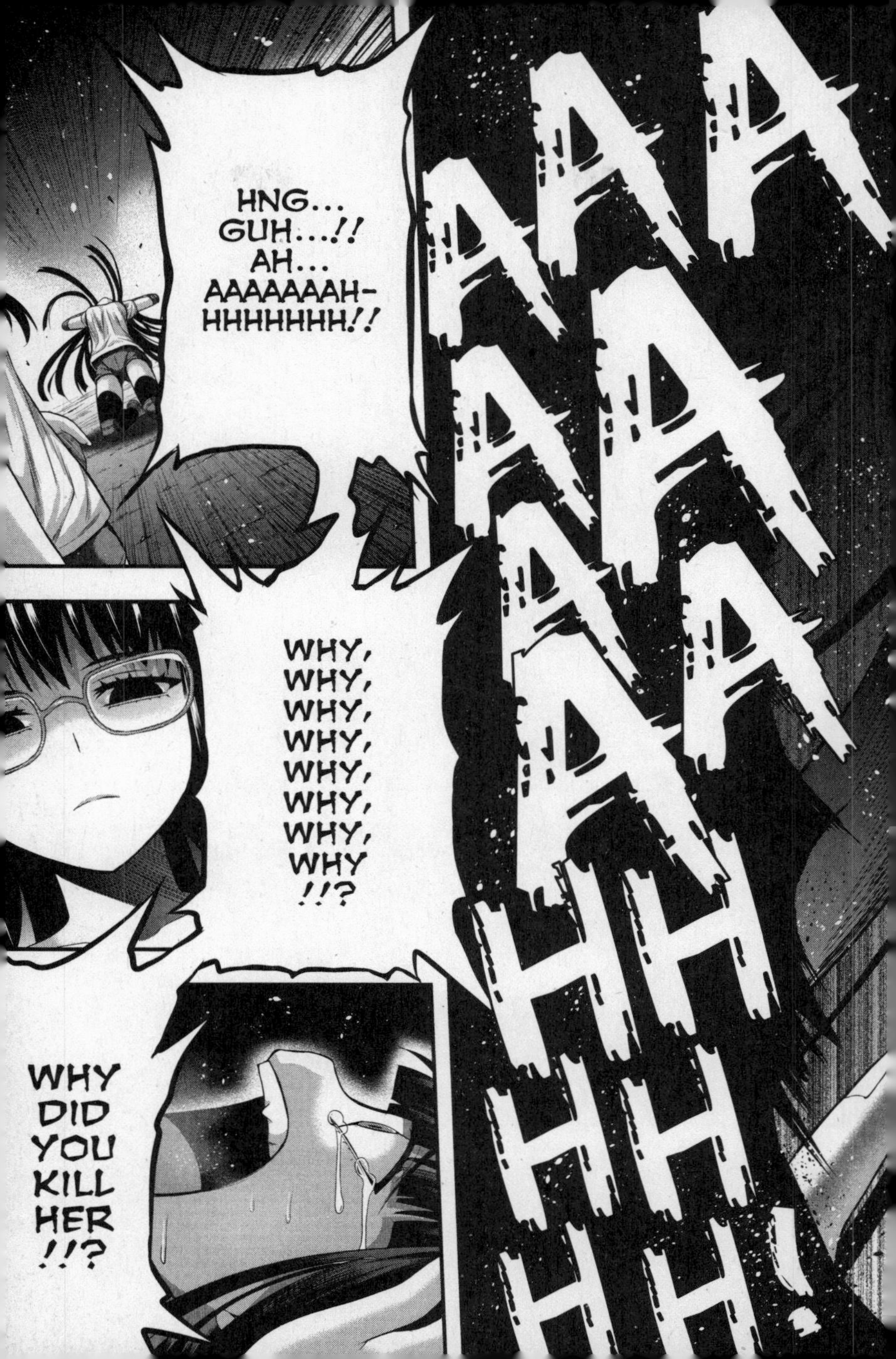
HNG... GUH...!! AH... AAAAAAAH-HHHHHHH!!
AAAAAAAAHHHHHH
WHY, WHY, WHY, WHY, WHY, WHY, WHY, WHY!!?
WHY DID YOU KILL HER!!?

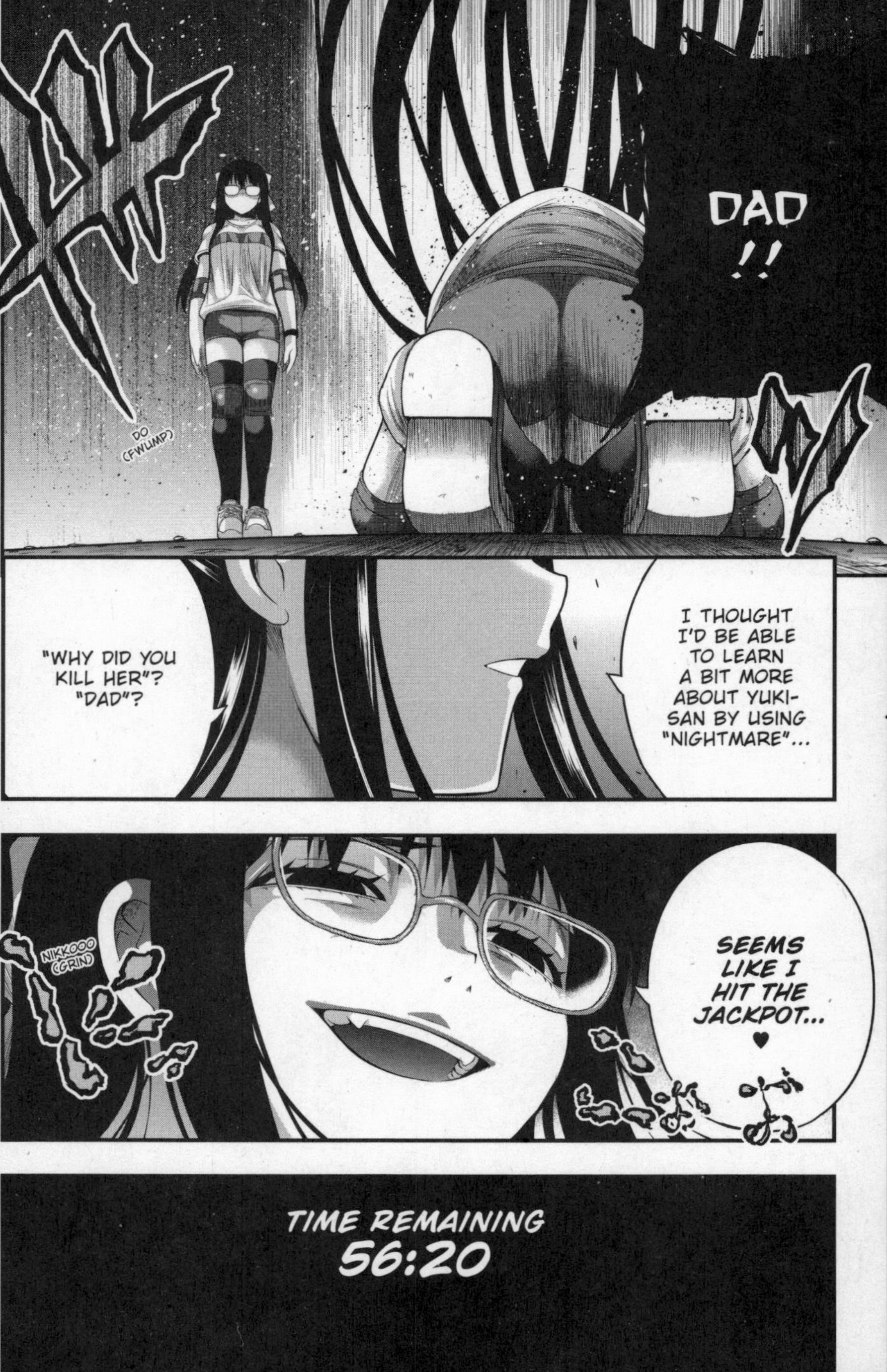
DAD!!
DO (FWUMP)
I THOUGHT I'D BE ABLE TO LEARN A BIT MORE ABOUT YUKI-SAN BY USING "NIGHTMARE"...
"WHY DID YOU KILL HER"? "DAD"?
SEEMS LIKE I HIT THE JACKPOT... ♥
NIKKOOO (GRIN)
TIME REMAINING 56:20

Though You May Burn to ASH

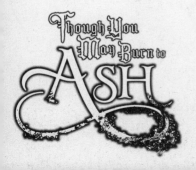

Though You May Burn to ASH

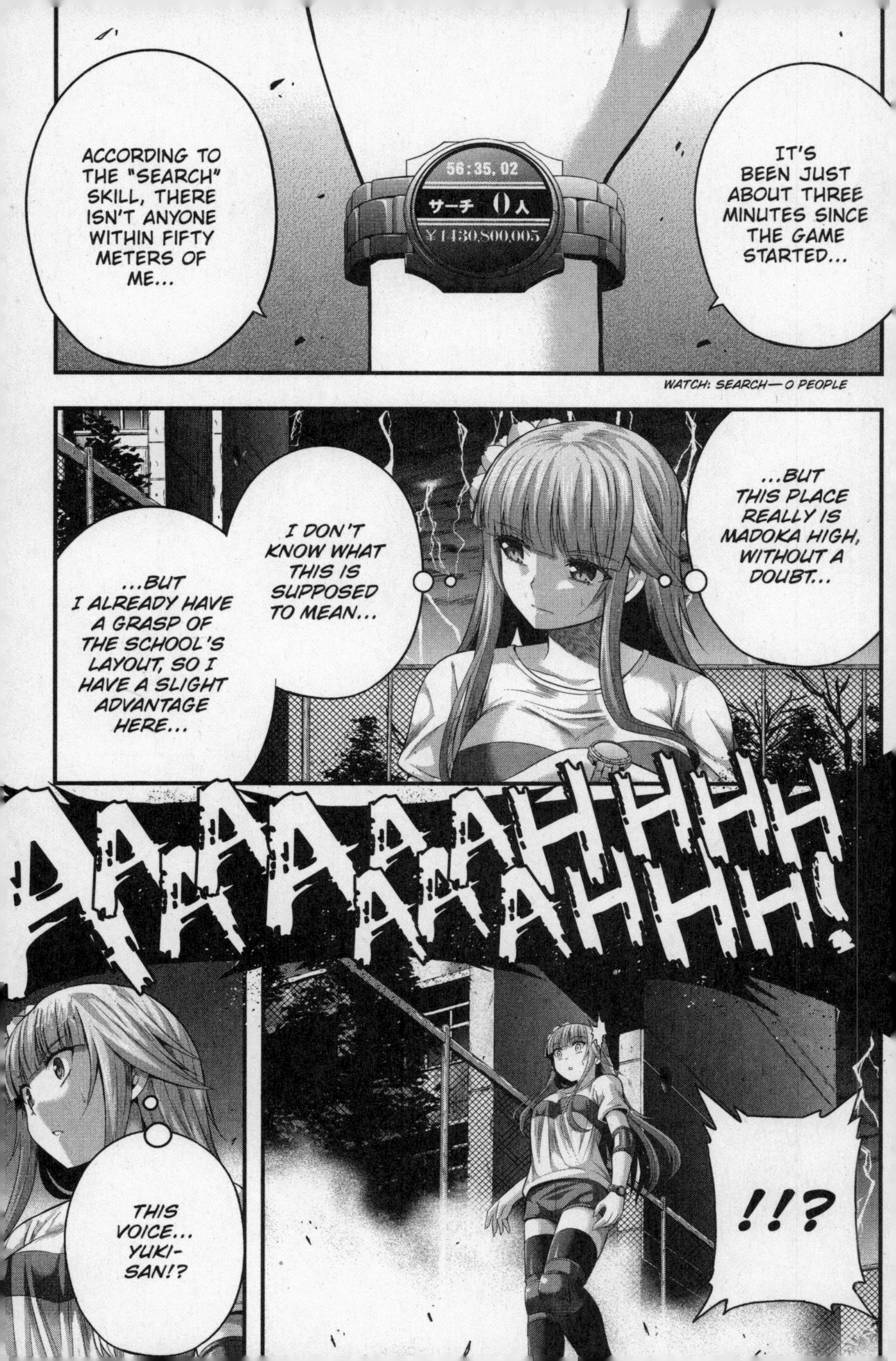
IT'S BEEN JUST ABOUT THREE MINUTES SINCE THE GAME STARTED...
56:35.02
サーチ 0人
¥1430,800,005
ACCORDING TO THE "SEARCH" SKILL, THERE ISN'T ANYONE WITHIN FIFTY METERS OF ME...
WATCH: SEARCH— 0 PEOPLE
...BUT THIS PLACE REALLY IS MADOKA HIGH, WITHOUT A DOUBT...
I DON'T KNOW WHAT THIS IS SUPPOSED TO MEAN...
...BUT I ALREADY HAVE A GRASP OF THE SCHOOL'S LAYOUT, SO I HAVE A SLIGHT ADVANTAGE HERE...
AAAAAAHHHHH AAAAAAHHHH!
!!?
THIS VOICE... YUKI-SAN!?

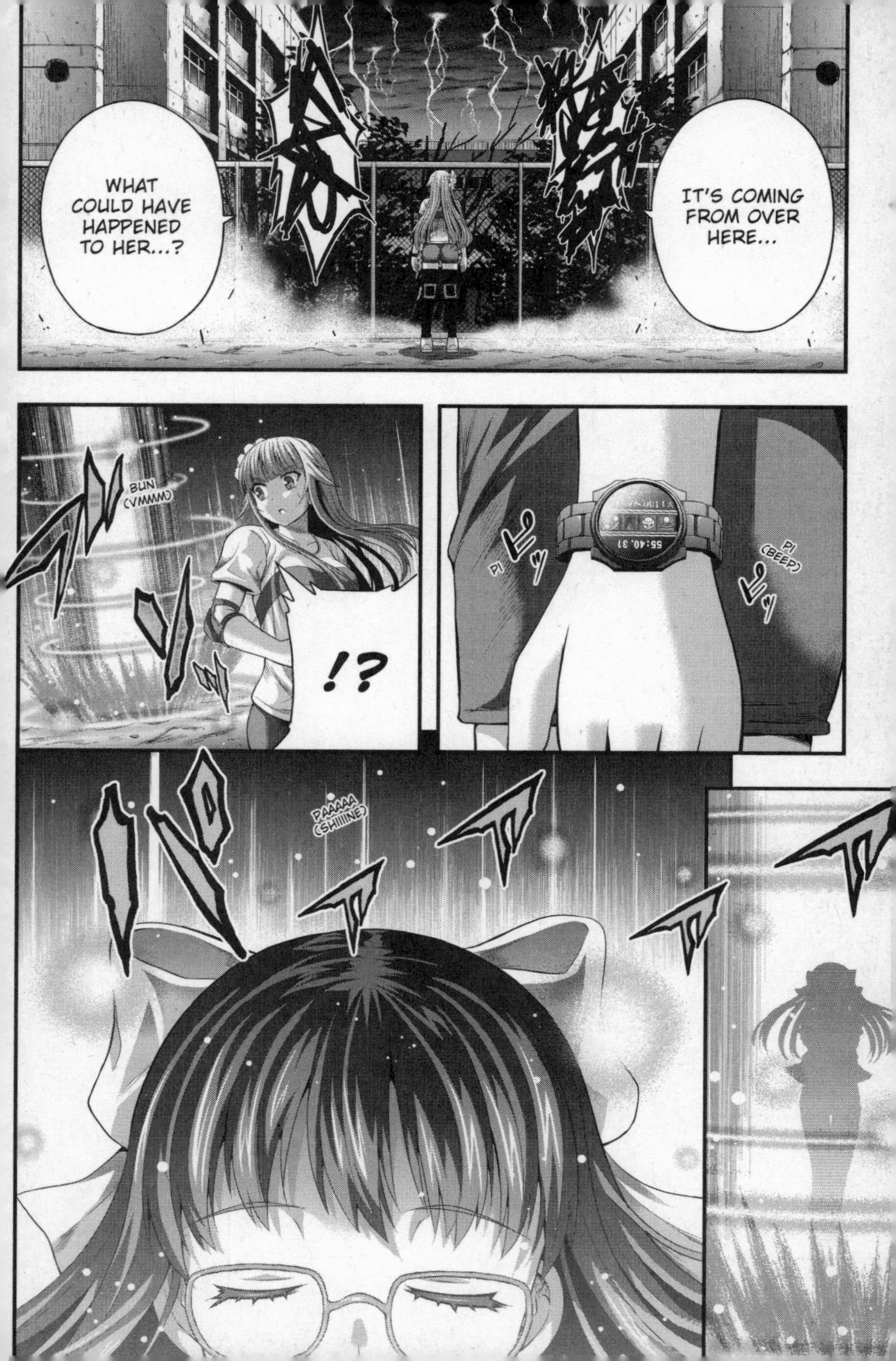
IT'S COMING FROM OVER HERE...
WHAT COULD HAVE HAPPENED TO HER...?
PI (BEEP)
PI
BUN (VMMMM)
!?
PAAAAA (SHIIIINE)

# CHAPTER 22: RED SKY AND TRUE MIND

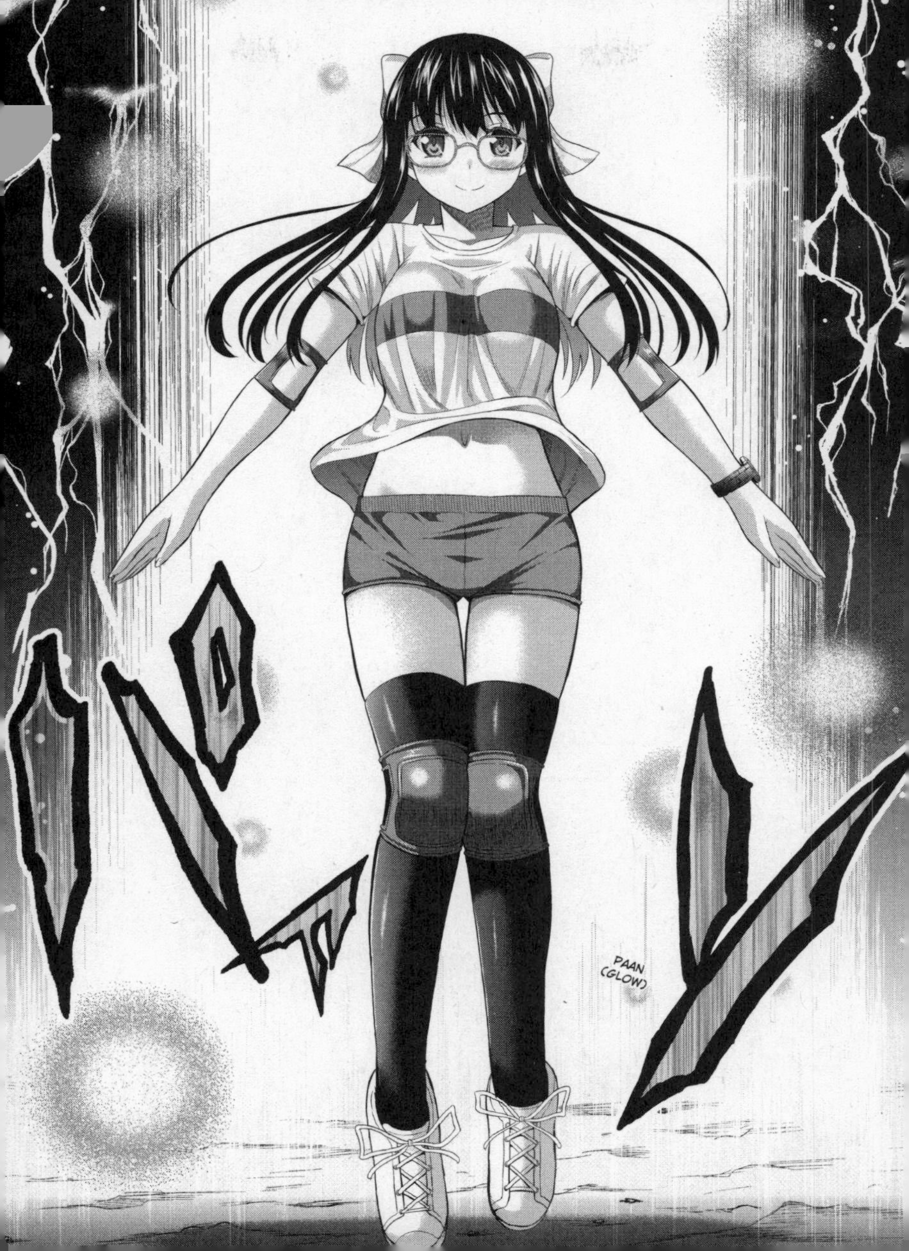
PAAN
(GLOW)

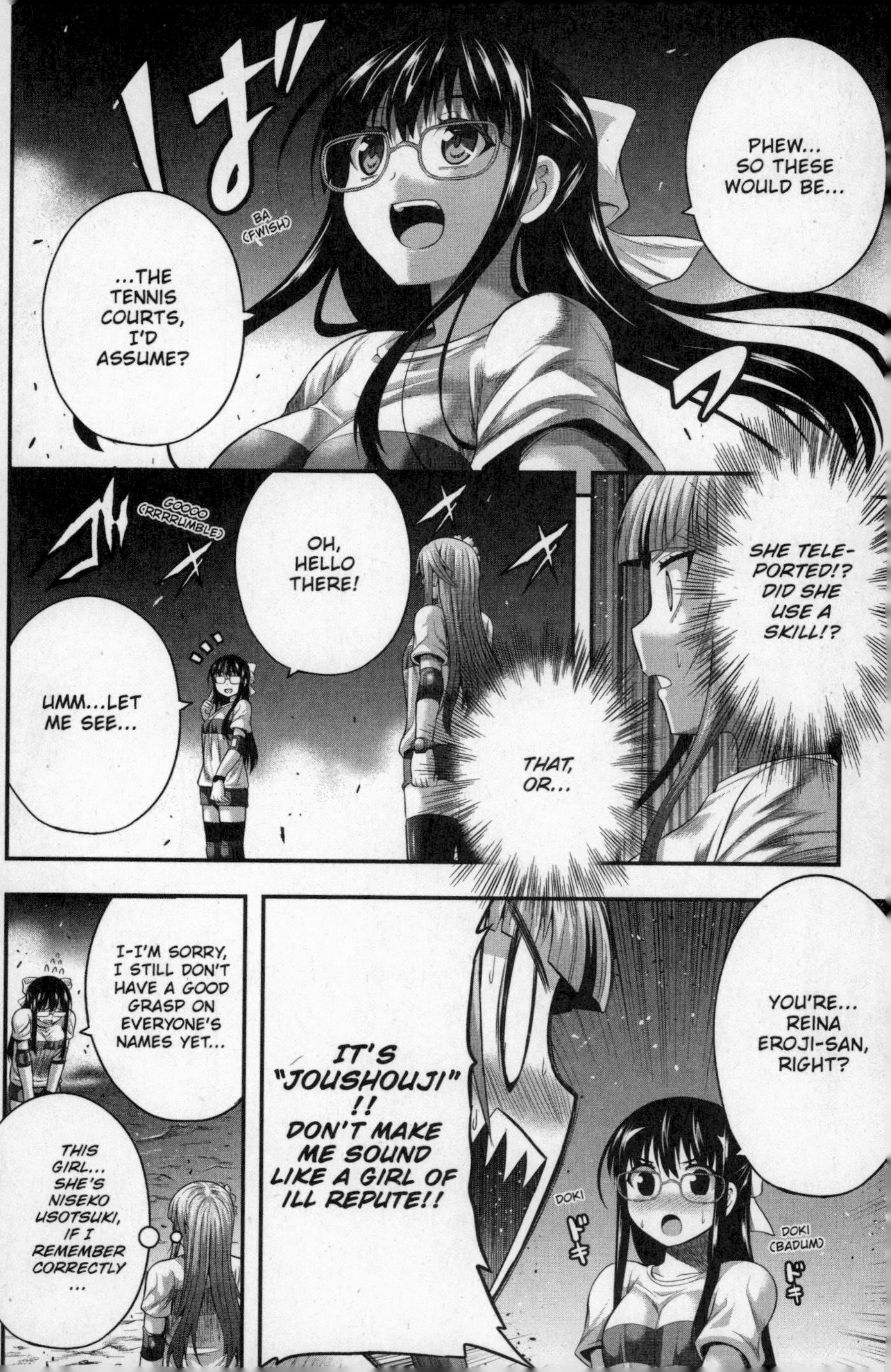
PHEW... SO THESE WOULD BE...
BA (FWISH)
...THE TENNIS COURTS, I'D ASSUME?
SHE TELE-PORTED!? DID SHE USE A SKILL!?
THAT, OR...
GOOOO (RRRRUMBLE)
OH, HELLO THERE!
UMM...LET ME SEE...
YOU'RE... REINA EROJI-SAN, RIGHT?
DOKI
DOKI (BADUM)
IT'S "JOUSHOUJI"!! DON'T MAKE ME SOUND LIKE A GIRL OF ILL REPUTE!!
I-I'M SORRY, I STILL DON'T HAVE A GOOD GRASP ON EVERYONE'S NAMES YET...
THIS GIRL... SHE'S NISEKO USOTSUKI, IF I REMEMBER CORRECTLY...

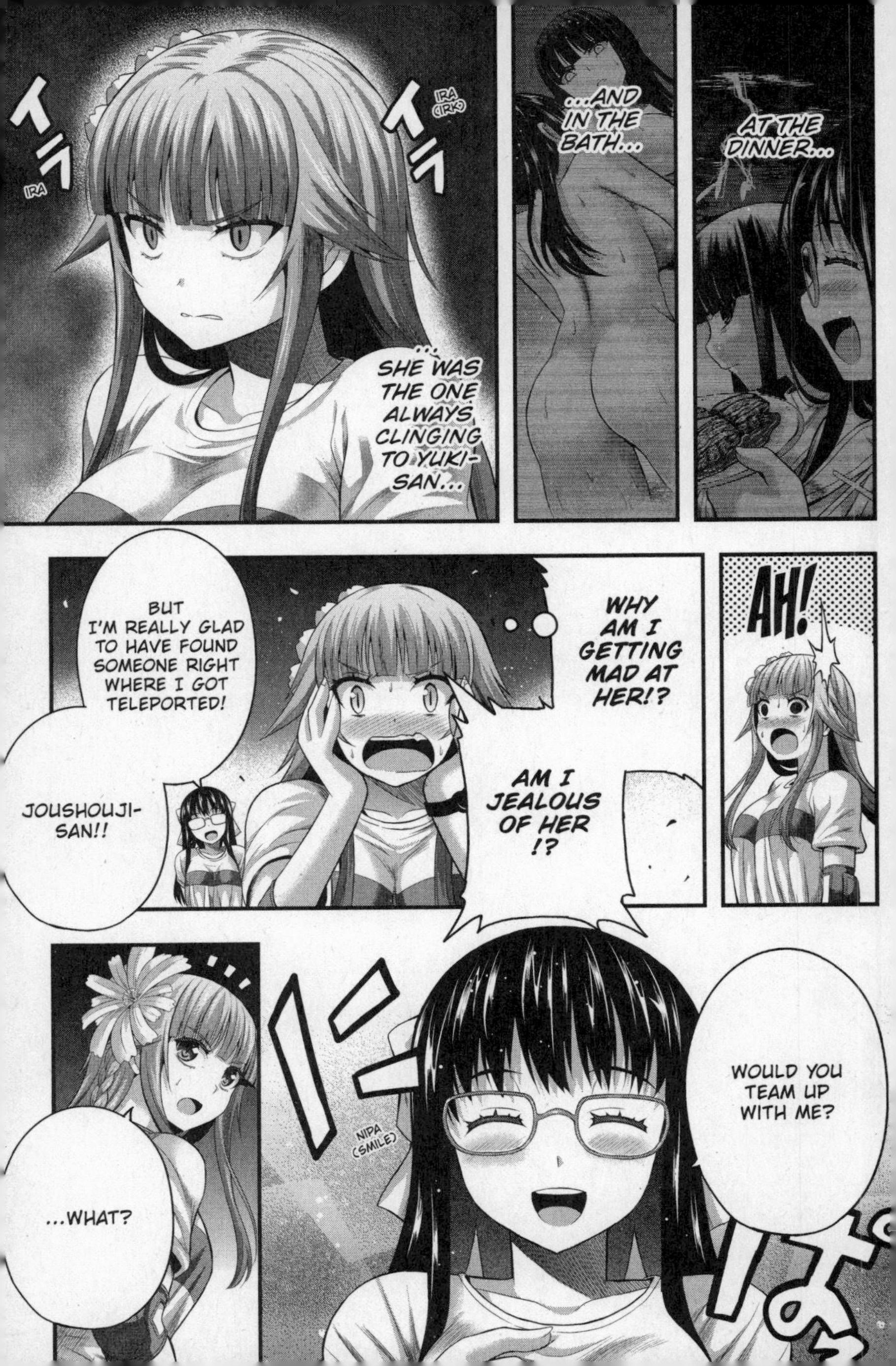
AT THE DINNER...
...AND IN THE BATH...
IRA (IRK)
IRA
...SHE WAS THE ONE ALWAYS CLINGING TO YUKI-SAN...
AH!
WHY AM I GETTING MAD AT HER!?
AM I JEALOUS OF HER!?
BUT I'M REALLY GLAD TO HAVE FOUND SOMEONE RIGHT WHERE I GOT TELEPORTED!
JOUSHOUJI-SAN!!
WOULD YOU TEAM UP WITH ME?
NIPA (SMILE)
...WHAT?

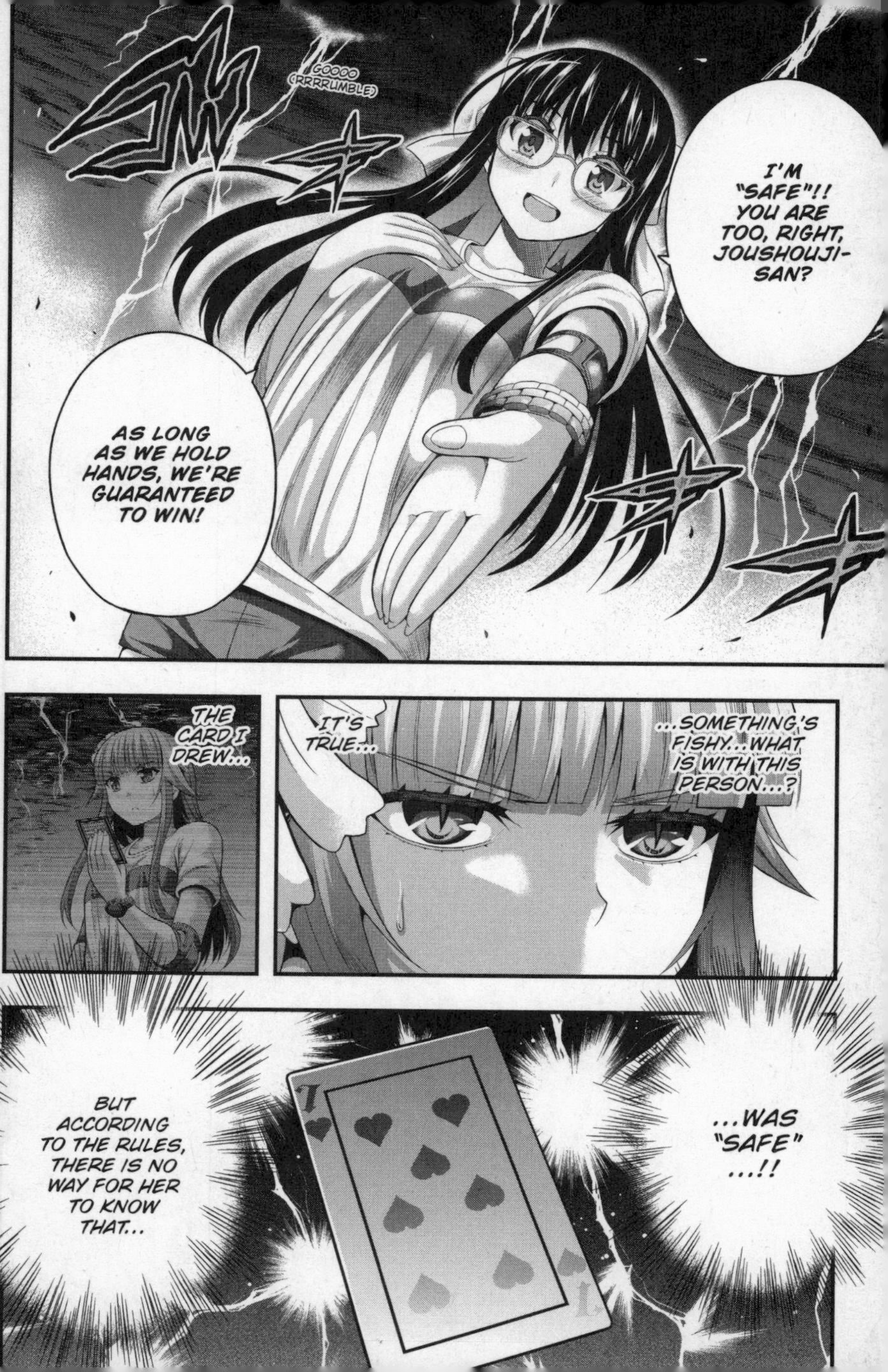
I'M "SAFE"!! YOU ARE TOO, RIGHT, JOUSHOUJI-SAN?
GOOOO (RRRRUMBLE)
AS LONG AS WE HOLD HANDS, WE'RE GUARANTEED TO WIN!
...SOMETHING'S FISHY...WHAT IS WITH THIS PERSON...?
IT'S TRUE...
THE CARD I DREW...
...WAS "SAFE" ...!!
BUT ACCORDING TO THE RULES, THERE IS NO WAY FOR HER TO KNOW THAT...

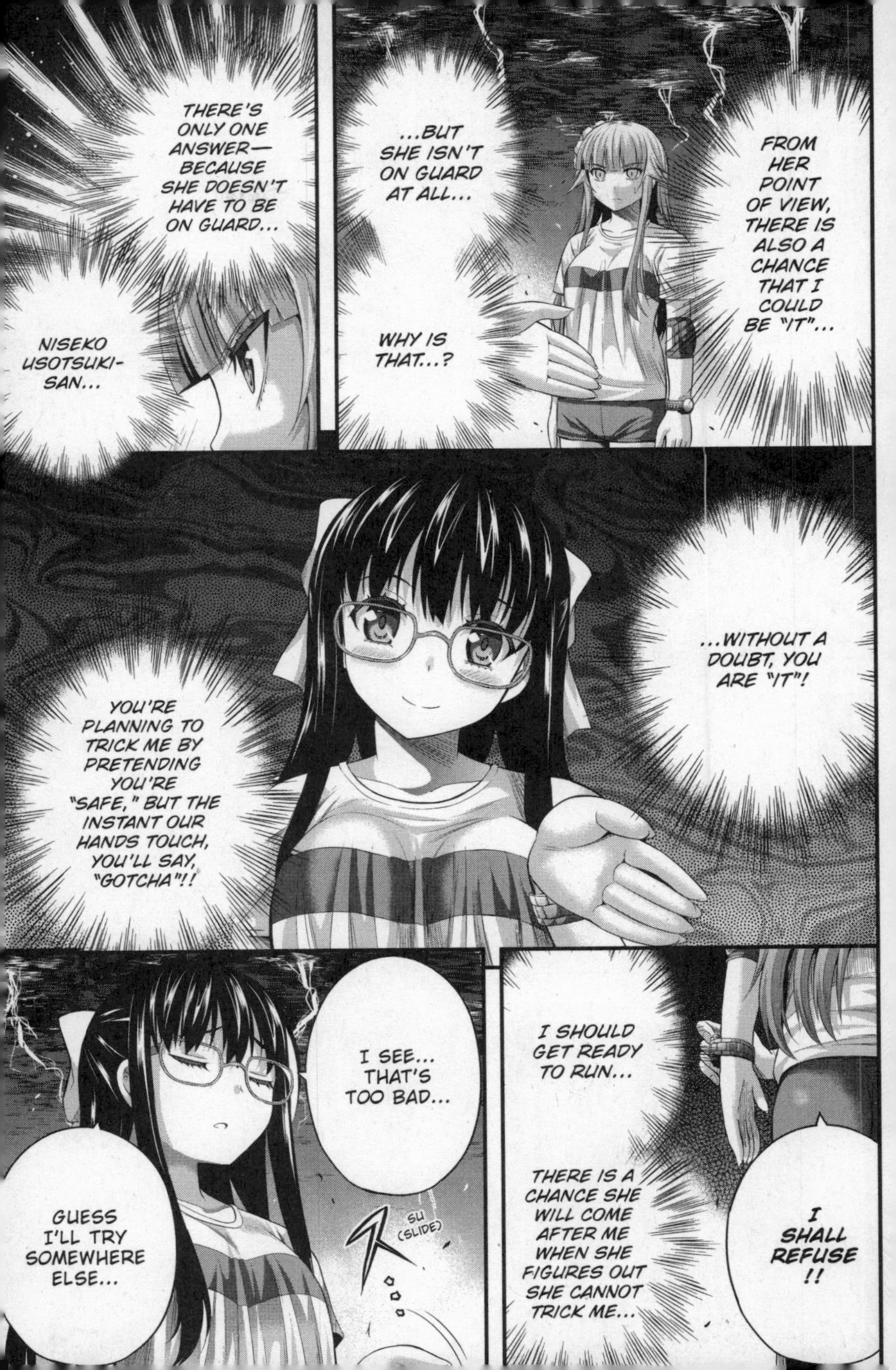
FROM HER POINT OF VIEW, THERE IS ALSO A CHANCE THAT I COULD BE "IT"...
...BUT SHE ISN'T ON GUARD AT ALL...
WHY IS THAT...?
THERE'S ONLY ONE ANSWER—BECAUSE SHE DOESN'T HAVE TO BE ON GUARD...
NISEKO USOTSUKI-SAN...
...WITHOUT A DOUBT, YOU ARE "IT"!
YOU'RE PLANNING TO TRICK ME BY PRETENDING YOU'RE "SAFE," BUT THE INSTANT OUR HANDS TOUCH, YOU'LL SAY, "GOTCHA"!!
I SHALL REFUSE!!
I SHOULD GET READY TO RUN...
THERE IS A CHANCE SHE WILL COME AFTER ME WHEN SHE FIGURES OUT SHE CANNOT TRICK ME...
I SEE... THAT'S TOO BAD...
SU (SLIDE)
GUESS I'LL TRY SOMEWHERE ELSE...

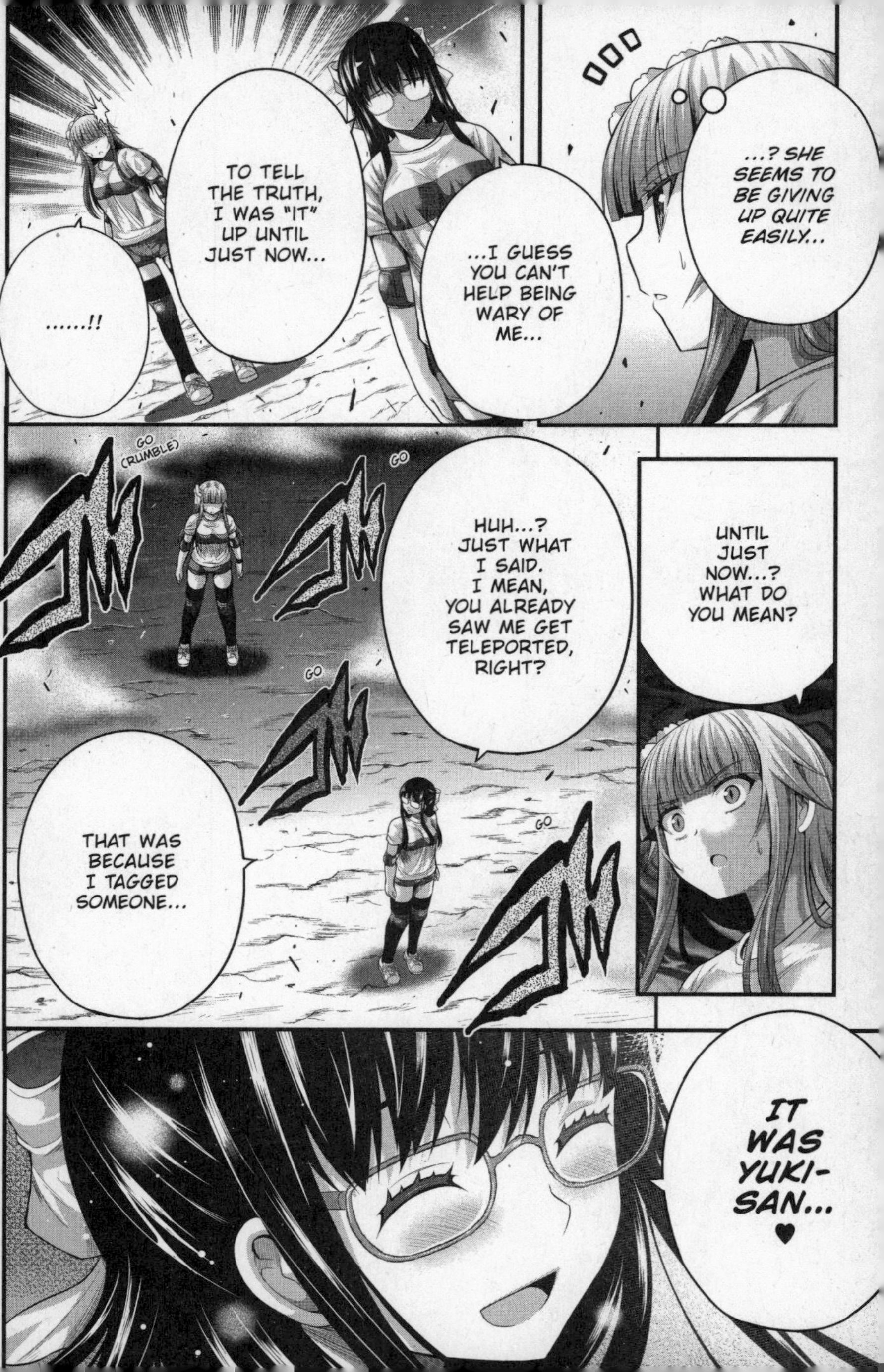
...? SHE SEEMS TO BE GIVING UP QUITE EASILY...
...I GUESS YOU CAN'T HELP BEING WARY OF ME...
TO TELL THE TRUTH, I WAS "IT" UP UNTIL JUST NOW...
......!!
UNTIL JUST NOW...? WHAT DO YOU MEAN?
GO
HUH...? JUST WHAT I SAID. I MEAN, YOU ALREADY SAW ME GET TELEPORTED, RIGHT?
GO (RUMBLE)
GO
GO
THAT WAS BECAUSE I TAGGED SOMEONE...
IT WAS YUKI-SAN... ♥

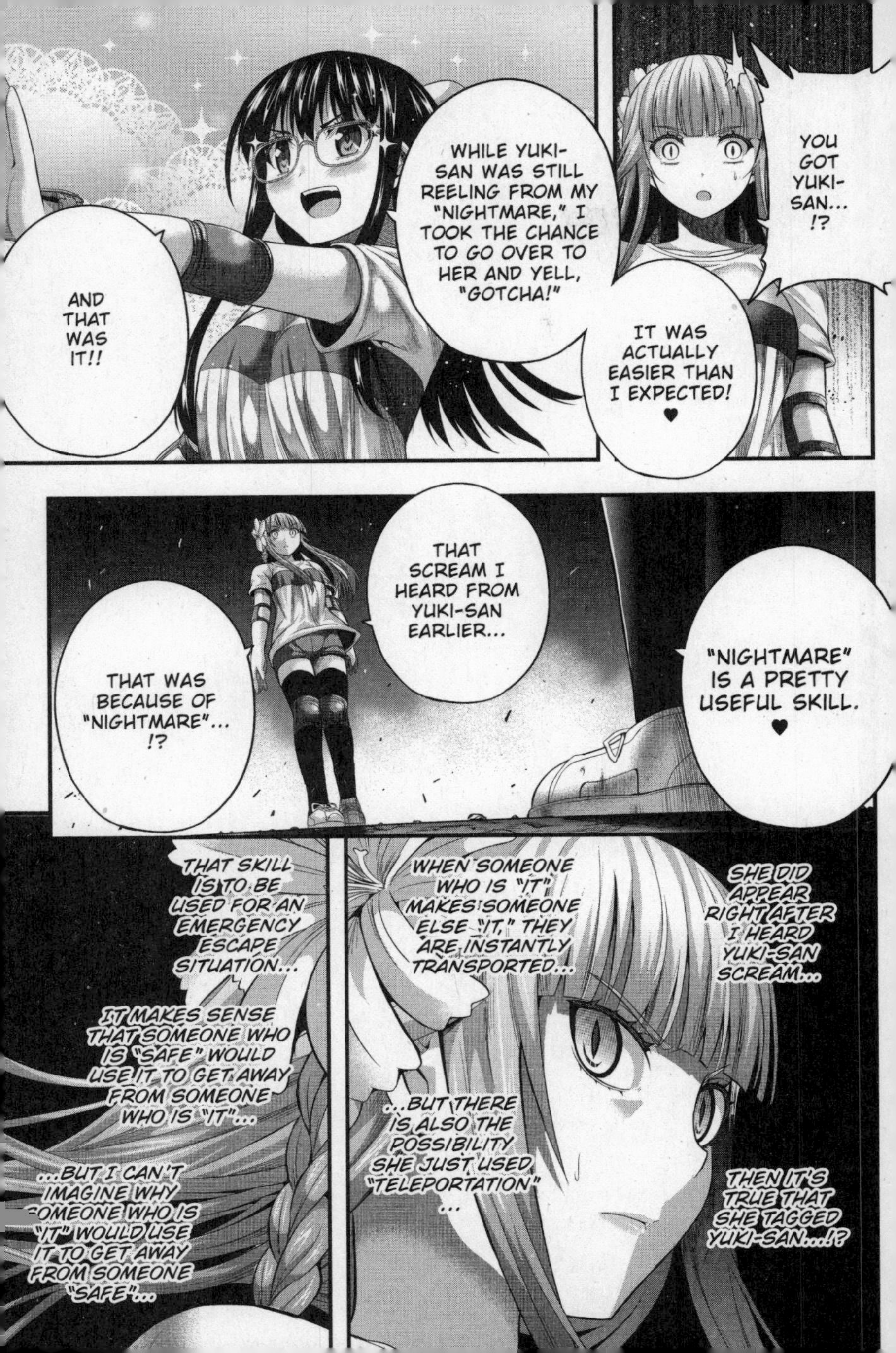
YOU GOT YUKI-SAN...!?
WHILE YUKI-SAN WAS STILL REELING FROM MY "NIGHTMARE," I TOOK THE CHANCE TO GO OVER TO HER AND YELL, "GOTCHA!"
AND THAT WAS IT!!
IT WAS ACTUALLY EASIER THAN I EXPECTED! ♥
"NIGHTMARE" IS A PRETTY USEFUL SKILL. ♥
THAT SCREAM I HEARD FROM YUKI-SAN EARLIER...
THAT WAS BECAUSE OF "NIGHTMARE"...!?
SHE DID APPEAR RIGHT AFTER I HEARD YUKI-SAN SCREAM...
WHEN SOMEONE WHO IS "IT" MAKES SOMEONE ELSE "IT," THEY ARE INSTANTLY TRANSPORTED...
...BUT THERE IS ALSO THE POSSIBILITY SHE JUST USED "TELEPORTATION"...
THAT SKILL IS TO BE USED FOR AN EMERGENCY ESCAPE SITUATION...
IT MAKES SENSE THAT SOMEONE WHO IS "SAFE" WOULD USE IT TO GET AWAY FROM SOMEONE WHO IS "IT"...
...BUT I CAN'T IMAGINE WHY SOMEONE WHO IS "IT" WOULD USE IT TO GET AWAY FROM SOMEONE "SAFE"...
THEN IT'S TRUE THAT SHE TAGGED YUKI-SAN...!?

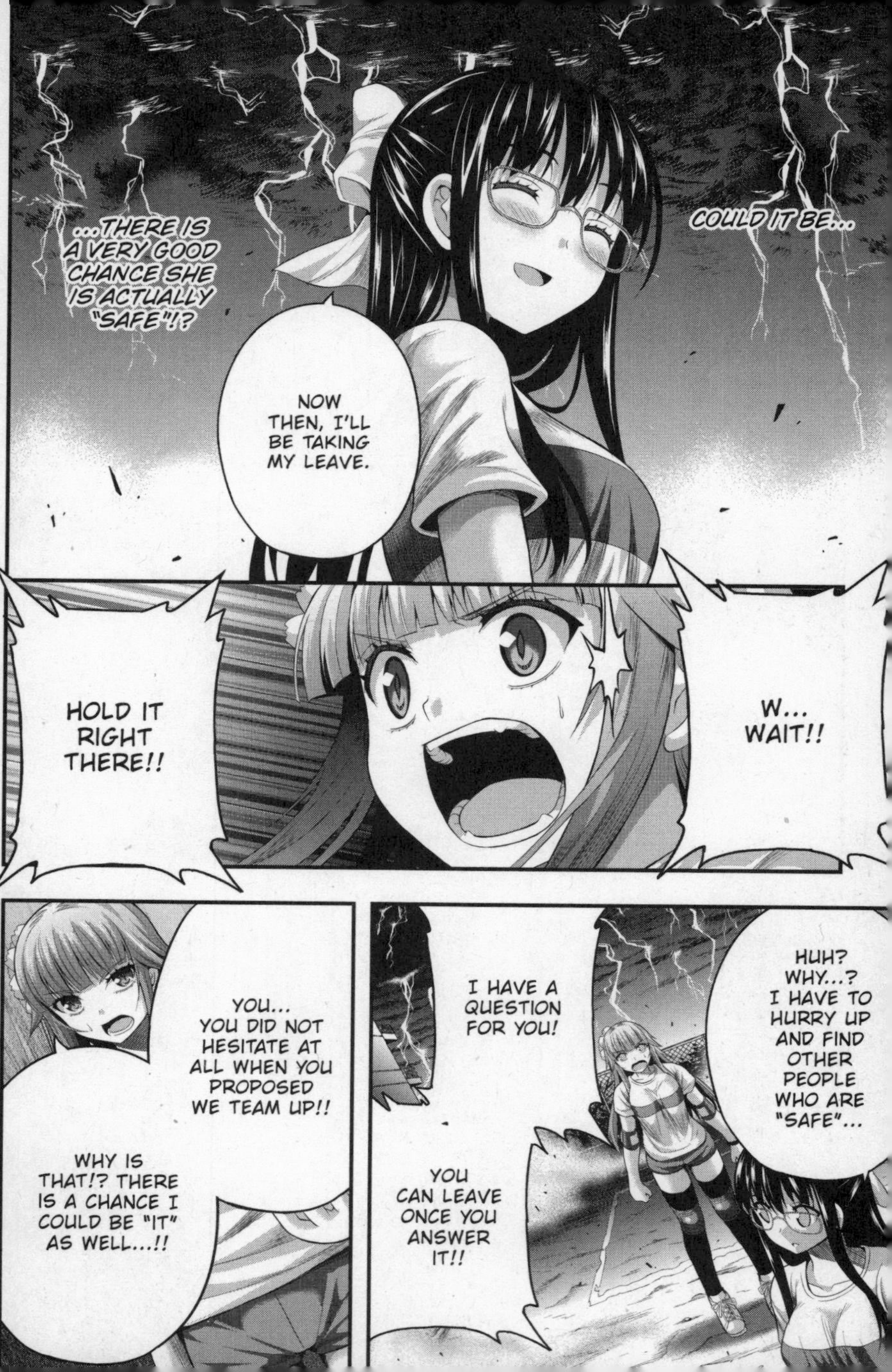
COULD IT BE...
...THERE IS A VERY GOOD CHANCE SHE IS ACTUALLY "SAFE"!?
NOW THEN, I'LL BE TAKING MY LEAVE.
W... WAIT!!
HOLD IT RIGHT THERE!!
HUH? WHY...? I HAVE TO HURRY UP AND FIND OTHER PEOPLE WHO ARE "SAFE"...
I HAVE A QUESTION FOR YOU!
YOU CAN LEAVE ONCE YOU ANSWER IT!!
YOU... YOU DID NOT HESITATE AT ALL WHEN YOU PROPOSED WE TEAM UP!!
WHY IS THAT!? THERE IS A CHANCE I COULD BE "IT" AS WELL...!!

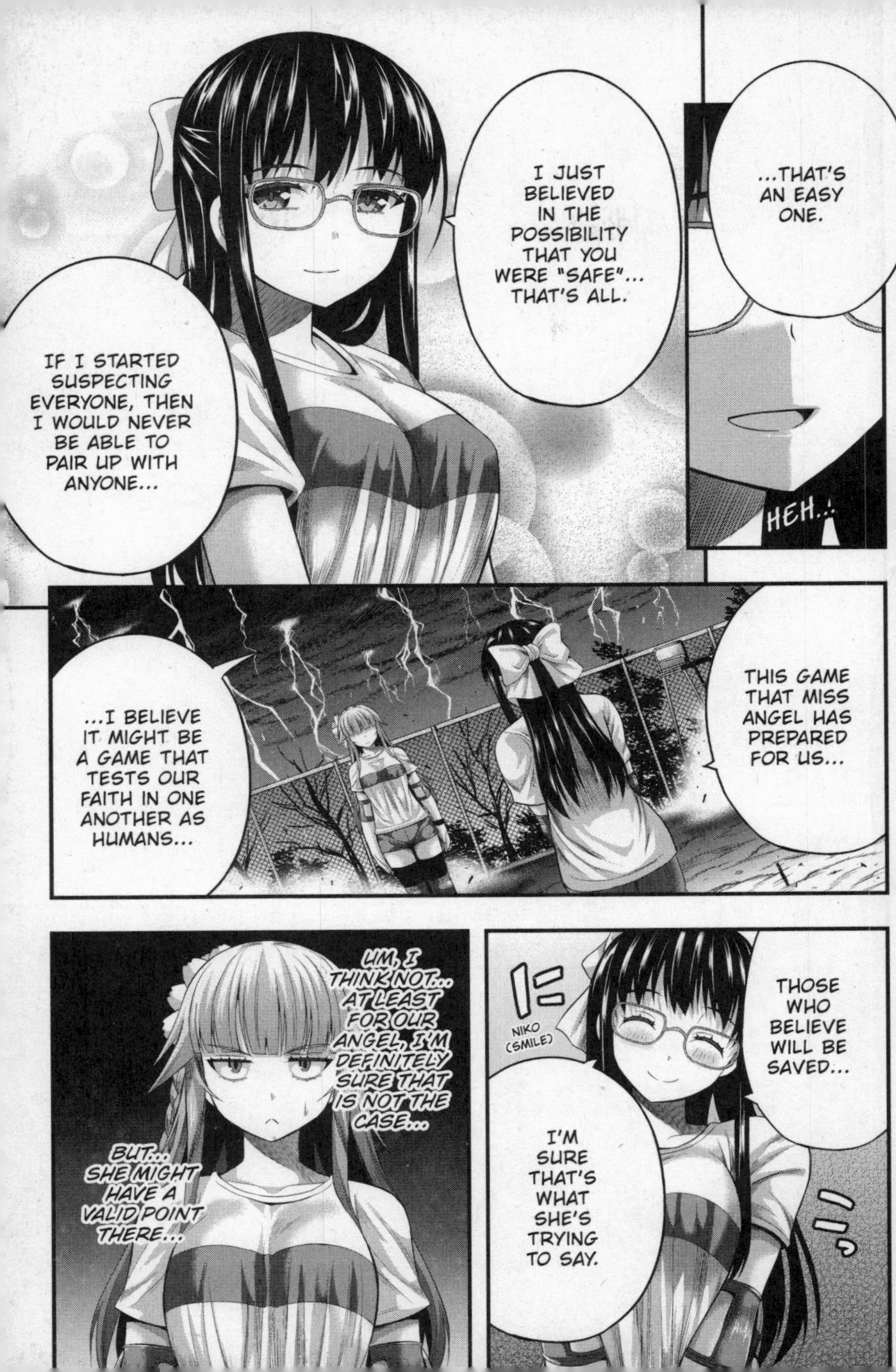
...THAT'S AN EASY ONE.
HEH...
I JUST BELIEVED IN THE POSSIBILITY THAT YOU WERE "SAFE"... THAT'S ALL.
IF I STARTED SUSPECTING EVERYONE, THEN I WOULD NEVER BE ABLE TO PAIR UP WITH ANYONE...
THIS GAME THAT MISS ANGEL HAS PREPARED FOR US...
...I BELIEVE IT MIGHT BE A GAME THAT TESTS OUR FAITH IN ONE ANOTHER AS HUMANS...
THOSE WHO BELIEVE WILL BE SAVED...
NIKO (SMILE)
I'M SURE THAT'S WHAT SHE'S TRYING TO SAY.
UM, I THINK NOT... AT LEAST FOR OUR ANGEL, I'M DEFINITELY SURE THAT IS NOT THE CASE...
BUT... SHE MIGHT HAVE A VALID POINT THERE...

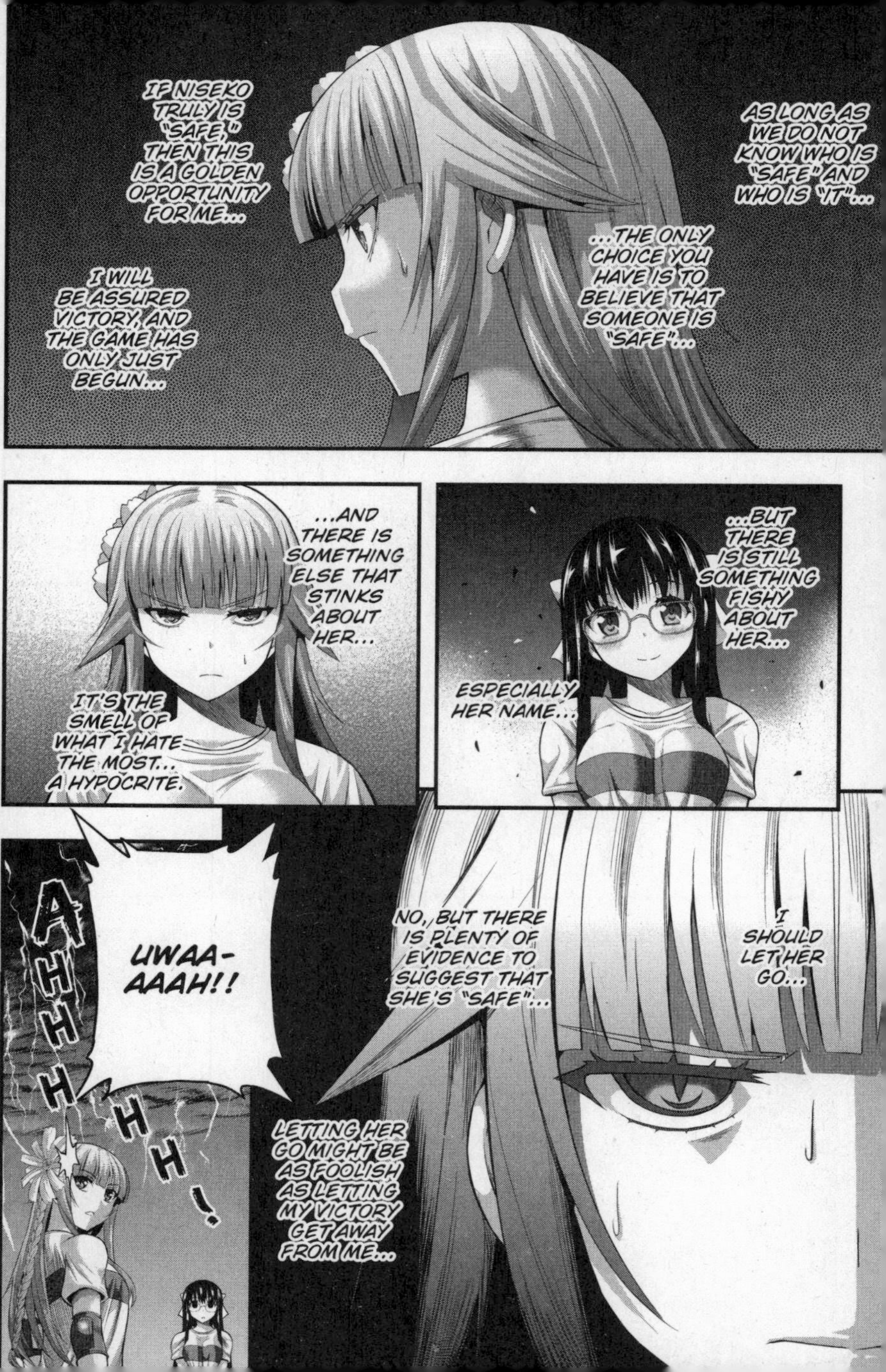
AS LONG AS WE DO NOT KNOW WHO IS "SAFE" AND WHO IS "IT"...
...THE ONLY CHOICE YOU HAVE IS TO BELIEVE THAT SOMEONE IS "SAFE"...
IF NISEKO TRULY IS "SAFE," THEN THIS IS A GOLDEN OPPORTUNITY FOR ME...
I WILL BE ASSURED VICTORY, AND THE GAME HAS ONLY JUST BEGUN...
...BUT THERE IS STILL SOMETHING FISHY ABOUT HER...
ESPECIALLY HER NAME...
...AND THERE IS SOMETHING ELSE THAT STINKS ABOUT HER...
IT'S THE SMELL OF WHAT I HATE THE MOST... A HYPOCRITE.
I SHOULD LET HER GO...
NO, BUT THERE IS PLENTY OF EVIDENCE TO SUGGEST THAT SHE'S "SAFE"...
LETTING HER GO MIGHT BE AS FOOLISH AS LETTING MY VICTORY GET AWAY FROM ME...
UWAA-AAAH!!
AHHHHHH!

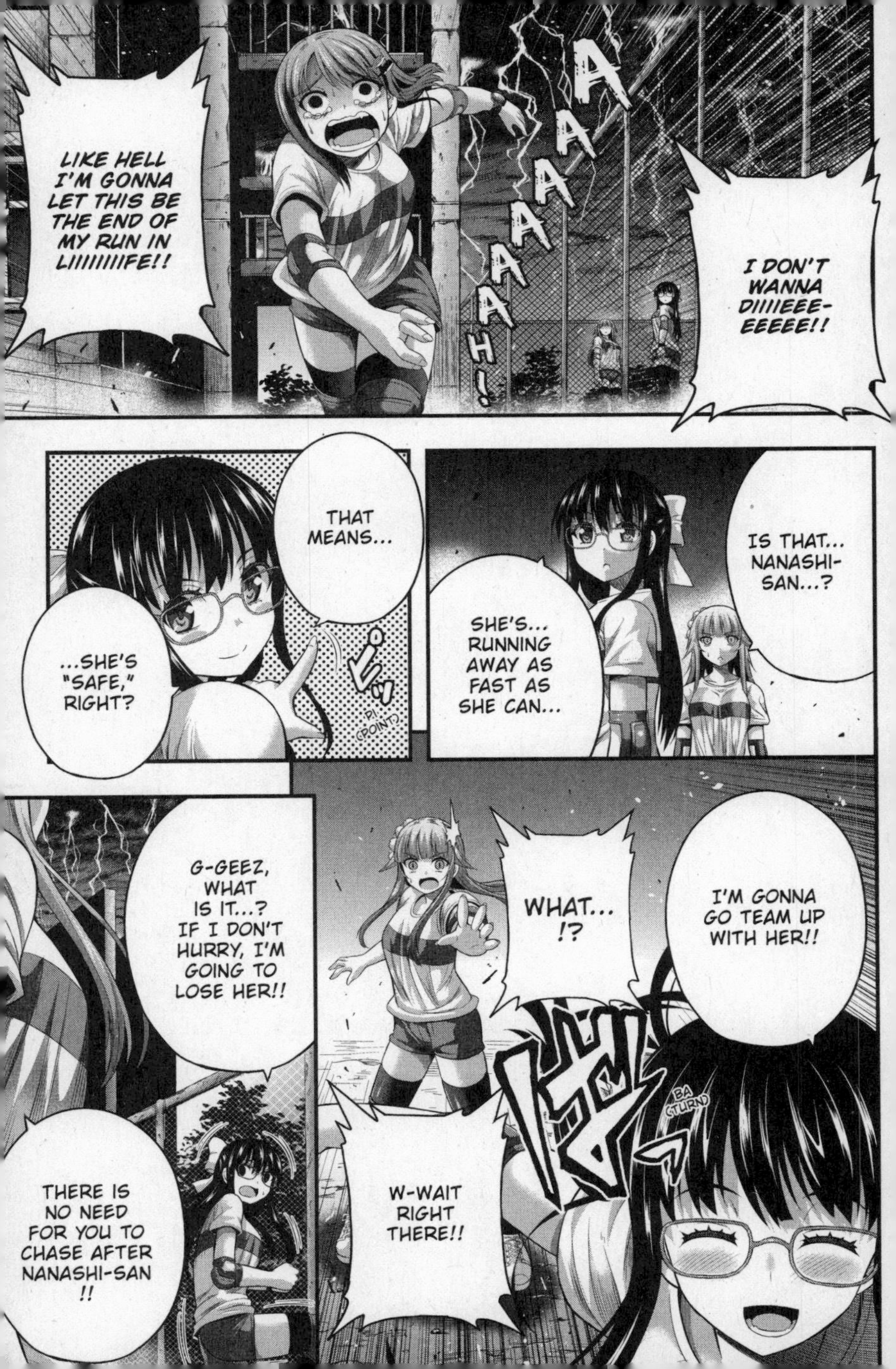

I DON'T WANNA DIIIIEEE-EEEEE!!
AAAAAAH!
LIKE HELL I'M GONNA LET THIS BE THE END OF MY RUN IN LIIIIIIIIFE!!
IS THAT... NANASHI-SAN...?
SHE'S... RUNNING AWAY AS FAST AS SHE CAN...
THAT MEANS...
...SHE'S "SAFE," RIGHT?
PI (POINT)
I'M GONNA GO TEAM UP WITH HER!!
WHAT... !?
BA (TURN)
W-WAIT RIGHT THERE!!
G-GEEZ, WHAT IS IT...? IF I DON'T HURRY, I'M GOING TO LOSE HER!!
THERE IS NO NEED FOR YOU TO CHASE AFTER NANASHI-SAN !!

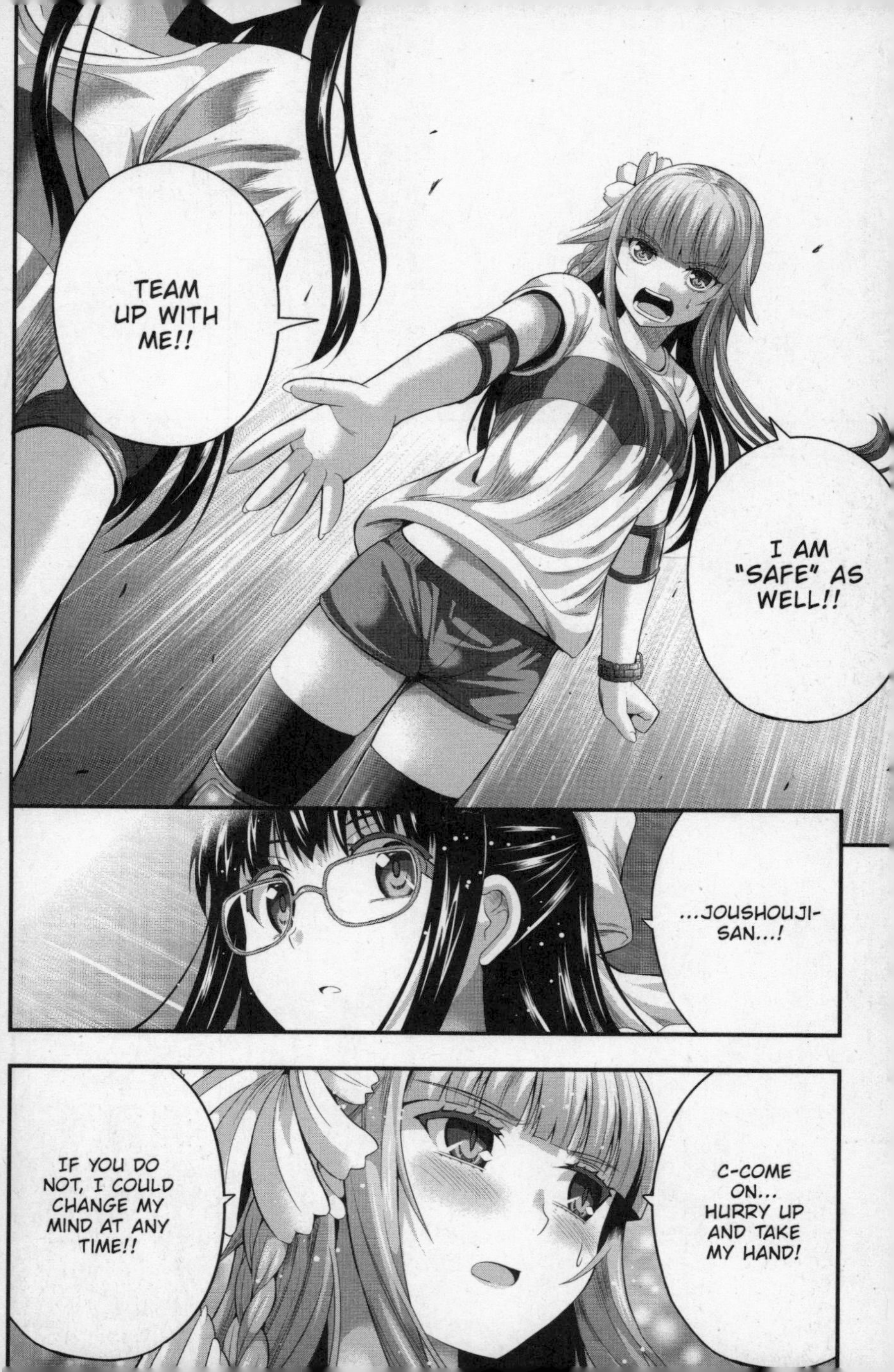
I AM "SAFE" AS WELL!!
TEAM UP WITH ME!!
...JOUSHOUJI-SAN...!
C-COME ON... HURRY UP AND TAKE MY HAND!
IF YOU DO NOT, I COULD CHANGE MY MIND AT ANY TIME!!

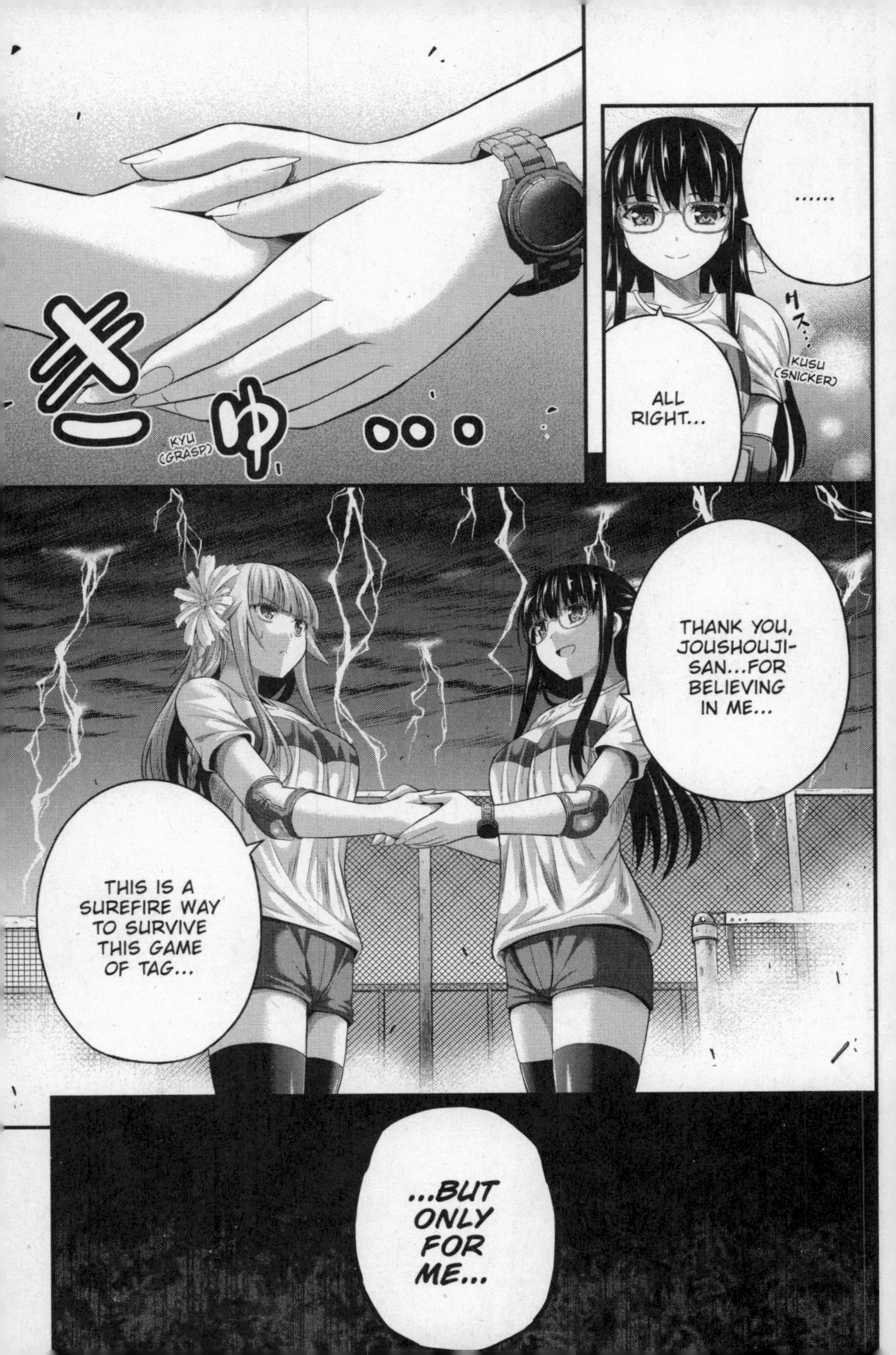
......
KUSU (SNICKER)
ALL RIGHT...
KYU (GRASP)
THANK YOU, JOUSHOUJI-SAN...FOR BELIEVING IN ME...
THIS IS A SUREFIRE WAY TO SURVIVE THIS GAME OF TAG...
...BUT ONLY FOR ME...

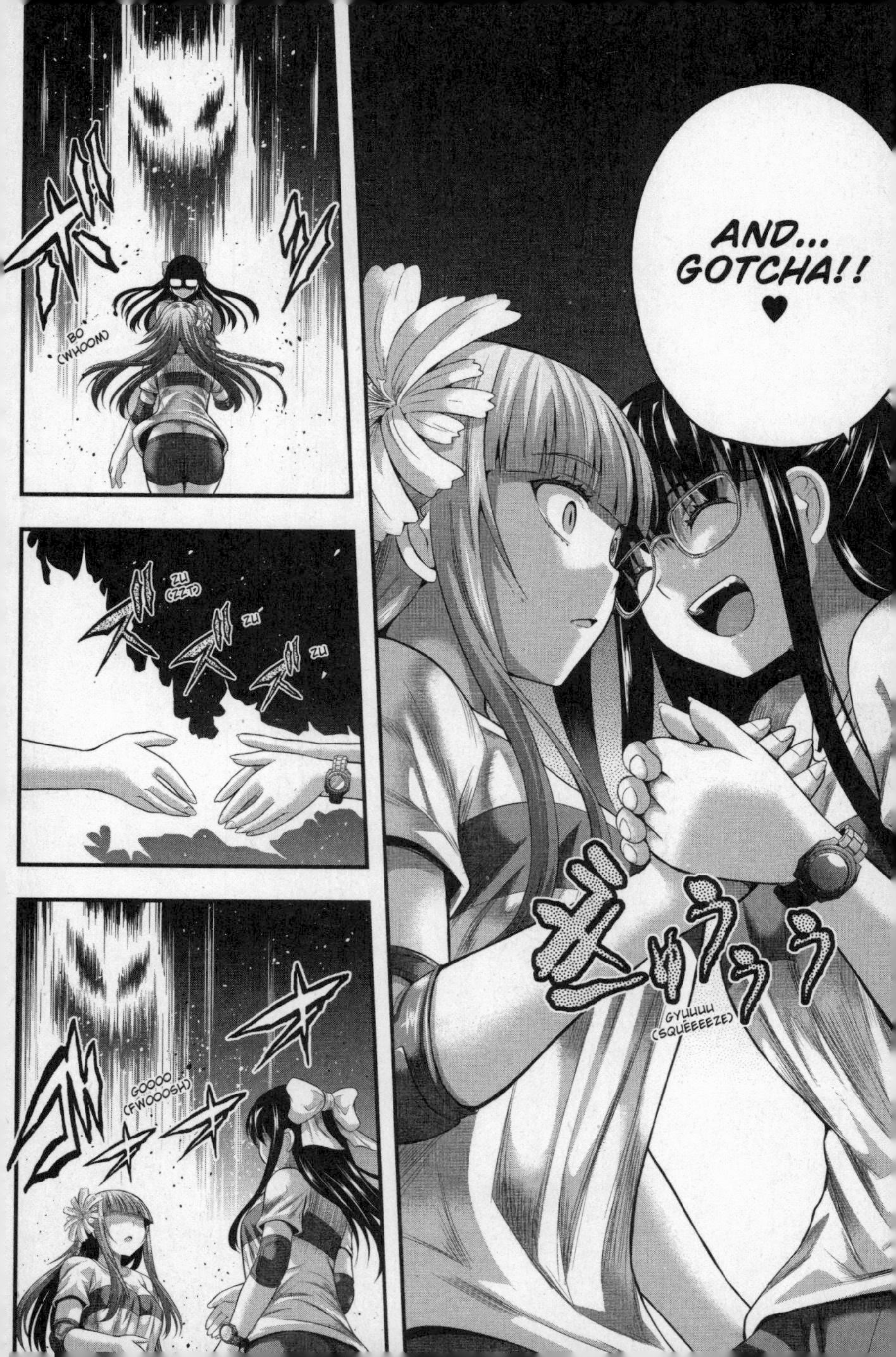
AND... GOTCHA!! ♥
GYUUUU (SQUEEEEZE)
BO (WHOOM)
ZU (ZZT)
ZU
ZU
GOOOO (FWOOOSH)

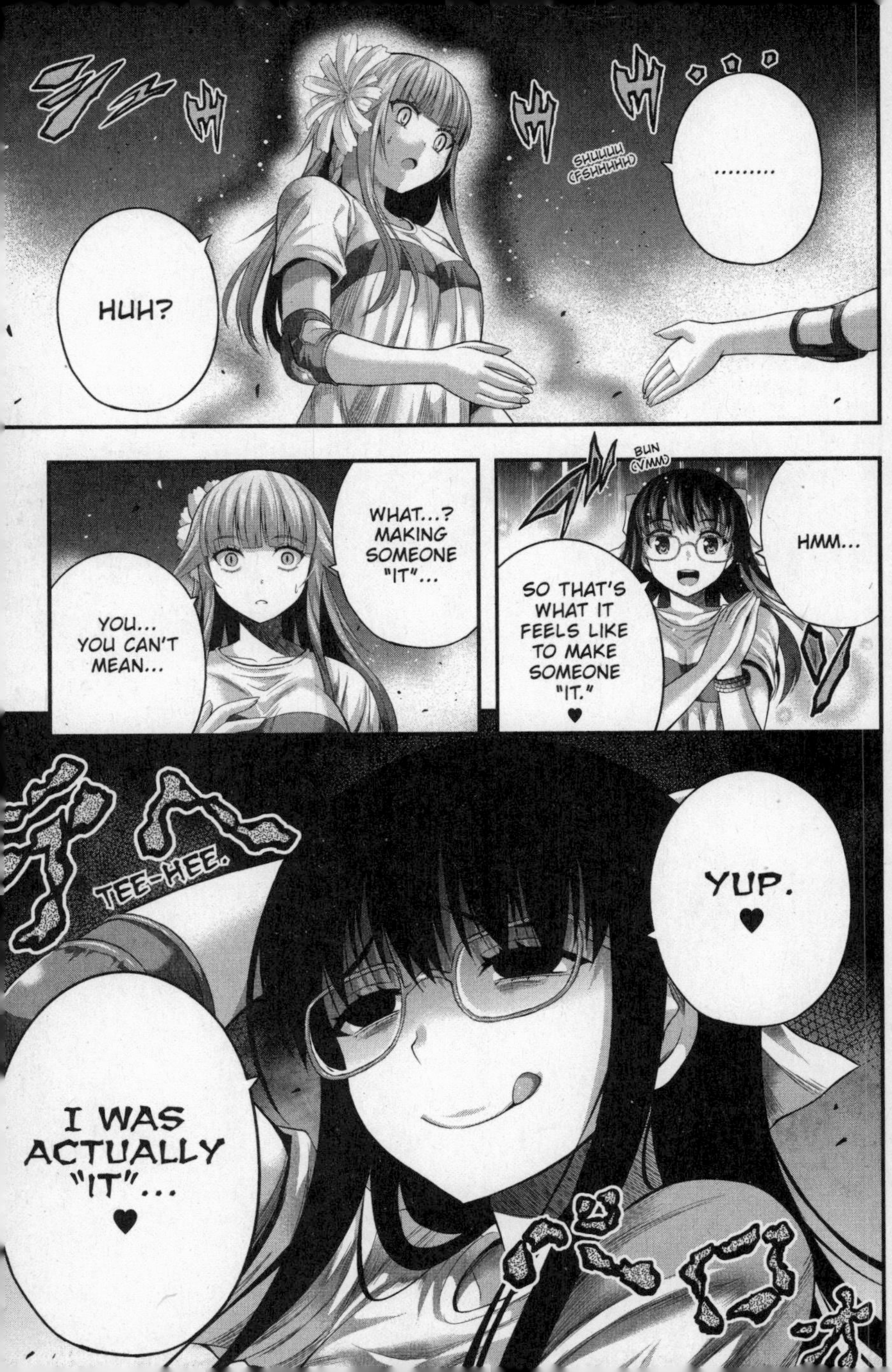
..........
SHUUUU (FSHHHHH)
HUH?
HMM...
SO THAT'S WHAT IT FEELS LIKE TO MAKE SOMEONE "IT." ♥
BUN (VMM)
WHAT...? MAKING SOMEONE "IT"...
YOU... YOU CAN'T MEAN...
YUP. ♥
TEE-HEE.
I WAS ACTUALLY "IT"... ♥

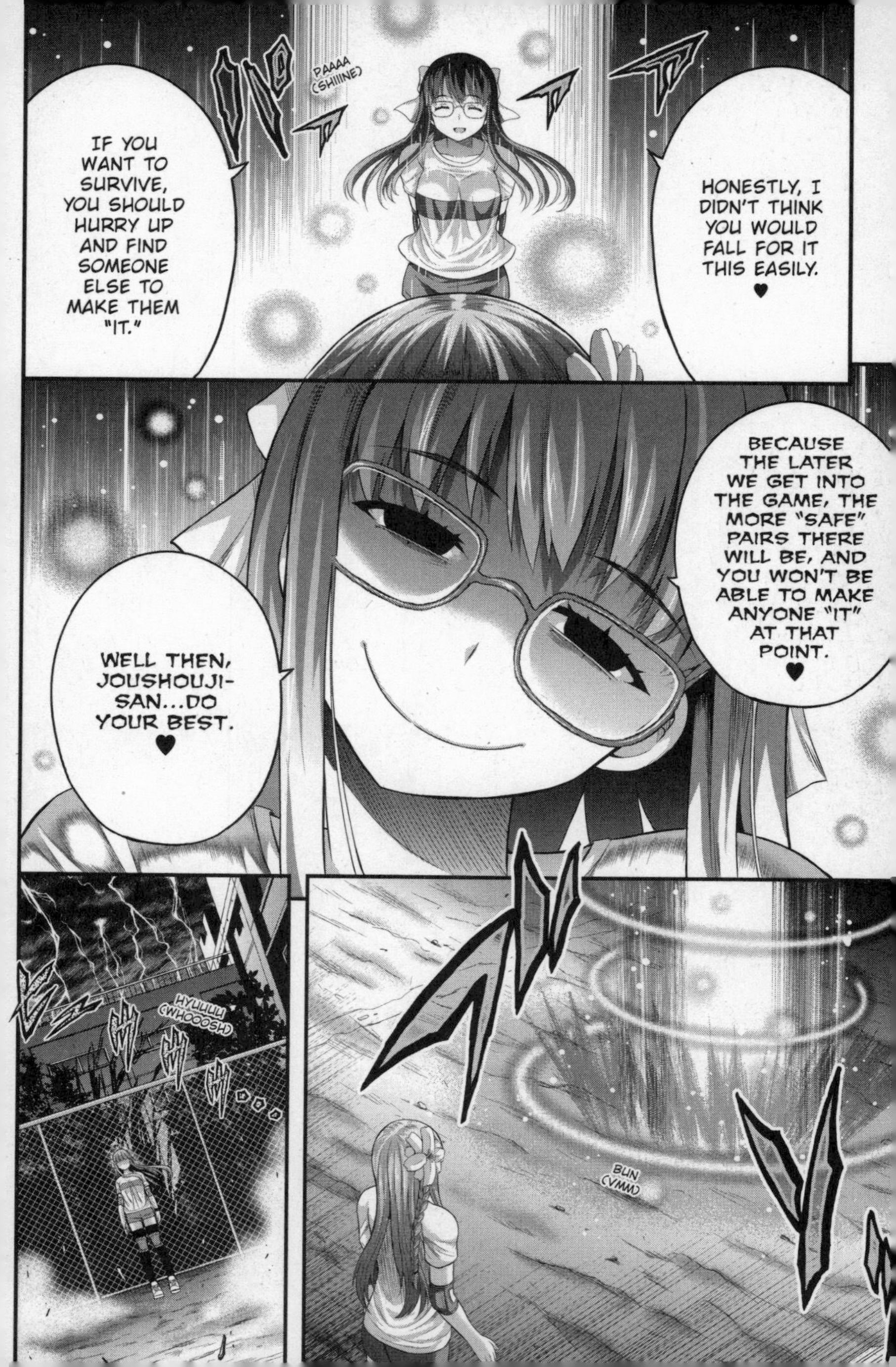
HONESTLY, I DIDN'T THINK YOU WOULD FALL FOR IT THIS EASILY. ♥
PAAAA (SHIIINE)
IF YOU WANT TO SURVIVE, YOU SHOULD HURRY UP AND FIND SOMEONE ELSE TO MAKE THEM "IT."
BECAUSE THE LATER WE GET INTO THE GAME, THE MORE "SAFE" PAIRS THERE WILL BE, AND YOU WON'T BE ABLE TO MAKE ANYONE "IT" AT THAT POINT. ♥
WELL THEN, JOUSHOUJI-SAN...DO YOUR BEST. ♥
BUN (VMM)
HYUUUU (WHOOOSH)

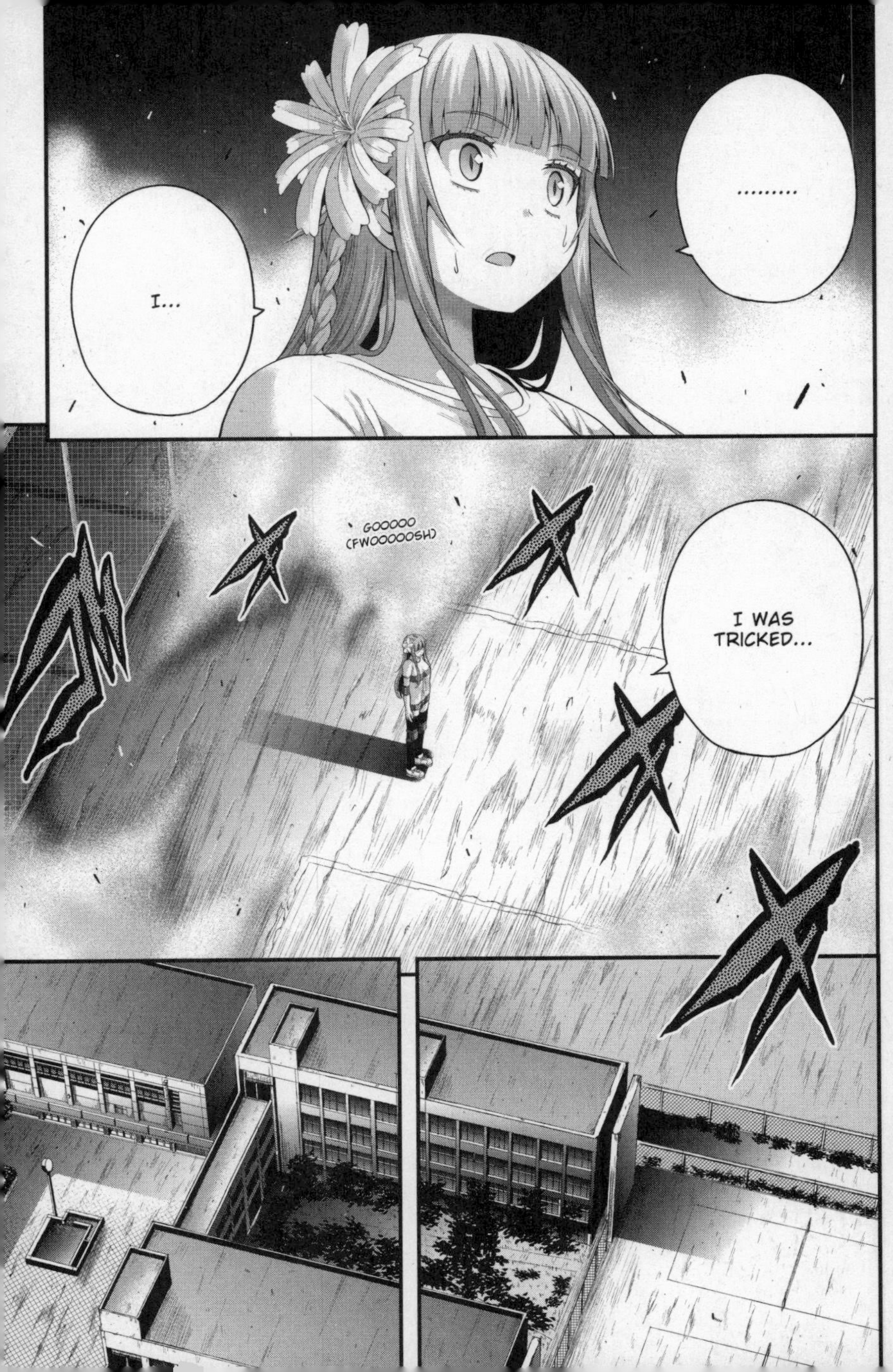

.........
I...
I WAS TRICKED...
GOOOOO (FWOOOOOSH)

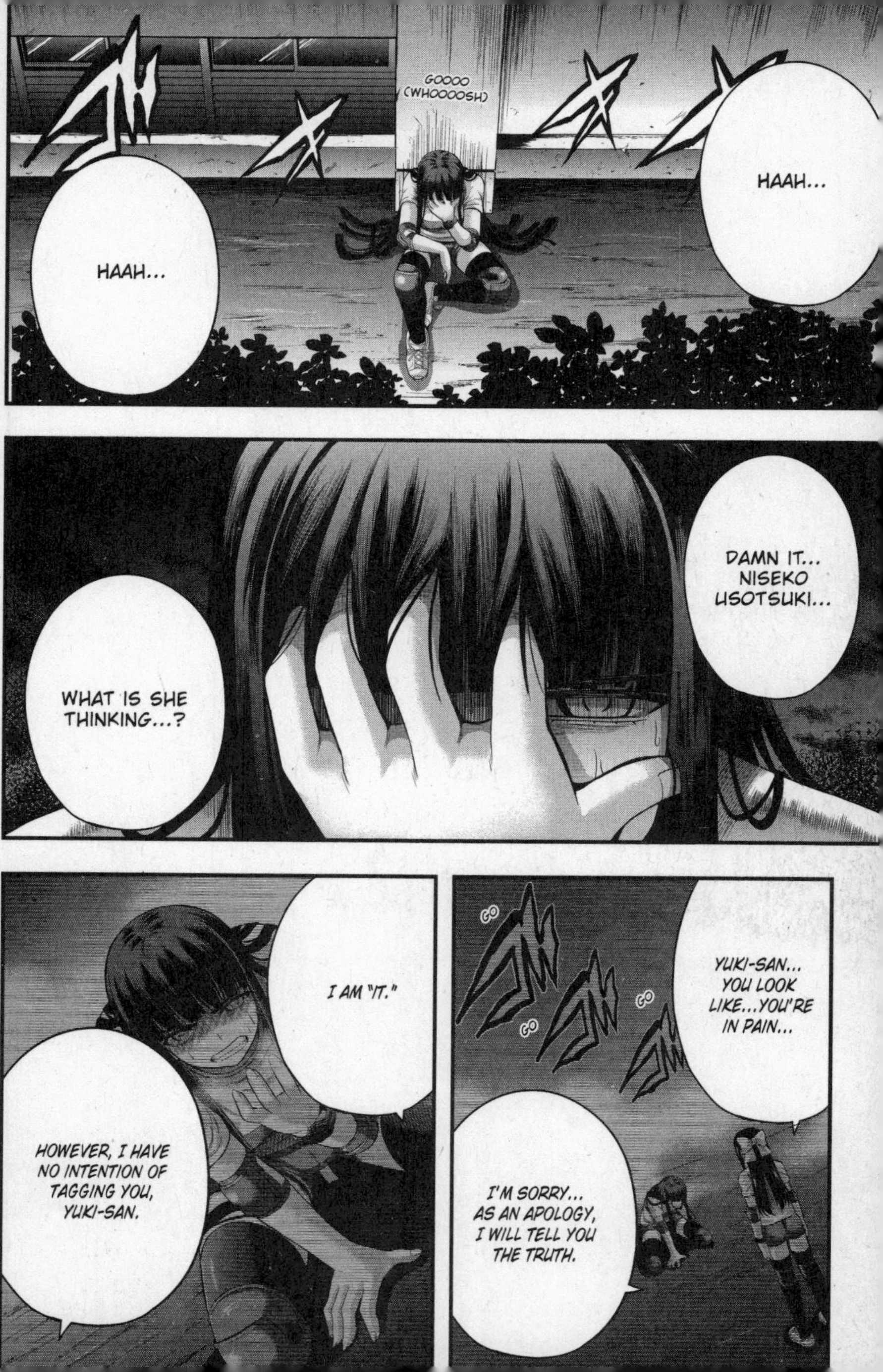
HAAH...
GOOOO (WHOOOOSH)
HAAH...
DAMN IT... NISEKO USOTSUKI...
WHAT IS SHE THINKING...?
YUKI-SAN... YOU LOOK LIKE...YOU'RE IN PAIN...
GO
GO
GO
I'M SORRY... AS AN APOLOGY, I WILL TELL YOU THE TRUTH.
I AM "IT."
HOWEVER, I HAVE NO INTENTION OF TAGGING YOU, YUKI-SAN.

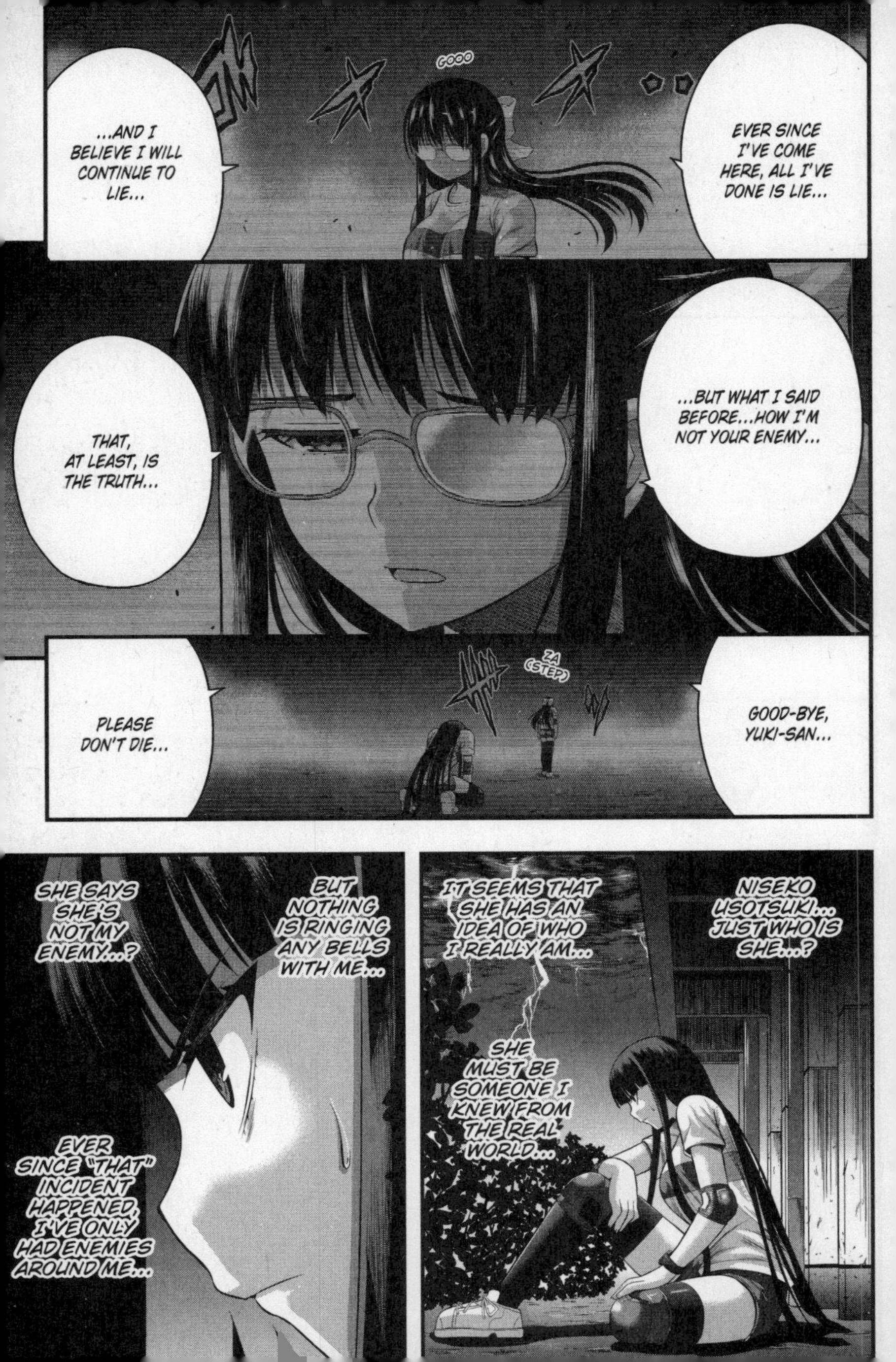
EVER SINCE I'VE COME HERE, ALL I'VE DONE IS LIE...
GOOO
...AND I BELIEVE I WILL CONTINUE TO LIE...
...BUT WHAT I SAID BEFORE...HOW I'M NOT YOUR ENEMY...
THAT, AT LEAST, IS THE TRUTH...
GOOD-BYE, YUKI-SAN...
ZA (STEP)
PLEASE DON'T DIE...
NISEKO USOTSUKI... JUST WHO IS SHE...?
IT SEEMS THAT SHE HAS AN IDEA OF WHO I REALLY AM...
SHE MUST BE SOMEONE I KNEW FROM THE REAL WORLD...
BUT NOTHING IS RINGING ANY BELLS WITH ME...
SHE SAYS SHE'S NOT MY ENEMY...?
EVER SINCE "THAT" INCIDENT HAPPENED, I'VE ONLY HAD ENEMIES AROUND ME...

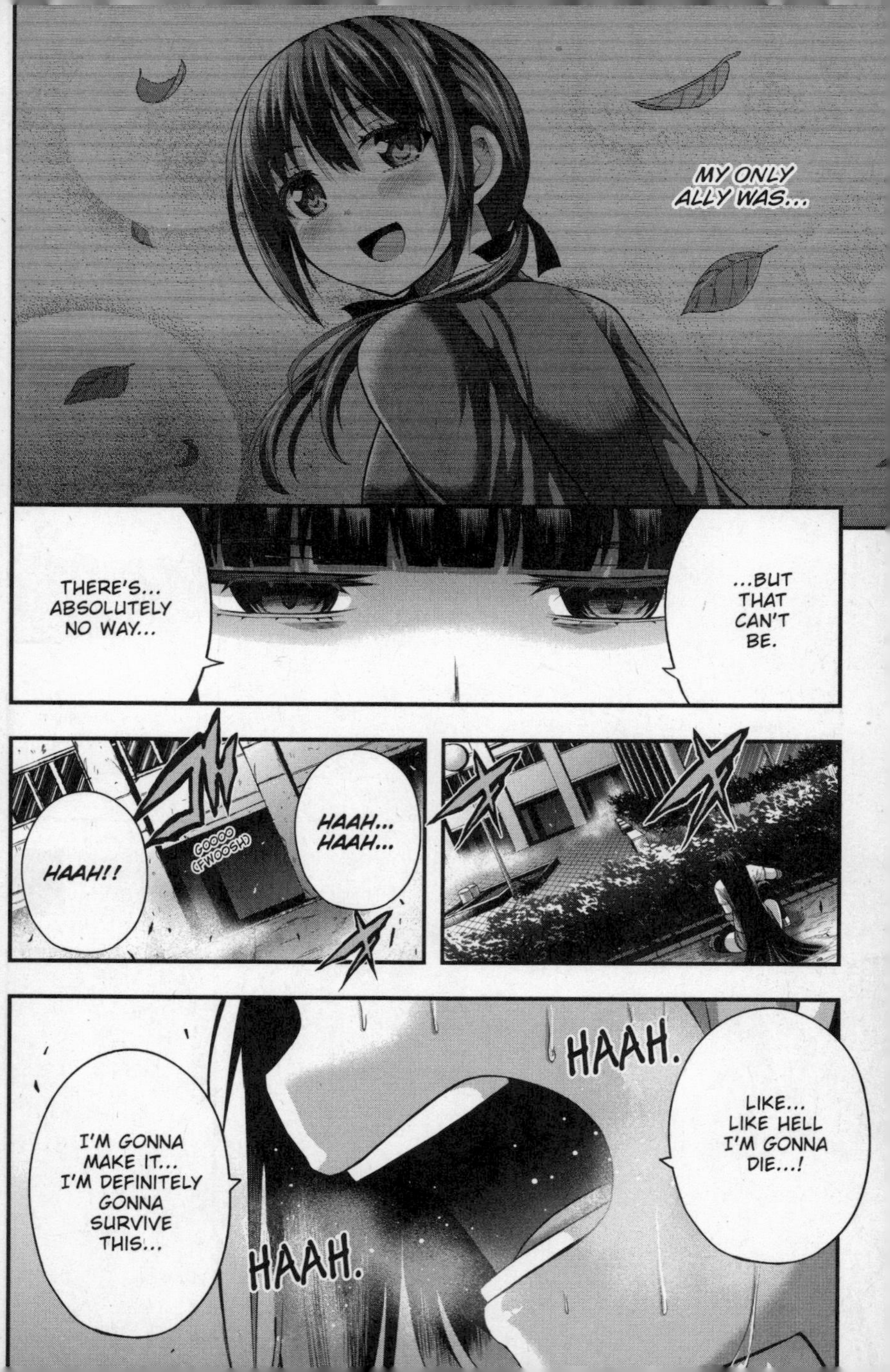
MY ONLY ALLY WAS...
...BUT THAT CAN'T BE.
THERE'S... ABSOLUTELY NO WAY...
HAAH... HAAH...
GOOOO (FWOOSH)
HAAH!!
LIKE... LIKE HELL I'M GONNA DIE...!
HAAH.
I'M GONNA MAKE IT... I'M DEFINITELY GONNA SURVIVE THIS...
HAAH.

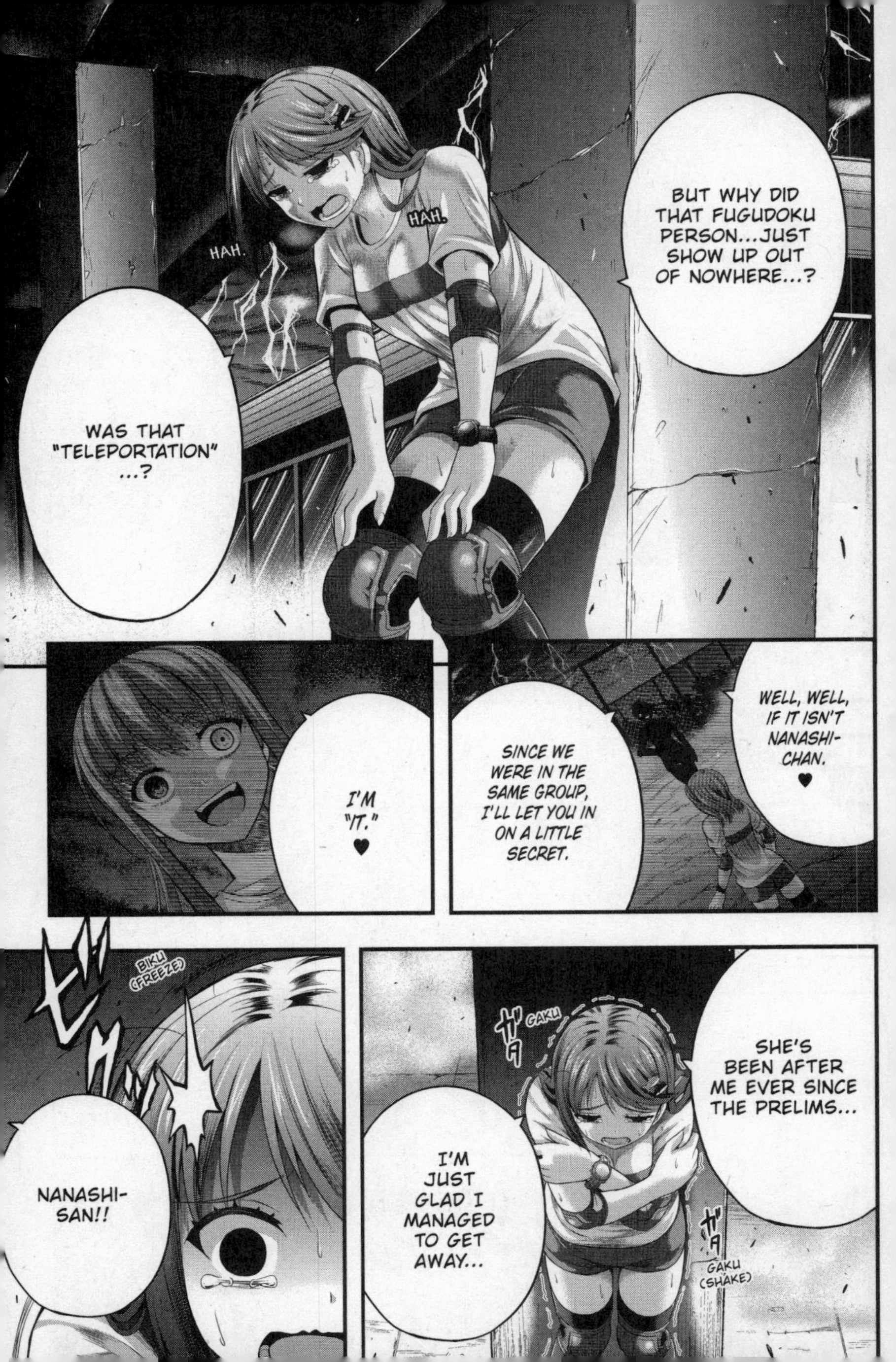
BUT WHY DID THAT FUGUDOKU PERSON...JUST SHOW UP OUT OF NOWHERE...?
HAH.
HAH.
WAS THAT "TELEPORTATION" ...?
WELL, WELL, IF IT ISN'T NANASHI-CHAN. ♥
SINCE WE WERE IN THE SAME GROUP, I'LL LET YOU IN ON A LITTLE SECRET.
I'M "IT." ♥
SHE'S BEEN AFTER ME EVER SINCE THE PRELIMS...
GAKU
I'M JUST GLAD I MANAGED TO GET AWAY...
GAKU (SHAKE)
BIKU (FREEZE)
NANASHI-SAN!!

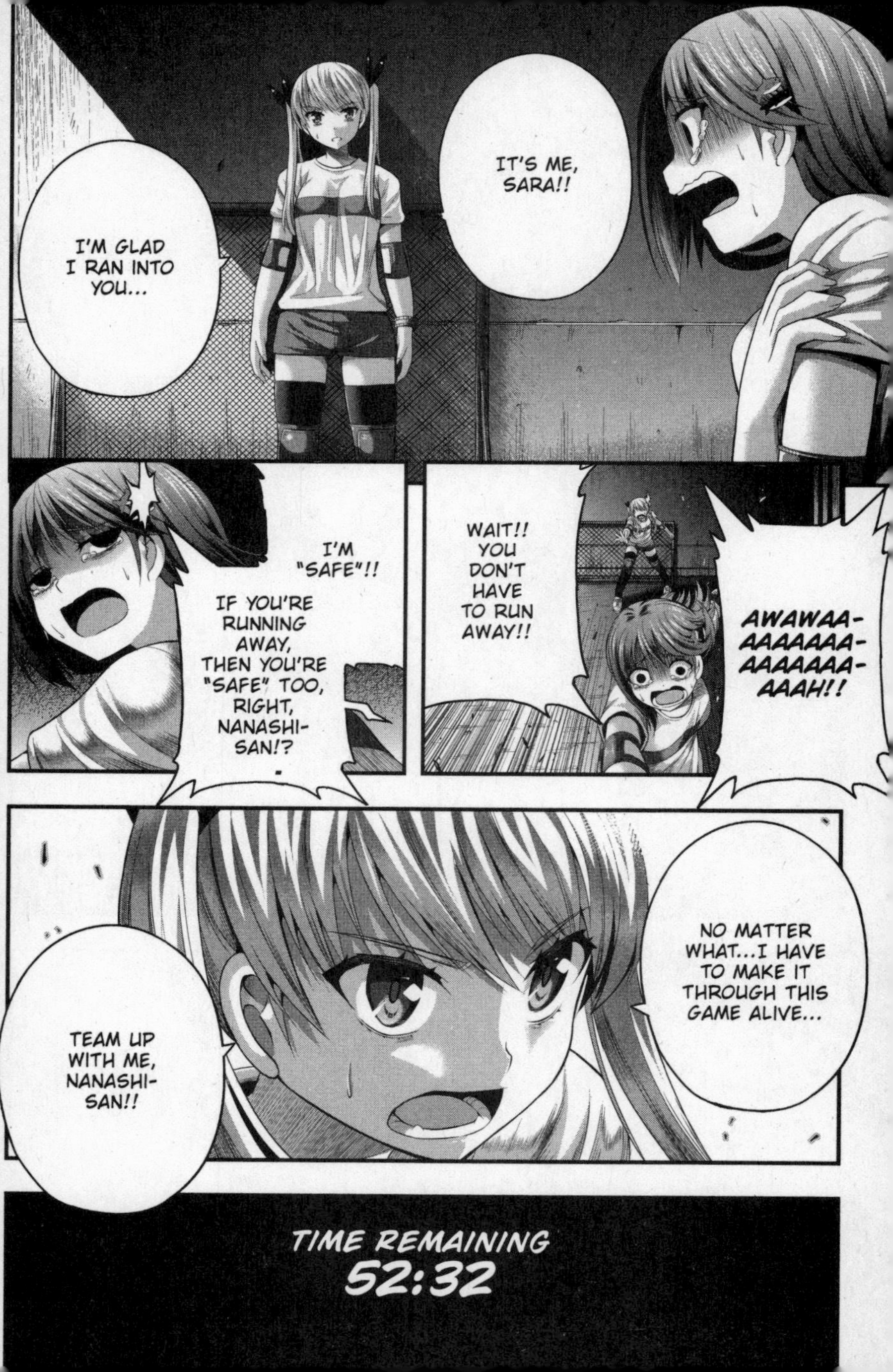
IT'S ME, SARA!!
I'M GLAD I RAN INTO YOU...
AWAWAA-AAAAAAA-AAAAAAA-AAAH!!
WAIT!! YOU DON'T HAVE TO RUN AWAY!!
I'M "SAFE"!!
IF YOU'RE RUNNING AWAY, THEN YOU'RE "SAFE" TOO, RIGHT, NANASHI-SAN!?
NO MATTER WHAT...I HAVE TO MAKE IT THROUGH THIS GAME ALIVE...
TEAM UP WITH ME, NANASHI-SAN!!
TIME REMAINING
52:32

Though You May Burn to Ash

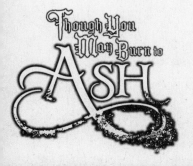

Though You May Burn to Ash

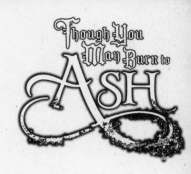

# CHAPTER 23: YOU GET WHAT YOU PAY FOR...

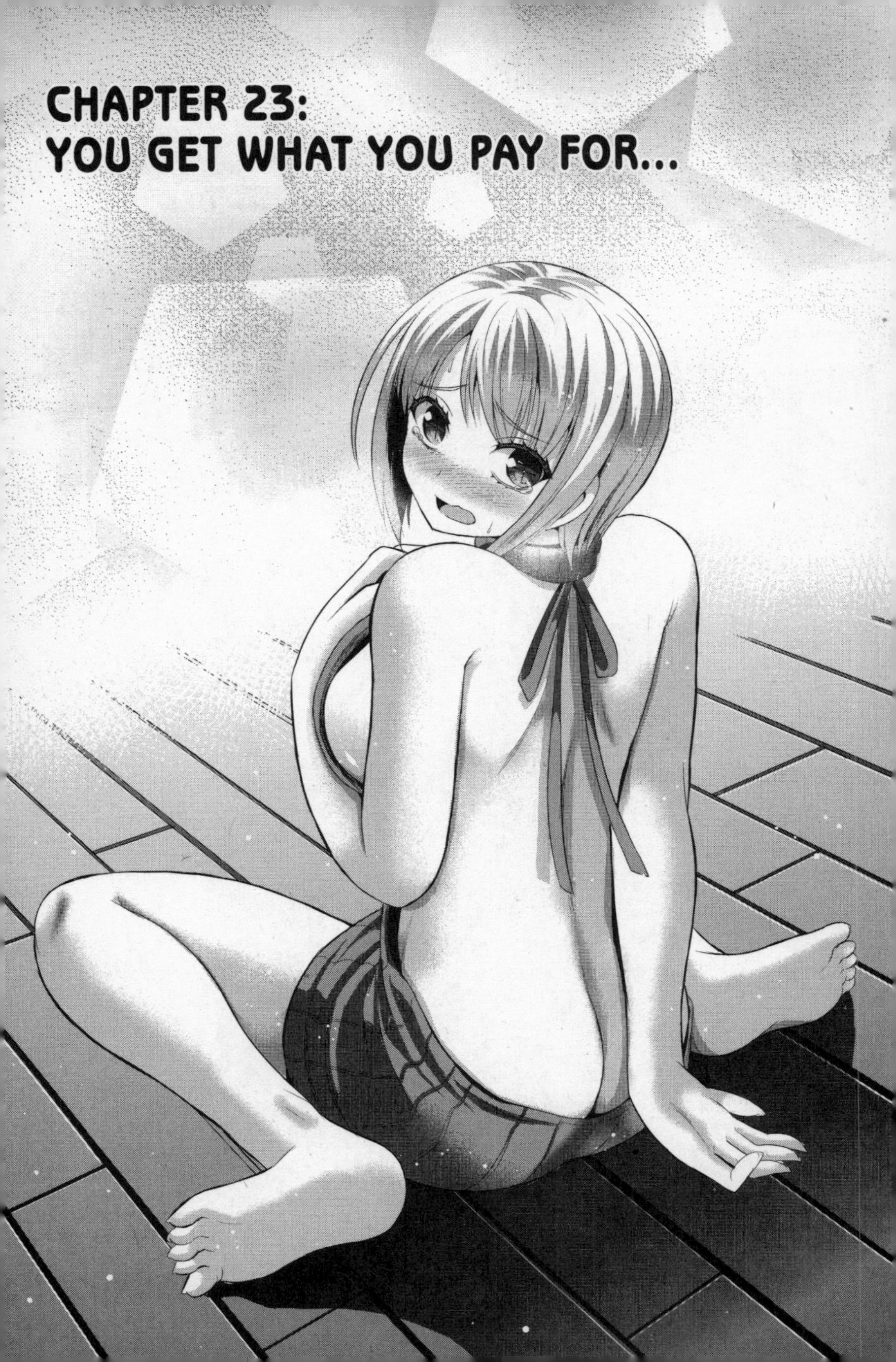

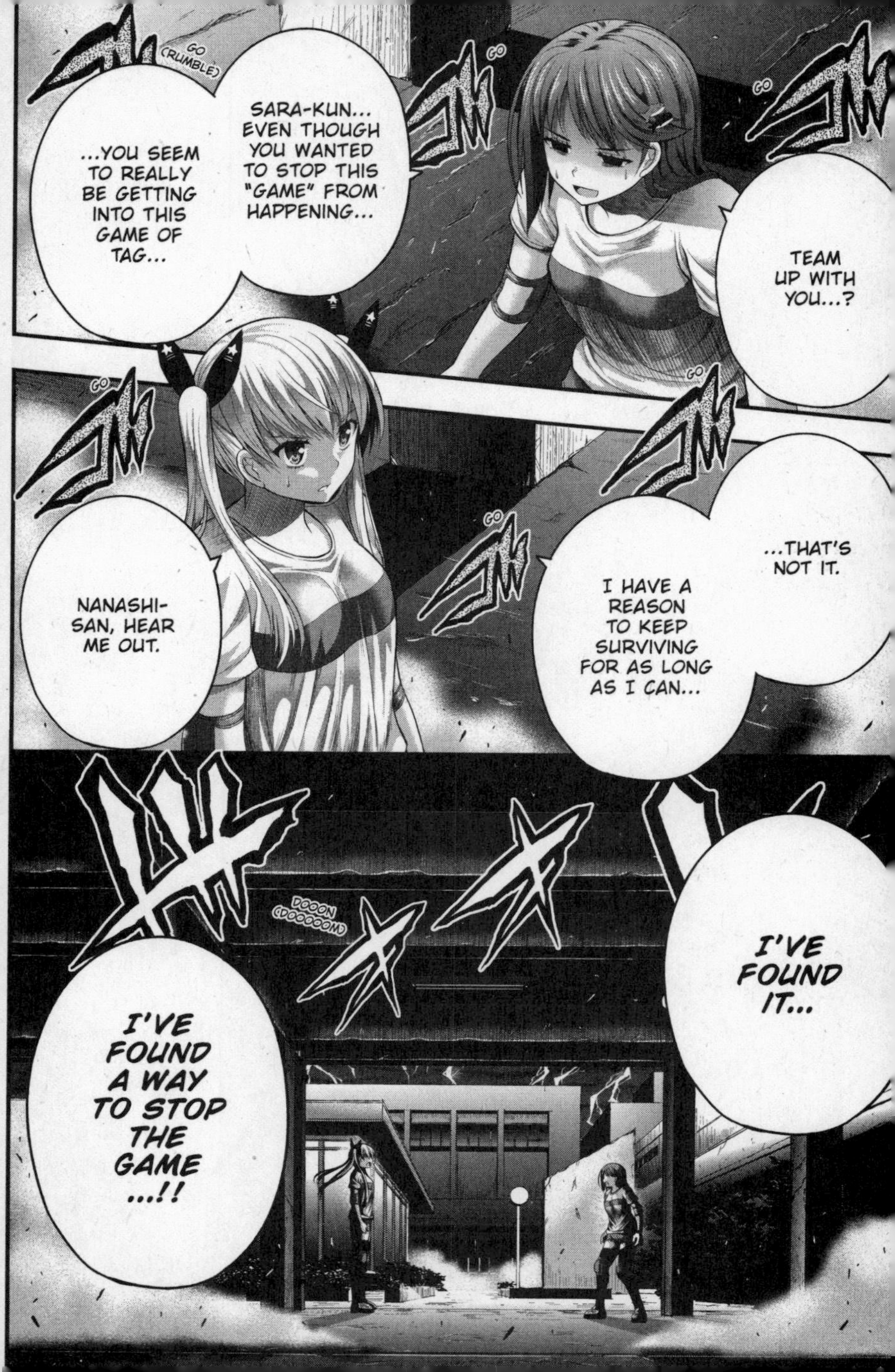
GO
GO
TEAM UP WITH YOU...?
SARA-KUN... EVEN THOUGH YOU WANTED TO STOP THIS "GAME" FROM HAPPENING...
...YOU SEEM TO REALLY BE GETTING INTO THIS GAME OF TAG...
GO (RUMBLE)
GO
...THAT'S NOT IT.
I HAVE A REASON TO KEEP SURVIVING FOR AS LONG AS I CAN...
GO
GO
NANASHI-SAN, HEAR ME OUT.
I'VE FOUND IT...
DOOON (DOOOOOM)
I'VE FOUND A WAY TO STOP THE GAME ...!!

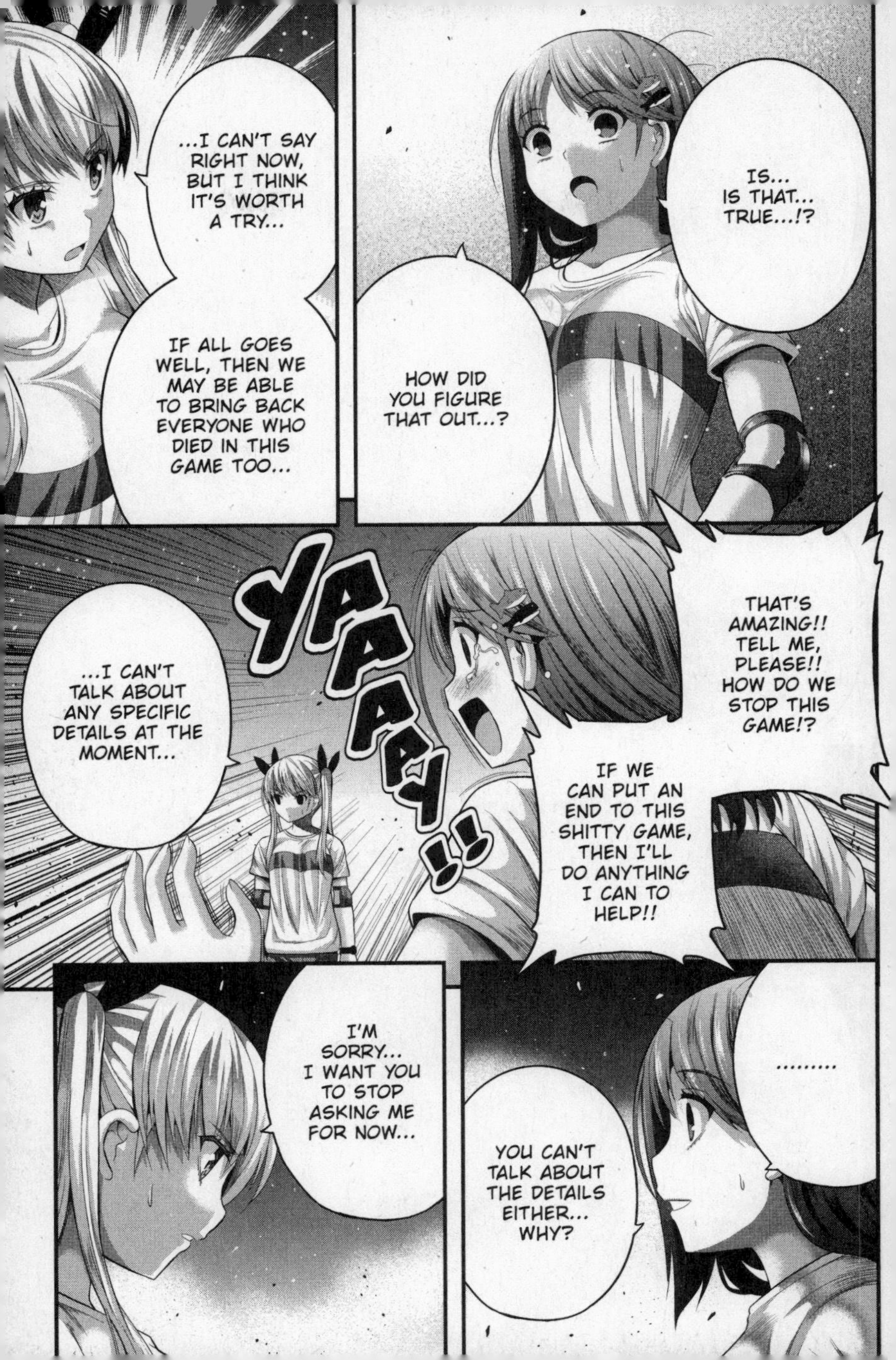
IS... IS THAT... TRUE...!?
HOW DID YOU FIGURE THAT OUT...?
...I CAN'T SAY RIGHT NOW, BUT I THINK IT'S WORTH A TRY...
IF ALL GOES WELL, THEN WE MAY BE ABLE TO BRING BACK EVERYONE WHO DIED IN THIS GAME TOO...
THAT'S AMAZING!! TELL ME, PLEASE!! HOW DO WE STOP THIS GAME!?
IF WE CAN PUT AN END TO THIS SHITTY GAME, THEN I'LL DO ANYTHING I CAN TO HELP!!
YAAAAY!!
...I CAN'T TALK ABOUT ANY SPECIFIC DETAILS AT THE MOMENT...
.........
YOU CAN'T TALK ABOUT THE DETAILS EITHER... WHY?
I'M SORRY... I WANT YOU TO STOP ASKING ME FOR NOW...

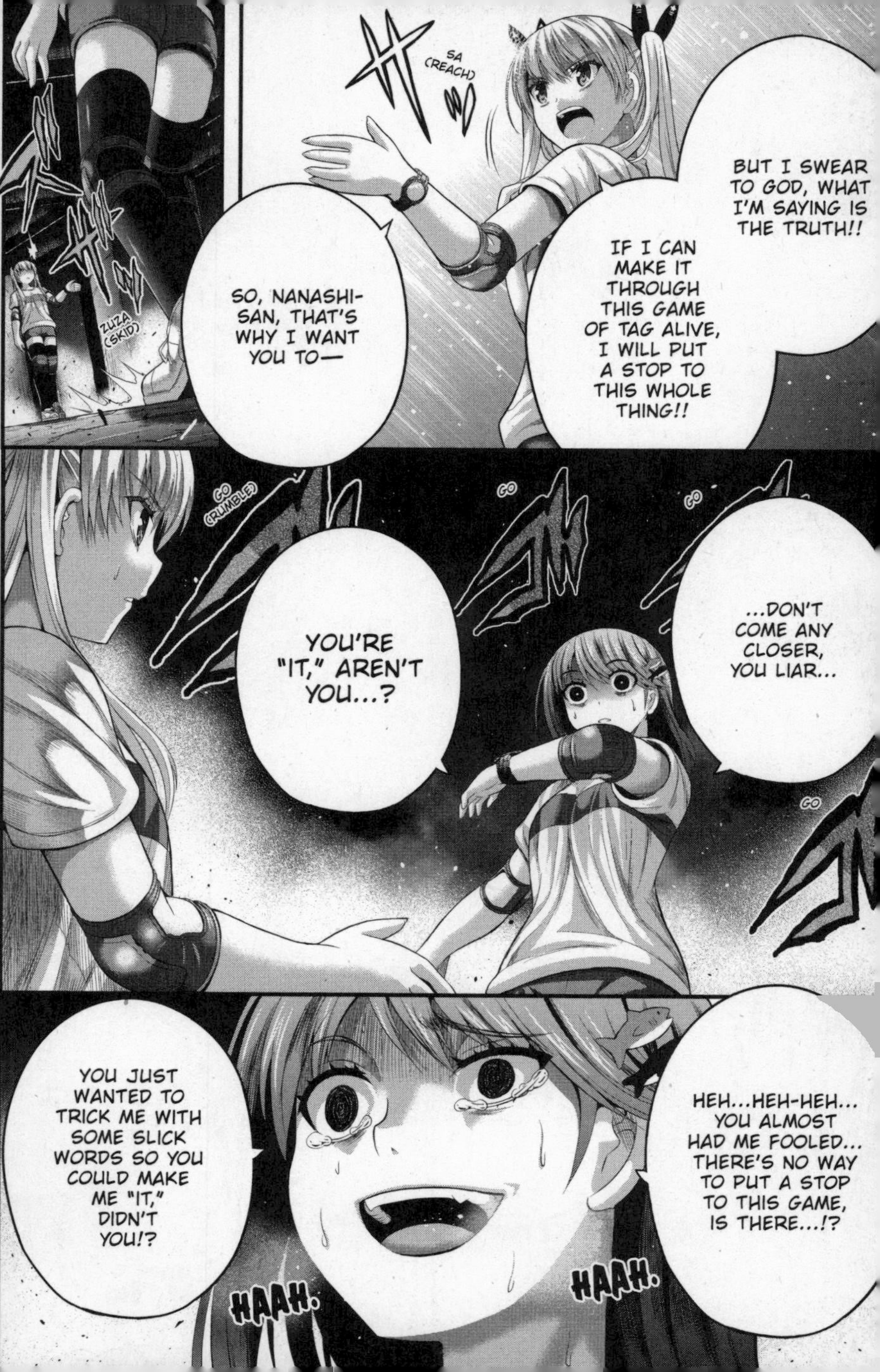
BUT I SWEAR TO GOD, WHAT I'M SAYING IS THE TRUTH!!
IF I CAN MAKE IT THROUGH THIS GAME OF TAG ALIVE, I WILL PUT A STOP TO THIS WHOLE THING!!
SA (REACH)
SO, NANASHI-SAN, THAT'S WHY I WANT YOU TO—
ZUZA (SKID)
...DON'T COME ANY CLOSER, YOU LIAR...
GO
GO
GO (RUMBLE)
YOU'RE "IT," AREN'T YOU...?
GO
HEH...HEH-HEH... YOU ALMOST HAD ME FOOLED... THERE'S NO WAY TO PUT A STOP TO THIS GAME, IS THERE...!?
HAAH.
YOU JUST WANTED TO TRICK ME WITH SOME SLICK WORDS SO YOU COULD MAKE ME "IT," DIDN'T YOU!?
HAAH.

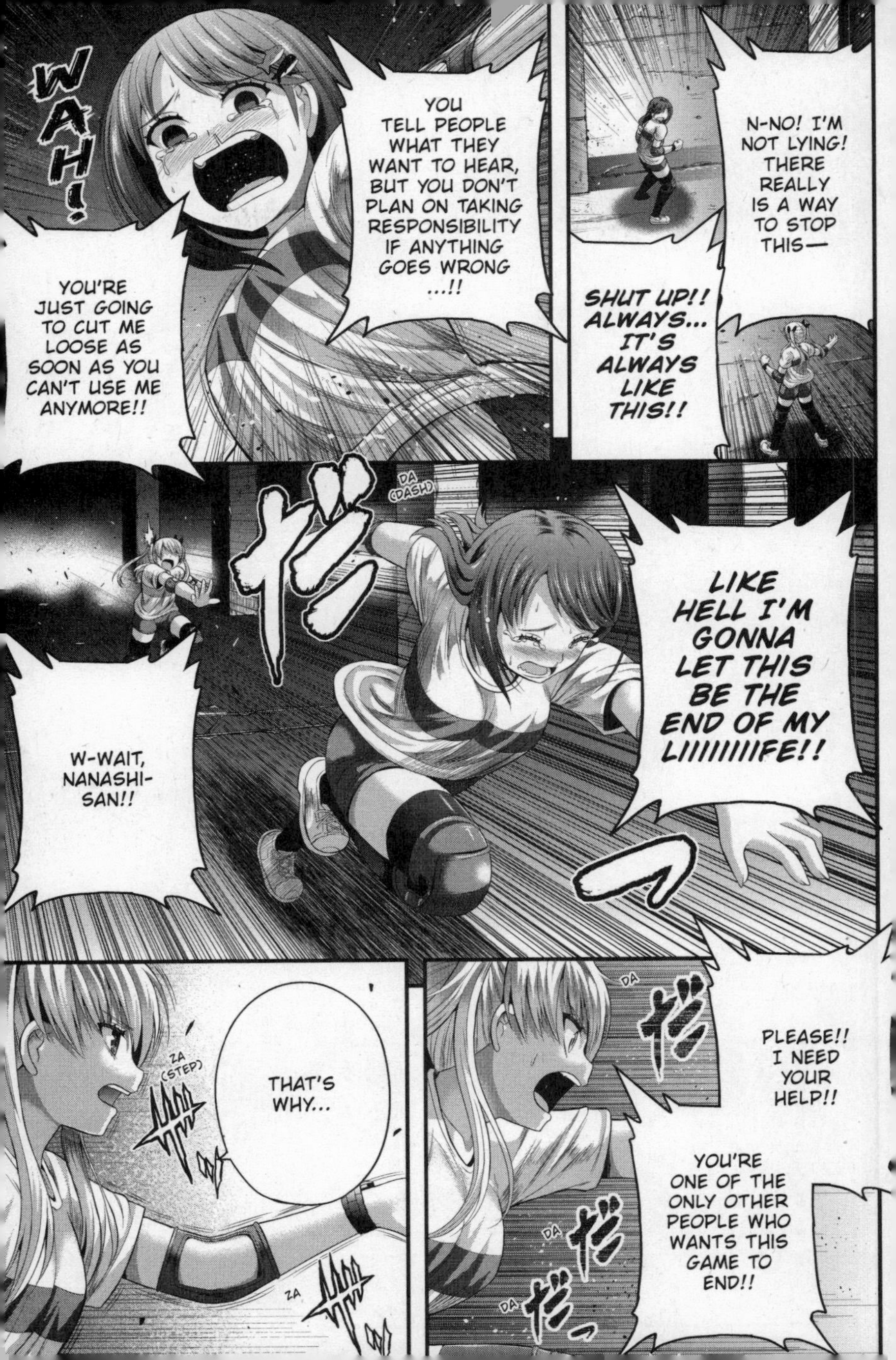
N-NO! I'M NOT LYING! THERE REALLY IS A WAY TO STOP THIS—
SHUT UP!! ALWAYS... IT'S ALWAYS LIKE THIS!!
WAH!
YOU TELL PEOPLE WHAT THEY WANT TO HEAR, BUT YOU DON'T PLAN ON TAKING RESPONSIBILITY IF ANYTHING GOES WRONG ...!!
YOU'RE JUST GOING TO CUT ME LOOSE AS SOON AS YOU CAN'T USE ME ANYMORE!!
LIKE HELL I'M GONNA LET THIS BE THE END OF MY LIIIIIIIIFE!!
DA (DASH)
W-WAIT, NANASHI-SAN!!
DA
PLEASE!! I NEED YOUR HELP!!
YOU'RE ONE OF THE ONLY OTHER PEOPLE WHO WANTS THIS GAME TO END!!
DA
DA
ZA (STEP)
THAT'S WHY...
ZA

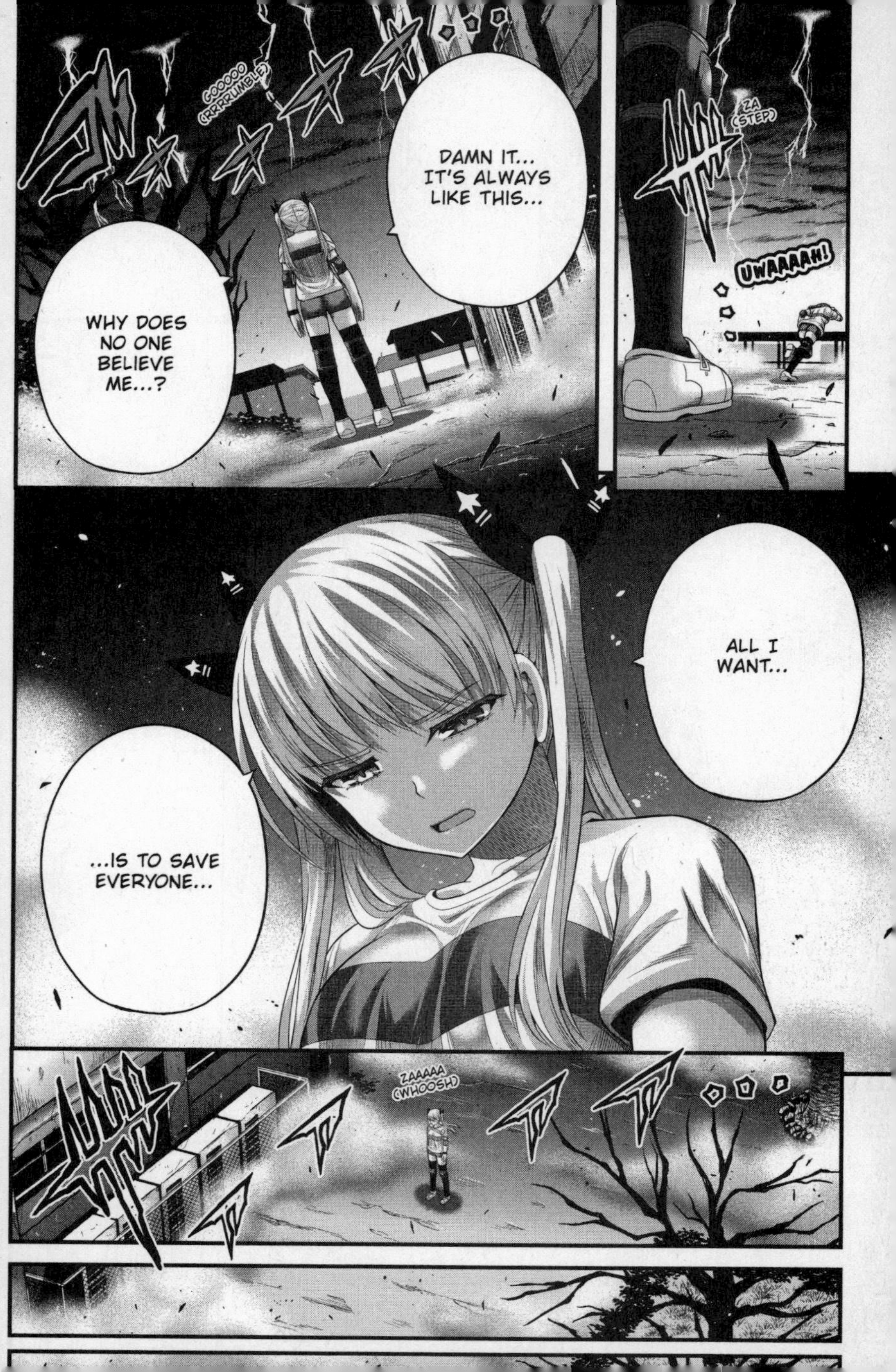
ZA (STEP)
UWAAAAH!
GOOOOOO (RRRRUMBLE)
DAMN IT... IT'S ALWAYS LIKE THIS...
WHY DOES NO ONE BELIEVE ME...?
ALL I WANT...
...IS TO SAVE EVERYONE...
ZAAAAA (WHOOSH)

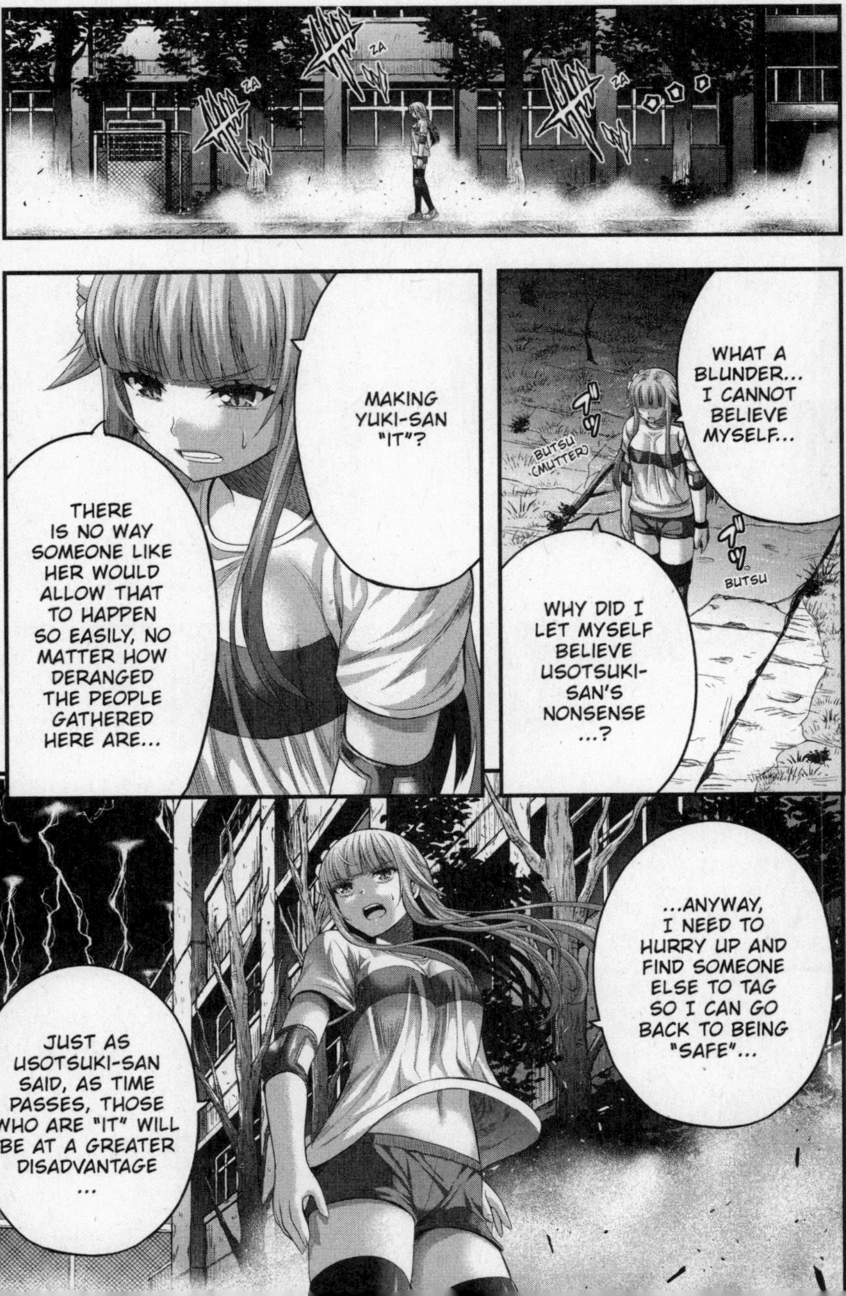
ZA
ZA
ZA
WHAT A BLUNDER... I CANNOT BELIEVE MYSELF...
BUTSU (MUTTER)
BUTSU
WHY DID I LET MYSELF BELIEVE USOTSUKI-SAN'S NONSENSE ...?
MAKING YUKI-SAN "IT"?
THERE IS NO WAY SOMEONE LIKE HER WOULD ALLOW THAT TO HAPPEN SO EASILY, NO MATTER HOW DERANGED THE PEOPLE GATHERED HERE ARE...
...ANYWAY, I NEED TO HURRY UP AND FIND SOMEONE ELSE TO TAG SO I CAN GO BACK TO BEING "SAFE"...
JUST AS USOTSUKI-SAN SAID, AS TIME PASSES, THOSE WHO ARE "IT" WILL BE AT A GREATER DISADVANTAGE ...

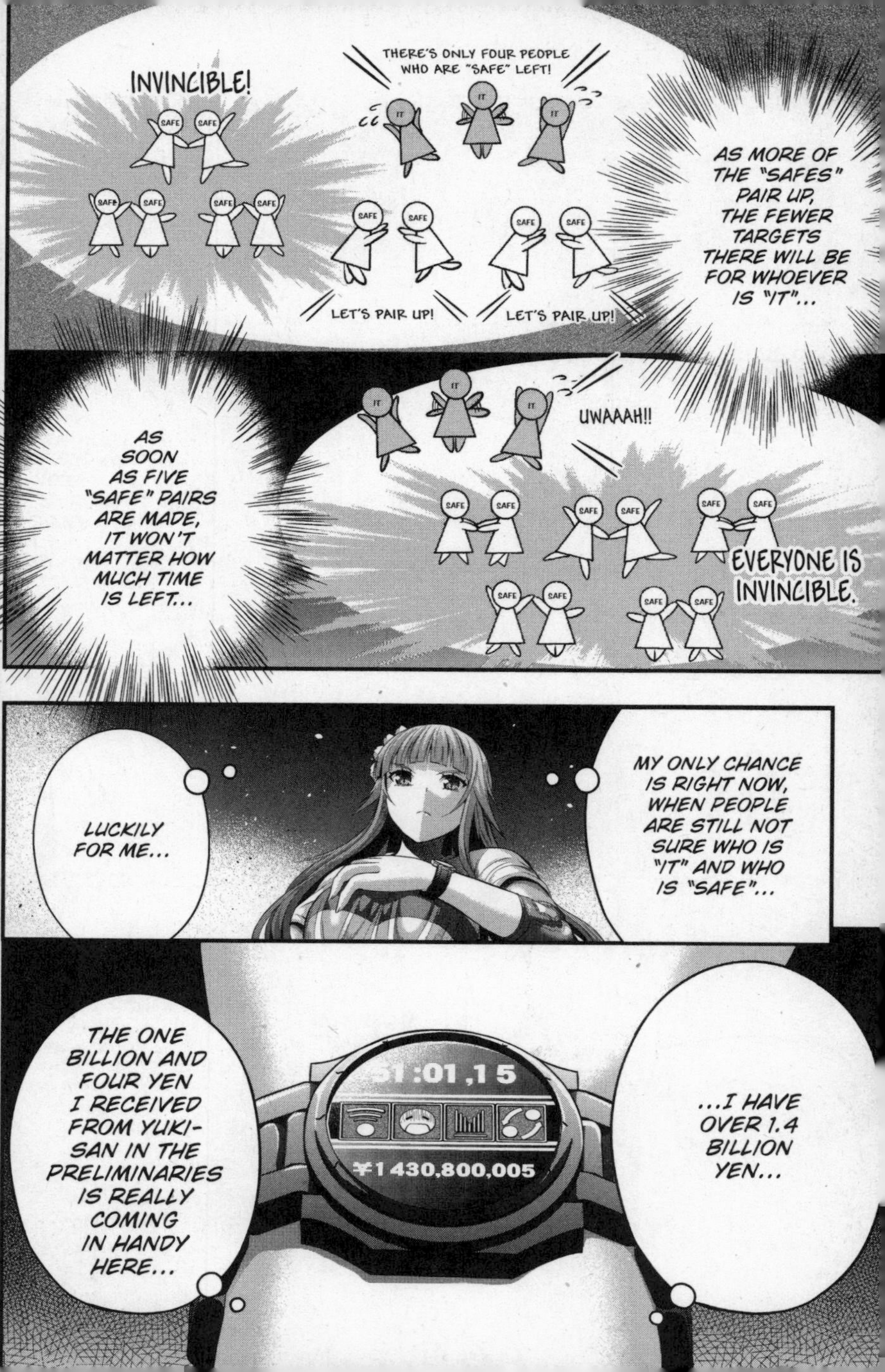
AS MORE OF THE "SAFES" PAIR UP, THE FEWER TARGETS THERE WILL BE FOR WHOEVER IS "IT"...
THERE'S ONLY FOUR PEOPLE WHO ARE "SAFE" LEFT!
INVINCIBLE!
LET'S PAIR UP!
LET'S PAIR UP!
UWAAAH!!
EVERYONE IS INVINCIBLE.
AS SOON AS FIVE "SAFE" PAIRS ARE MADE, IT WON'T MATTER HOW MUCH TIME IS LEFT...
MY ONLY CHANCE IS RIGHT NOW, WHEN PEOPLE ARE STILL NOT SURE WHO IS "IT" AND WHO IS "SAFE"...
LUCKILY FOR ME...
...I HAVE OVER 1.4 BILLION YEN...
¥1430,800,005
THE ONE BILLION AND FOUR YEN I RECEIVED FROM YUKI-SAN IN THE PRELIMINARIES IS REALLY COMING IN HANDY HERE...

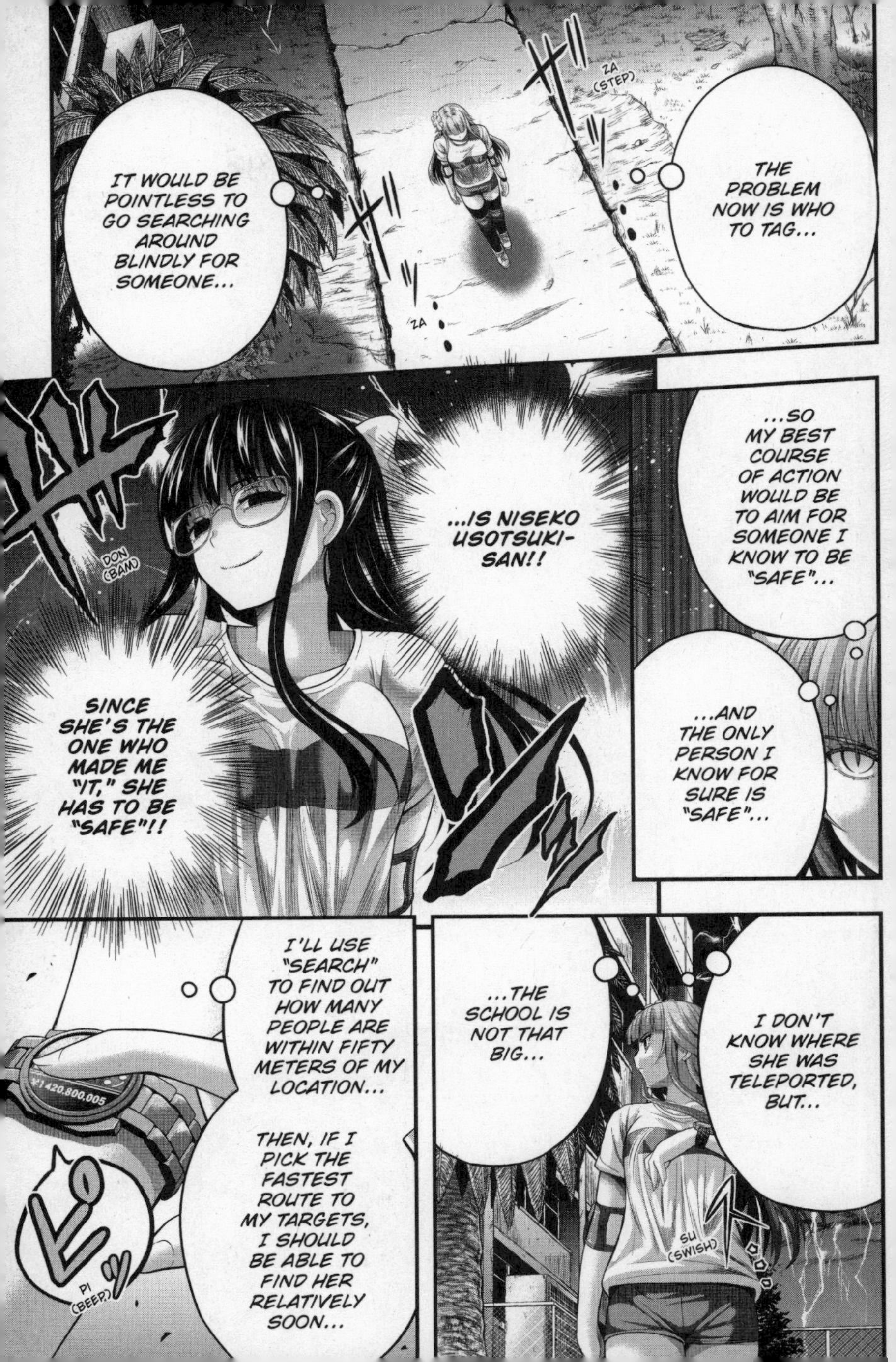
ZA (STEP)
THE PROBLEM NOW IS WHO TO TAG...
IT WOULD BE POINTLESS TO GO SEARCHING AROUND BLINDLY FOR SOMEONE...
ZA
...SO MY BEST COURSE OF ACTION WOULD BE TO AIM FOR SOMEONE I KNOW TO BE "SAFE"...
...AND THE ONLY PERSON I KNOW FOR SURE IS "SAFE"...
...IS NISEKO USOTSUKI-SAN!!
DON (BAM)
SINCE SHE'S THE ONE WHO MADE ME "IT," SHE HAS TO BE "SAFE"!!
I DON'T KNOW WHERE SHE WAS TELEPORTED, BUT...
...THE SCHOOL IS NOT THAT BIG...
SU (SWISH)
I'LL USE "SEARCH" TO FIND OUT HOW MANY PEOPLE ARE WITHIN FIFTY METERS OF MY LOCATION...
THEN, IF I PICK THE FASTEST ROUTE TO MY TARGETS, I SHOULD BE ABLE TO FIND HER RELATIVELY SOON...
¥1420.800.005
PI (BEEP)

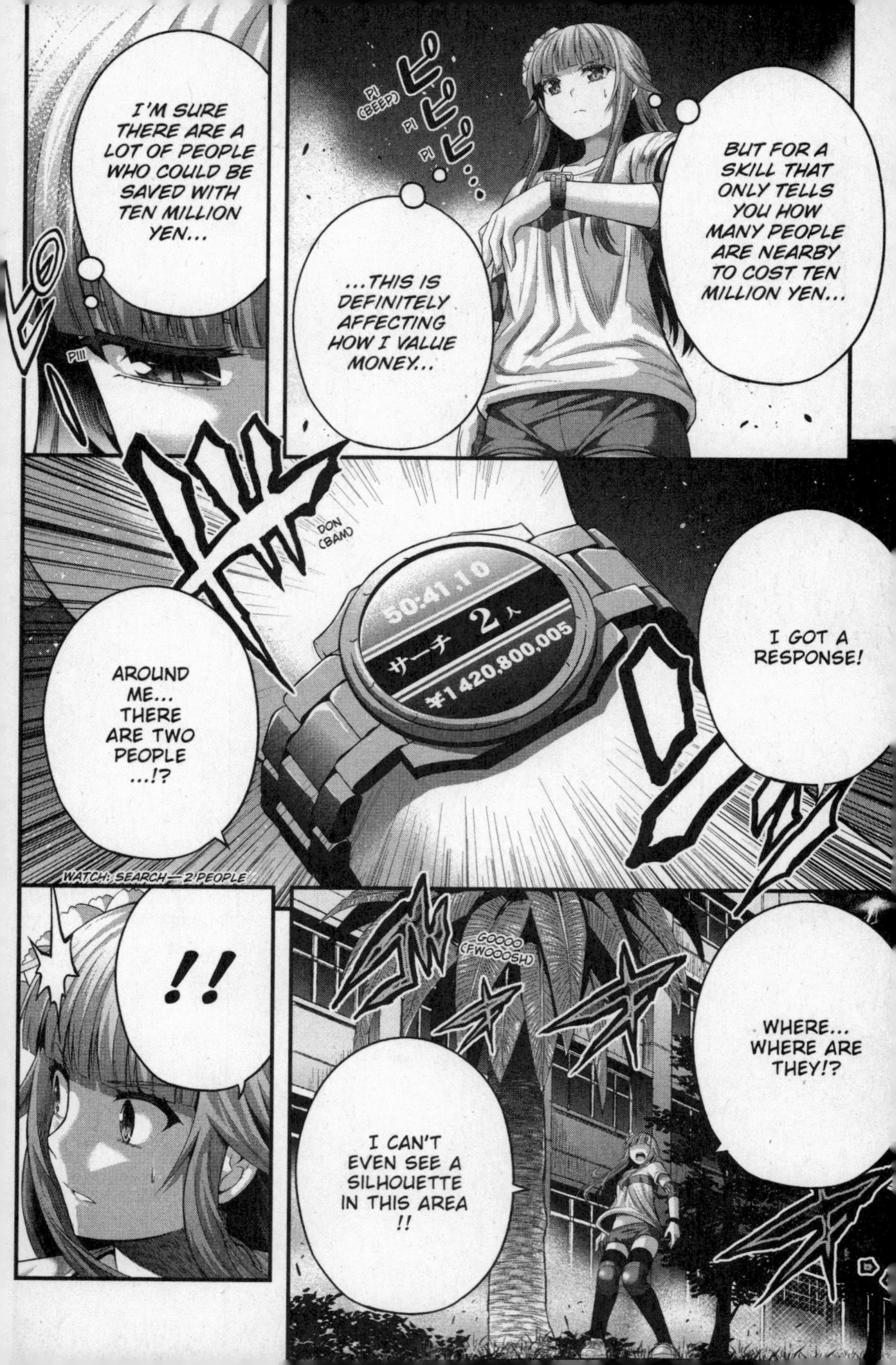
PI (BEEP) PI PI
BUT FOR A SKILL THAT ONLY TELLS YOU HOW MANY PEOPLE ARE NEARBY TO COST TEN MILLION YEN...
...THIS IS DEFINITELY AFFECTING HOW I VALUE MONEY...
I'M SURE THERE ARE A LOT OF PEOPLE WHO COULD BE SAVED WITH TEN MILLION YEN...
PIII
I GOT A RESPONSE!
50:41.10
サーチ 2人
¥1420,800,005
DON (BAM)
AROUND ME... THERE ARE TWO PEOPLE ...!?
WATCH: SEARCH—2 PEOPLE
GOOOO (FWOOOSH)
WHERE... WHERE ARE THEY!?
I CAN'T EVEN SEE A SILHOUETTE IN THIS AREA !!
!!

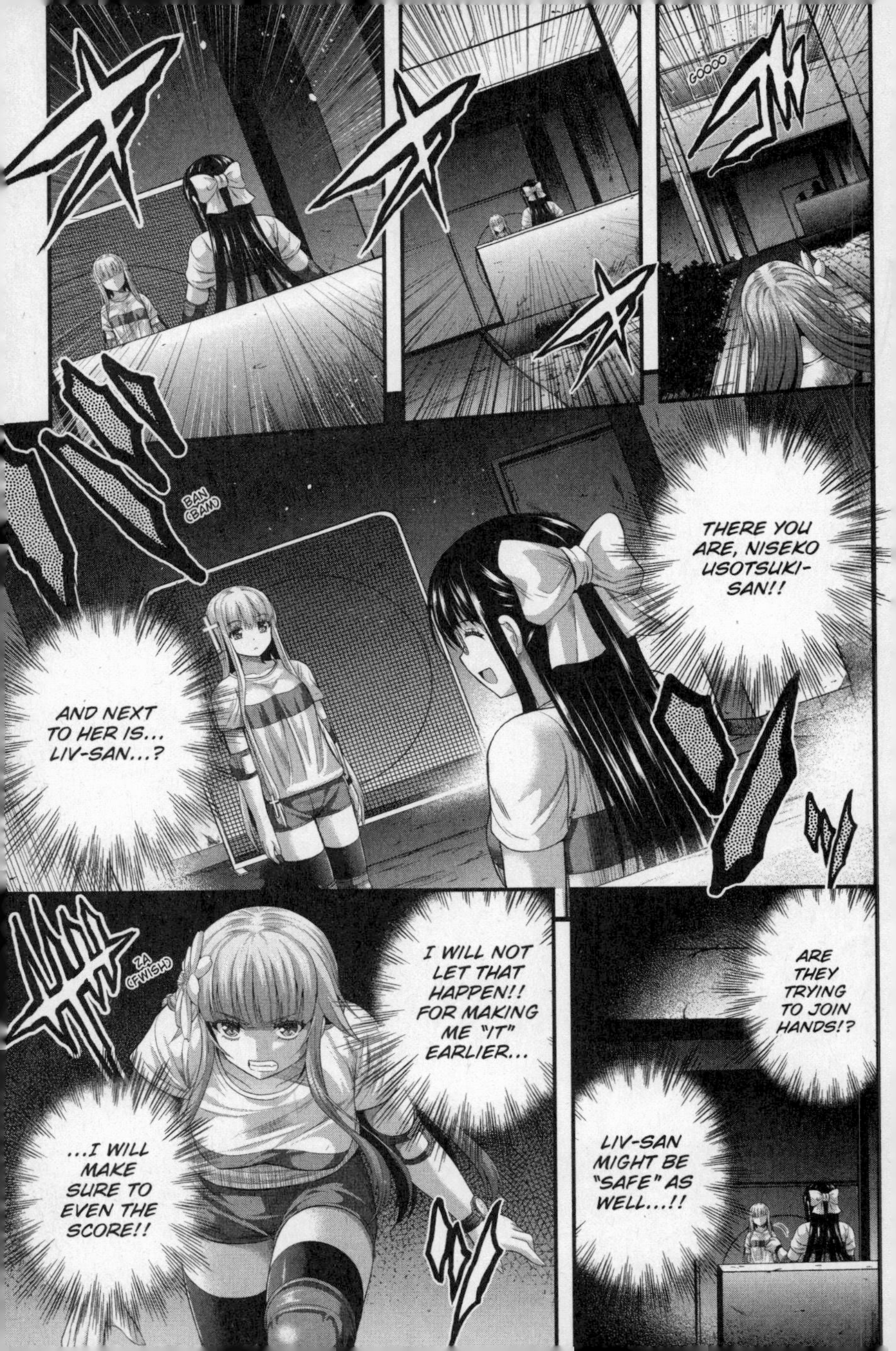
GOOOO
THERE YOU ARE, NISEKO USOTSUKI-SAN!!
BAN (BAM)
AND NEXT TO HER IS... LIV-SAN...?
ARE THEY TRYING TO JOIN HANDS!?
LIV-SAN MIGHT BE "SAFE" AS WELL...!!
I WILL NOT LET THAT HAPPEN!! FOR MAKING ME "IT" EARLIER...
ZA (FWISH)
...I WILL MAKE SURE TO EVEN THE SCORE!!

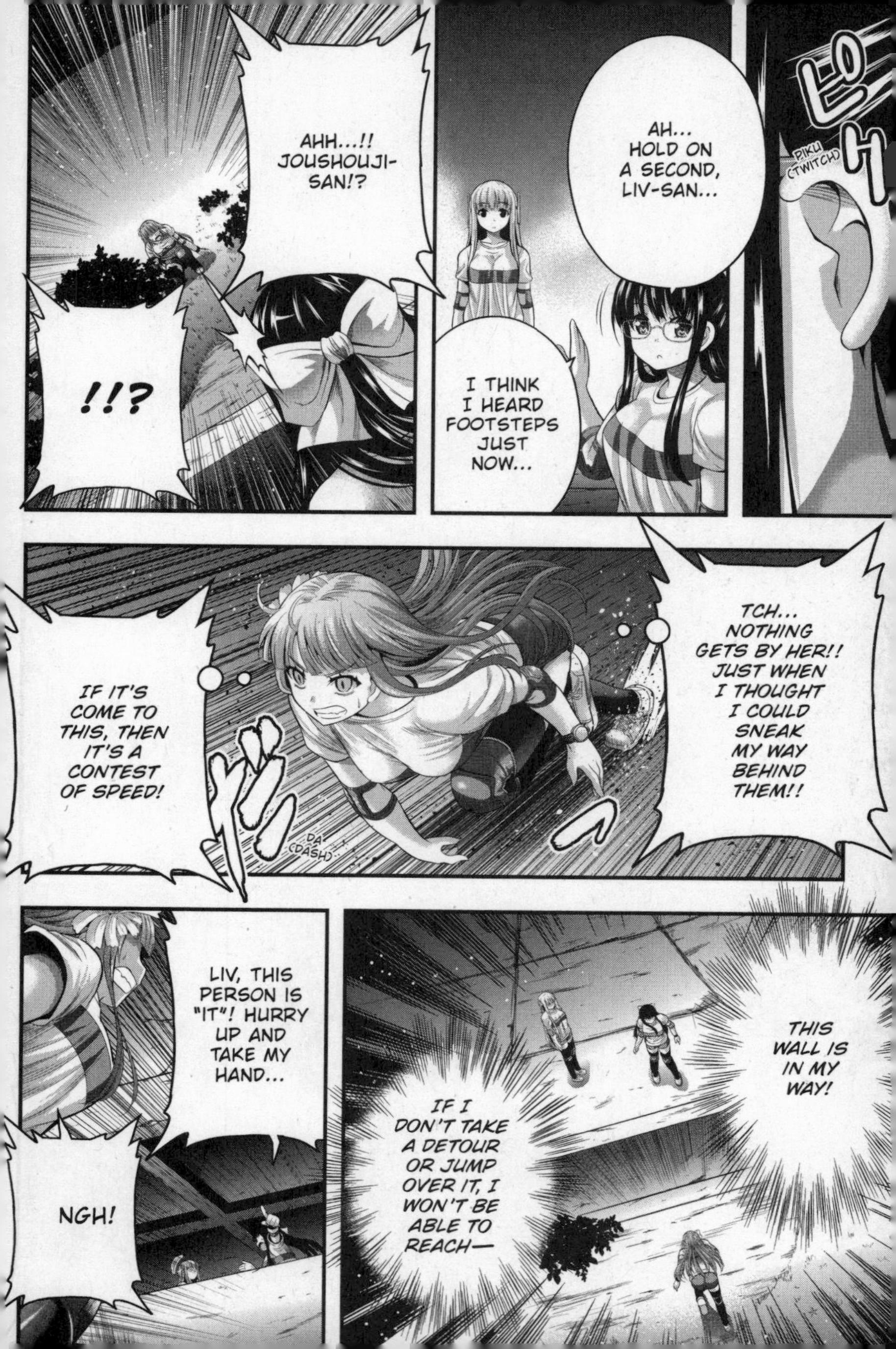
PIKU (TWITCH)
AH... HOLD ON A SECOND, LIV-SAN...
I THINK I HEARD FOOTSTEPS JUST NOW...
AHH...!! JOUSHOUJI-SAN!?
!!?
TCH... NOTHING GETS BY HER!! JUST WHEN I THOUGHT I COULD SNEAK MY WAY BEHIND THEM!!
DA (DASH)
IF IT'S COME TO THIS, THEN IT'S A CONTEST OF SPEED!
THIS WALL IS IN MY WAY!
IF I DON'T TAKE A DETOUR OR JUMP OVER IT, I WON'T BE ABLE TO REACH—
LIV, THIS PERSON IS "IT"! HURRY UP AND TAKE MY HAND...
NGH!

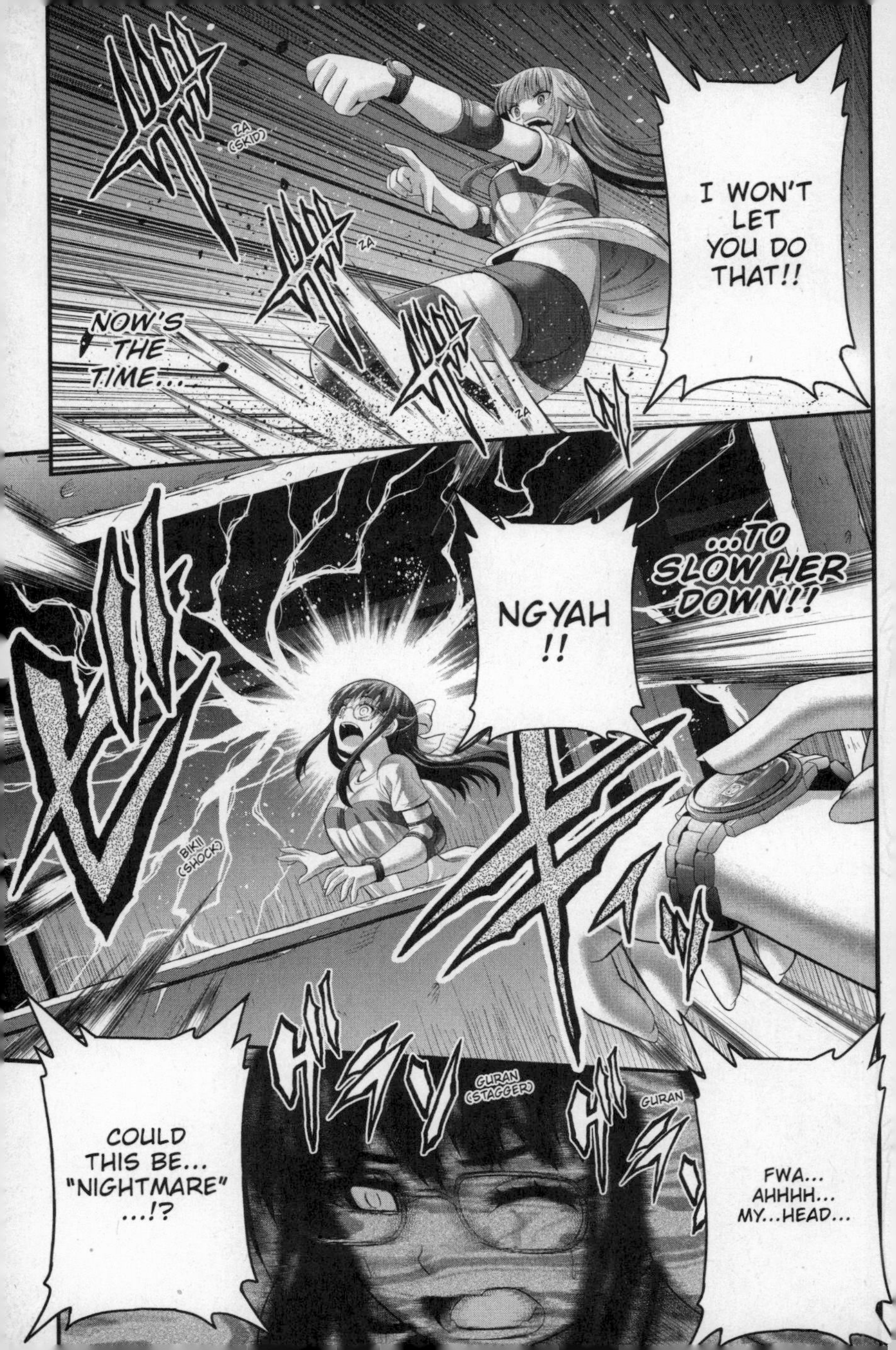
I WON'T LET YOU DO THAT!!
ZA (SKID)
ZA
ZA
NOW'S THE TIME...
...TO SLOW HER DOWN!!
NGYAH!!
BIKII (SHOCK)
FWA... AHHHH... MY...HEAD...
GURAN
GURAN (STAGGER)
COULD THIS BE... "NIGHTMARE" ...!?

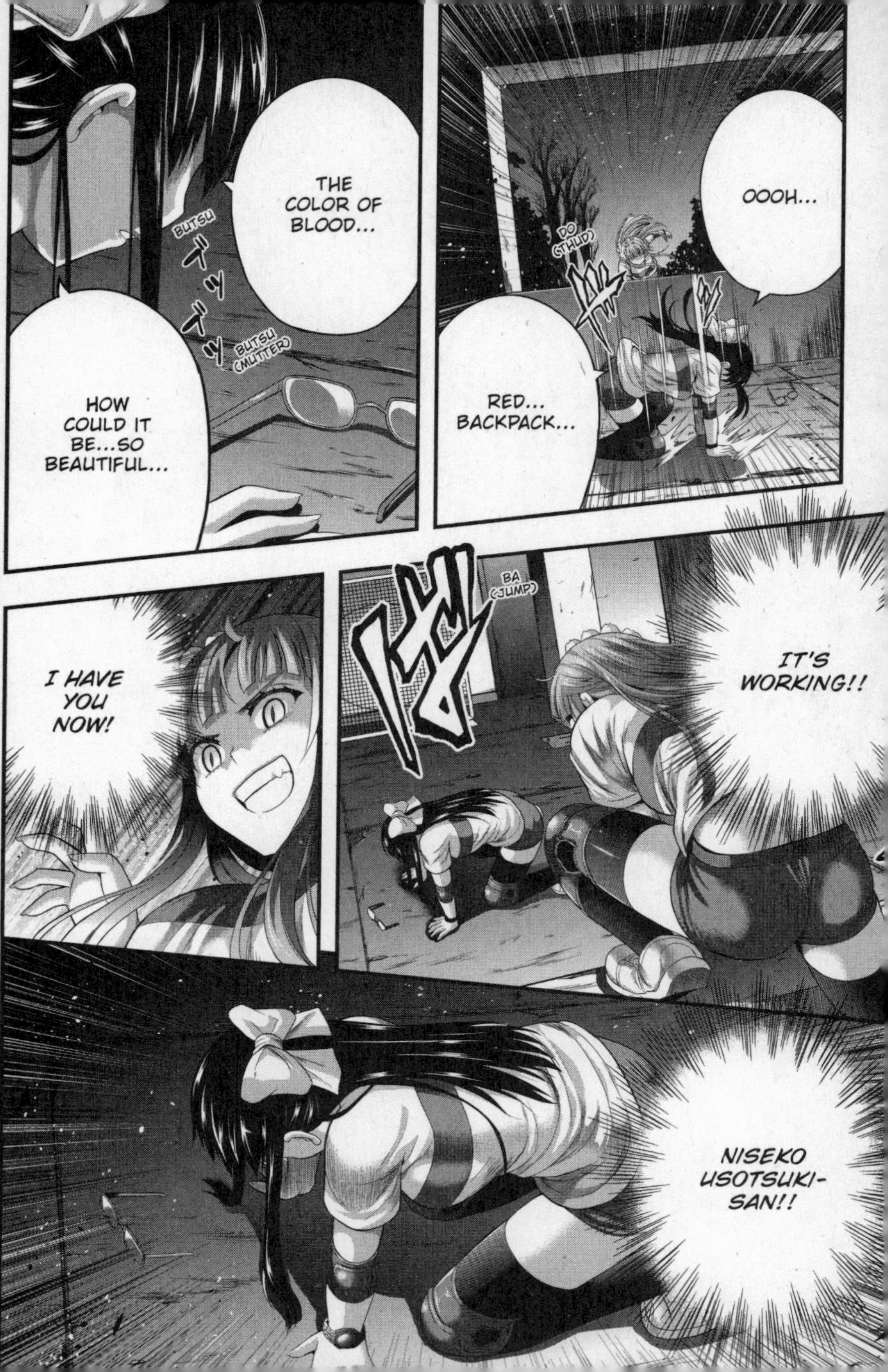
OOOH...
DO (THUD)
RED... BACKPACK...
THE COLOR OF BLOOD...
BUTSU
BUTSU (MUTTER)
HOW COULD IT BE...SO BEAUTIFUL...
IT'S WORKING!!
BA (JUMP)
I HAVE YOU NOW!
NISEKO USOTSUKI-SAN!!

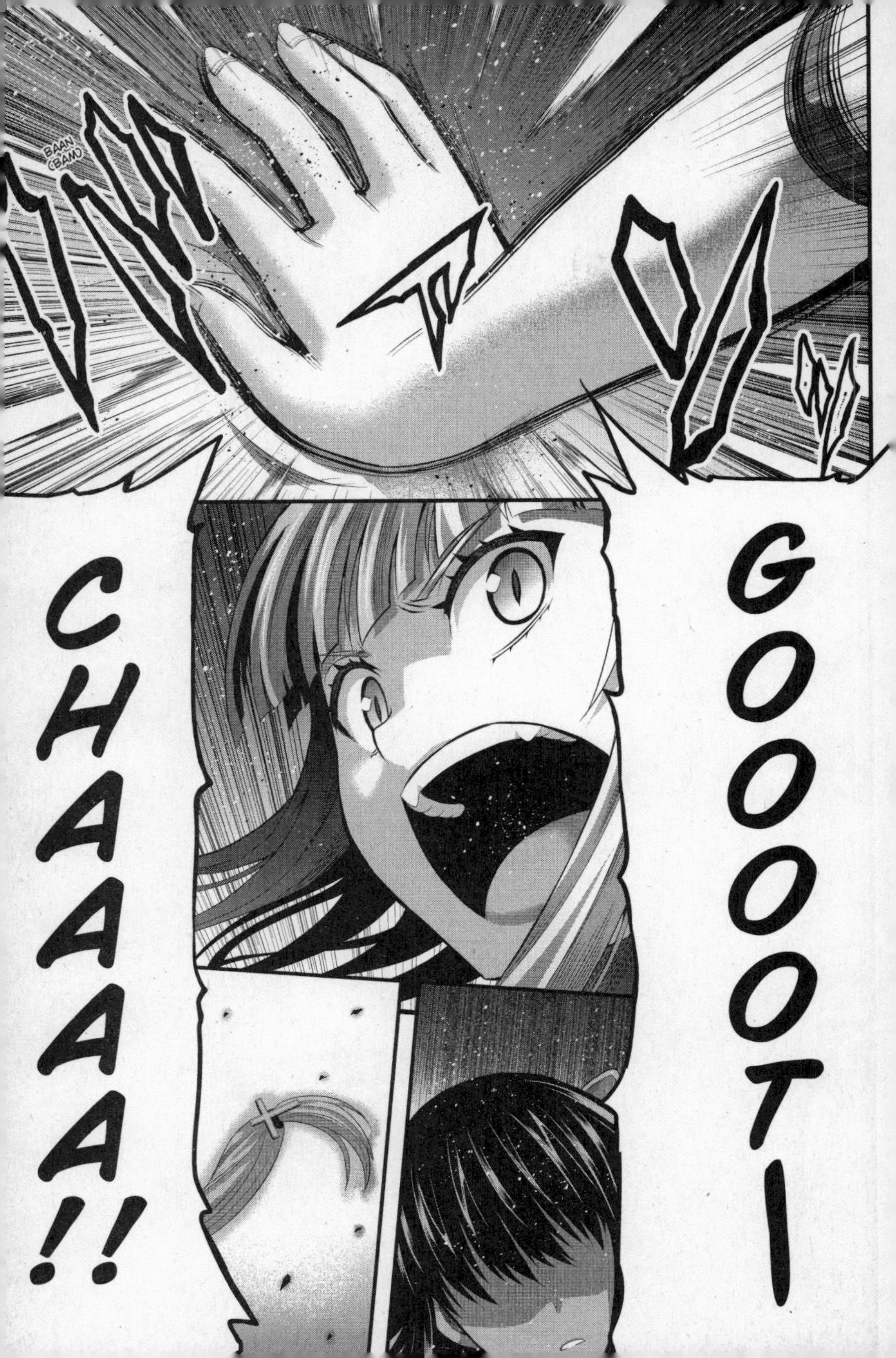
BAAN
(BAM)
GOOOOTI
CHAAAA!!

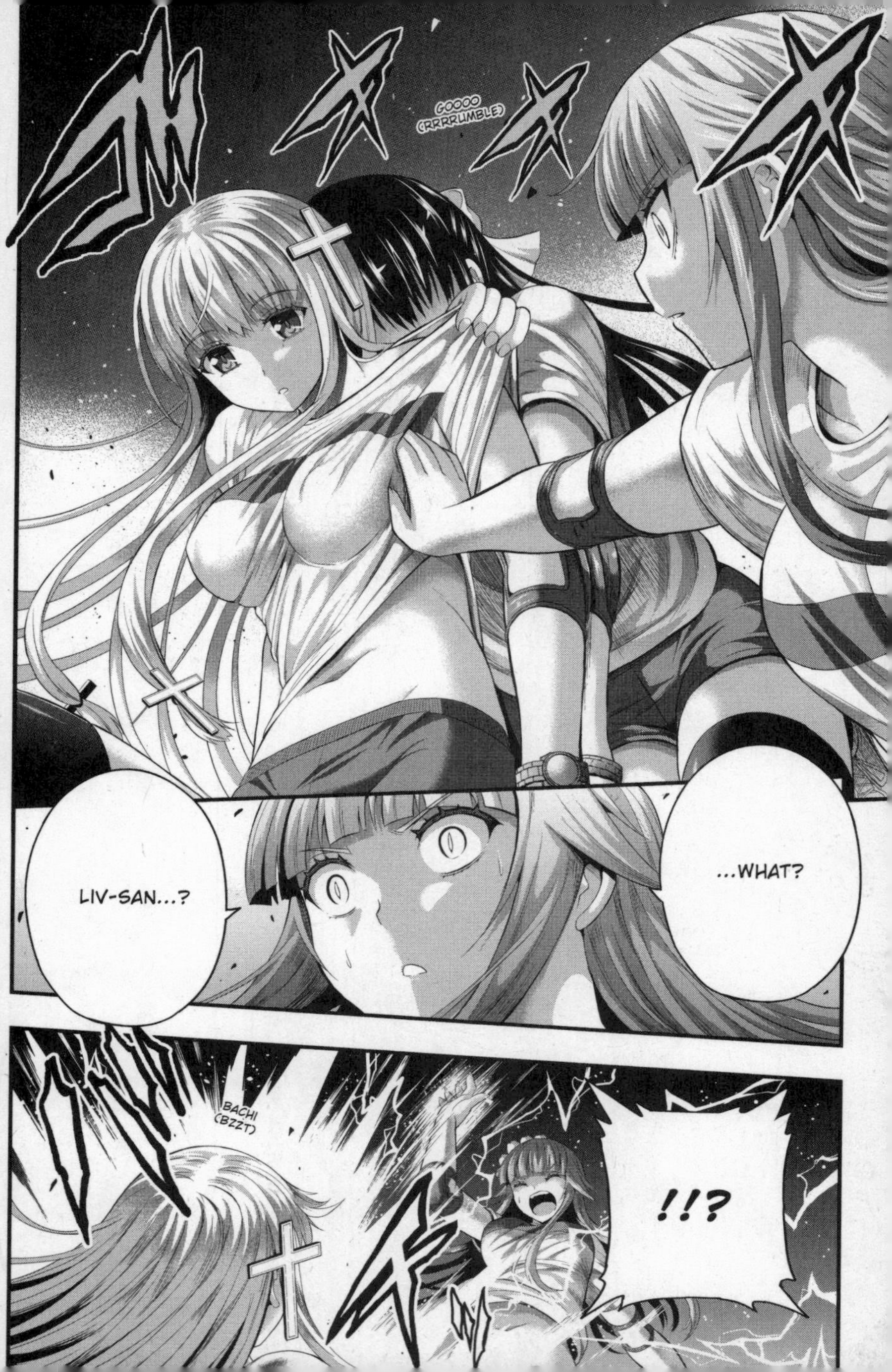
GOOOO (RRRRUMBLE)
...WHAT?
LIV-SAN...?
BACHI (BZZT)
!!?

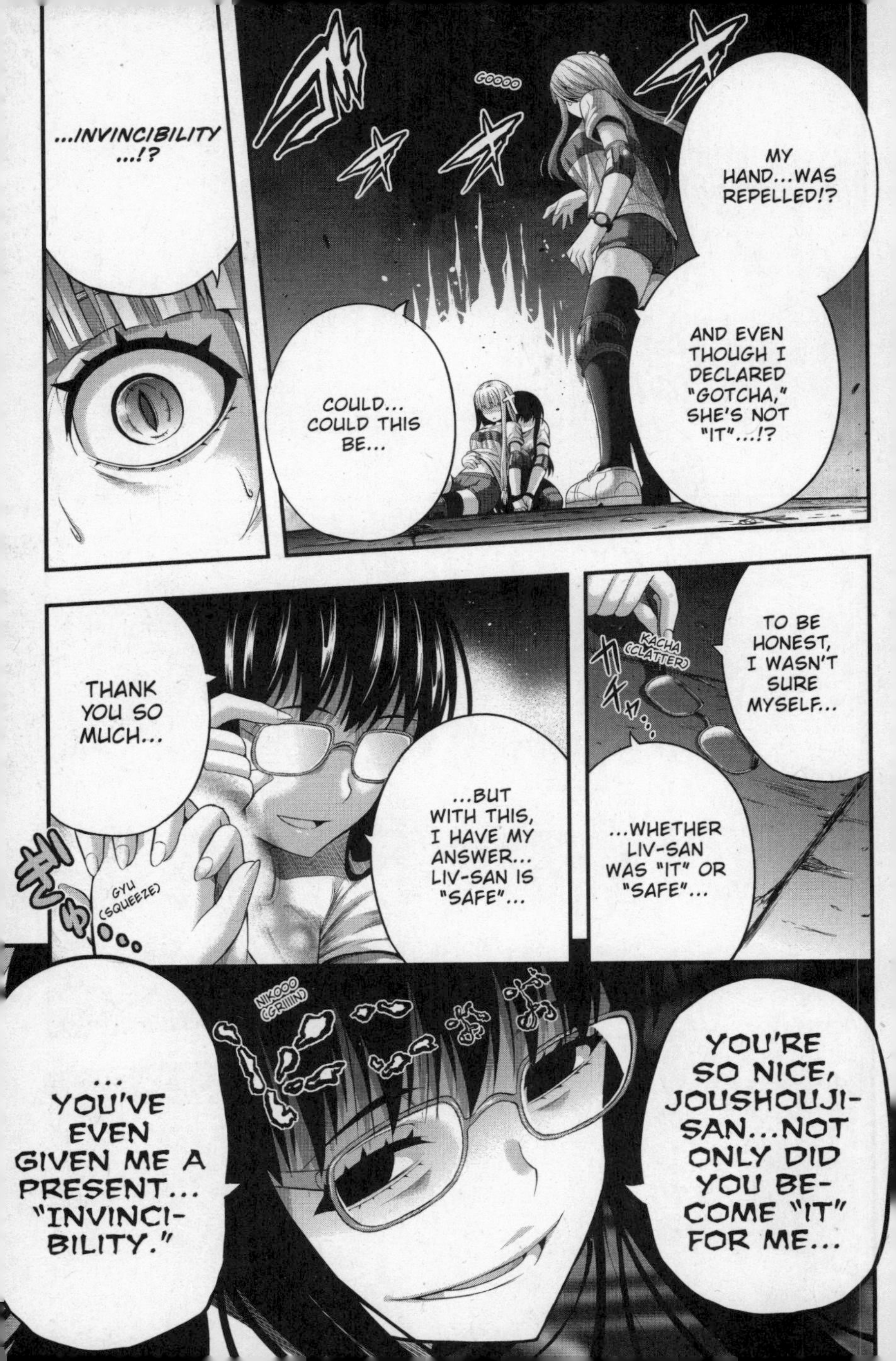
GOOOO
MY HAND...WAS REPELLED!?
AND EVEN THOUGH I DECLARED "GOTCHA," SHE'S NOT "IT"...!?
COULD... COULD THIS BE...
...INVINCIBILITY ...!?
TO BE HONEST, I WASN'T SURE MYSELF...
KACHA (CLATTER)
...WHETHER LIV-SAN WAS "IT" OR "SAFE"...
...BUT WITH THIS, I HAVE MY ANSWER... LIV-SAN IS "SAFE"...
THANK YOU SO MUCH...
GYU (SQUEEZE)
NIKOOO (GRIIIIN)
YOU'RE SO NICE, JOUSHOUJI-SAN...NOT ONLY DID YOU BE-COME "IT" FOR ME...
...YOU'VE EVEN GIVEN ME A PRESENT... "INVINCI-BILITY."

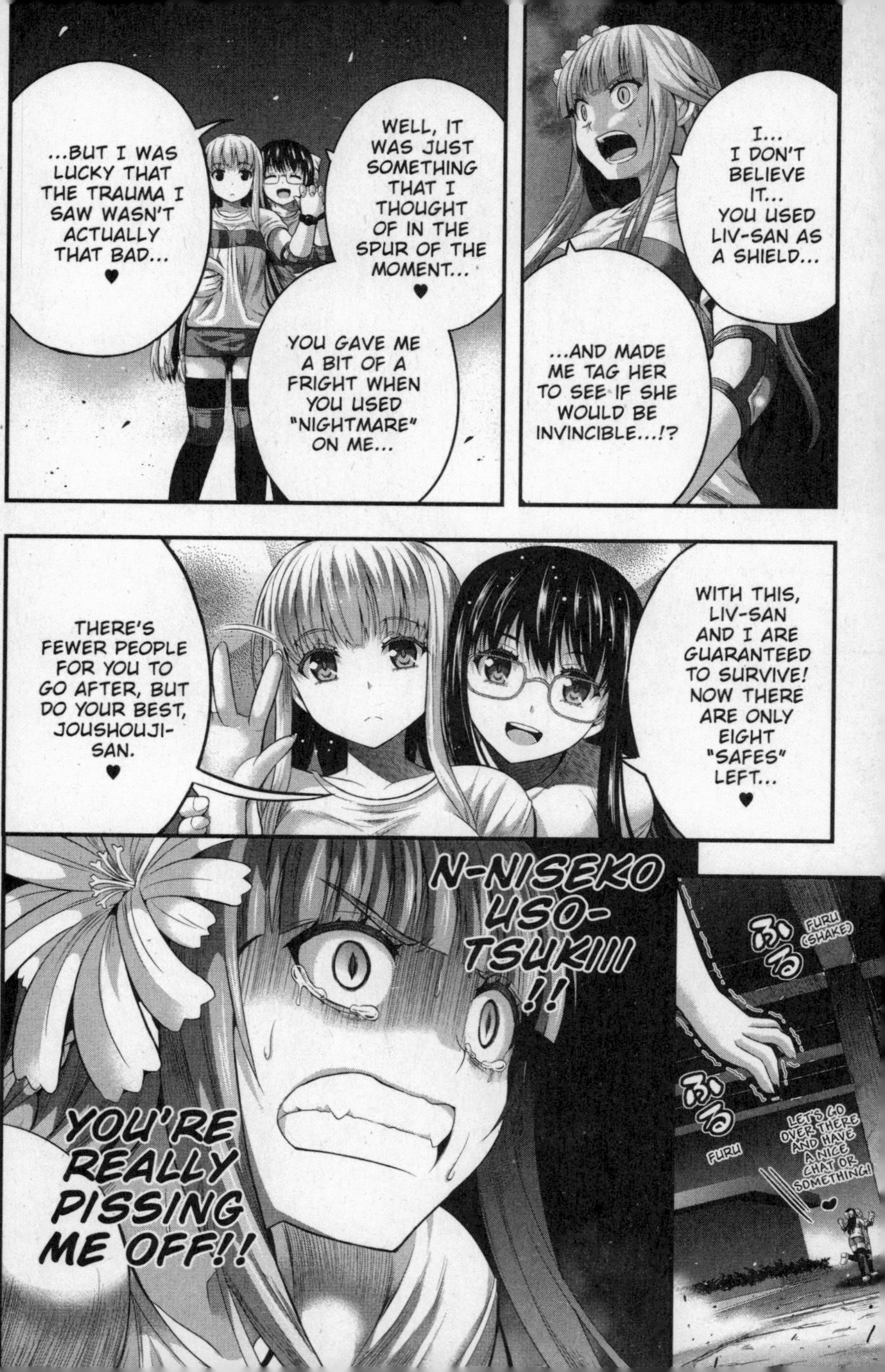
I... I DON'T BELIEVE IT... YOU USED LIV-SAN AS A SHIELD...
...AND MADE ME TAG HER TO SEE IF SHE WOULD BE INVINCIBLE...!?
WELL, IT WAS JUST SOMETHING THAT I THOUGHT OF IN THE SPUR OF THE MOMENT... ♥
...BUT I WAS LUCKY THAT THE TRAUMA I SAW WASN'T ACTUALLY THAT BAD... ♥
YOU GAVE ME A BIT OF A FRIGHT WHEN YOU USED "NIGHTMARE" ON ME...
WITH THIS, LIV-SAN AND I ARE GUARANTEED TO SURVIVE! NOW THERE ARE ONLY EIGHT "SAFES" LEFT... ♥
THERE'S FEWER PEOPLE FOR YOU TO GO AFTER, BUT DO YOUR BEST, JOUSHOUJI-SAN. ♥
ふる
FURU (SHAKE)
ふる
FURU
LET'S GO OVER THERE AND HAVE A NICE CHAT OR SOMETHING!
N-NISEKO USO-TSUKIII!!
YOU'RE REALLY PISSING ME OFF!!

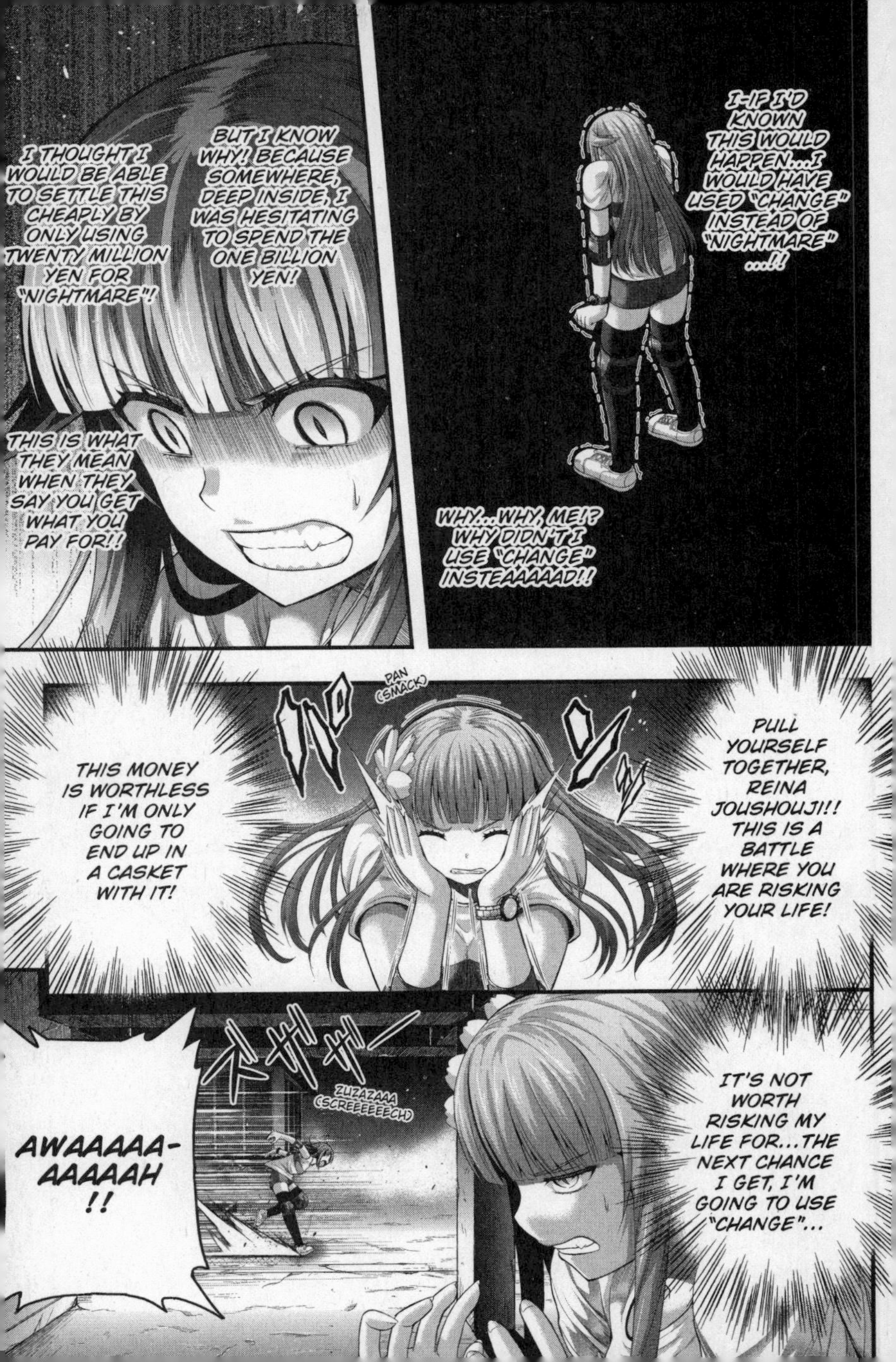
I-IF I'D KNOWN THIS WOULD HAPPEN...I WOULD HAVE USED "CHANGE" INSTEAD OF "NIGHTMARE" ...!!
WHY...WHY, ME!? WHY DIDN'T I USE "CHANGE" INSTEAAAAAD!!
I THOUGHT I WOULD BE ABLE TO SETTLE THIS CHEAPLY BY ONLY USING TWENTY MILLION YEN FOR "NIGHTMARE"!
BUT I KNOW WHY! BECAUSE SOMEWHERE, DEEP INSIDE, I WAS HESITATING TO SPEND THE ONE BILLION YEN!
THIS IS WHAT THEY MEAN WHEN THEY SAY YOU GET WHAT YOU PAY FOR!!
PULL YOURSELF TOGETHER, REINA JOUSHOUJI!! THIS IS A BATTLE WHERE YOU ARE RISKING YOUR LIFE!
PAN (SMACK)
THIS MONEY IS WORTHLESS IF I'M ONLY GOING TO END UP IN A CASKET WITH IT!
IT'S NOT WORTH RISKING MY LIFE FOR...THE NEXT CHANCE I GET, I'M GOING TO USE "CHANGE"...
ZUZAZAAA (SCREEEEEECH)
AWAAAAA-AAAAAH !!

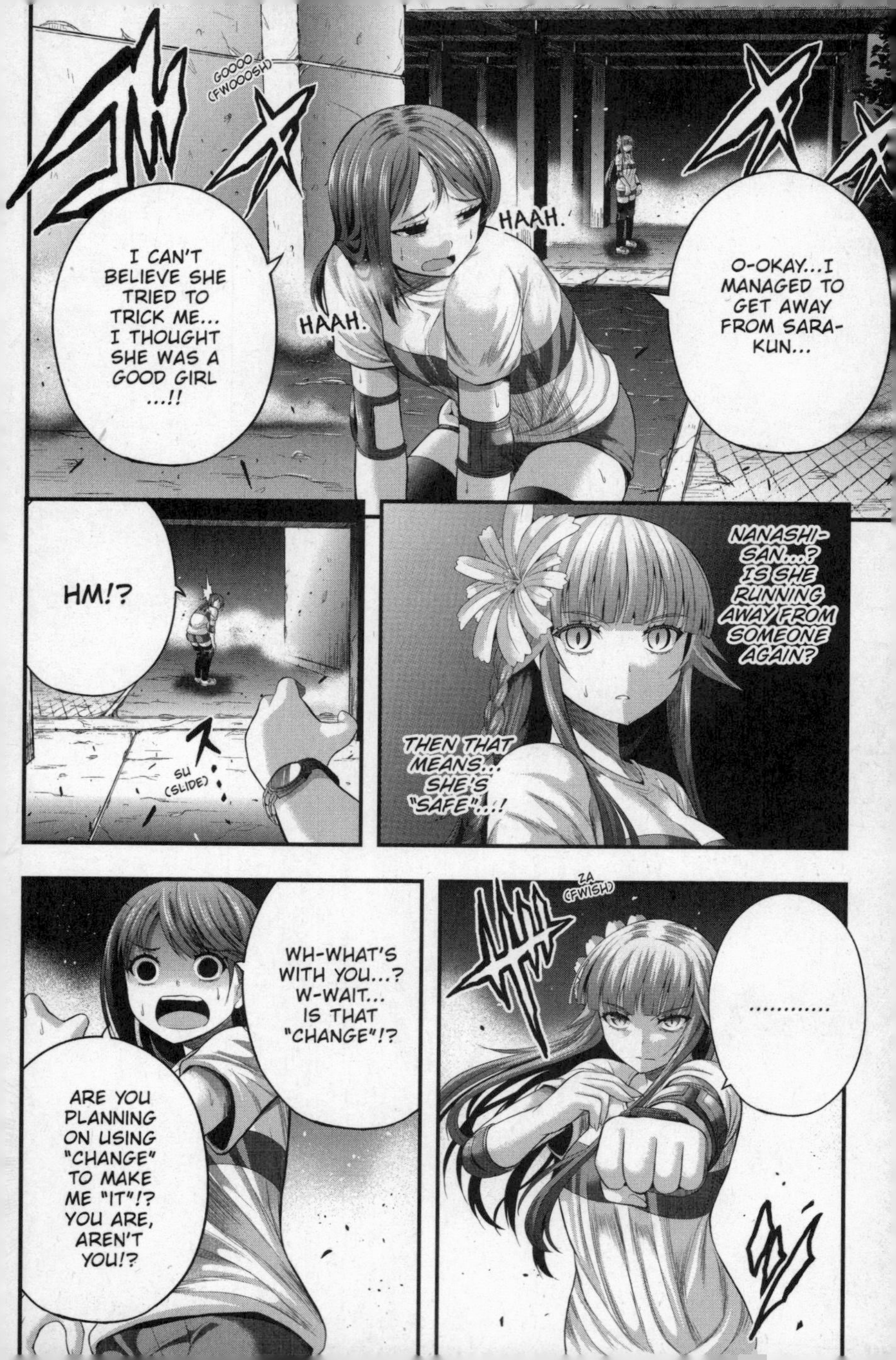

O-OKAY...I MANAGED TO GET AWAY FROM SARA-KUN...
HAAH.
GOOOO (FWOOOSH)
I CAN'T BELIEVE SHE TRIED TO TRICK ME... I THOUGHT SHE WAS A GOOD GIRL ...!!
HAAH.
NANASHI-SAN...? IS SHE RUNNING AWAY FROM SOMEONE AGAIN?
THEN THAT MEANS... SHE'S "SAFE"...!
HM!?
SU (SLIDE)
ZA (FWISH)
............
WH-WHAT'S WITH YOU...? W-WAIT... IS THAT "CHANGE"!?
ARE YOU PLANNING ON USING "CHANGE" TO MAKE ME "IT"!? YOU ARE, AREN'T YOU!?

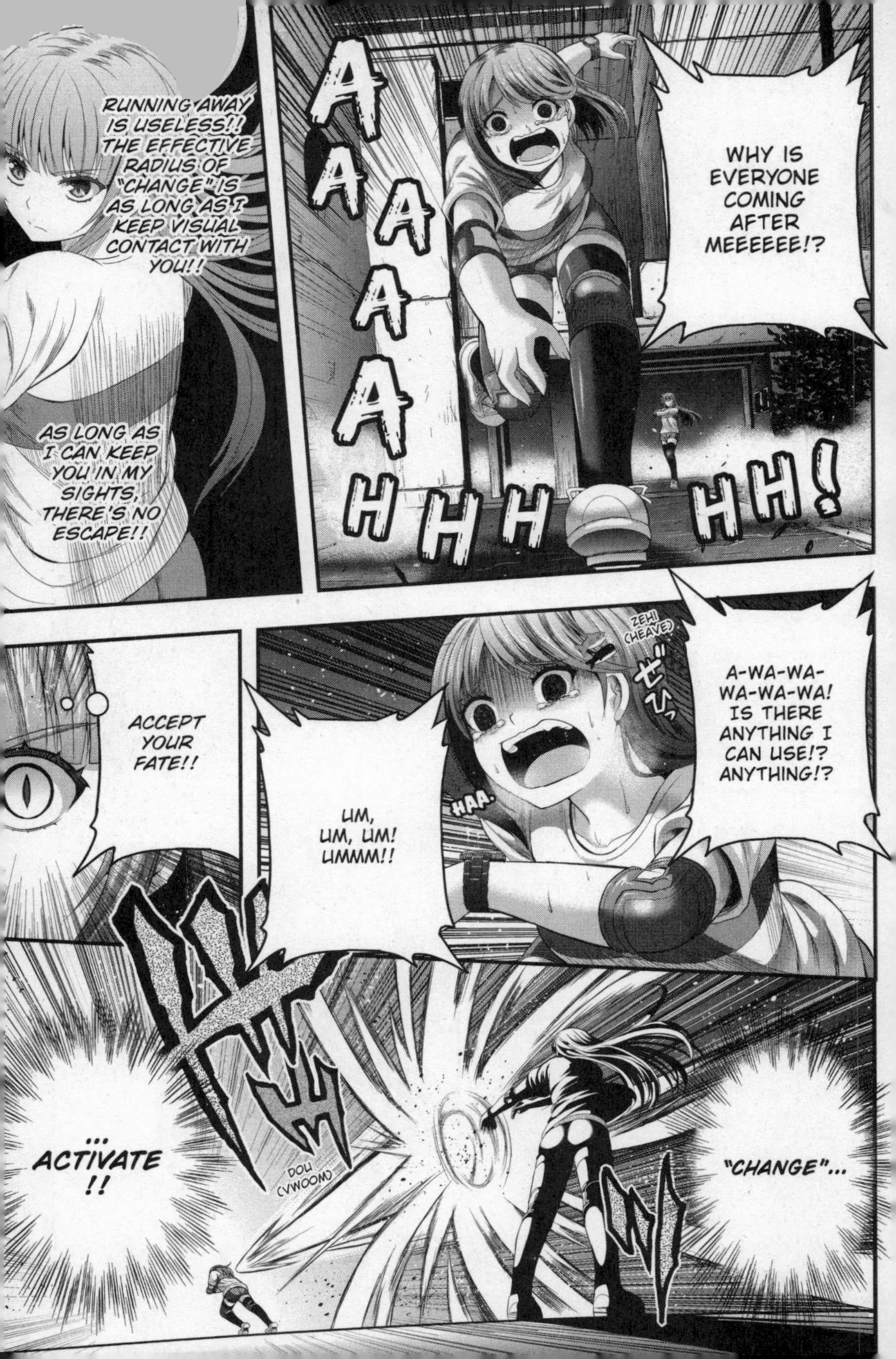
AAAAAHHHHH!
WHY IS EVERYONE COMING AFTER MEEEEEE!?
RUNNING AWAY IS USELESS!! THE EFFECTIVE RADIUS OF "CHANGE" IS AS LONG AS I KEEP VISUAL CONTACT WITH YOU!!
AS LONG AS I CAN KEEP YOU IN MY SIGHTS, THERE'S NO ESCAPE!!
A-WA-WA-WA-WA-WA! IS THERE ANYTHING I CAN USE!? ANYTHING!?
ZEHI (HEAVE)
HAA.
UM, UM, UM! UMMM!!
ACCEPT YOUR FATE!!
"CHANGE"...
DOU (VWOOM)
... ACTIVATE !!

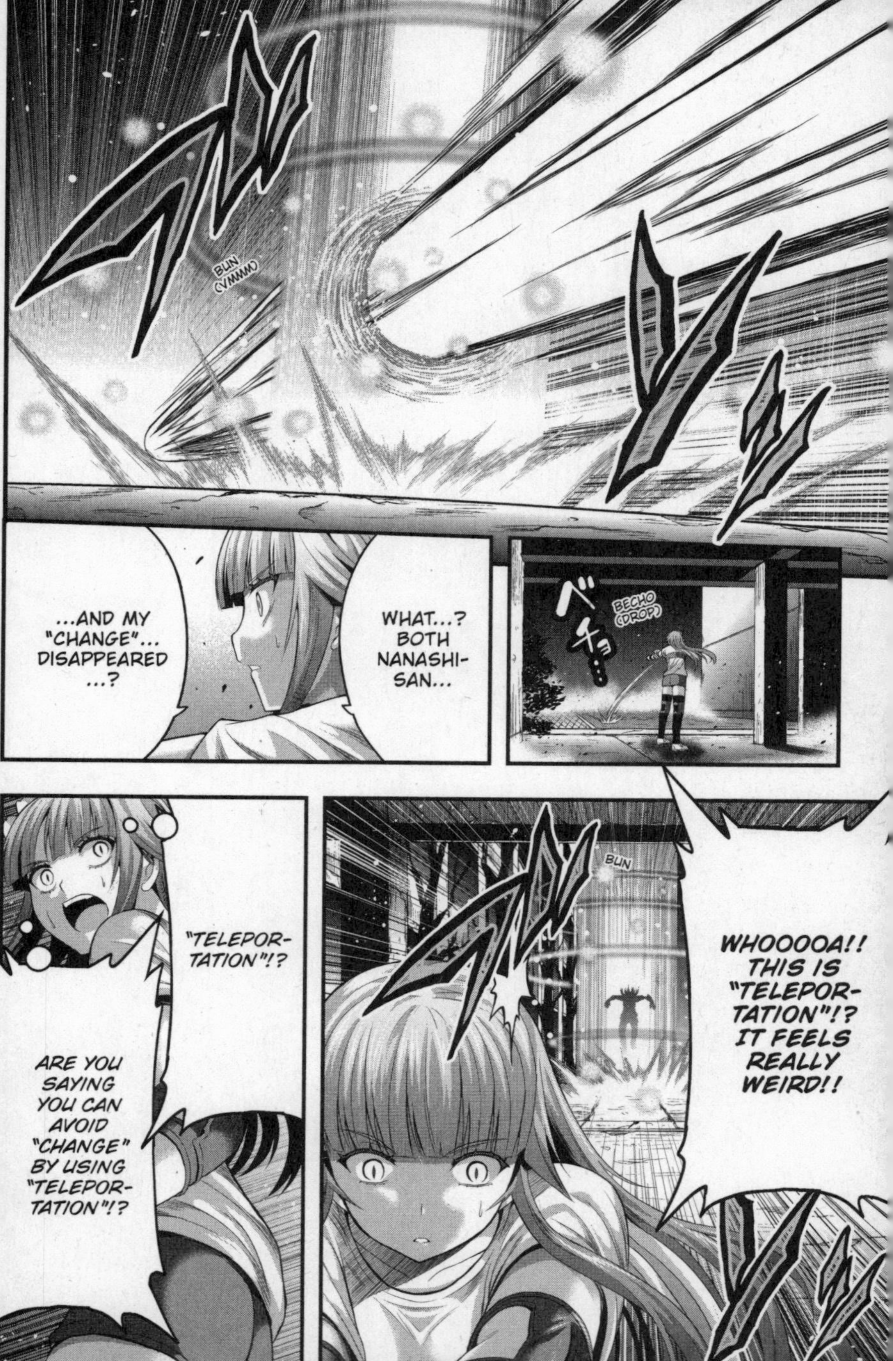
BUN (VMMMM)
BECHO (DROP)
WHAT...? BOTH NANASHI-SAN...
...AND MY "CHANGE"... DISAPPEARED ...?
BUN
WHOOOOA!! THIS IS "TELEPOR-TATION"!? IT FEELS REALLY WEIRD!!
"TELEPOR-TATION"!?
ARE YOU SAYING YOU CAN AVOID "CHANGE" BY USING "TELEPOR-TATION"!?

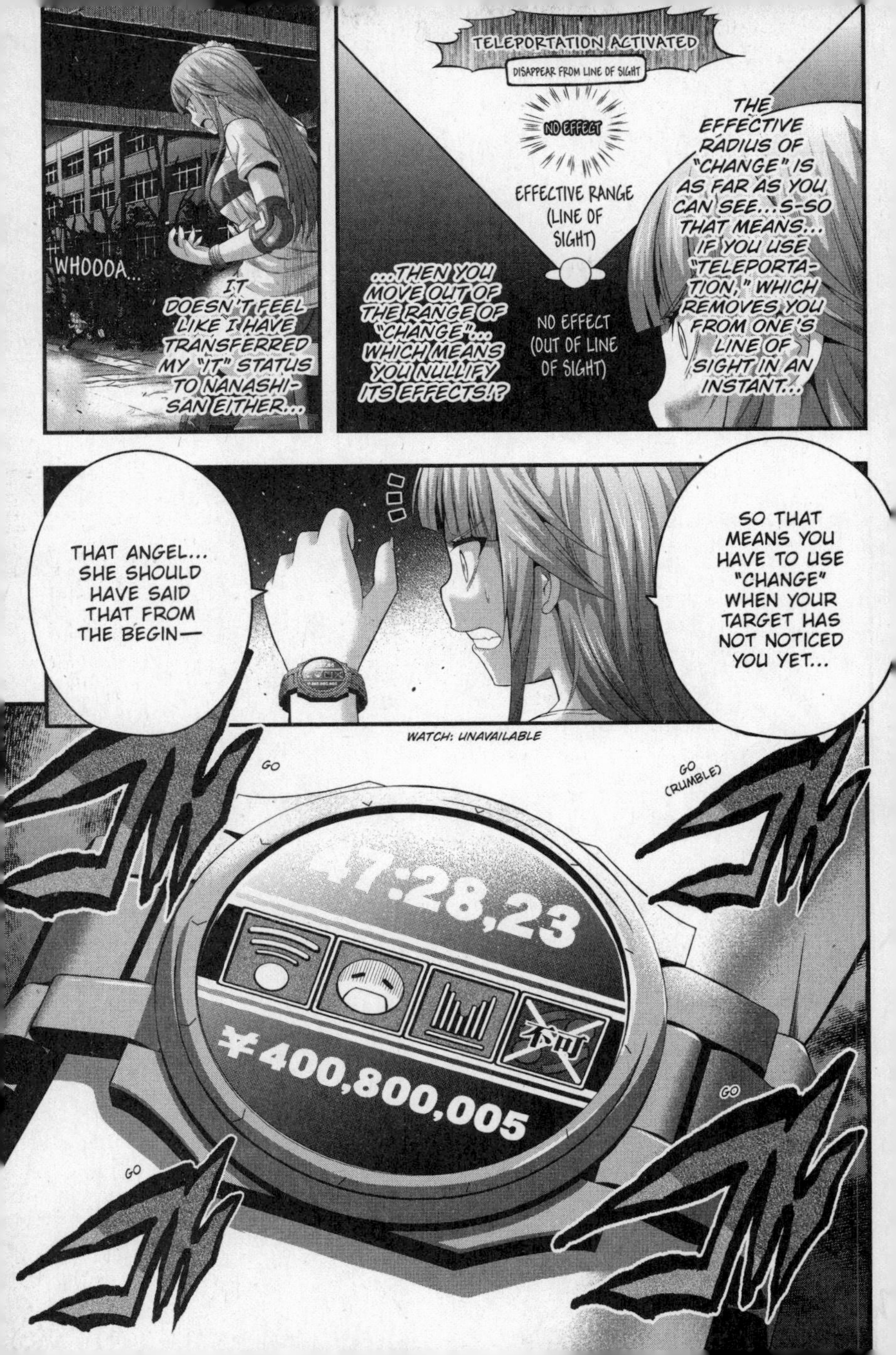
TELEPORTATION ACTIVATED
DISAPPEAR FROM LINE OF SIGHT
THE EFFECTIVE RADIUS OF "CHANGE" IS AS FAR AS YOU CAN SEE...S-SO THAT MEANS... IF YOU USE "TELEPORTATION," WHICH REMOVES YOU FROM ONE'S LINE OF SIGHT IN AN INSTANT...
NO EFFECT
EFFECTIVE RANGE (LINE OF SIGHT)
NO EFFECT (OUT OF LINE OF SIGHT)
...THEN YOU MOVE OUT OF THE RANGE OF "CHANGE"... WHICH MEANS YOU NULLIFY ITS EFFECTS!?
WHOOOA...
IT DOESN'T FEEL LIKE I HAVE TRANSFERRED MY "IT" STATUS TO NANASHI-SAN EITHER...
SO THAT MEANS YOU HAVE TO USE "CHANGE" WHEN YOUR TARGET HAS NOT NOTICED YOU YET...
THAT ANGEL... SHE SHOULD HAVE SAID THAT FROM THE BEGIN—
WATCH: UNAVAILABLE
GO (RUMBLE)
GO
47:28,23
¥400,800,005
GO
GO

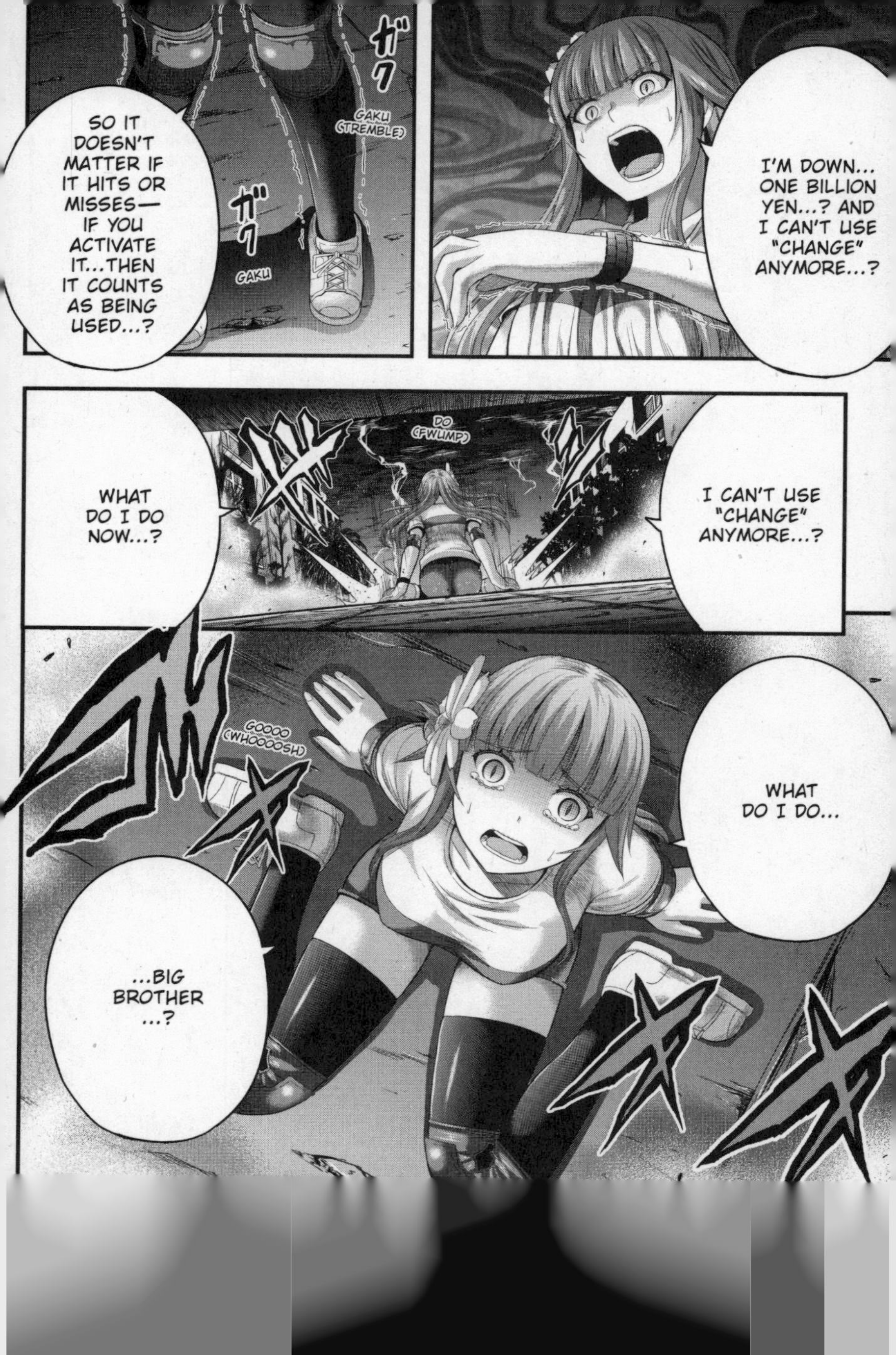
I'M DOWN... ONE BILLION YEN...? AND I CAN'T USE "CHANGE" ANYMORE...?
ガク
GAKU (TREMBLE)
ガク
GAKU
SO IT DOESN'T MATTER IF IT HITS OR MISSES—IF YOU ACTIVATE IT...THEN IT COUNTS AS BEING USED...?
I CAN'T USE "CHANGE" ANYMORE...?
DO (FWUMP)
WHAT DO I DO NOW...?
WHAT DO I DO...
GOOOO (WHOOOOSH)
...BIG BROTHER ...?

Though You May Burn to ASH

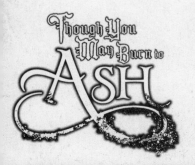

Though You May Burn to Ash

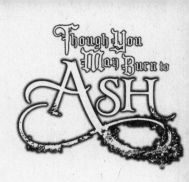

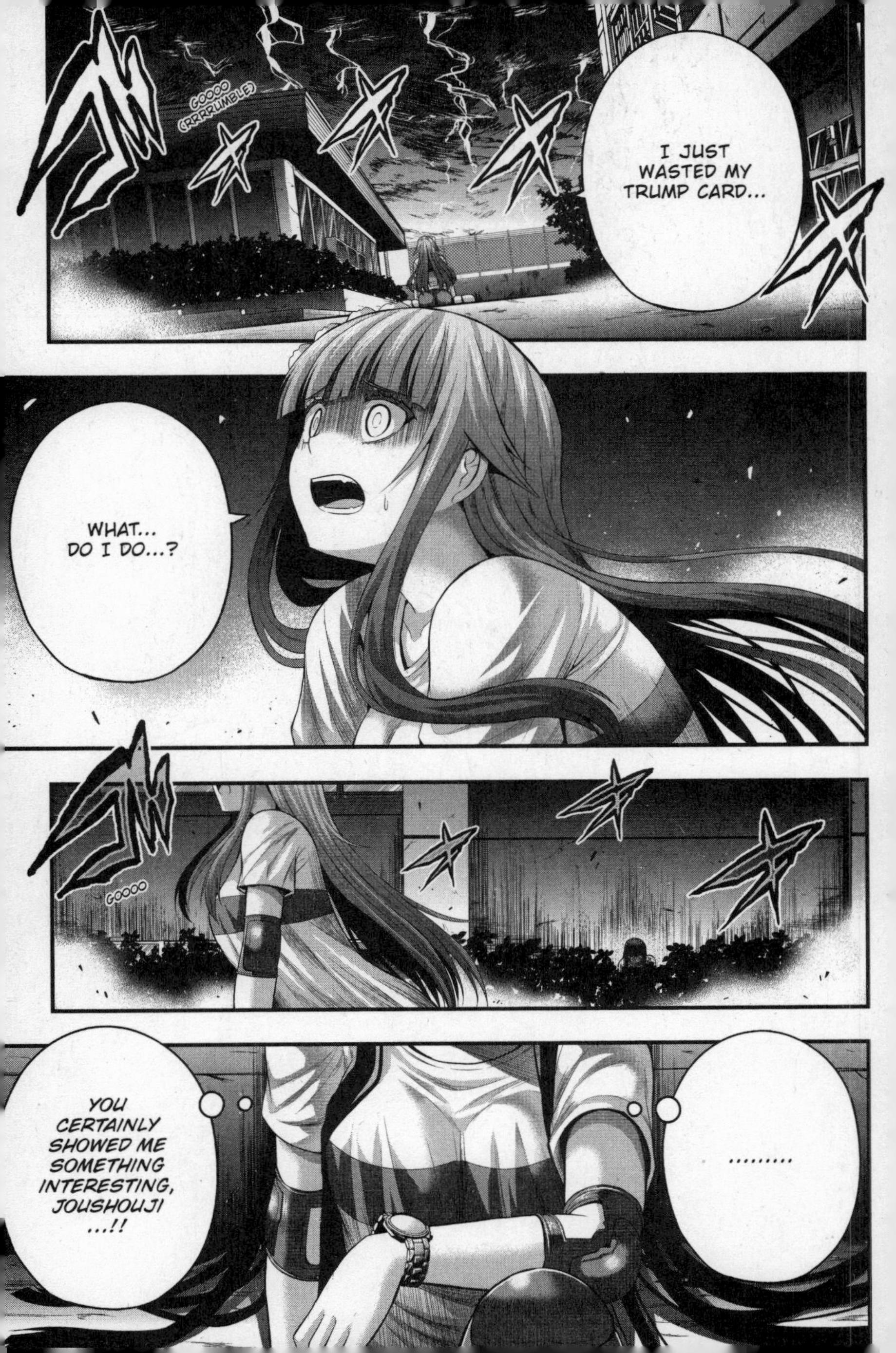
I JUST WASTED MY TRUMP CARD...
GOOOO (RRRRUMBLE)
WHAT... DO I DO...?
GOOOO
..........
YOU CERTAINLY SHOWED ME SOMETHING INTERESTING, JOUSHOUJI ...!!

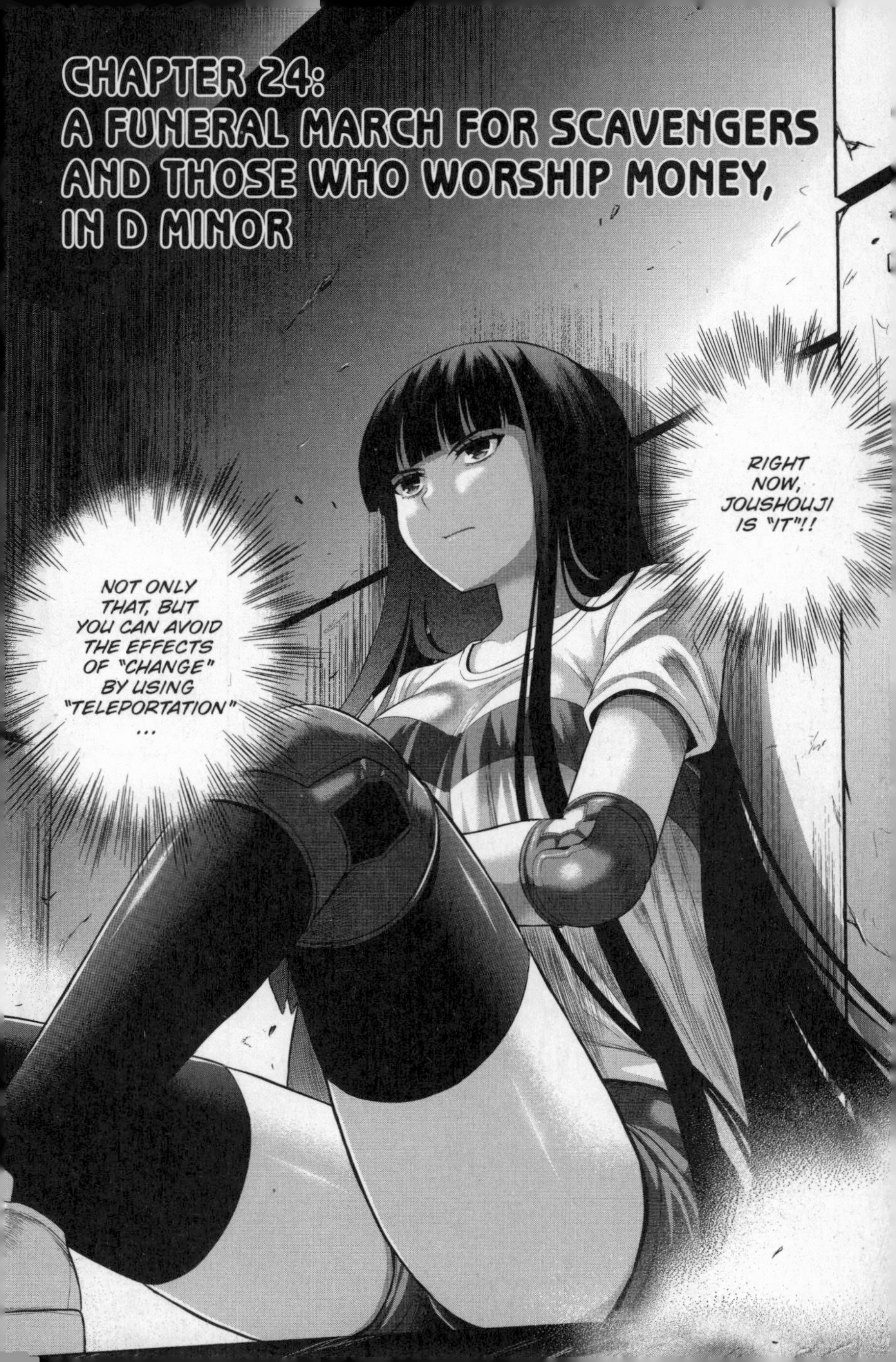
CHAPTER 24: A FUNERAL MARCH FOR SCAVENGERS AND THOSE WHO WORSHIP MONEY, IN D MINOR
RIGHT NOW, JOUSHOUJI IS "IT"!!
NOT ONLY THAT, BUT YOU CAN AVOID THE EFFECTS OF "CHANGE" BY USING "TELEPORTATION" ...

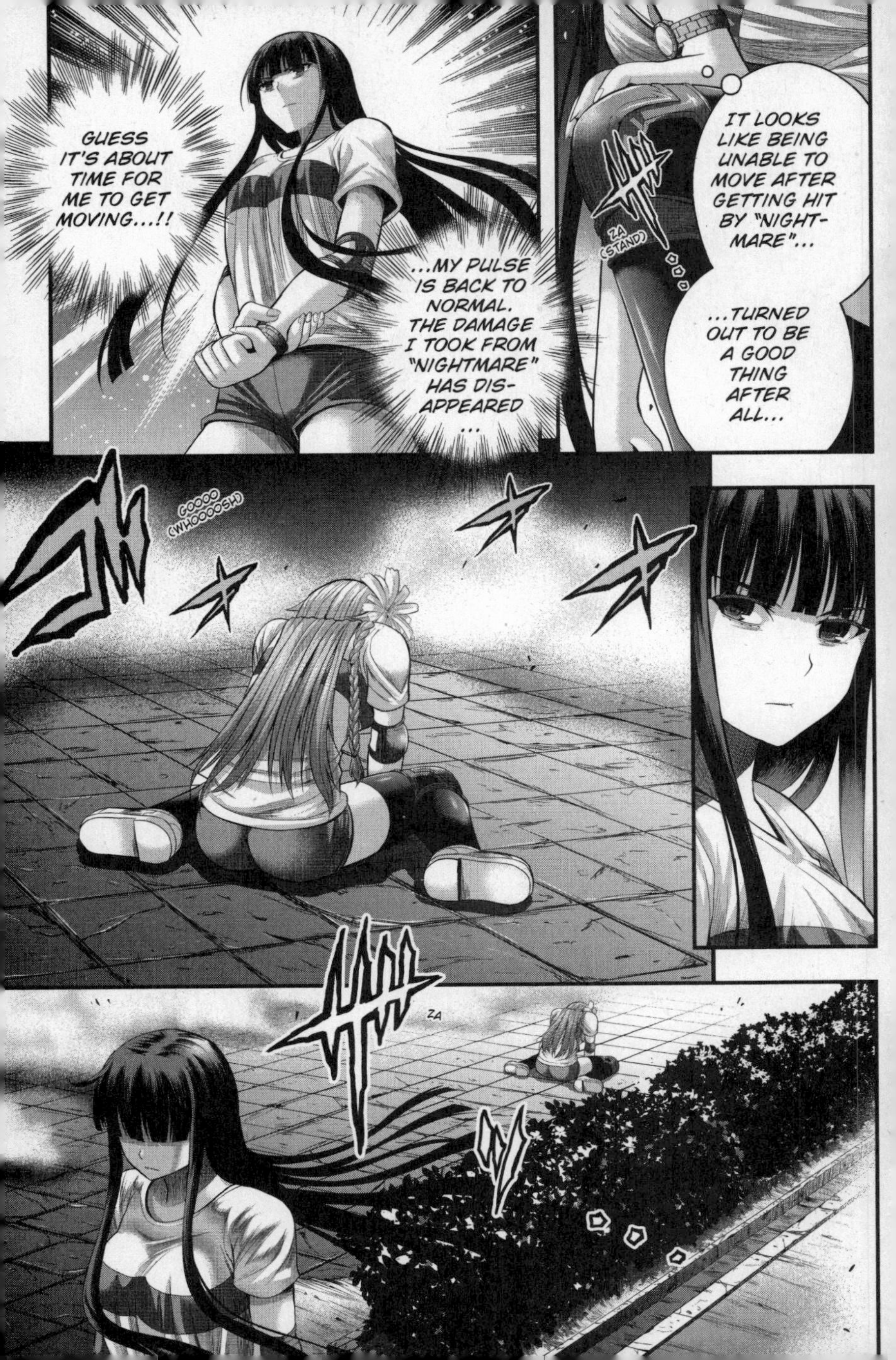
IT LOOKS LIKE BEING UNABLE TO MOVE AFTER GETTING HIT BY "NIGHT-MARE"...
ZA (STAND)
...TURNED OUT TO BE A GOOD THING AFTER ALL...
...MY PULSE IS BACK TO NORMAL. THE DAMAGE I TOOK FROM "NIGHTMARE" HAS DIS-APPEARED...
GUESS IT'S ABOUT TIME FOR ME TO GET MOVING...!!
GOOOO (WHOOOOSH)
ZA

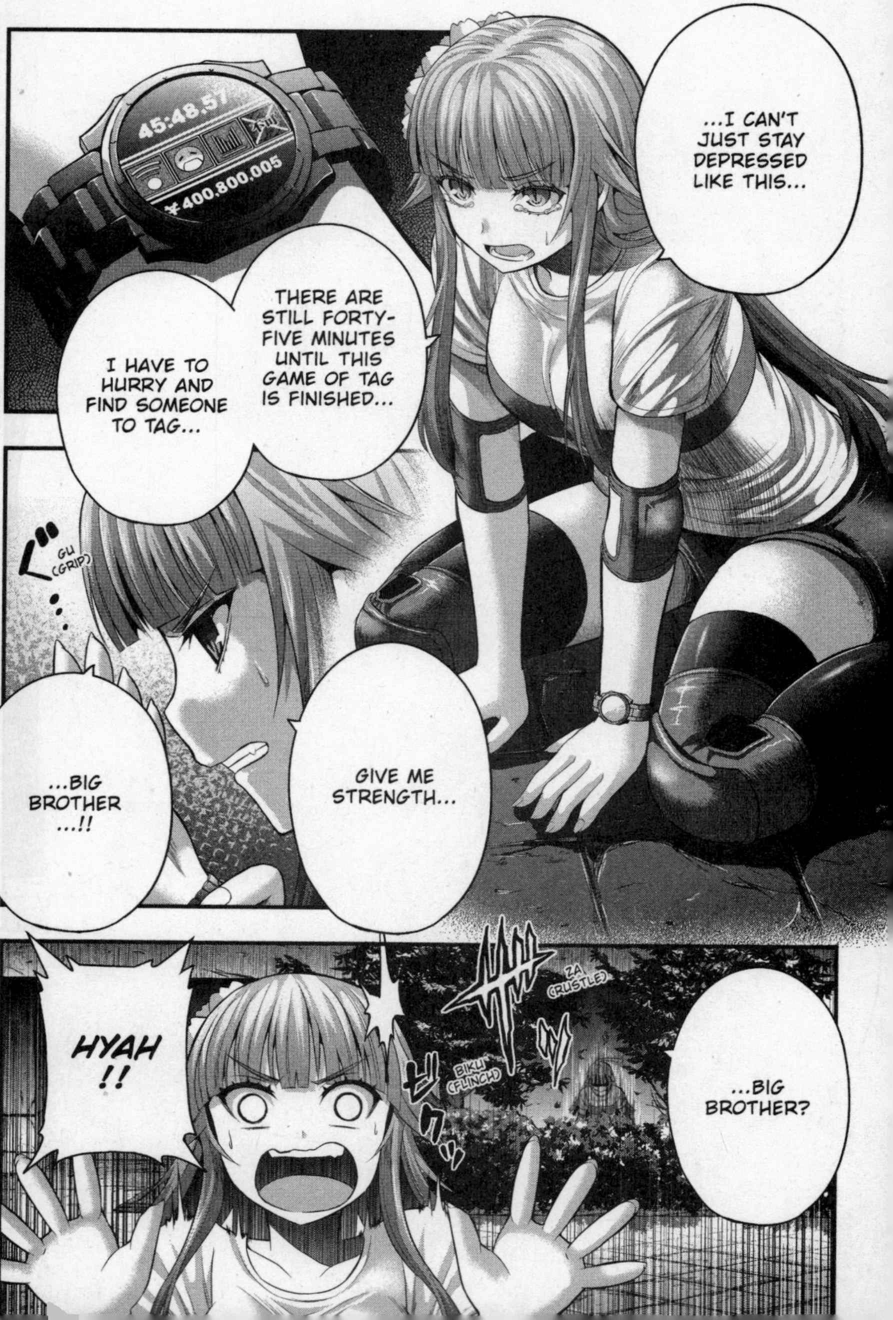

...I CAN'T JUST STAY DEPRESSED LIKE THIS...
45:48.57
¥400,800,005
THERE ARE STILL FORTY-FIVE MINUTES UNTIL THIS GAME OF TAG IS FINISHED...
I HAVE TO HURRY AND FIND SOMEONE TO TAG...
GU (GRIP)
...
GIVE ME STRENGTH...
...BIG BROTHER ...!!
...BIG BROTHER?
ZA (RUSTLE)
BIKU (FLINCH)
HYAH!!

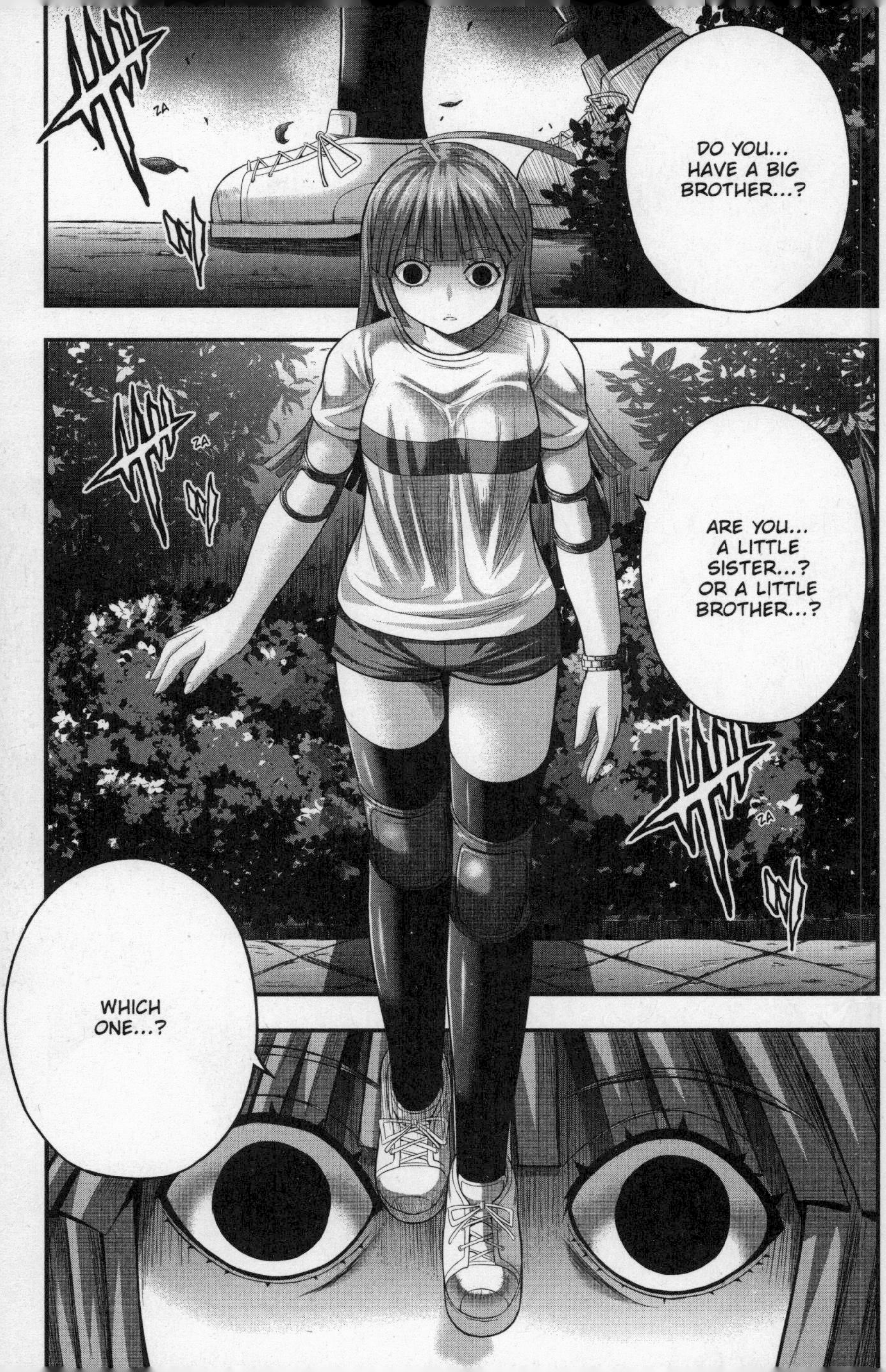
ZA
DO YOU... HAVE A BIG BROTHER...?
ZA
ARE YOU... A LITTLE SISTER...? OR A LITTLE BROTHER...?
ZA
WHICH ONE...?

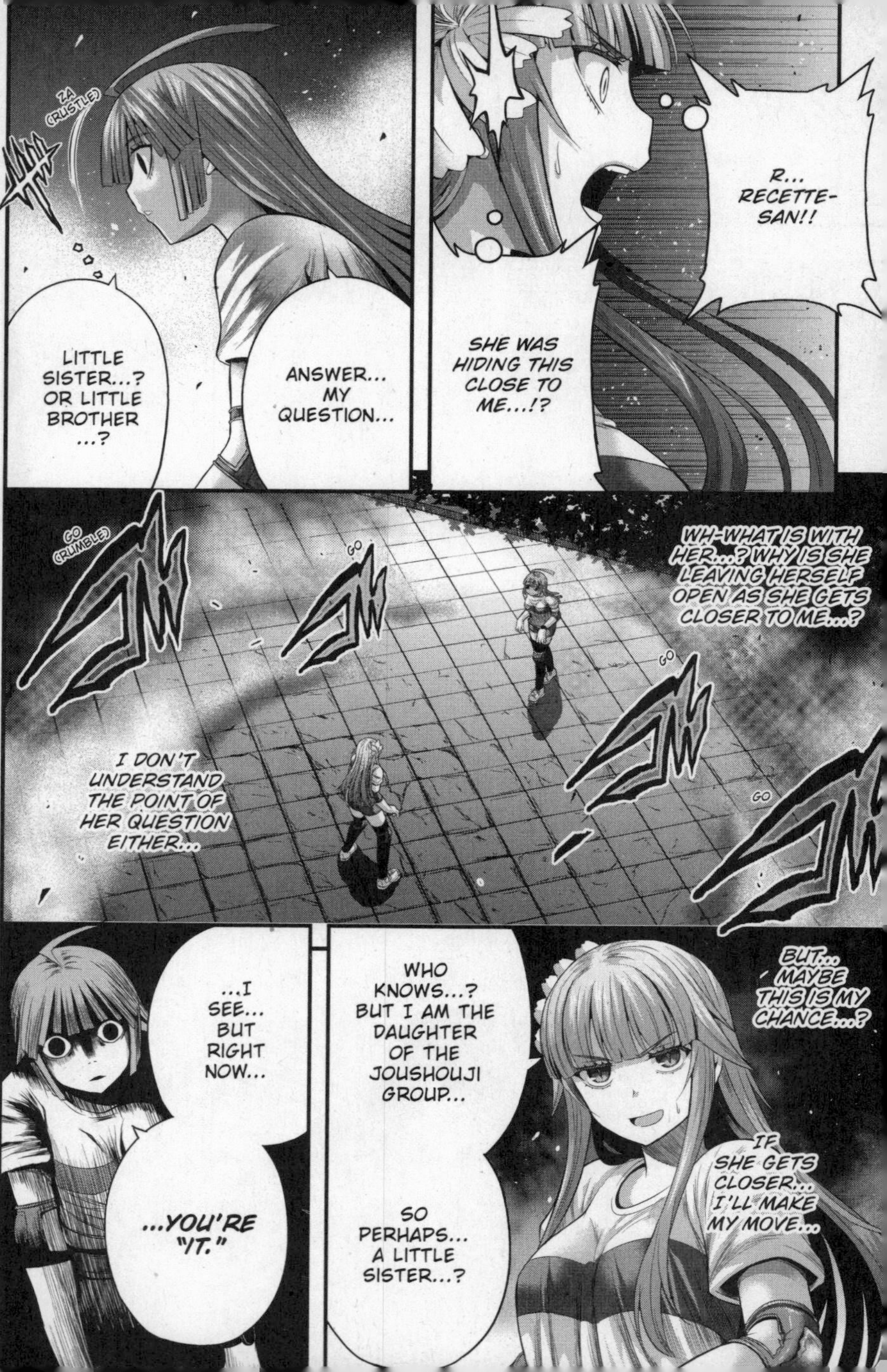
R... RECETTE-SAN!!
SHE WAS HIDING THIS CLOSE TO ME...!?
ZA (RUSTLE)
ANSWER... MY QUESTION...
LITTLE SISTER...? OR LITTLE BROTHER ...?
WH-WHAT IS WITH HER...? WHY IS SHE LEAVING HERSELF OPEN AS SHE GETS CLOSER TO ME...?
GO (RUMBLE)
GO
GO
GO
I DON'T UNDERSTAND THE POINT OF HER QUESTION EITHER...
BUT... MAYBE THIS IS MY CHANCE...?
WHO KNOWS...? BUT I AM THE DAUGHTER OF THE JOUSHOUJI GROUP...
SO PERHAPS... A LITTLE SISTER...?
IF SHE GETS CLOSER... I'LL MAKE MY MOVE...
...I SEE... BUT RIGHT NOW...
...YOU'RE "IT."

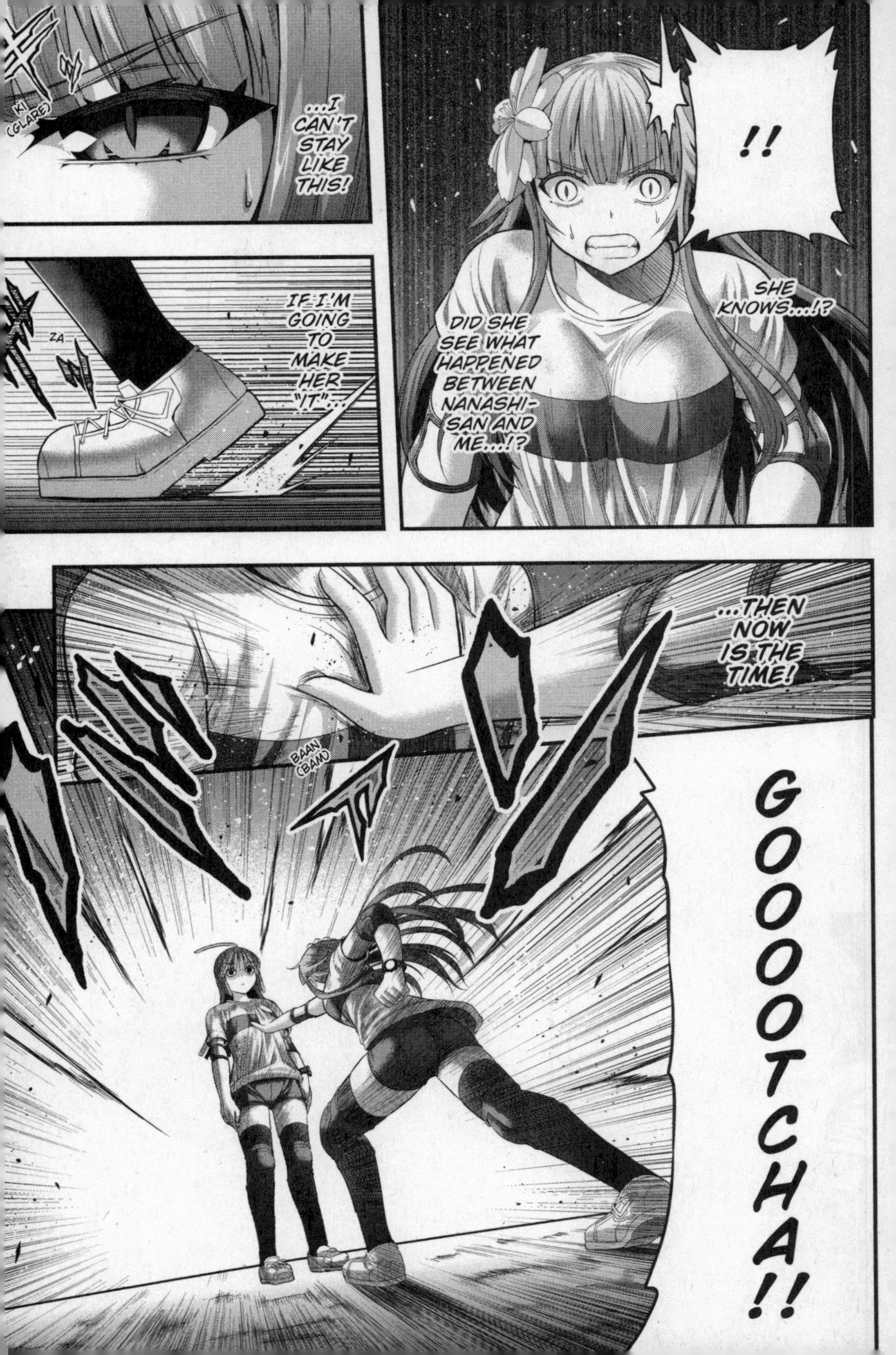
!!
SHE KNOWS...!?
DID SHE SEE WHAT HAPPENED BETWEEN NANASHI-SAN AND ME...!?
...I CAN'T STAY LIKE THIS!
KI (GLARE)
IF I'M GOING TO MAKE HER "IT"...
ZA
...THEN NOW IS THE TIME!
GOOOOOTCHA!!
BAAN (BAM)

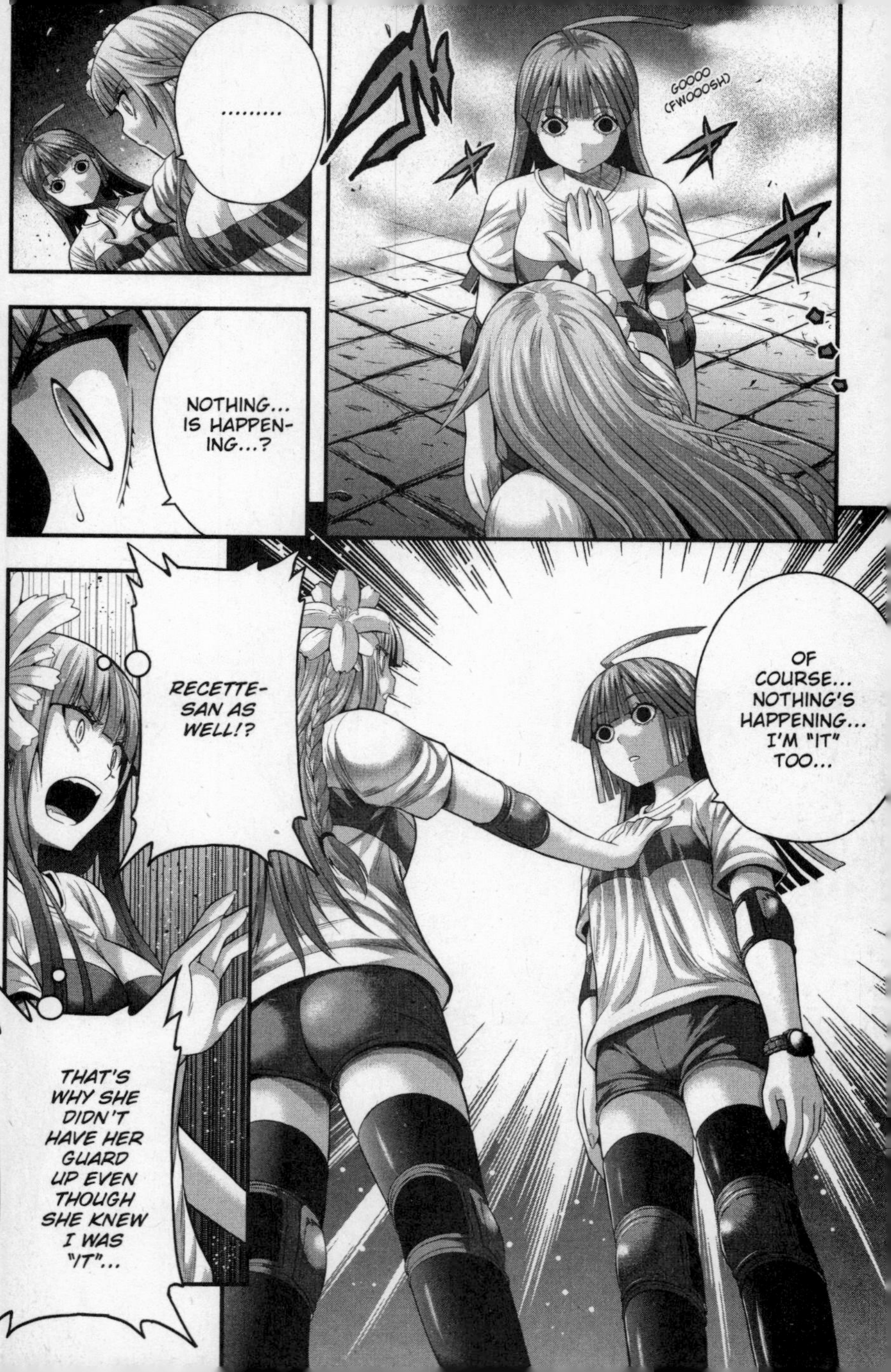
GOOOO (FWOOOSH)
..........
NOTHING... IS HAPPEN-ING...?
OF COURSE... NOTHING'S HAPPENING... I'M "IT" TOO...
RECETTE-SAN AS WELL!?
THAT'S WHY SHE DIDN'T HAVE HER GUARD UP EVEN THOUGH SHE KNEW I WAS "IT"...

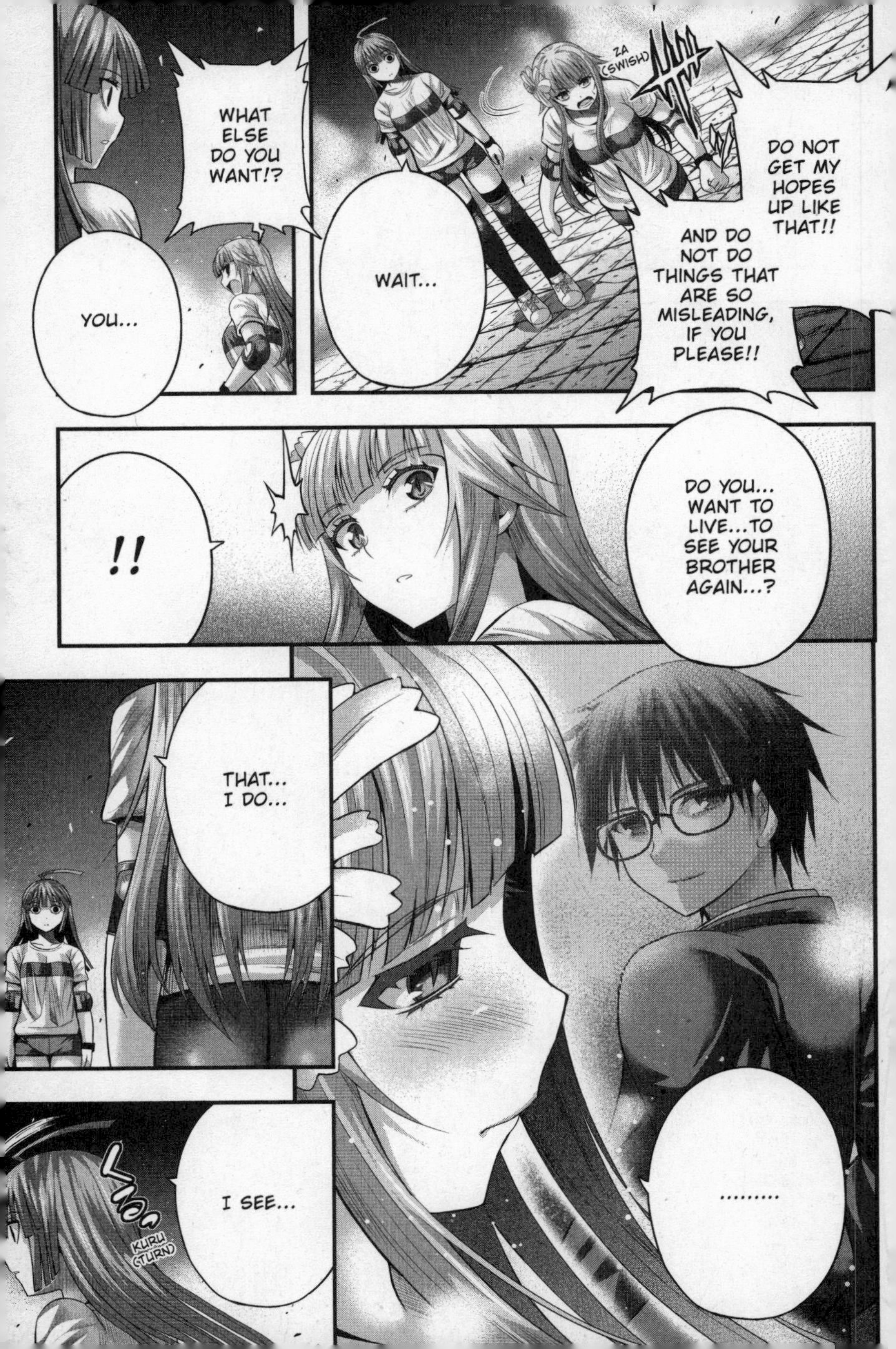
ZA (SWISH)
DO NOT GET MY HOPES UP LIKE THAT!!
AND DO NOT DO THINGS THAT ARE SO MISLEADING, IF YOU PLEASE!!
WAIT...
WHAT ELSE DO YOU WANT!?
YOU...
DO YOU... WANT TO LIVE...TO SEE YOUR BROTHER AGAIN...?
!!
.........
THAT... I DO...
I SEE...
KURU (TURN)

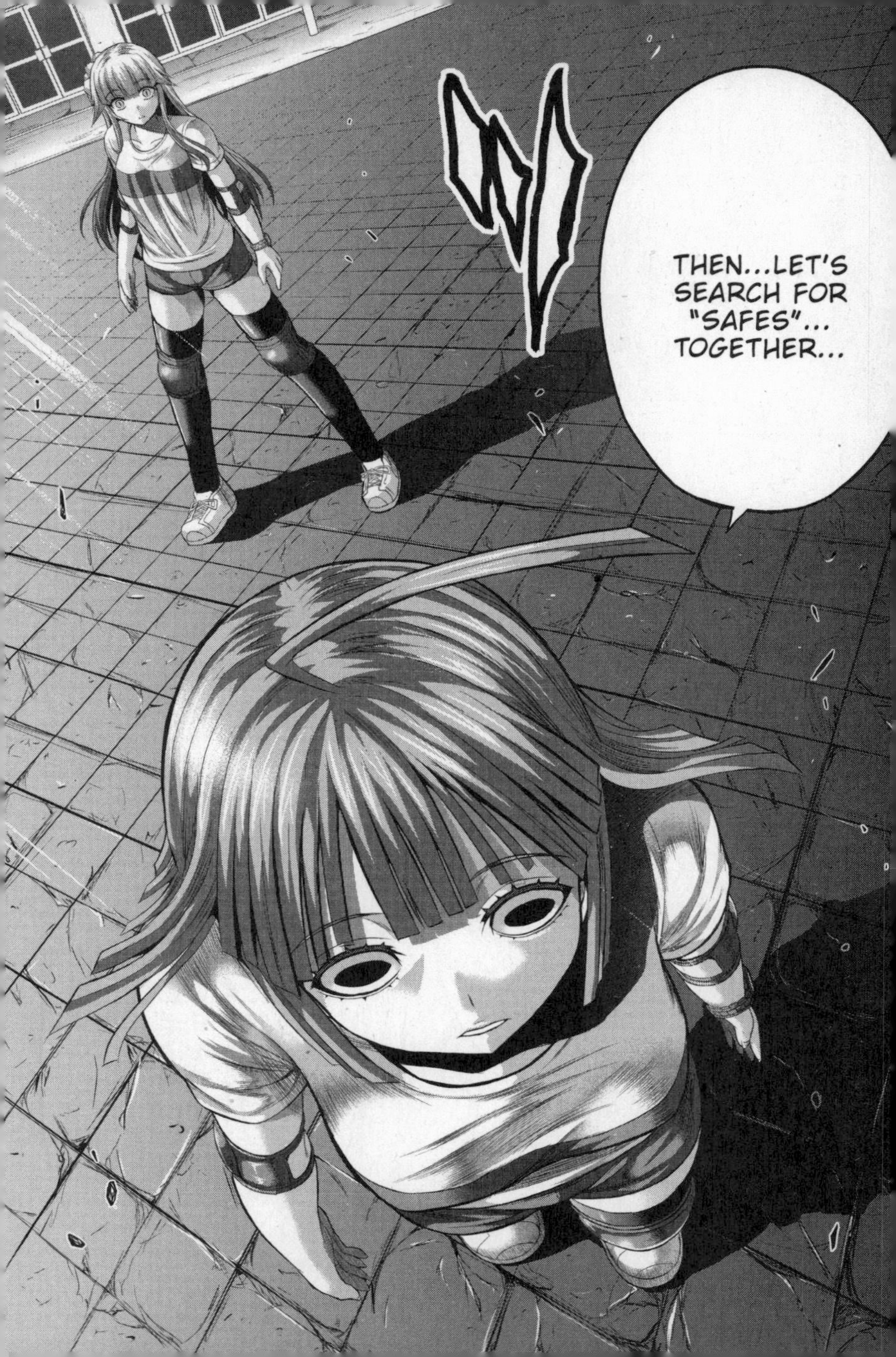
THEN...LET'S SEARCH FOR "SAFES"... TOGETHER...

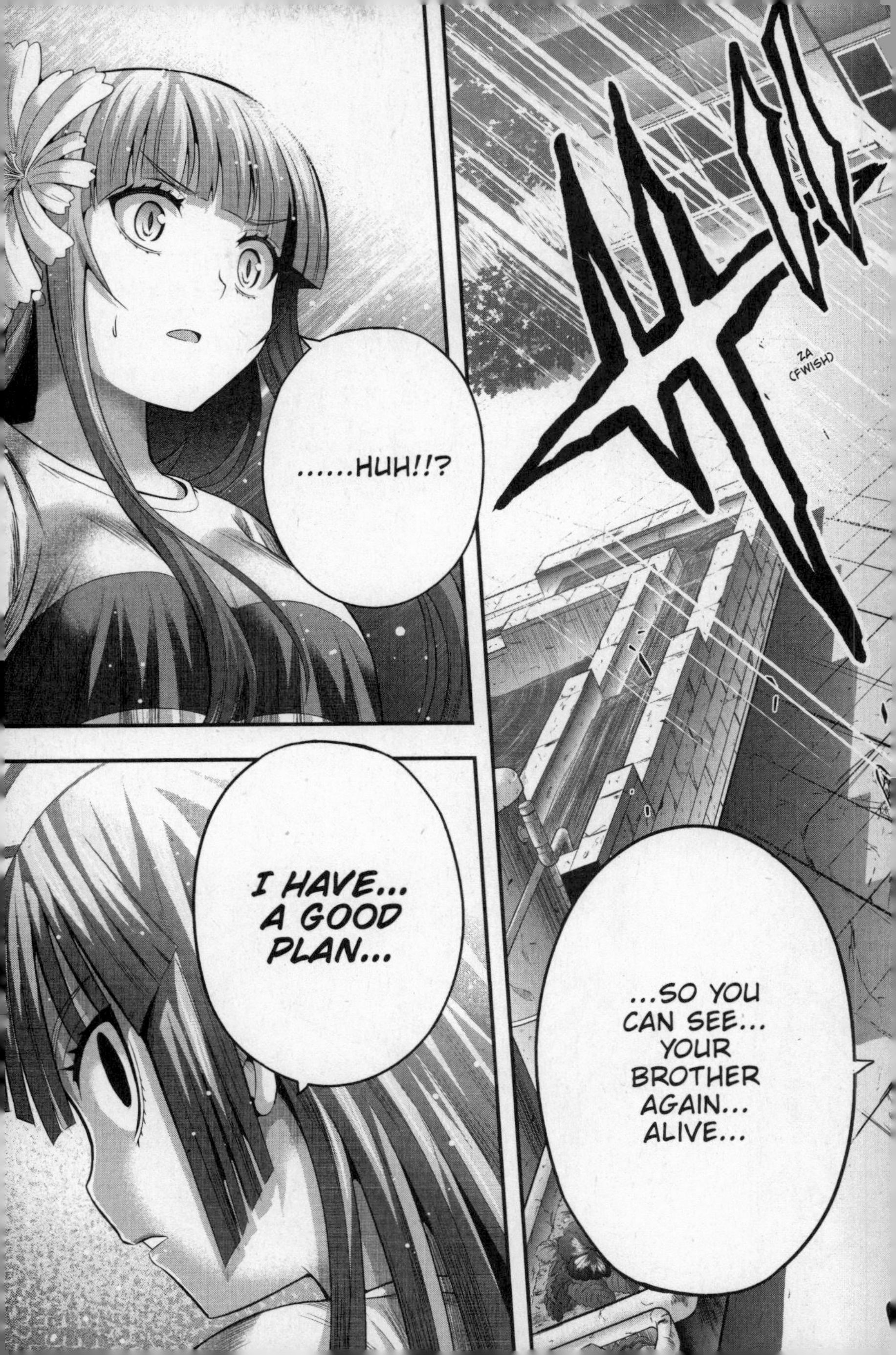
ZA (FWISH)
...SO YOU CAN SEE... YOUR BROTHER AGAIN... ALIVE...
......HUH!!?
I HAVE... A GOOD PLAN...

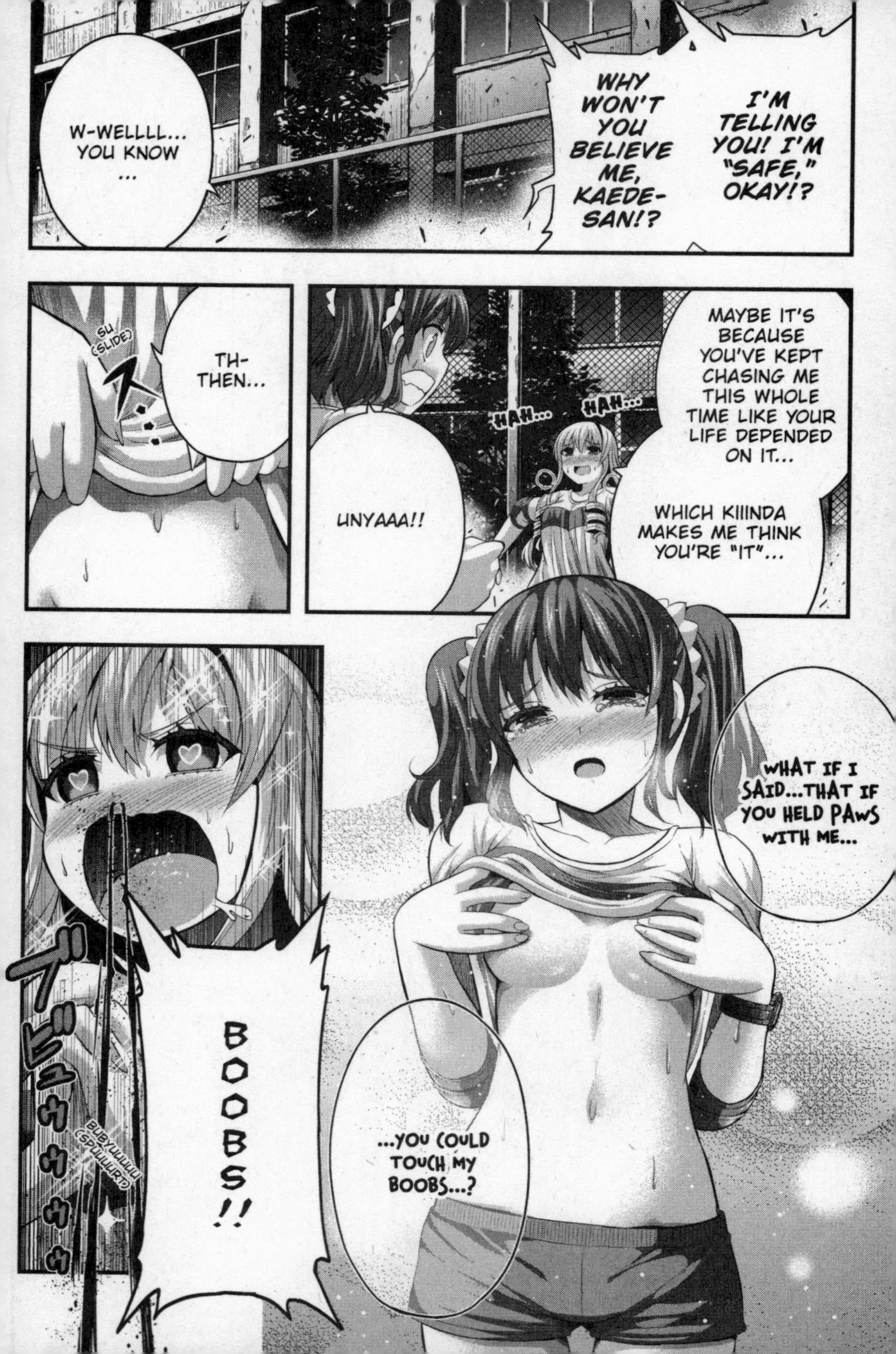

I'M TELLING YOU! I'M "SAFE," OKAY!?
WHY WON'T YOU BELIEVE ME, KAEDE-SAN!?
W-WELLLL... YOU KNOW ...
MAYBE IT'S BECAUSE YOU'VE KEPT CHASING ME THIS WHOLE TIME LIKE YOUR LIFE DEPENDED ON IT...
WHICH KIIINDA MAKES ME THINK YOU'RE "IT"...
HAH... HAH...
UNYAAA!!
SU (SLIDE)
TH-THEN...
WHAT IF I SAID...THAT IF YOU HELD PAWS WITH ME...
...YOU COULD TOUCH MY BOOBS...?
BOOBS!!
BUBYUUUUU (SPUUUURT)

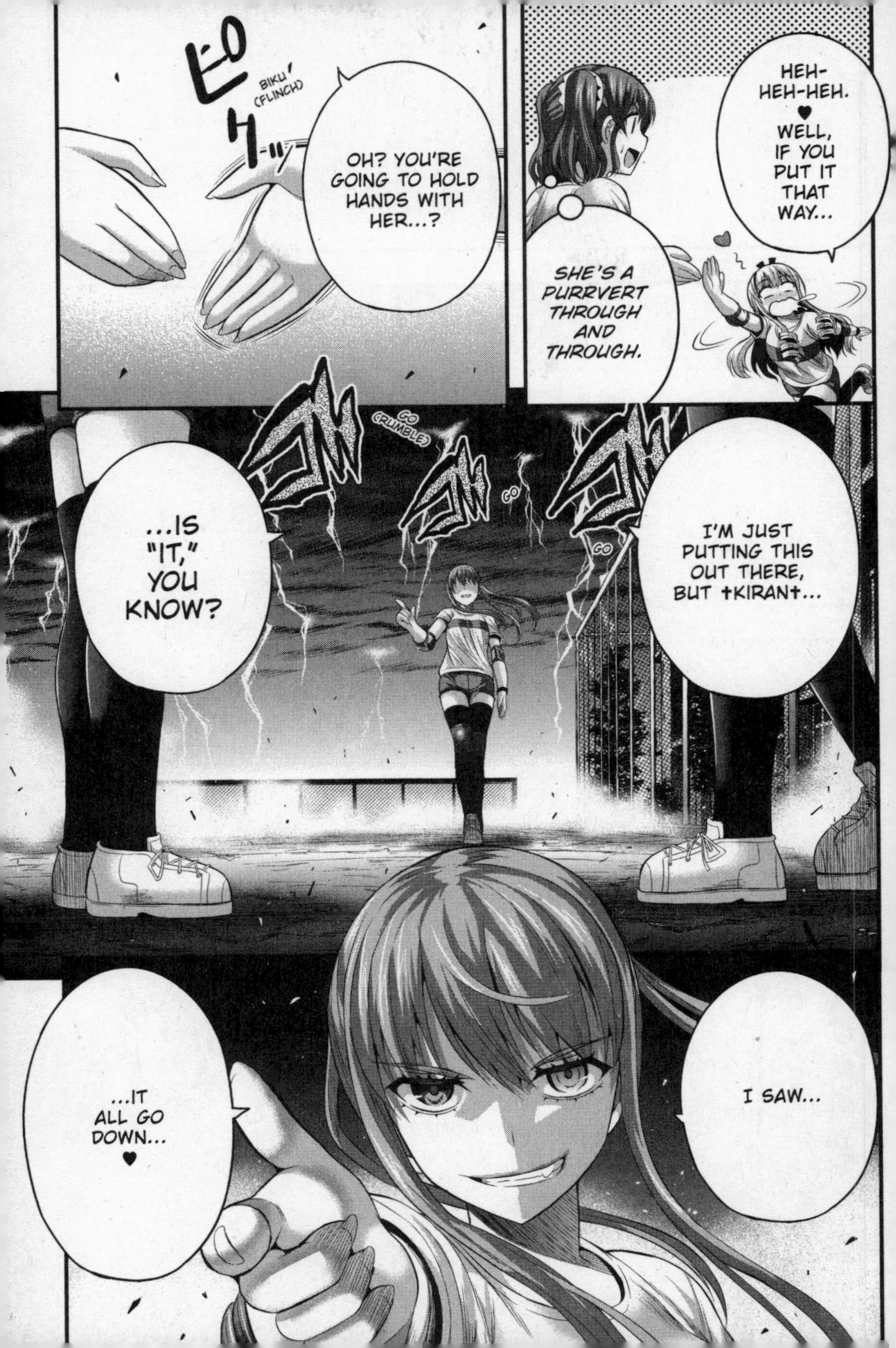
HEH-HEH-HEH. ♥ WELL, IF YOU PUT IT THAT WAY...
SHE'S A PURRVERT THROUGH AND THROUGH.
ビクッ
BIKU' (FLINCH)
OH? YOU'RE GOING TO HOLD HANDS WITH HER...?
I'M JUST PUTTING THIS OUT THERE, BUT †KIRAN†...
GO
GO
GO (RUMBLE)
...IS "IT," YOU KNOW?
I SAW...
...IT ALL GO DOWN... ♥

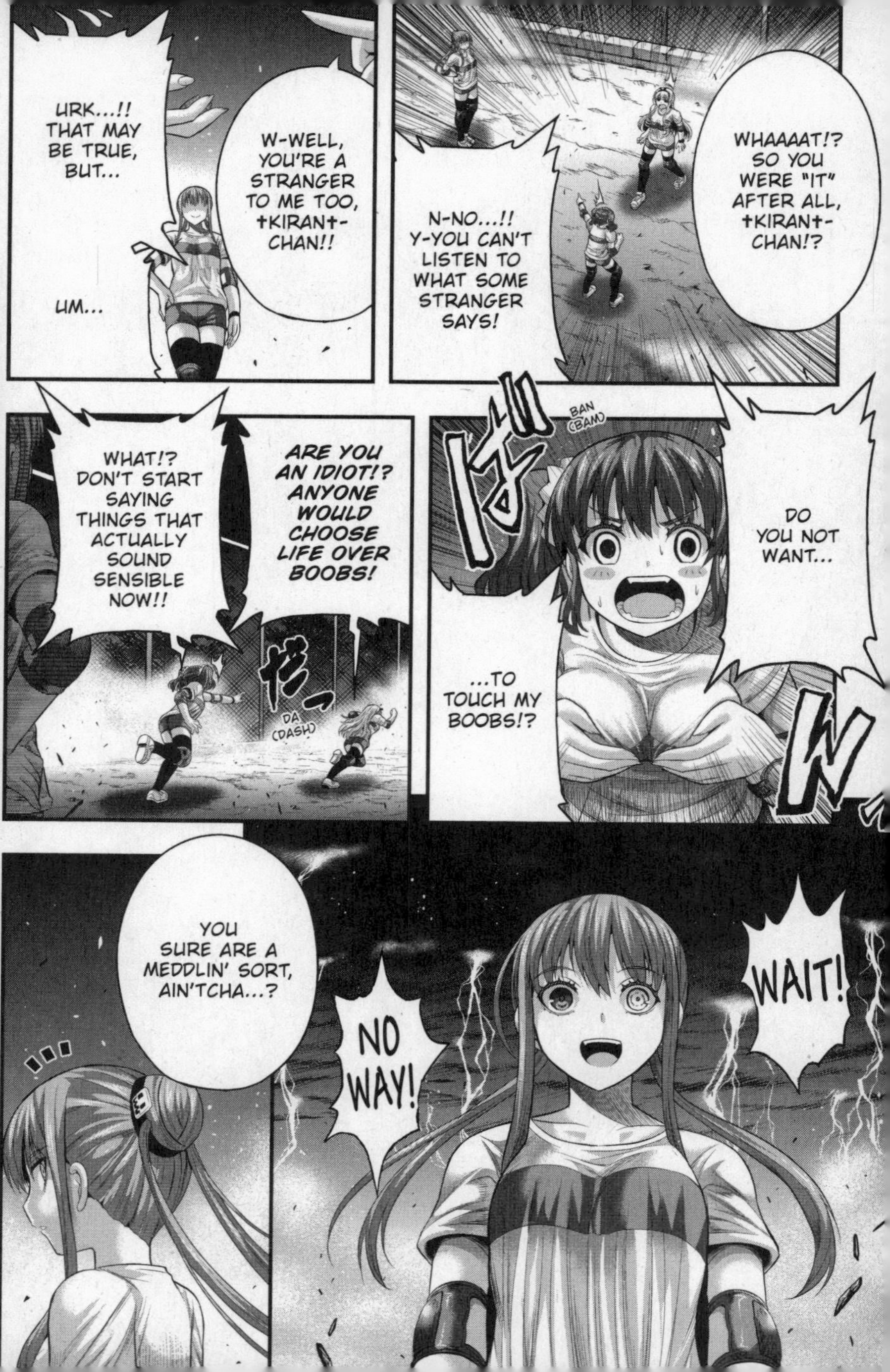
WHAAAAT!? SO YOU WERE "IT" AFTER ALL, †KIRAN†-CHAN!?
N-NO...!! Y-YOU CAN'T LISTEN TO WHAT SOME STRANGER SAYS!
W-WELL, YOU'RE A STRANGER TO ME TOO, †KIRAN†-CHAN!!
URK...!! THAT MAY BE TRUE, BUT...
UM...
BAN (BAM)
DO YOU NOT WANT...
...TO TOUCH MY BOOBS!?
ARE YOU AN IDIOT!? ANYONE WOULD CHOOSE LIFE OVER BOOBS!
WHAT!? DON'T START SAYING THINGS THAT ACTUALLY SOUND SENSIBLE NOW!!
DA (DASH)
WAIT!
NO WAY!
YOU SURE ARE A MEDDLIN' SORT, AIN'TCHA...?
...

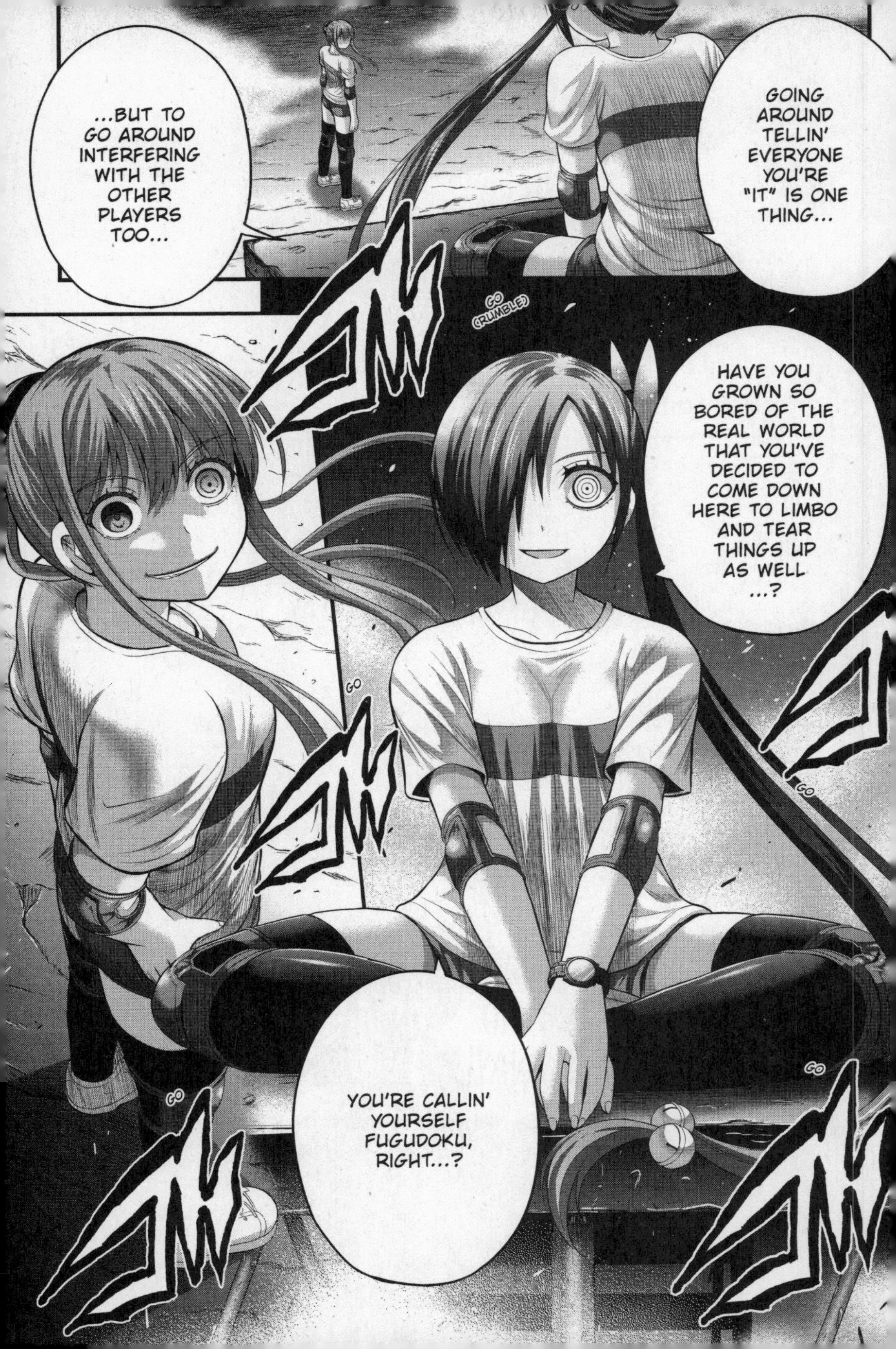
GOING AROUND TELLIN' EVERYONE YOU'RE "IT" IS ONE THING...
...BUT TO GO AROUND INTERFERING WITH THE OTHER PLAYERS TOO...
GO (RUMBLE)
HAVE YOU GROWN SO BORED OF THE REAL WORLD THAT YOU'VE DECIDED TO COME DOWN HERE TO LIMBO AND TEAR THINGS UP AS WELL ...?
GO
GO
GO
GO
YOU'RE CALLIN' YOURSELF FUGUDOKU, RIGHT...?

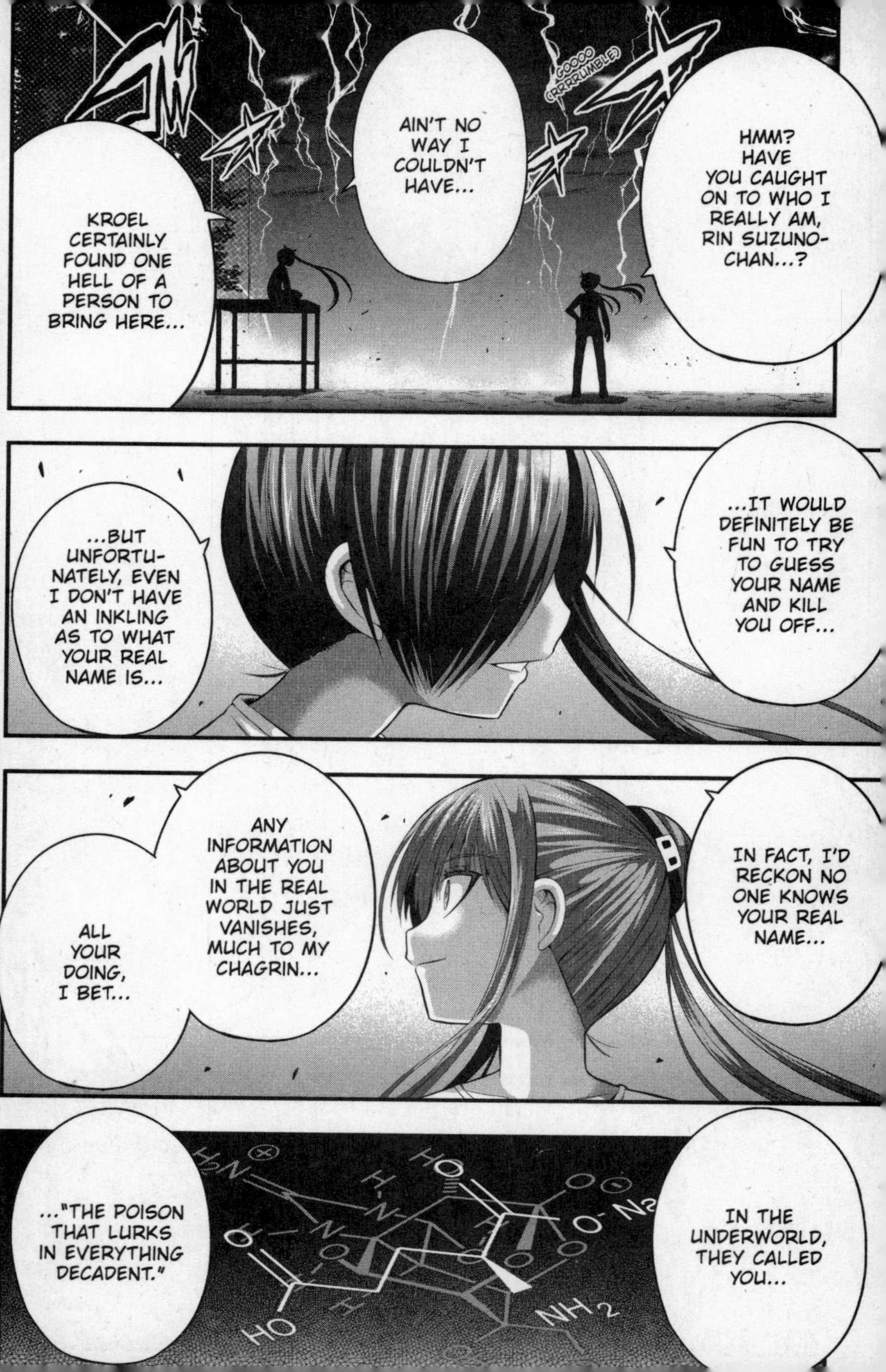
HMM? HAVE YOU CAUGHT ON TO WHO I REALLY AM, RIN SUZUNO-CHAN...?
GOOOO (RRRRUMBLE)
AIN'T NO WAY I COULDN'T HAVE...
KROEL CERTAINLY FOUND ONE HELL OF A PERSON TO BRING HERE...
...IT WOULD DEFINITELY BE FUN TO TRY TO GUESS YOUR NAME AND KILL YOU OFF...
...BUT UNFORTU-NATELY, EVEN I DON'T HAVE AN INKLING AS TO WHAT YOUR REAL NAME IS...
IN FACT, I'D RECKON NO ONE KNOWS YOUR REAL NAME...
ANY INFORMATION ABOUT YOU IN THE REAL WORLD JUST VANISHES, MUCH TO MY CHAGRIN...
ALL YOUR DOING, I BET...
IN THE UNDERWORLD, THEY CALLED YOU...
..."THE POISON THAT LURKS IN EVERYTHING DECADENT."

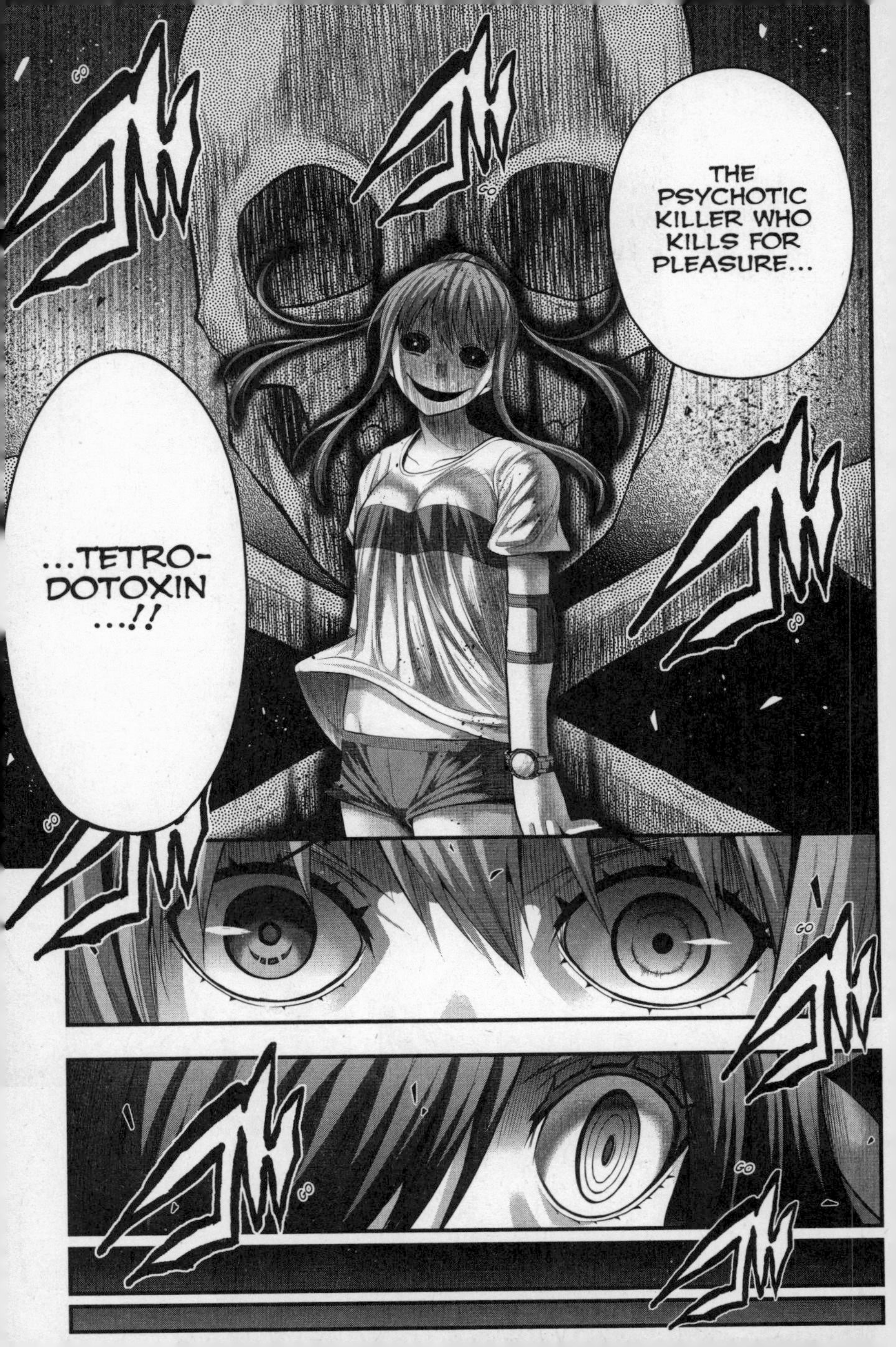
GO
GO
THE PSYCHOTIC KILLER WHO KILLS FOR PLEASURE...
...TETRO-DOTOXIN ...!!
GO
GO
GO
GO
GO

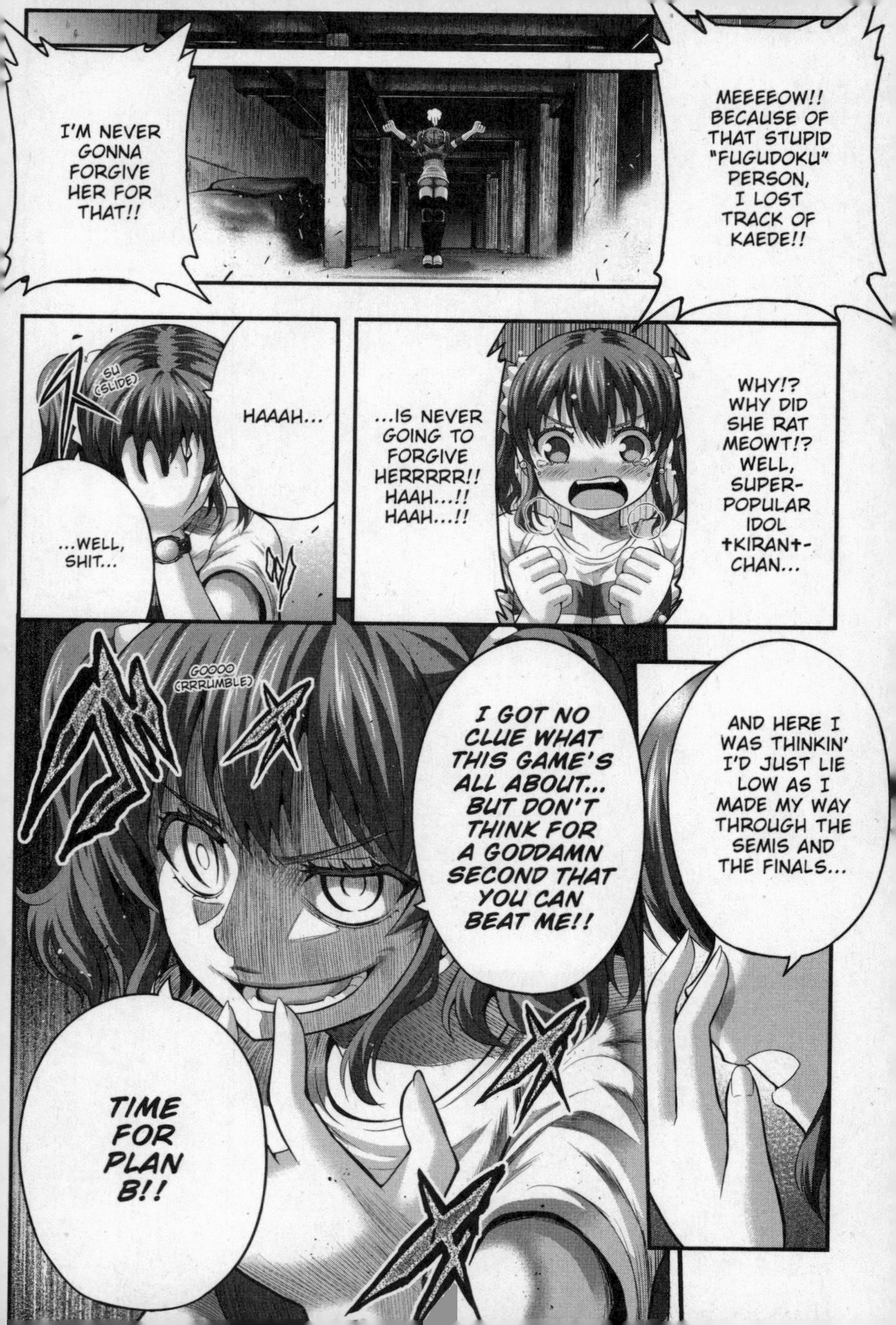
MEEEEOW!! BECAUSE OF THAT STUPID "FUGUDOKU" PERSON, I LOST TRACK OF KAEDE!!
I'M NEVER GONNA FORGIVE HER FOR THAT!!
WHY!? WHY DID SHE RAT MEOWT!? WELL, SUPER-POPULAR IDOL †KIRAN†-CHAN...
...IS NEVER GOING TO FORGIVE HERRRRR!! HAAH...!! HAAH...!!
HAAAH...
SU (SLIDE)
...WELL, SHIT...
AND HERE I WAS THINKIN' I'D JUST LIE LOW AS I MADE MY WAY THROUGH THE SEMIS AND THE FINALS...
I GOT NO CLUE WHAT THIS GAME'S ALL ABOUT... BUT DON'T THINK FOR A GODDAMN SECOND THAT YOU CAN BEAT ME!!
GOOOO (RRRUMBLE)
TIME FOR PLAN B!!

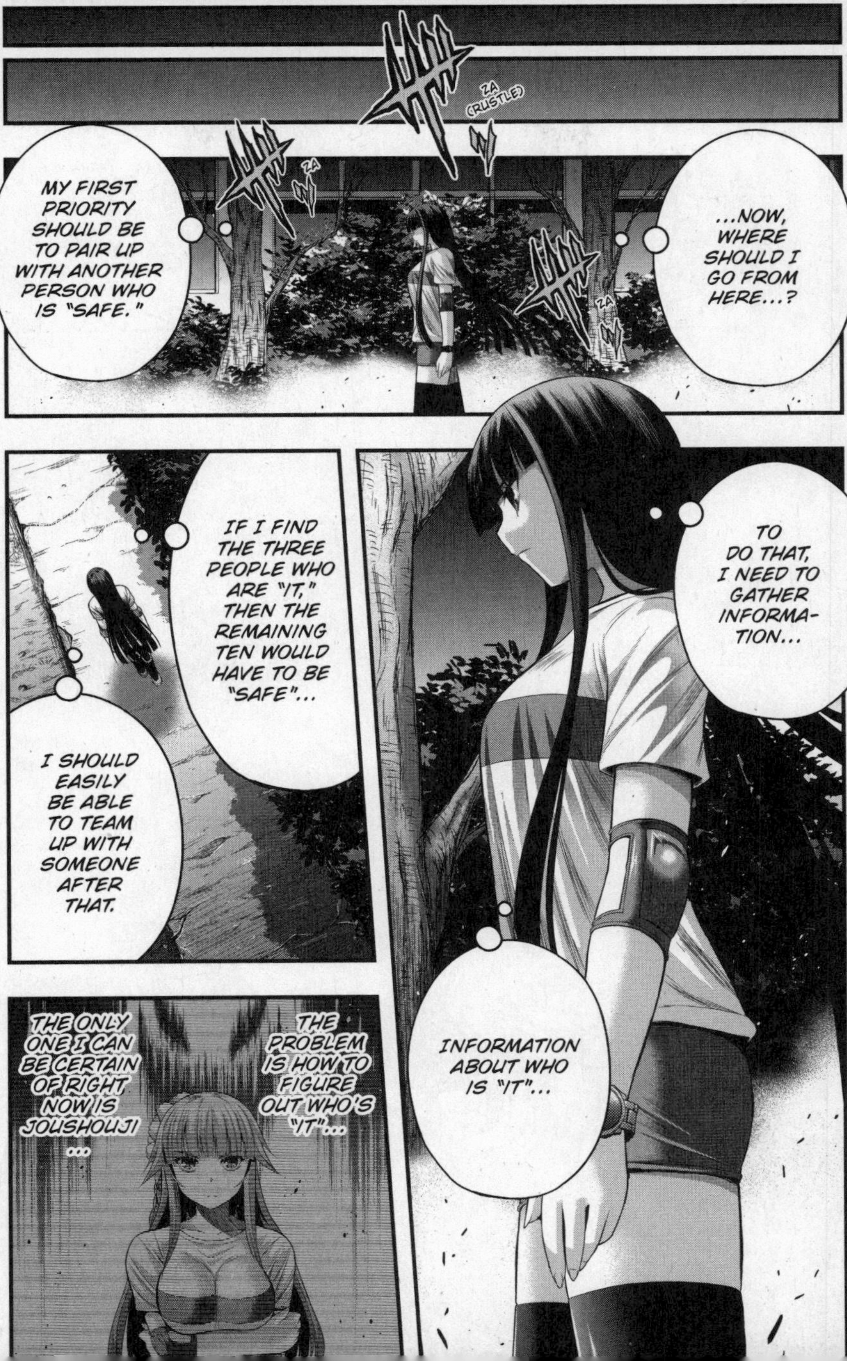
ZA (RUSTLE)
...NOW, WHERE SHOULD I GO FROM HERE...?
ZA
ZA
MY FIRST PRIORITY SHOULD BE TO PAIR UP WITH ANOTHER PERSON WHO IS "SAFE."
TO DO THAT, I NEED TO GATHER INFORMATION...
INFORMATION ABOUT WHO IS "IT"...
IF I FIND THE THREE PEOPLE WHO ARE "IT," THEN THE REMAINING TEN WOULD HAVE TO BE "SAFE"...
I SHOULD EASILY BE ABLE TO TEAM UP WITH SOMEONE AFTER THAT.
THE PROBLEM IS HOW TO FIGURE OUT WHO'S "IT"...
THE ONLY ONE I CAN BE CERTAIN OF RIGHT NOW IS JOUSHOUJI...

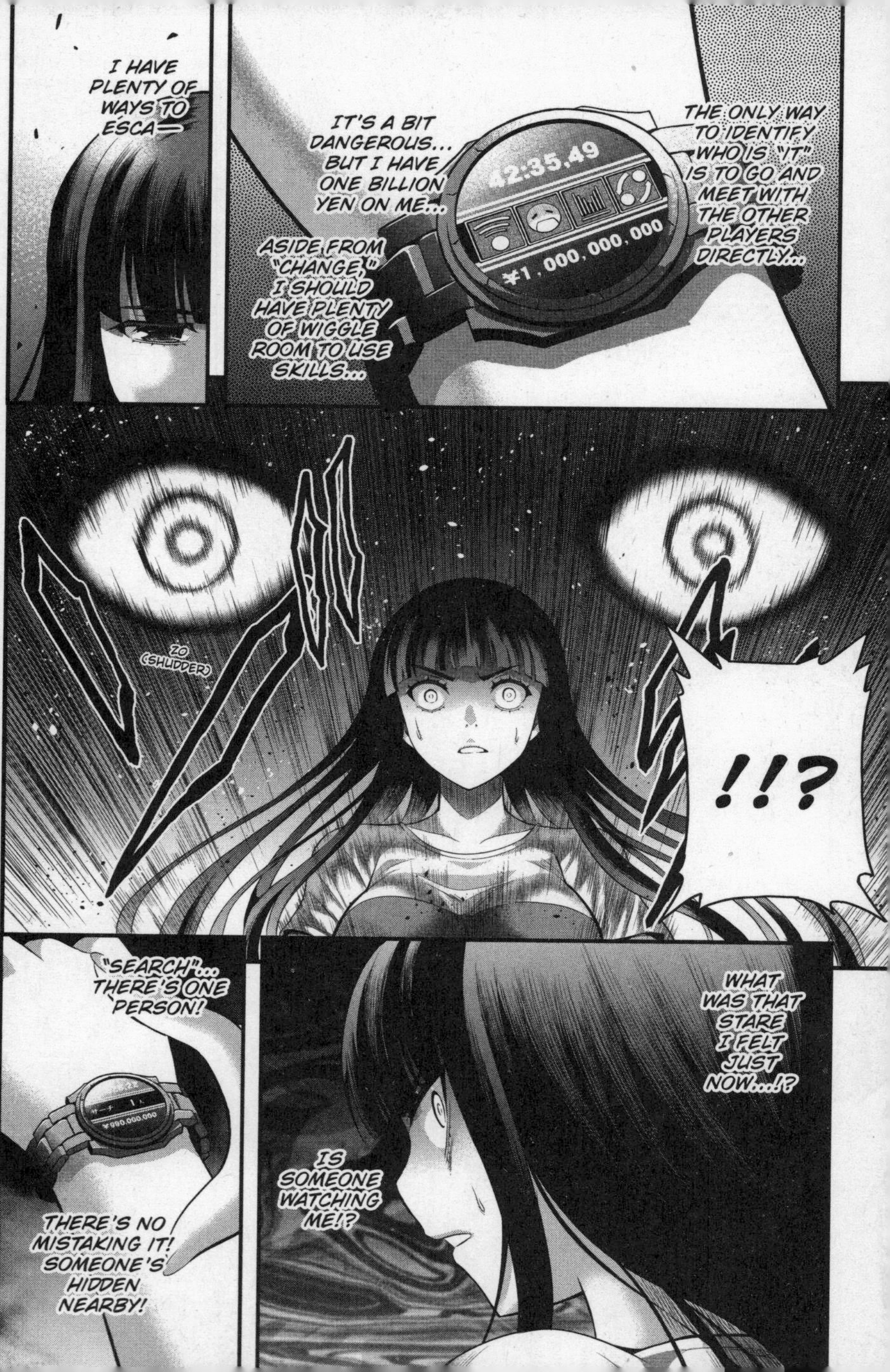
THE ONLY WAY TO IDENTIFY WHO IS "IT" IS TO GO AND MEET WITH THE OTHER PLAYERS DIRECTLY...
IT'S A BIT DANGEROUS... BUT I HAVE ONE BILLION YEN ON ME...
42:35.49
¥1,000,000,000
ASIDE FROM "CHANGE," I SHOULD HAVE PLENTY OF WIGGLE ROOM TO USE SKILLS...
I HAVE PLENTY OF WAYS TO ESCA—
!!?
ZO (SHUDDER)
WHAT WAS THAT STARE I FELT JUST NOW...!?
IS SOMEONE WATCHING ME!?
"SEARCH"... THERE'S ONE PERSON!
¥990,000,000
THERE'S NO MISTAKING IT! SOMEONE'S HIDDEN NEARBY!

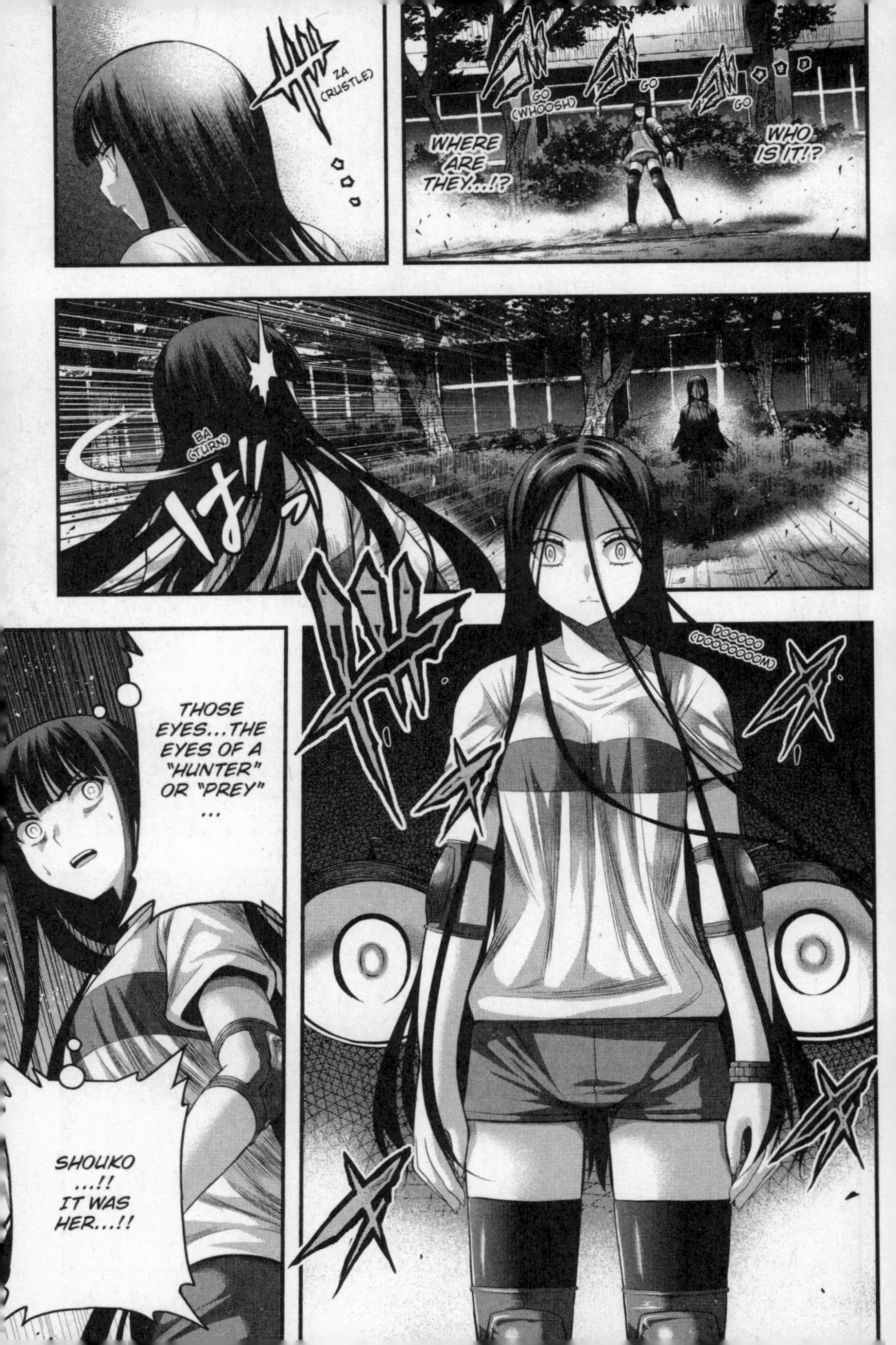
GO
GO
GO (WHOOSH)
WHO IS IT!?
WHERE ARE THEY...!?
ZA (RUSTLE)
BA (TURN)
DOOOOO (DOOOOOOOOM)
THOSE EYES...THE EYES OF A "HUNTER" OR "PREY" ...
SHOUKO ...!! IT WAS HER...!!

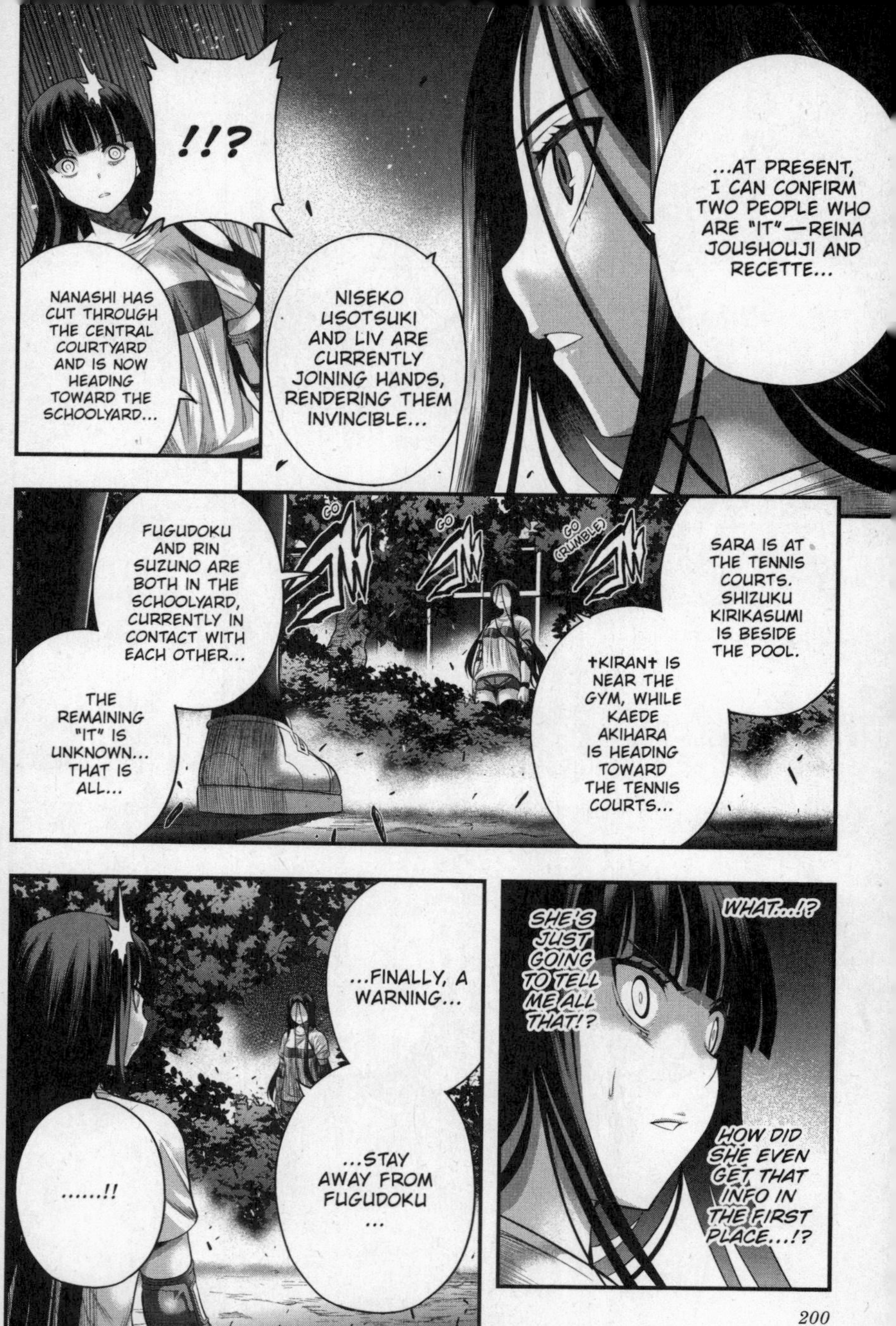
...AT PRESENT, I CAN CONFIRM TWO PEOPLE WHO ARE "IT"—REINA JOUSHOUJI AND RECETTE...
NISEKO USOTSUKI AND LIV ARE CURRENTLY JOINING HANDS, RENDERING THEM INVINCIBLE...
!!?
NANASHI HAS CUT THROUGH THE CENTRAL COURTYARD AND IS NOW HEADING TOWARD THE SCHOOLYARD...
SARA IS AT THE TENNIS COURTS. SHIZUKU KIRIKASUMI IS BESIDE THE POOL.
†KIRAN† IS NEAR THE GYM, WHILE KAEDE AKIHARA IS HEADING TOWARD THE TENNIS COURTS...
GO (RUMBLE)
GO
GO
FUGUDOKU AND RIN SUZUNO ARE BOTH IN THE SCHOOLYARD, CURRENTLY IN CONTACT WITH EACH OTHER...
THE REMAINING "IT" IS UNKNOWN... THAT IS ALL...
WHAT...!?
SHE'S JUST GOING TO TELL ME ALL THAT!?
HOW DID SHE EVEN GET THAT INFO IN THE FIRST PLACE...!?
...FINALLY, A WARNING...
...STAY AWAY FROM FUGUDOKU...
......!!

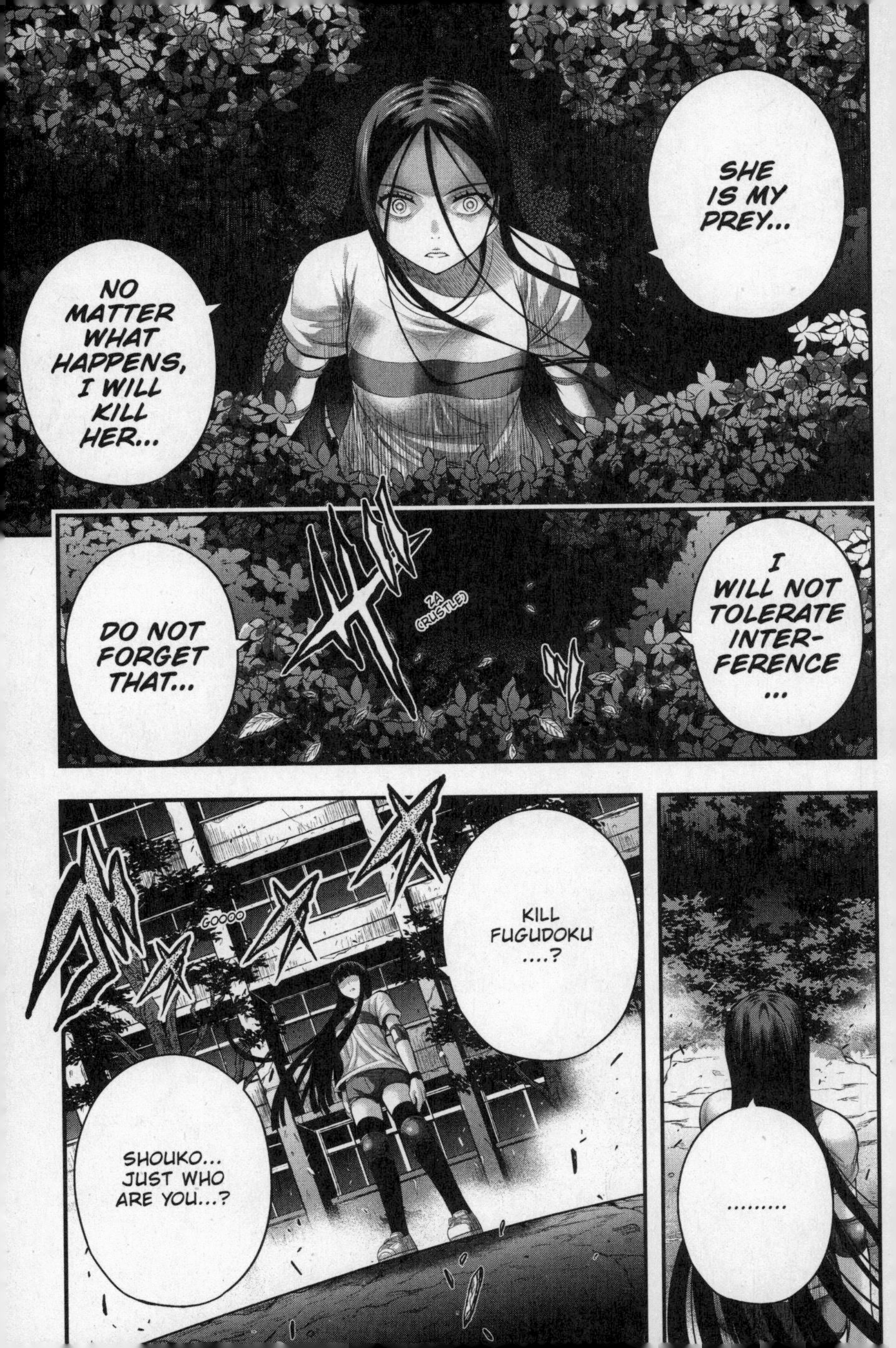
SHE IS MY PREY...
NO MATTER WHAT HAPPENS, I WILL KILL HER...
I WILL NOT TOLERATE INTER-FERENCE...
ZA (RUSTLE)
DO NOT FORGET THAT...
.........
KILL FUGUDOKU ....?
GOOOO
SHOUKO... JUST WHO ARE YOU...?

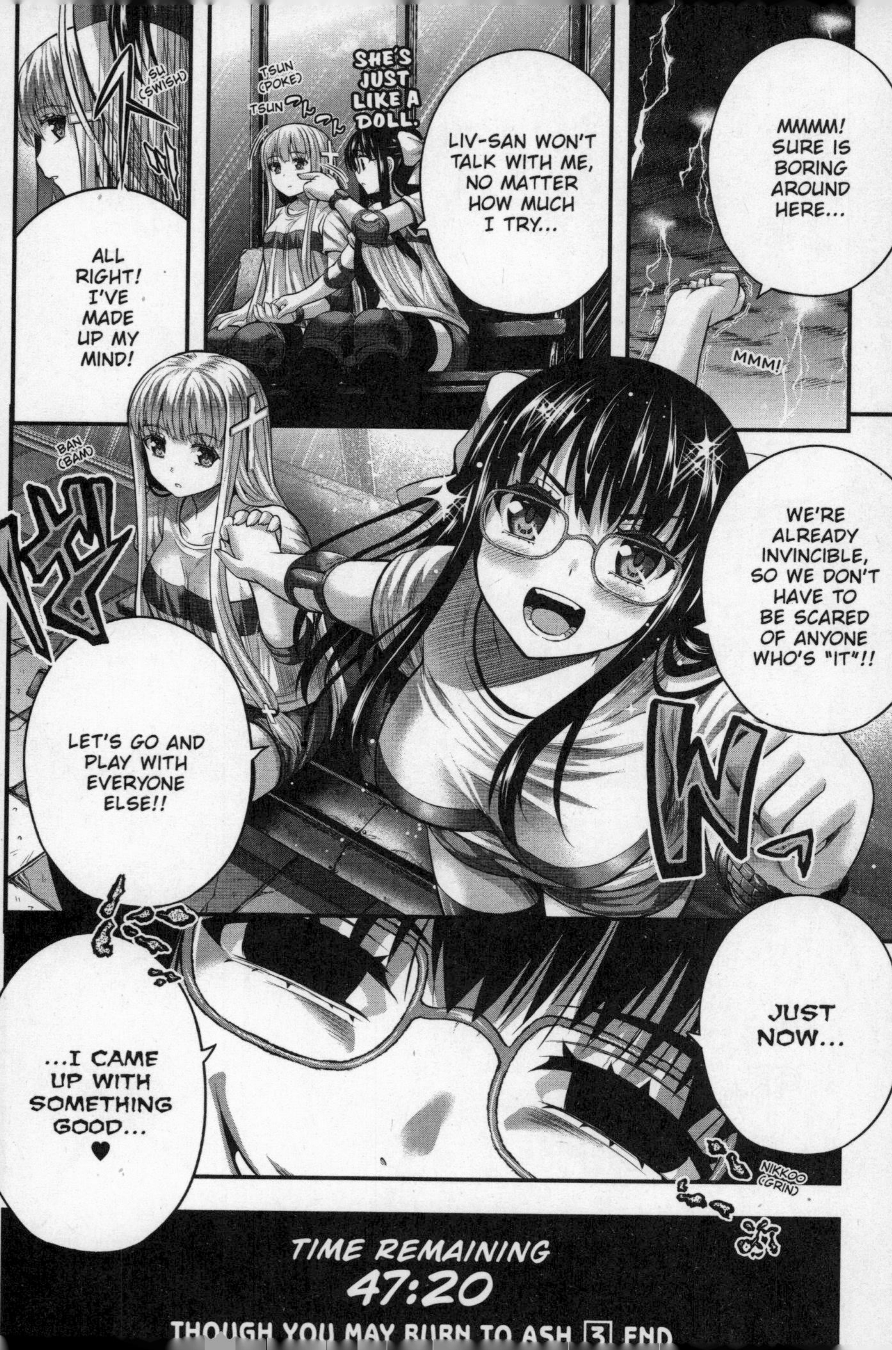
MMMM! SURE IS BORING AROUND HERE...
MMM!
LIV-SAN WON'T TALK WITH ME, NO MATTER HOW MUCH I TRY...
SHE'S JUST LIKE A DOLL.
TSUN (POKE)
TSUN
SU (SWISH)
ALL RIGHT! I'VE MADE UP MY MIND!
WE'RE ALREADY INVINCIBLE, SO WE DON'T HAVE TO BE SCARED OF ANYONE WHO'S "IT"!!
BAN (BAN)
LET'S GO AND PLAY WITH EVERYONE ELSE!!
JUST NOW...
NIKKOO (GRIN)
...I CAME UP WITH SOMETHING GOOD... ♥
TIME REMAINING
47:20
THOUGH YOU MAY BURN TO ASH 3 END

Though You May Burn to Ash

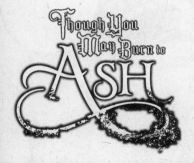

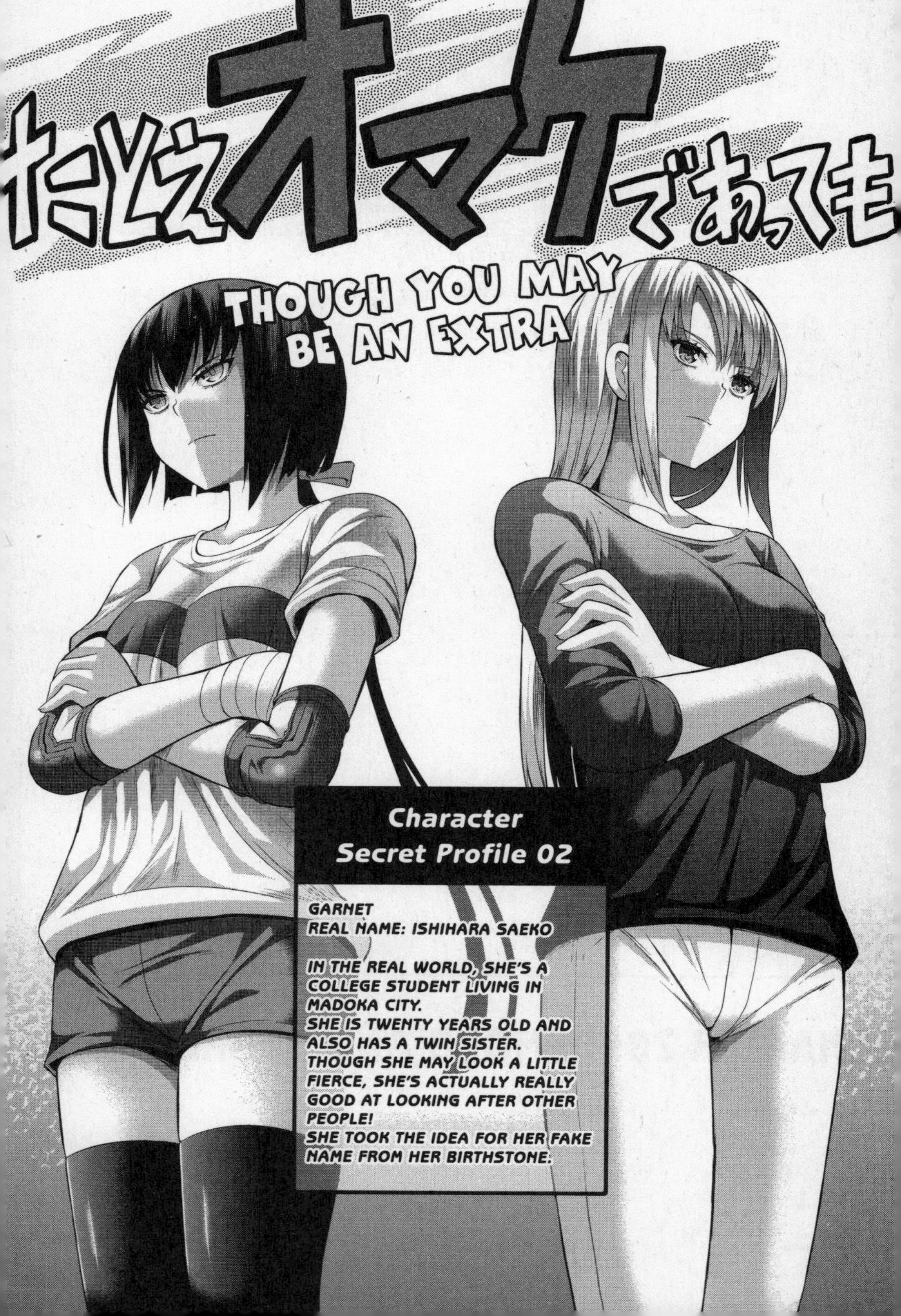
たとえオマケであっても
THOUGH YOU MAY BE AN EXTRA
Character Secret Profile 02
GARNET
REAL NAME: ISHIHARA SAEKO
IN THE REAL WORLD, SHE'S A COLLEGE STUDENT LIVING IN MADOKA CITY.
SHE IS TWENTY YEARS OLD AND ALSO HAS A TWIN SISTER.
THOUGH SHE MAY LOOK A LITTLE FIERCE, SHE'S ACTUALLY REALLY GOOD AT LOOKING AFTER OTHER PEOPLE!
SHE TOOK THE IDEA FOR HER FAKE NAME FROM HER BIRTHSTONE.

# CHAPTER 17: MANIPULATING LIFE AND DEATH

And now for Volume 3's commentary-ish segment!
Pawsitively pleased to meetcha!
Here, we find everyone getting along and enjoying a nice dinner together as they show off their individual personalities.
By the way, just as Recette-san said, all the meat being served was pork.
The flesh of everyone who died in the game is being used as fertilizer by Shiroel for her flower garden, which is very important to her.
It's the circle of life.

# CHAPTER 18: A LITTLE BOYISH, A LITTLE GIRLISH...

The first fan-service scene (?) in *Though You May Burn to Ash*.
In case you were wondering, I do draw all the bits that have been blocked out by the steam in my original pages.
For a pro's pages, I feel that you shouldn't not draw something, even if it ends up not being visible. (?)

# CHAPTER 19: THE ONLY GOOD ANGEL IS A DEAD ANGEL

Since Kroel won't die, that means she's not a good angel.
But it doesn't mean she's a bad angel, either.
Kroel's power isn't to create multiple bodies that all share the same memories and consciousness, by the way.
The existence called "Kroel" isn't a completely stable entity in the first place and has to use probabilities to make itself appear.
Even if those probabilities come close to zero, they will never actually become zero itself.
That's why she can't die. (?)

# CHAPTER 20: DEMONS AND SNAKES

The quarterfinals are finally getting started.
To be completely honest, at the end of Chapter 19, I had no idea what kind of game everyone would be playing.
Actually, I was thinking of a completely different game to use.
The idea of "Wouldn't a game of tag where you didn't know who was 'it' be really interesting!?" coming to me from the heavens was really a sudden event.
Manga truly is a living thing.

# CHAPTER 21: SHOW ME A LIAR, AND I'LL SHOW YOU A THIEF

I actually don't really enjoy drawing girls' faces
in weird ways, but Usotsuki-san's grinning face
is cute. I like it.
Usotsuki-san is one of my favorite characters,
so I tend to draw her in a lot of scenes.

# CHAPTER 22: RED SKY AND TRUE MIND

Niseko Usotsuki, the participant full of mysteries.
Her design is based off a character from a four-
panel manga I drew a looong time ago.
But my drawing style has really changed since then,
and I'm sad because no one can recognize who it is.

# CHAPTER 23: YOU GET WHAT YOU PAY FOR...

Looking at Nanashi-san running all over the place and panting
everywhere kind of makes me feel bad for her.
I want to make her feel at ease soon...

# CHAPTER 24: A FUNERAL MARCH FOR SCAVENGERS AND THOSE WHO WORSHIP MONEY, IN D MINOR

This chapter has a long-ass subtitle.
Just an example of me trying to go for
something cool that sounds like a classical
piece of music...and failing.

# AFTERWORD

YAHOOOOO!! CAN EVERYONE SEE ME?
I'M KAKASHI ONIYAZU.
I MANAGED TO GET VOLUME 3 OUT!
TODAY IS ALSO THE DAY VISION FINALLY RETURNED TO MY LEFT EYE.
HOW IS EVERYONE DOING? I AM KAKASHI ONIYAZU.

IT'S ONLY VOLUME 3 AND I'VE RUN OUT OF THINGS TO WIRTE IN MY
AFTERWORD.
JUST HOW LITTLE DO YOU ACTUALLY GET OUTSIDE, YOU IDIOT!?
IT'S BECAUSE I STAY INSIDE ALL DAY DRAWING MANGA.
PLEASE FORGIVE ME.

THAT SAID, I'M THE TYPE OF PERSON WHO PLANS TO GET OUT AND DO A
BUNCH OF THINGS WHILE WORKING ON A DEADLINE, BUT THEN JUST END UP
LAZING AROUND ONCE I ACTUALLY GET THE FREE TIME.
I'M JUST NOT VERY GOOD AT LIVING WELL.

PUTTING THAT ASIDE, *THOUGH YOU MAY BURN TO ASH* IS ENTERING THE TAG
ARC.
WHICH THREE PEOPLE SHOULD DIE?
HOW ARE THE THIRTEEN PARTICIPANTS CONNECTED IN THE REAL WORLD?
WHY DOES NISEKO USOTSUKI HANG AROUND YUKI SO MUCH?
HOW DOES SARA PLAN TO STOP THE GAME?
WELL, IT'D MAKE ME VERY HAPPY IF YOU'D LET YOUR IMAGINATION RUN WILD
AND LOOK FORWARD TO THE ANSWERS AS YOU READ ALONG.

AND THERE YOU HAVE IT. I LOOK FORWARD TO SEEING YOU AGAIN IN
VOLUME 4 AND BEYOND, MY GOOD SIR OR MADAM!
HEH...HEH-HEH!!

YEEEEAAAAAAHHH!!
I MANAGED TO FILL UP THE AFTERWORD!!
NOW I HAVE TO GO REVISE THE REST OF THE VOLUME. AAAHHHHHHH!
AND WITH THAT, I HOPE TO SEE YOU AGAIN IN VOLUME 4.

## ✧ SPECIAL THANKS ✧

KAORU NAKAGAWA-SAMA     KAZUNARI TAKAHASHI-SAMA          CHOUNIKU-SAMA

   SASAKI-SAN-SAMA          ASAKI NAKAMA-SAMA     YAMAGUCHI OPTOMETRY-SAMA

   HIROSHI ETOU-SAMA          SOUICHI ITOU-SAMA          MAKOTO ETOU-SAMA

# TRANSLATION NOTES

## COMMON HONORIFICS

no honorific: Indicates familiarity or closeness; if used without permission or reason, addressing someone in this manner would constitute an insult.

-*san*: The Japanese equivalent of Mr./Mrs./Miss. If a situation calls for politeness, this is the fail-safe honorific.

-*kun*: Used most often when referring to boys, this indicates affection or familiarity. Occasionally used by older men among their peers, but it may also be used by anyone referring to a person of lower standing.

-*chan*: An affectionate honorific indicating familiarity used mostly in reference to girls; also used in reference to cute persons or animals of either gender.

-*sensei*: A respectful term for teachers, artists, or high-level professionals.

### Page 18

**†Kiran†**'s manner of speech is a bit strange—she ends all her sentences in *nya*, which translates to "meow," hence the assortment of feline phrases scattered throughout her lines.

### Page 19

**Kaede** is certainly doing a poor job of playing a girl, as she constantly uses the male pronoun *boku* to refer to herself before correcting to *watashi*, which, while gender-neutral, is what women normally use.

### Page 72

If you're wondering why Kroel is giving herself horns as she says "tag," it's because "tag" in Japanese is *onigokko*, with *oni* meaning "demon." If you're "it," you're the demon tasked with chasing the children, who are the "safe" players.

### Page 129

**Red Sky and True Mind** is a play on the song "Blue Sky and True Mind" by The Yellow Monkey, a '90s rock group from Japan that has sold over ten million albums.

### Page 130

What Niseko actually called Reina here is *ojouji*, which means "love affair" and isn't too far off from "Joushouji."

Though You May Burn to ASH

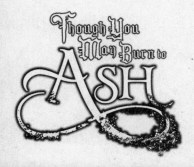

# Though You May Burn to Ash 3

## Kakashi Oniyazu

TRANSLATION: GARRISON DENIM ☠ LETTERING: ANDWORLDDESIGN

TATOE HAI NI NATTEMO vol. 3
© 2017 Kakashi Oniyazu / SQUARE ENIX CO., LTD.
First published in Japan in 2017 by SQUARE ENIX CO., LTD.
English translation rights arranged with SQUARE ENIX CO., LTD.
and Yen Press, LLC through Tuttle-Mori Agency, Inc.

English translation © 2018 by SQUARE ENIX CO., LTD.

Yen Press
1290 Avenue of the Americas
New York, NY 10104

Visit us at yenpress.com
facebook.com/yenpress
twitter.com/yenpress
yenpress.tumblr.com
instagram.com/yenpress

First Yen Press Edition: September 2018

Yen Press is an imprint of Yen Press, LLC.
The Yen Press name and logo are trademarks of Yen Press, LLC.

Library of Congress Control Number: 2017954641

ISBNs: 978-1-9753-2740-8 (paperback)
        978-1-9753-2741-5 (ebook)

10 9 8 7 6 5 4 3 2 1

WOR

Printed in the United States of America